"*A Taste of Puerto Rico* will not only be greatly enjoyed by current aficionados of Caribbean cuisine but will win over a new audience." —Jacques Pépin

"A splendid book for anyone interested in the delectable foods the Caribbean has to offer."
—Elizabeth Lambert Ortiz, author of
The Complete Book of Caribbean Cooking

"Yvonne Ortiz has done a wonderful job—she is a shining star from the Shining Star." —Lyn Stallworth,
author of *The Brooklyn Cookbook*

"Finally—an authentic Puerto Rican cookbook with a complete culinary history and recipes for us all to enjoy."
—Linnette Creen, author of *A Taste of Cuba*

"For years Yvonne has been my guide to a treasure hunt of riches—and now she has guided me into my own kitchen for a taste of the island at home."
—Betty Fussell, author of *The Story of Corn*

"A rich and delicious compilation of recipes."
—Christopher Idone

YVONNE ORTIZ is a regular contributor to *Gourmet*, *Cook's Illustrated*, and the *New York Times*, as well as to *El Diario/La Prensa*, the country's largest national Spanish-language daily newspaper. She was born in New York City, raised in Cayey, Puerto Rico, and now lives in Jersey City, New Jersey.

Traditional and New Dishes
from the
Puerto Rican Community

A Taste of Puerto Rico

Yvonne Ortiz

A PLUME BOOK

PLUME
Published by the Penguin Group
Penguin Books USA Inc., 375 Hudson Street,
New York, New York 10014, U.S.A.
Penguin Books Ltd, 27 Wrights Lane, London W8 5TZ, England
Penguin Books Australia Ltd, Ringwood, Victoria, Australia
Penguin Books Canada Ltd, 10 Alcorn Avenue,
Toronto, Ontario, Canada M4V 3B2
Penguin Books (N.Z.) Ltd, 182–190 Wairau Road, Auckland 10, New Zealand

Penguin Books Ltd, Registered Offices: Harmondsworth, Middlesex, England

Published by Plume, an imprint of Dutton Signet,
a division of Penguin Books USA Inc.
Previously published in a Dutton edition.

First Plume Printing, April, 1997

30 29 28 27 26 25 24

℗ REGISTERED TRADEMARK—MARCA REGISTRADA

The Library of Congress has catalogued the Dutton edition as follows:
Ortiz, Yvonne.
    A taste of Puerto Rico : traditional and new dishes from the Puerto Rican
    community / Yvonne Ortiz.
        p.   cm.
    ISBN 0-525-93812-5 (hc.)
    ISBN 0-452-27548-2 (pbk.)
    1. Cookery. Puerto Rican.   I. Title.
TX716.P8078   1994
641.597295—dc20   93–46165
                                                              CIP

Printed in the United States of America
Original hardcover design by Eve L. Kirch

BOOKS ARE AVAILABLE AT QUANTITY DISCOUNTS WHEN USED TO PROMOTE
PRODUCTS OR SERVICES. FOR INFORMATION PLEASE WRITE TO PREMIUM MARKETING
DIVISION, PENGUIN BOOKS USA INC., 375 HUDSON STREET, NEW YORK, NY 10014.

To my son, Alexito,
and all the Puerto Ricans on the U.S.A. mainland
who need to learn about our culinary traditions
from a distance.

Acknowledgments

In 1989 this book seemed only a dream. Since then, many people have worked hard to make it a happy reality. I am grateful to you all. I would like to acknowledge:

My son for being patient and understanding. Madeline Morel, my agent, and Carole DeSanti and Julia Moskin, my editors; Sharon Pinsker, Ed Manchess, Eric Weinstein, and all the residents of Su Casa; John Haney, my proofreader, who also assisted in the recipe testing and development; Federica Bennett for turning a mess of notes into a manuscript; Dolores Gonzalez, my kitchen assistant; Yoly Sanchez and Milagros Marcano for research material; Dr. Maricel Precilla, my mentor; Fern Berman, Dalia Carmel, Elsa Ayala, and Angel Alvelo; Cara DeSilva at *New York Newsday*; my mother, father, and brother; and Mauricio Redondo.

Contents

Contents

Introduction

When I was growing up in Cayey, Puerto Rico, I could only sample the island's vast and diverse cuisines. Cayey is a small town located in the center of the island. It is surrounded by mountains and situated near the coastal town of Salinas. Its location gives the town a breezy warmth year-round that feels like spring on the mainland. During my childhood, the town consisted of only a few streets, a main plaza, and a church. There were only three restaurants, which served what would be considered "home cooking."

Even though the island is only a hundred miles long and thirty-five miles wide, there are marked regional differences in the names given to foods, their preparation, and the dishes themselves. It was when I entered the University of Puerto Rico in 1974 and went to live in a boardinghouse that my first real exposure to the diversity of our cuisine started.

Girls from all over the island attended the university. By becoming friends with many of them I was able to visit towns that otherwise would still be unknown to me except for the names on the map. Every town, or almost every one, is renowned for a special dish, fruit, or vegetable. For example, I tasted *mabí*, a fermented drink made from the bark of the *mabí* tree, which is somewhat like a cross between root beer and sarsaparilla, in Juana Díaz. Many people claim it is the best *mabí* in Puerto Rico. I also tried Villaalba's tomatoes; Ponce's *quenepas*, a fruit with a big pit and pink flesh; and Vieques's famous *bilí*, *quenepas* soaked in rum and marinated in the bottle for a few weeks. The rum is then strained and served.

When I was younger, I visited my maternal grandmother in Humacao every summer. As a curious teenager I wandered around the town looking for something interesting to do. One possibility was to eat lunch in the *fonda*, a kind of casual restaurant like the French *bistro* or Italian *trattoria*. The menu usually had typical peasant fare: tripe soup, boiled root vegetables, and rice and beans. These occasions became a ritual for me every summer, something I looked forward to all year.

Little did I know that some ten years later I would not only become a chef, but that I would also be an ambassador for our food. After completing my graduate studies, and feeling very sure of myself, I came to New York to pursue a dream: to study the culinary arts. I went through the entire spectrum, institutional as well as commercial cooking.

My training in classical French cuisine and its basic techniques allowed me to enter a new world. As a Puerto Rican I learned to cook for the American palate, but always with a tropical splash that was instinctive to me. One day I decided that it was time to go back to my ethnic and culinary roots. I was already fascinated with other countries' food histories. Why not investigate my people and how our food habits came to be what they are today?

For many years Puerto Ricans have been characterized as eating only rice and beans. Even though Puerto Ricans form the largest group of Hispanics living in cities like New York, little or nothing was known about the richness of our food culture. The traditional cuisine is the result of three heritages: the native, the Spanish, and the African. The cuisine is accentuated by features here and there from other groups who, even though they may have stayed for only a short time, left us some gastronomic presents. We even have some Italian and Chinese influences.

The growing number of second- and third-generation Puerto Ricans, including my son, on the mainland inspired me to write this book. Five centuries of culinary history have brought about significant changes in our eating habits. From the natives, with their mostly vegetarian diet, to the thousands of people in New York who celebrate the annual Puerto Rican Day Parade, we have a rainbow of flavors and traditions. With my most sincere intention of sharing all the valuable information that I have come across in recent years, this book was born. I hope it will give a better understanding of why we are the rainbow people and why our cuisine is diverse in colors and flavors.

Yvonne Ortiz
New York City
June 1994

1

A Historical and Culinary Journey

Christopher Columbus discovered the island of Puerto Rico on his second voyage while looking for new lands to claim for the Spanish king and queen. When Spanish explorers (and later settlers) came to Puerto Rico, they found the Taíno people, members of the Arawak tribe, living there. The Arawaks were the dominant group in the Caribbean at that time; the Spanish called them "Indians," because Columbus was not at all correct in guessing where he was.

The Taínos had a structured society with a chief called a *cacique*. They grew food in gardens next to the *bohíos* (huts) in which they lived. The carefully tended gardens were known as *kunukus*. The main crops cultivated by the Taínos were *yuca* (cassava), corn, yams, and *yautía* (taro root). They also grew peanuts and a vegetable similar to the water chestnut called *lerén*. Fruits such as guava, soursop, pineapple, and sea grapes grew wild. Other foods that grew wild were black-eyed peas and lima beans.

Yuca was a staple food of the Taínos. The main food prepared with *yuca* was *casabe*, a flat bread that was eaten daily.

Yuca was an important staple because wheat did not grow well in the soil of the island and had to be imported from Spain. There were periods as long as eight years when a supply ship would not come! *Casabe* was often the only bread available; it was even used as the Host for Holy Communion. It is still eaten today. Taínos also used *yuca* to make vinegar, which was an important seasoning since they did not use salt in cooking. *Ajíes caballeros*, very hot peppers, were another popular seasoning.

Corn was a major food in the Taíno diet. Foods to be cooked on an open fire were wrapped in corn husks, later replaced by plantain leaves brought to the island by African slaves, but the grain was very important to the island diet and culture.

Taínos used very little domestic equipment in food preparation. The two main cooking utensils, the *olla* (pot) and the *burén* (flat griddle put directly on the fire), used for toasting, pan-broiling, and making *casabe*, were made of clay. Taínos cooked their food over a *fogón*, a hearth of three stones, with a fire made from leaves and sticks. The natives' diet was mainly vegetarian. They did, however, eat some meat, such as iguana, and they hunted and fished for shellfish, tortoise, seabirds, and other game.

Foods introduced by the Spanish include chick-peas, cilantro, eggplant, onions, and garlic. Many foods native to Mexico and South America came to the island during the European explorations of the seventeenth and eighteenth centuries. Potatoes came from the Andes, passion fruit from Brazil, chayote, papaya, avocado, and cocoa from Mexico. Breadfruit was brought from Tahiti to feed the African slaves in the eighteenth century and remained a staple when slavery was abolished in the nineteenth century. The coconut palm tree was introduced by the Spanish, but fruits like pears, peaches, and apples did not adapt well to the growing conditions on the island. Two other foods, essential to the Spanish daily diet, that did not thrive at all in the island's soil were olives and grapes. Without olive oil, lard became the cooking fat of choice.

Coffee came in 1736, and along with sugarcane was the

backbone of the island's economy through the first half of this century. Rum, introduced to the island by the Spanish, has become the favorite liquor over the years. Today Puerto Rico is the biggest producer of rum in the world.

The African slave trade brought important foods and techniques to the island's cuisine. The most significant of the former were green pigeon peas, plantain, yams, and okra. The African population also developed many coconut dishes, which are still quite popular. Their favorite technique was frying, which quickly became our most popular way of cooking.

Other groups that visited the island and left culinary presents were the Dutch (Edam cheese), the Italians (macaroni and chicken), and the Chinese (dumplings). The Chinese came to the area after slavery had been abolished. They worked in the sugar and coffee fields. By the end of the nineteenth century all these elements had shaped what we consider our national cuisine. By 1848 the first restaurant, La Mallorquina, was established in Old San Juan. *El Cocinero Puertorriqueño*, the island's first cookbook, was published in 1849.

In a traditional Puerto Rican diet, a typical breakfast consists of *café con leche* (coffee with hot milk) and a piece of bread with butter. Today the morning meal is more American style: bacon, eggs, home fries, and pancakes. Once, lunch would have been boiled root vegetables and codfish. To these have now been added fast-food items such as pizza, burgers, sandwiches, and the very popular salads sold in salad bars. Dinner almost always consists of rice, beans, and a meat dish, preceded by a soup. Other choices include *tostones* (fried green plantains), fried yellow plantains, and *yuca con mojo* (cassava in garlic sauce).

Traditionally, Puerto Rican cuisine did not include much in the way of vegetables. A typical green salad would consist of lettuce, tomatoes, cucumbers, and canned peas and corn. Other vegetables eaten were *chayote* and eggplant. They were usually part of a stewed dish.

Nouvelle Cuisine brought a new spectrum of foods to the island. From breakfast to dessert, different choices are now available. Fresh pasta, salmon, lamb, and a better variety of vegetables can now be purchased. Today at the typical restaurant you can get dishes like shrimp in creole sauce, served with broccoli or cauliflower. Typical desserts such as *flan* (egg custard), *tembleque* (coconut custard), and guava with white cheese have been replaced by lighter and more sophisticated preparations. Mango jelly roll, passion fruit cheesecake, and fresh fruit salad with kiwi are part of the present repertoire.

Holidays and festive occasions have a special menu: roast suckling pig, rice with green pigeon peas, and goat or veal stew. This menu is still followed even on the mainland. American holidays like Thanksgiving and Easter have become part of our traditional celebrations, but we give them a very Puerto Rican touch. Turkey is seasoned with *adobo*, the stuffing is made with beef *picadillo*, and roast pork is eaten on Easter Sunday.

Although we are not big on dairy products, we do produce a white cheese called *queso de hoja*. On the island it is sold fresh; here on the mainland we can get it packaged. Among the typical food establishments are the *fonda* (diner-type restaurant) and the *plaza de mercado* (indoor farmers' market that usually includes stands to buy prepared food).

The last element in our cuisine is American. When we became part of the United States in 1898, American foods and eating habits were combined with traditional ones. After the Depression we suffered the effects of the Second World War and a massive migration to the United States.

By 1950 things were changing on the island. The electric blender replaced the *pilón* (mortar and pestle) in making important basics such as *recaíto*, as women started to enter the work force. At the same time, tourism became an important factor in the island's economy. With the boom, our cuisine had to be adapted to suit the palates of our visitors. It was also a time when the first significant cookbooks written by Puerto Rican women were published. On the mainland, Puerto Ricans struggled to get used to the new environment. La Marketa was established in New York in 1936. This market, located under the train tracks of Metro North in East Harlem, became a way of preserving the diet and the culinary traditions of the Caribbean. It was and is a primary meeting place, routinely drawing shoppers from all over the city. Until recently, ingredients such as cilantro, sweet chili peppers, and *mabí* could be found only in La Marketa.

The *bodegas*, small grocery stores, became a symbol of our cultural identity. These stores, started by Spanish immigrants at the end of the nineteenth century, were located at the heart of prominent Puerto Rican neighborhoods like the Lower East Side and South Brooklyn. The best thing about *bodegas* is that they make Puerto Rican ingredients widely available.

Puerto Rican New Cuisine showed up around 1978, an offshoot of Nouvelle Cuisine, which started in France, then spread to the United States, and soon reached the island. This movement brought about a considerable refinement of our traditional peasant dishes. There were innovative combinations of ingredients and more elegant presentations. Fruits found their way into classical sauces; recipes were lighter. There were fewer fried foods; lard was almost completely eliminated. Balsamic vinegar and kiwi fruit were introduced. People started to become more educated about the dining experience. Magazines such as *Bon Appétit* and *Cuisine* became available in San Juan. It was just the beginning of a new era for our gastronomy. Puerto Rican New Cuisine, although not yet well known outside the island, started to redefine our food culture. Chefs like Giovanna Huyke and Alfredo Ayala are considered the pioneers of the movement.

In the 1980s our diet was redefined, especially by health issues that slowly started to make an impression in the last ten years. Lard, used for centuries, was replaced by corn and olive oils. (Traditionally, olive oil was used only for salads and pickling.) Low-cholesterol cooking and foods gradually became part of the daily diet. Our famous fritters are now made with annatto oil instead of lard!

Back on the mainland at about the same time, the *casita* concept was born. It is truly a phenomenon of our culture. *Casitas* are little houses that resemble the traditional *bohíos*, the huts that date back to Taíno times. They are built in gardens throughout New York and are used for community activities like after-school programs, voter-registration drives, and big day-long picnics. Food, of course, plays an important and essential role in the *casitas*. Traditions are strengthened through special activities such as the celebration of Three Kings Day (Epiphany) and the Puerto Rican Day Parade, as well as daily activities.

The 1990s brought back to the island's cuisine the *fonda*, or traditional family-style restaurant. Casita Blanca, the best-known *fonda* in San Juan, has become a showcase for our rediscovered traditional foods.

Puerto Ricans travel constantly between the island and the mainland. A melding of new and traditional cooking in many homes as well as in food establishments has resulted. I hope to reflect this trend in *A Taste of Puerto Rico*.

THE BASICS: THE PUERTO RICAN PANTRY
(La Despensa Puertorriqueña)

Like every cuisine, Puerto Rican cooking has some staple ingredients. These are a result of five hundred years of culinary exchanges. Although some ingredients have been replaced because of health concerns and lifestyle changes, the basic staples are fairly consistent with those of our ancestors.

Some ingredients may not be immediately familiar to you, although most of them are readily available. I have included a mail-order guide to help those who live in areas where the ingredients might not be easy to obtain.

The ingredients used in traditional Puerto Rican cooking, like the dishes that showcase them, are a result of a wonderfully tangled heritage. These are everyday grocery items for people on the island as well as here in the United States. Sweet chili peppers, passion fruit, and papayas add color and fragrance to produce counters throughout the country. Varieties of these foods grown in the United States make them easier to find and more affordable.

Besides finding typical foods when you shop for Puerto Rican pantry items, you will find a reflection of our culture and cuisine. You will have the opportunity to see, touch, and smell the ingredients that make our dishes unique.

Aceite de maíz (corn oil) has replaced lard as the cooking fat of choice. It is used for frying, cooking rice, stewing, and braising.

Adobo is a basic dry seasoning mix made of salt, black pepper, garlic, and onion powder. It is used for meats, poultry, pork, and seafood. *Adobo* can be purchased bottled, with or without black pepper. (See recipe, page 15.)

Alcaparrado, a bottled mixture of olives, capers, and diced pimiento imported from Spain, is used mainly in bean stews, pickled fish, and braised meat dishes.

Annatto or *achiote* seeds have been used for centuries. Annatto replaced hard-to-find saffron in colonial cooking. The seeds can be ground and sprinkled or mixed into soups, pastry dough, or stews. Annatto does not have the delicate flavor of saffron but imparts a bright yellow color that can turn an everyday dish into a festive presentation. To make annatto oil, heat two cups of olive oil in a small saucepan. Add ½ cup annatto seeds (available at all *bodegas* and many supermarkets) and cook about 5 minutes over low heat. When the oil is a rich orange color, remove, let cool, and strain.

Bacalao is dry salted codfish. It is always soaked in water and cooked before being incorporated into recipes. It is usually sold whole, with some bones and skin, or as a fillet, skinless and with few or no bones. The two main preparations in which *bacalao* is used are salads and stews.

To cook *bacalao*, first soak it in water to cover overnight. Then put it in a pot with cold water to cover, and bring to a boil. When the water boils, pour it off and repeat with fresh cold water. Repeat once more, then taste the *bacalao*. If it still seems excessively salty, repeat one more time, then cool and shred.

Calabaza is West Indian pumpkin, a vegetable with green skin and bright, firm yellow flesh. It is used mainly in stews. It can also be used to make fritters, soups, and custards. *Calabaza* is available year-round and is sold whole or cut in pieces.

The whole squash can be round or pear-shaped. It can be somewhat difficult to determine if it is ripe and ready to use. Look for a squash with a dull rind and a solid stem attached. It should be heavy for its size. If you are buying just a piece, look for bright yellow flesh. A whole squash can be stored at room temperature for up to a month. Cut it into pieces, remove all of the seeds, wrap it tightly in plastic wrap, and refrigerate. Pieces can be stored this way for up to a week. It can also be frozen. If *calabaza* is not available, you can substitute acorn squash.

Cilantro (coriander), is also known as *cilantrillo* or *culantrillo*. It is an herb with green leaves that looks somewhat like parsley. Cilantro is available year-round almost everywhere. Make sure the roots are still attached. To store, wrap in moist paper towel and place in the refrigerator. Wash well and let sit in cold water just before use.

Coco is coconut. That used for cooking purposes is in the mature stage and has a hairy brown surface. It is also known as *coco seco* (dry coconut). Coconut milk is the liquid extracted from the coconut meat. Coconut cream, a very sweet canned coconut product, is used mostly in the preparation of drinks like the *piña colada*. Both are available in supermarkets.

Gandules (green pigeon peas) are our national bean. They are used to prepare our famous dish, *arroz con gandules*—yellow rice with green pigeon peas (see recipe, page 171.) These peas, of African origin, are sold on the island fresh, canned, or frozen. On the mainland you will most likely find them frozen or canned. They are also sold dried.

Guanábana, soursop, a fruit with green skin and white, sweet pulp, was traditionally used to make drinks, including the popular *champola*. Fresh soursops are hard to find on the mainland, but frozen pulp and concentrate are available year-round.

Habichuelas (beans) are part of the real basic Puerto Rican cuisine. The most popular beans on the island are the *rosada* (pink), *blanca* (white), *marca diablo* (red kidney), and *garbanzo* (chick-pea). In traditional cooking, dried beans were soaked overnight, cooked, and incorporated into the recipe. (See recipe for cooking dried beans, page 172.) Canned beans can also be used.

Jamón de cocinar is a cured (smoked) ham usually sold in thick slices. It is an essential ingredient in the traditional *sofrito*. It is also used as a flavor enhancer in stews, yellow-rice dishes, and braised meats such as Puerto Rican pot roast (*carne mechada*). (See recipe, page 148.) If smoked ham is not available, you can use ham steak or any other lightly smoked ham.

Lechosa, papaya, grown on the island is very different from the type we are used to seeing here on the mainland. When mature, the skin color is a much brighter color (almost golden) than the Hawaiian fruit that is so common in the United States. The flesh is thick, with an almost coral-red color. Another big difference is the size. Puerto Rican papayas can reach 20 inches in length and weigh as much as 10 pounds. We eat papaya fresh as is or in milkshakes. Green papaya is cooked with sugar and spices. It is a traditional dessert served with white cheese. This variety of papaya is also grown in Florida, Mexico, and the Philippines. Hispanic markets carry it mostly during the summer months. Hawaiian papaya, available almost year-round, can be substituted. Look for a fruit that is almost yellow. If it is only partly ripe, leave it at room temperature for a few more days. Refrigerate only when the fruit is completely ripe.

Parcha, passion fruit, is an oval-shaped fruit, native to Brazil. The variety grown on the island has a light yellow color. The ones we get here come mostly from New Zealand and are purple. Both types have a hard shell with seeds surrounded by fleshy deep-orange pulp. For many years passion fruit was used mainly to prepare a delicious thirst-quenching juice, *refresco de parcha*. As the New Cuisine became popular on the island, this "liquid gold" found its way into ice creams, sorbets, and innovative sauces. The fresh fruit can be expensive, but today passion fruit concentrate is available almost everywhere. It is sold frozen or in liquid form.

If you are lucky enough to find fresh passion fruit, look for ones that are large and heavy. They are usually sold by the piece. The fruit will be ripe when the skin is wrinkled. It can be kept at room temperature for a few days until you are ready to use it. It will also keep for about a week in the refrigerator. You can freeze the whole fruit in a plastic bag. When ready to use, simply cut in half and defrost the pulp.

Pimientos de cocinar, Italian frying peppers, are peppers with a thin skin and a mild flavor. They are usually from 3 to 5 inches long and about 2 inches wide. Their color varies from light green to bright red. Italian frying peppers are available fresh year-round. Look for shiny skin with no wrinkles. Store them in the refrigerator.

Plátano, plantain, is a relative of the banana. It is eaten green or ripe. Green plantain, or *plátano verde*, is the plantain at the unripened stage. It has a thick green skin and firm cream-colored flesh with a starchy taste. Store green plantains at room temperature; they will ripen slowly. If you refrigerate green plantains they will not ripen. Green plantain is used to make *mofongo*, *tostones*, and *pasteles*. (See Glossary.) *Plátano maduro* or *amarillo*, the yellow plantain at the ripe stage, has a sweet taste. When the plantain is greenish yellow it is called *pintón*. This means that it has black spots throughout the yellow skin. When the plantain is fully ripe it is also called *maduro*. Most dishes are made with the plantain at this stage, when the flesh is still firm. When the plantain turns completely black, it is made into a dessert called *dulce de plátano*. Ripe yellow plantains can be fried, baked, or boiled. They are also used in dishes like yellow plantain and meat pie. (See recipe, page 94.)

Recaíto is a raw mixture of Old and New World ingredients: *Recao* (green spiny leaf), *ajíes dulces* (sweet chili peppers), and *pimientos de cocinar* (Italian frying peppers) are native to the Caribbean. Garlic, onions, and cilantro came from Europe. Combined with tomato sauce, *alcaparrado*, and ham or fatback, and cooked slightly, *recaíto* becomes *sofrito*.

Salchichas, Vienna sausages, are a popular combination of beef, pork, and chicken sausage in a broth. They are only available canned.

Salsa de tomate, canned tomato sauce "Spanish style," is used in all stewed and braised dishes.

Sofrito consists of *recaíto* mixed with cooking ham or fatback, *alcaparrado*, and tomato sauce. This mixture is traditionally lightly sautéed in lard. Today lard has been replaced by corn or olive oil, and the fatback and ham have been largely eliminated. The Spanish settlers brought the *sofrito* (slightly cooked) concept to the island and adapted it to the new ingredients they found there.

Tamarindo, tamarind, is a pod-shaped fruit with brown skin. Large pits hold the pulp, which tends to be somewhat sour. It is eaten as a fruit, added to drinks, and mixed with sugar to make a compote. Store tamarind at room temperature or in the refrigerator.

Tocino, dry salt-cured pork (fatback), is a major ingredient of the traditional *sofrito* and yellow-rice dishes. White rice is also cooked with *tocino*. The fatback is diced and sautéed over medium heat. The fat rendered is then used to prepare other dishes. The golden brown, crispy pieces can be removed or incorporated into the dish.

Fatback is no longer used as often as it was in the past. Cholesterol-conscious cooks now opt for healthier versions of *sofrito* made with corn or olive oil. Store fatback wrapped in plastic in the refrigerator.

Viandas is the collective name for the many root vegetables and tubers that have been an important feature of Puerto Rican cooking since the time of the Taínos. Included in this category are *yautía, yuca, chayote, calabaza, apio, batata*, and *ñame*. All are starchy vegetables that should be bought when firm, and can be kept indefinitely in a cool place if left whole. They are used in *sancocho* and many other stews and soups. American pumpkin, potatoes, and sweet potatoes are acceptable substitutes, but you will sacrifice some flavor.

Vinagre generally means cider vinegar and is used mainly to marinate cubed steak and salad dressings. White vinegar is used to prepare *escabeche* dishes. Today balsamic and raspberry vinegars are used in dishes like pickled green bananas. (See recipe, page 37.)

3

SAUCES, DRESSINGS, SEASONINGS, AND MARINADES
(Salsas, Aderezos, y Marinadas)

The basic sauces in traditional Puerto Rican cooking are those based on *sofrito, escabeche, ajilimójili, mojito de ajo,* and *mojito isleño.* Our main sauce is a *sofrito* base that is used in stewing and braising.

Escabeche, a combination of olive oil, white vinegar, and spices, is used mainly for marinating. It is essential in seafood dishes eaten during Lent, such as *pescado en escabeche.*

Ajilimójili, a combination of sweet chili peppers, lemon, and garlic, is a sauce that can be improvised with freshly picked ingredients.

Mojito de ajo is a basic dipping sauce made with fresh garlic and olive oil. *Mojito de ajo* and *ajilimójili* do not require any cooking.

Mojito isleño is our best-known sauce. A combination of onions, olives, and tomato sauce, it is served with fritters and fried fish.

Other sauces have become part of our repertoire as part of the new Puerto Rican cuisine. Fruits have been incorporated into sauces like barbecue, Hollandaise, or vinaigrette, and Italian pesto has been adapted using cilantro instead of basil.

Adobo

Adobo is a basic seasoning in Puerto Rican cooking. It can be used for meats, poultry, pork, or seafood.

- 1 **tablespoon garlic powder**
- 1 **tablespoon onion powder**
- 1 **tablespoon dried oregano**
- ½ **tablespoon salt**
- ½ **tablespoon black pepper**

Mix all of the ingredients in a food processor or shake well in a glass jar.

Makes 4 tablespoons

Basic Recaíto
(Recaíto Básico)

This is the base for sofrito. It can be made in large batches and frozen.

½ medium yellow onion, diced
1 Italian frying pepper, seeded and diced
2 garlic cloves, peeled
3 sweet chili peppers, seeded
3 *recao* leaves (if *recao* leaves are unavailable, triple the amount of cilantro)
1 sprig cilantro

Combine all of the ingredients in a blender or food processor.

Makes ½ cup

NOTE: If using a blender, add some water or oil to the machine before mixing the ingredients.

Escabeche Sauce
(Salsa de Escabeche)

When Cara DeSilva, New York Newsday food writer, interviewed me about Puerto Rican cuisine for the first time, she was fascinated with the many dishes we make escabeche style.

Escabeche sauce is common throughout the island. White vinegar is used in traditional versions. New variations are being made with balsamic, red wine, and raspberry vinegars.

1 cup olive oil
3 medium yellow onions, sliced
½ cup white vinegar
½ tablespoon salt
1 tablespoon black peppercorns
4 bay leaves
5 garlic cloves, peeled and chopped
1 cup *alcaparrado*, drained and rinsed

Heat the oil in a nonreactive pan. Add the onion and sauté for 5 minutes. Reduce the heat. Add the remaining ingredients and cook over medium heat for 10 minutes.

Makes 3½ cups

NOTE: This sauce can be used with fried fish, poached chicken, or boiled *viandas* (root vegetables).

Sofrito Dipping Sauce
(Salsa de Sofrito)

A habit-forming sauce! Serve it with fish sticks or chicken cracklings.

- **1 tablespoon corn oil**
- **2 tablespoons Basic *Recaíto* (see page 16)**
- **1 tablespoon tomato paste**
- **1 tablespoon ketchup**

Heat the oil. Add the remaining ingredients and sauté lightly over medium heat for 3 minutes.

Makes ⅓ cup

Ajilimójili Sauce
(Salsa de Ajilimójili)

This traditional sauce is usually served with meats and fried fish. It is also good with tostones *(fried green plantain) or simply boiled* viandas *(root vegetables).*

   3 garlic cloves, peeled
 10 sweet chili peppers, seeded
   1 teaspoon salt
   1 teaspoon black pepper
      Juice of 3 lemons
 ½ cup olive oil

Grind all the dry ingredients in a mortar. Add the lemon juice and oil and mix well.

Makes 1 cup

NOTE: This sauce can also be prepared in a blender or food processor.

Traditional Garlic Dipping Sauce
(Mojito de Ajo Tradicional)

This is the classic sauce served over tostones *(fried green plantains).
It can also be used for* viandas *(root vegetables). Watch out, it's habit
forming!*

6 garlic cloves, peeled
1 cup olive oil
1 teaspoon salt

Crush the garlic cloves in a mortar. Add the oil and salt.
Store, tightly covered, in the refrigerator.

Makes 1 cup

NOTE: This sauce can also be made in a blender or food
processor.

Mojito Isleño

This traditional sauce comes from Salinas, a town on the southern coast of Puerto Rico. Almost everyone has a recipe for it. My version was inspired by the members of Villa Puerto Rico, one of the casitas (see page 5). Many of them come from this beautiful part of the island. Mojito Isleño can be served with any of our classic fritters, such as bacalaítos *(salt-cod fritters),* almojábanas *(rice-flour fritters) or* sorullitos *(cornmeal sticks).*

⅓ cup corn oil
1 medium yellow onion, chopped
1 cup tomato sauce
⅓ cup *alcaparrado*, drained, or manzanilla olives
2 bay leaves
2 Italian frying peppers, seeded and chopped
1 teaspoon salt
2 teaspoons black pepper
2 roasted red peppers, drained and cut into strips

Heat the oil in a heavy pot. Add the onion and sauté over medium heat until translucent. Add the rest of the ingredients and bring to a boil. Reduce the heat to low and cook for 15 minutes.

Makes 2⅓ cups

NOTE: You can use green bell peppers instead of the frying peppers and red onions instead of yellow, if desired.

Guava Barbecue Sauce
(Salsa de Guayaba para La Barbacoa)

Guavas grow wild on the island. Here they are rather expensive and sometimes hard to find. Frozen guava pulp works just fine in this delicious sauce. Brush this over ribs or chicken.

1 cup frozen guava pulp, thawed
1 cup ketchup
1 tablespoon Dijon mustard
2 tablespoons sherry

Thoroughly combine all of the ingredients.

Makes 2 cups

Guava Hollandaise Sauce
(Salsa Holandesa de Guayaba)

Here is a variation of the classic French sauce. It works well with poached lobster or shrimp and is also good over grilled fish, chicken, or beef. When I first made this sauce I asked my son, Alex, to help me peel the shrimp that would accompany it. He agreed because he couldn't resist the fragrant smell of guava!

3 **egg yolks**
1 **tablespoon fresh lemon juice**
3 **tablespoons frozen guava pulp, thawed (found in the juice section of the supermarket)**
¼ **pound (1 stick) unsalted butter**
½ **teaspoon salt**
½ **teaspoon white pepper**

Blend the egg yolks with the lemon juice and guava con-centrate in a food processor or blender for about 10 seconds. Melt the butter over medium-low heat until it starts to bubble. While the butter is still bubbling, pour it slowly through the feed tube of the processor or into the running blender, until the sauce thickens. Season with salt and pepper.

Makes 1 cup

Guava Butter
(Mantequilla de Guayaba)

Guava preserves combined with butter and golden rum make a delicious spread for breakfast toast.

- ½ cup (1 stick) butter
- 3 tablespoons guava preserves
- ½ tablespoon golden rum

Combine all of the ingredients in a food processor.

Makes ¾ cup

Mango Vinaigrette
(Vinagreta de Mango)

When I was working for A Sense of Taste caterers, Cheryl Kleinman introduced me to sauces made with fresh mango.

Every time I go back home to Puerto Rico, I can't think of enough uses for the mangoes in my mother's backyard. This dressing is good with a simple salad of arugula, carrots, and celery.

1 **cup mango purée (2 medium mangoes puréed in food processor)**
⅓ **cup cider vinegar**
⅔ **cup sunflower oil**
3 **tablespoons honey**
1 **teaspoon salt**
1 **teaspoon white pepper**
2 **tablespoons chopped fresh scallion for garnish**

Combine all of the ingredients, except the scallion, in a blender or food processor. Transfer the mixture to a bowl and garnish with the scallion.

Makes 1¾ cups

Mango Mojito
(Mojito de Mango)

Mangoes came to the island via Brazil. The best ones are from Mayaguez, a town on the west coast. Mangoes and ginger are combined here to create a delicious condiment. Serve it with grilled fish or chicken.

> 1 **tablespoon brown sugar**
> **Juice of 2 limes**
> 1 **tablespoon chopped fresh ginger**
> 1 **scallion, chopped**
> ¼ **cup roughly chopped cilantro**
> 2 **medium mangoes, peeled and diced**
> **Pinch salt**

Thoroughly combine all of the ingredients.

Makes 1½ cups

Papaya and Tarragon Sauce
(Salsa de Papaya y Estragón)

Tarragon's delicate flavor combines perfectly with papaya. This sauce, with its subtle yellow color, offers an interesting alternative to our everyday red sauces and is very good with grilled fish or roasted chicken.

  2 **medium papayas, peeled and diced**
1¼ **cups heavy cream**
  ¼ **cup dry sherry**
  2 **tablespoons fresh tarragon or 2 teaspoons dried**
       tarragon leaves
  1 **teaspoon salt**
  1 **teaspoon white pepper**

Purée the papaya and press through a sieve; set aside. In a saucepan over medium heat, reduce the heavy cream by about half. Add the remaining ingredients. Turn the heat to low and cook for 5 minutes. Cool the sauce to room temperature. Strain before serving.

Makes 2 cups

27

Cilantro Pesto
(Pesto de Cilantro)

This variation of the classic Italian sauce can be spread on grilled chicken or fish. For an interesting salad, combine it with cooked chayote and plum tomatoes.

- 2 cups cilantro
- ½ cup grated Parmesan cheese
- ⅓ cup chopped walnuts
- ¾ cup olive oil
- 4 garlic cloves, peeled
- 1 teaspoon black pepper
- Juice of 2 lemons

Thoroughly combine all of the ingredients in a food processor or blender.

Makes 1¼ cups

Cilantro Aïoli
(Aïoli de Cilantro)

This sauce is where the Mediterranean meets the Caribbean!

- 6 egg yolks
- 1 teaspoon Dijon mustard
  Salt and black pepper to taste
- 1 tablespoon fresh lemon juice
- 3 garlic cloves, peeled and crushed
- 1 cup loosely packed cilantro
- 1 cup light olive oil combined with 1 cup regular olive oil
- 1 tablespoon hot water

Place the egg yolks, mustard, salt, pepper, lemon juice, garlic, and cilantro in a blender or food processor. Process until the leaves are finely chopped. With the processor still running, slowly add the oil. The mixture should have the consistency of mayonnaise. Add the hot water, blend, and transfer to a glass container. Cover and refrigerate until ready to use.

Makes 2½ cups

Green Sauce
(Salsa Verde)

Nydia Velazquez, the first Puerto Rican woman to be elected to the U.S. Congress, likes to prepare mixed seafood cooked in salsa verde. You can also serve it over grilled fish, shrimp, or steamed lobster.

- ½ cup cilantro
- 5 garlic cloves
- 1 teaspoon salt
- 1⅓ cups olive oil
- ⅓ cup fresh lemon juice
- ½ teaspoon salt
- 2 teaspoons capers for garnish

Combine all of the ingredients except the capers in a food processor. Garnish with the capers.

Makes 1¾ cups

Butter-Rum Seafood Sauce
(Salsa de Mantequilla y Ron para Mariscos)

A simple sauce that enhances the flavor of poached seafood.

1½ cups fish stock
1 tablespoon golden rum (or to taste)
1 tablespoon all-purpose flour combined with 1
    tablespoon melted butter
1 teaspoon salt
1 teaspoon black pepper
Chopped parsley for garnish

Bring the stock and rum to a boil. Turn the heat to low and whisk in the flour-butter mixture, a little at a time, until the sauce thickens. Turn the heat to medium-low and cook for 5 minutes, stirring constantly. Add the salt and pepper. Add parsley for garnish.

Makes 1½ cups

4

APPETIZERS AND FRITTERS
(Aperitivos y Frituras)

Fritters are everyday food in Puerto Rico. They are sold at fritter stands and incorporated into the daily menus in most homes. They are also served as appetizers.

Meat turnovers, or *empanadas*, fritters common to all Latin cuisines, are often eaten for breakfast. Seafood *empanadas* are usually eaten for lunch. Guava turnovers (made with puff pastry) are served for dessert, sprinkled with confectioners' sugar. Our most famous fritters, *tostones* (fried green plantains), are a traditional side dish. They are served with rice and beans, onion steak, or fried pork chops.

The Puerto Rican New Cuisine has turned this peasant fritter into a gourmet presentation by adding items like caviar and fancy seafoods. Other traditional appetizers are chicken nuggets and pickled green bananas. The latter are now combined with new ingredients like flavored vinegars to create interesting variations that can be found in elegant restaurants and on caterers' menus in the United States.

Note that unripe (green) bananas and plantains are *not* the same! See "The Basics" (page 11) for information.

Stuffed Papaya
(Papaya Rellena)

A light and refreshing brunch dish!

>   Boston lettuce
> 6   small papayas, peeled, halved lengthwise, and seeded
> 6   tablespoons cottage cheese combined with 3
>   tablespoons mango, banana, kiwi, or strawberries,
>   diced
>   Ground nutmeg for garnish

Arrange the lettuce on a platter. Put the papaya halves on top and stuff with the cottage-cheese mixture. Sprinkle with nutmeg to taste.

Serves 6

Puerto Rican White Cheese Marinated in Fresh Herbs

(Queso Blanco Puertorriqueño Marinado en Hierbas Frescas)

In this variation of fresh mozzarella cheese marinated in fresh herbs, the cilantro gives just the right tropical touch.

1½ **pounds Puerto Rican white cheese**
3 **cups olive oil**
4 **tablespoons coarsely chopped fresh basil**
4 **tablespoons coarsely chopped fresh cilantro**
2 **tablespoons coarsely chopped fresh thyme**
   Pinch black pepper

Set the cheese in a bowl. In another bowl, combine the oil, herbs, and pepper, then pour the mixture over the cheese. Marinate in the refrigerator overnight. Drain the cheese and slice.

Serves 6

Puerto Rican White Cheese and Tomato Salad

(Ensalada de Tomate y Queso Blanco Puertorriqueño)

Classical tomato salad with a Puerto Rican touch, served with cilantro pesto.

      2 **7-ounce packages Puerto Rican white cheese, sliced**
3 or 4 **medium tomatoes, sliced**
    ¼ **cup Cilantro Pesto (see page 28)**

Arrange the cheese and tomato slices on a platter. Pour the cilantro pesto over them. Refrigerate, covered, for at least 1 hour before serving.

Serves 6

Traditional Pickled Green Bananas
(Guineos Verdes en Escabeche)

This dish is a holiday staple on the island. You can prepare it with almost any root vegetable. You can use the basic Escabeche Sauce (see page 17) or the following combination.

  4 pounds unripe (green) bananas, unpeeled, cooked for
    20 minutes in 2 cups of milk plus 2 quarts of water
⅔ cup white vinegar
1⅓ cups olive oil
  1 tablespoon salt
½ tablespoon black pepper
  1 cup *alcaparrado*
  4 bay leaves

Peel the bananas and cut them into ½-inch-thick slices. Combine the remaining ingredients in a nonreactive bowl. Add the bananas and toss well. Marinate for at least 1 hour before serving. Even better, marinate overnight.

Serves 6

NOTE: A variation of this traditional dish is made with balsamic vinegar and black Kalamata olives. See the following recipe.

Green Bananas in Balsamic Vinaigrette

(Guineos Verdes con Vinagre Balsámico)

Faintly resembling potato salad, this dish makes an intriguing tropical side dish for grilled chicken, fish, or beef. Sweet balsamic vinegar from Italy and Kalamata olives from Greece add a cross-cultural dimension to this version of the classic escabeche, *pickled green bananas.*

> 2 cups milk
> 2 quarts water
> 1 tablespoon salt
> 4 pounds unpeeled unripe (green) bananas, halved crosswise (do not peel)
> ⅔ cup balsamic vinegar
> ½ tablespoon black pepper
> 1⅓ cups light olive oil
> 1 cup Kalamata olives, pitted and sliced
> 4 bay leaves

In a soup kettle or large pot, bring the milk and water to a boil. Add the salt and bananas. Bring to a boil again, then reduce the heat, and simmer until the bananas are cooked but firm, 20 to 25 minutes.

Drain and peel the bananas, and cut them into ½-inch-thick slices. In a large nonreactive bowl, mix the vinegar with the black pepper. Whisk in the oil. Add the olives, bay leaves, and bananas and toss well. Let stand at room temperature for at least 1 hour before serving. This dish can be refrigerated overnight.

Serves 6

Traditional Tostones
(Tostones Tradicionales)

Traditionally, tostones *were eaten as a side dish with* bistec
encebollado *(onion steak), a dish as standard as American meat and
potatoes.* Tostones *can also be considered our French fries. Twice
fried,* tostones *are crispy on the outside and meaty inside. They recently have become star appetizers in the new culinary repertoire of
the island.*

2 cups corn oil
3 green plantains, peeled and cut in 1-inch diagonal
    slices

In a deep heavy skillet, heat the oil until it is very hot but
not smoking. Drop in the plantain slices and brown on all
sides. Remove with a slotted spoon, but maintain the oil temperature. Using a *tostonera* (see Glossary) or two pieces of
waxed paper, flatten the plantain slices to ¼ inch thick. Refry
until golden brown on both sides. Remove and drain on paper
towels.

Serves 6

NOTE: For a more sophisticated dish, arrange the *tostones* on
a platter and top each with 1 teaspoon of sour cream and ½
teaspoon black or red caviar. Delicious!

Stuffed Tostones
(Tostones Rellenos)

I tried the most delicious stuffed tostones at Restaurant El Jibarito in Chicago. Carmen, the chef, produces culinary wonders from a very small kitchen!

STUFFING
- 1 tablespoon annatto oil (see page 8)
- 1 fresh plum tomato, chopped
- 1 tablespoon tomato paste
- 1½ tablespoons Basic *Recaíto* (see page 16)
- ½ pound large shrimp, peeled, cleaned, and diced

- 3 green plantains
- 1 cup corn oil

Heat the annatto oil in a medium skillet. Add the remaining stuffing ingredients. Cook over medium heat for 5 minutes, or until the shrimp turn pink. Set aside. Peel the plantains and cut them into ½-inch rounds. Prepare as for Traditional *Tostones* (see page 39).

Place 1 teaspoon of the shrimp mixture on a *tostón*. Put another *tostón* on top and secure with a toothpick.

Makes 30 stuffed tostones.

NOTE: You can also stuff the *tostones* with seafood salad.

Plantain Chips
(Platanutres)

These have been called Puerto Rican potato chips. They are an excellent party food and are habit forming!

3 green plantains
Ice water
2 cups corn oil
Adobo **to taste (see page 15)**

Peel the plantains and slice them paper thin. Place in a bowl of ice water for 20 minutes. Drain and dry the plantain slices. Heat the oil until hot but not smoking and fry the chips briefly, until golden brown and crispy.

Remove from the pan and drain on paper towels. Sprinkle the chips with *adobo*.

Makes about ½ pound

Loíza Crab Burgers
(Tortitas de Cangrejo de Loíza)

The first time I tried crab cakes they were prepared by Rod Avilés, a very talented Puerto Rican chef in New York City. Since I grew up eating crab fritters in Loíza, I thought of them as Loíza crab burgers.

Fresh crumbs made from corn bread or muffins and cilantro give the perfect touch. Serve with fresh avocado slices.

- 1½ **pounds crabmeat**
- 3 **tablespoons mayonnaise**
- 2 **tablespoons Dijon mustard**
- 2 **eggs, beaten**
- ½ **cup chopped cilantro**
- ½ **cup fresh, frozen, or canned corn kernels**
- 1 **teaspoon salt**
- ½ **teaspoon chili powder**
- 1 **cup corn-bread crumbs**
- 2 **cups plain (white) bread crumbs**
- ½ **tablespoon black pepper**
- ¼ **cup corn oil**

Combine the first 8 ingredients and refrigerate for 30 minutes. Form patties with 2 tablespoons of crab mix for each. Combine the bread crumbs and black pepper on a plate and lightly bread each crab patty. Heat 1 tablespoon of the oil in a skillet and pan-fry the patties until golden brown on each side, adding oil as needed.

Makes 30 crab fritters for hors d'oeuvres; serves 6 to 8 as a main dish

Salt Codfish Fritters
(Bacalaítos)

Fritters are an everyday food on the island. At the fiestas patron-ales, the towns' celebrations to honor their patron saints, street ven-dors offer different versions of this traditional appetizer. This recipe was inspired by the feasts of Cataño, a town located on the north coast, across the bay from Old San Juan.

½ pound salt *bacalao*, cooked and shredded (see page 8)
2 cups all-purpose flour
1 teaspoon salt
½ teaspoon black pepper
½ teaspoon baking powder
3 garlic cloves, peeled and chopped
2 tablespoons Basic *Recaíto* (see page 16)
½ yellow and ½ red bell pepper, seeded and diced
2 cups water
2 cups corn oil

Combine the *bacalao*, flour, salt, pepper, baking powder, gar-lic, *recaíto*, and bell pepper in a bowl. Add the water and mix well. Let stand at room temperature for 30 minutes.

Heat the oil in a frying pan until hot but not smoking. Drop the batter by spoonfuls and fry until golden brown on both sides. Drain on paper towels. Keep the fritters warm in a low oven until you finish frying.

Serves 6

Rice-Flour Fritters

(Almojábanas)

This traditional appetizer uses white cheese. These fritters are often served with Mojito Isleño *(see page 21).*

1½ **cups rice flour**
½ **cup all-purpose flour**
2 **teaspoons baking powder**
1 **teaspoon salt**
1 **teaspoon black pepper**
¾ **cup milk**
3 **eggs**
½ **pound Puerto Rican white cheese, grated**
3 **cups corn oil**

Combine all of the dry ingredients in a large bowl; add the milk. Beat the eggs into the mixture one at a time. Add the cheese and let the mixture sit at room temperature for at least 2 hours before frying.

Heat the oil in a frying pan until hot but not smoking. Drop the fritters by spoonfuls and fry until golden brown on both sides. Drain on paper towels.

Makes 40 to 45 fritters

Alcapurría

This traditional fritter can also be stuffed with canned corned beef or chicken instead of picadillo.

1¾ **pounds** *yautía* **(taro root)**
3 **pounds unripe (green) bananas**
2 **teaspoons salt**
3 **tablespoons annatto oil (see page 8) plus some to coat aluminum foil**
1 **recipe Basic Beef** *Picadillo* **(see page 180)**
2 **cups corn oil**

Peel the *yautía*, and the green bananas. Grate each vegetable separately on the finest (smallest) side of the grater. Combine the grated vegetables with the salt and annatto oil in a large bowl. Cover with plastic wrap and refrigerate overnight.

Brush a small amount of oil on an 8 × 10-inch square of aluminum foil. Spread on ¼ cup of the dough. Place 1 tablespoon of *picadillo* on top. Fold the foil so the filling is completely covered. Smooth the fritter out with the back of a spoon. Repeat the process with the rest of the dough. When ready to fry, carefully remove the fritters from the foil. In a skillet, heat the corn oil until hot but not smoking. Fry a few *alcapurrías* at a time until golden brown. Drain on paper towels.

Makes 18 alcapurrías.

Shredded Green Plantain Fritters
(Arañitas de Plátano)

Arañitas *means "little spiders." Traditionally, this is one of the favorite ways to use plantains on the island. After Hurricane Hugo destroyed many of the plantain fields, these became a gourmet item on island tables.*

- **6 tablespoons butter, melted**
- **2 garlic cloves, peeled and chopped**
- **1 tablespoon brandy (optional)**
- **3 medium green plantains, peeled**
  Salt and black pepper to taste
- **3 tablespoons corn or vegetable oil**

Combine 4 tablespoons of the butter with the garlic and brandy and set aside. Coarsely grate the plantains into a bowl and season with the salt and pepper to taste. Heat the oil in a skillet until it is hot but not smoking. Press ¼ cup of the grated plantain at a time in your hands to form a small patty. Fry in the hot oil until golden brown, turning once to make sure it cooks evenly. Repeat with the remaining *arañitas*.

To serve, arrange the *arañitas* on a platter and brush with the remaining melted butter.

Makes 8 to 10 fritters

Meat Turnovers
(*Pastelillos de Carne*)

Known as empanadas *throughout Latin America, pastelillos are street food on the island. Traditional fillings include beef, seafood, and cheese. The small ones are eaten as snacks or appetizers. Larger ones can be a meal with a crisp garden salad.*

1 pound frozen puff pastry, thawed
1 cup Basic Beef *Picadillo* (see page 180)
1 egg, beaten

Preheat the oven to 375°F. Roll the dough ⅛ inch thick and cut out circles about 4½ inches wide. Fill one side of each circle with 1½ tablespoons of *picadillo*.

Brush the dough edges with the egg. Fold and press the dough to form a half moon and place on an ungreased cookie sheet. Bake for 30 minutes, or until golden brown.

Makes 10 pastelillos

Rice-Flour Crêpes Stuffed with Shrimp

(Crepas de Harina de Arroz Rellenas de Camarones)

STUFFING
- 1 tablespoon annatto oil
- 1 fresh plum tomato, chopped
- 1 tablespoon tomato paste
- 1½ tablespoons Basic *Recaíto* (see page 16)
- ½ pound large shrimp, cleaned, deveined, and chopped

CRÊPE BATTER
- 1½ cups rice flour
- ½ cup all-purpose flour
- 2 teaspoons baking powder
- ½ teaspoon black pepper
- 1 cup milk
- 3 eggs
- ½ pound Puerto Rican white cheese, grated
  Olive oil for frying

Heat the annatto oil in a large skillet. Add the plum tomato, tomato paste, and *recaíto*. Cook over medium heat for 3 minutes. Stir in the shrimp and cook until they just turn pink. Set aside.

Sift the dry ingredients together. With a wooden spoon, slowly stir in the milk, then the eggs. Continue stirring until the mixture is smooth and free of lumps. Add the grated cheese. Let the batter rest for 1 hour in the refrigerator.

Heat a 7-inch frying pan and coat it with 1 tablespoon of olive oil. Pour in ¼ cup of the crêpe batter and cook briefly, until golden brown on one side. Turn the crêpe over and cook for 1 minute. Repeat the process, adding more oil as needed, with the remaining batter.

To assemble the crêpes, place 2 teaspoons of the stuffing on one side of each crêpe. Lift the edges and roll. Secure with a toothpick. Serve at room temperature or rewarm in a very low oven.

Makes 15 to 20 crêpes

Cornsticks
(Sorullitos de Maíz)

The most famous cornsticks come from La Parguera, the phosphorescent bay located on the southwest coast. They are served with a sauce made from ketchup and mayonnaise known as Sauce Andaluse.

- 2 **cups water**
- 1 **teaspoon salt or** *Adobo* **(see page 15)**
- 1½ **cups yellow cornmeal**
- ½ **cup grated Cheddar cheese**
- 3 **cups corn oil**

Bring the water and salt to a boil in a small saucepan. Add the cornmeal. Reduce the heat to low and cook, stirring constantly, for 3 to 5 minutes, until thickened. Remove the pot from the heat and add the grated cheese. Let the mixture cool a little. Shape 2 tablespoons of dough into a stick about 3 inches long. Repeat with the remaining dough. Heat the oil in a skillet until hot but not smoking and fry until golden brown on all sides.

Makes 18 to 20 sticks

NOTE: You can also use Parmesan, Edam, or white cheese.

Chicken "Cracklings"
(Chicharrones de Pollo)

The word chicharrón *makes me think right away of the famous pork cracklings sold by street vendors in Bayamón, a town on the north coast of the island.*

In this case it refers to one of our most famous traditional dishes, small pieces of chicken that are crispy on the outside but very moist and tender inside. This recipe was inspired by Rosa Franco, the owner of a small factory that manufactures flanes *(custards) in Connecticut.*

1 3½-pound chicken, cut in small pieces
   Salt, black pepper, and dried oregano to taste
3 garlic cloves, peeled and chopped
½ cup golden rum
   Juice of 3 lemons
1 cup all-purpose flour
2 teaspoons salt
2 teaspoons black pepper
¼ cup corn oil

Sprinkle the chicken with salt, pepper, oregano, and garlic. Marinate in the rum and lemon juice for 30 minutes. Drain. In a plastic bag, combine the flour with the salt and pepper and dredge the chicken pieces, shaking off the excess. Heat the oil in a large skillet until hot but not smoking and fry the chicken pieces, a few at a time, until all sides are golden brown. Serve at once.

Serves 6

NOTE: You can use brandy instead of rum.

5

SOUPS
(Sopas)

Our national soup is *asopao* (chicken soup). Most traditional soups, somewhere between soups and stews, are based on a combination of assorted root vegetables, meats, and a *sofrito*-based sauce.

New soups, like sauces, use fruits as main ingredients. Cream soups have also resulted from the new trends. Cold soups, very appropriate for the warm climate, have now become quite popular.

Chicken Soup
(Asopao de Pollo)

Our national soup asopao is a medley of chicken, rice, and seasonings that nourishes the body and soul.

During the Christmas season, when groups of family and friends
get together at the asaltos (singing Christmas carols from house to
house), the best way to end the evening is with a big pot of steaming
asopao. Not only is it great party food, but it tastes better when re-
heated the next day.

1   3-pound chicken, cut into serving pieces
    Adobo to taste (see page 15)
3   tablespoons annatto oil
4   ounces smoked ham, diced
½   cup Basic Recaíto (see page 16)
1   cup tomato sauce
½   cup alcaparrado
6   cups water
2   cups short-grain rice
2   teaspoons salt
1   teaspoon black pepper
½   cup green peas, cooked, for garnish
½   cup diced pimientos for garnish

Season the chicken with the adobo. Set aside. Heat the oil in
a large soup pot and sauté the ham over medium heat. Add
the recaíto, tomato sauce, and alcaparrado. Cook for 5 minutes.

Add the chicken and water, and bring to a boil. Stir in the
rice, salt, and pepper, and turn the heat to medium-low. Cover
and simmer for 30 minutes, or until the rice is done.

The soup should have a thick consistency. Serve in bowls
and garnish with the peas and pimientos.

Serves 6 to 8

NOTE: If you want to prepare this soup for a party, double the recipe. For a new twist you can add blanched broccoli florets. You can also make *asopao* with shrimp, lobster, or salt codfish, instead of chicken.

Puerto Rican Chicken Noodle Soup
(Sopa de Fideos y Pollo)

This is another Puerto Rican version of the cure-all soup. It is one of the first solid foods given to babies, as well as the classic remedy for colds.

  2 **pounds boneless chicken breast, cut into pieces**
    ***Adobo* to taste (see page 15)**
  8 **cups chicken stock**
  ½ **cup Basic *Recaíto* (see page 16)**
  4 **ounces angel hair pasta, crushed**
1¼ **pounds potatoes, peeled and diced**
  ¼ **cup short-grain rice**
  2 **teaspoons salt, or to taste**
  2 **teaspoons black pepper**
  2 **sprigs cilantro**

Season the chicken with the *adobo*. Bring the chicken, water, and *recaíto* to a boil in a soup kettle. Add the remaining ingredients and bring to another boil. Reduce the heat to low and cook for 20 minutes, or until the rice and noodles are cooked.

Serves 6 to 8

Green Pigeon Pea Soup
(Asopao de Gandules)

This is a variation of our national soup, asopao de pollo. For vegetarians, like my friend Judith Velez, this soup, made with water instead of stock, is a real treat.

My mother used to pick fresh gandules *pods from the beautiful trees in our backyard. I would gather the* recao, *sweet chili peppers, and cilantro for her. My father's job was to shell and pick over the green pigeon peas.*

  1 **14-ounce package frozen** *gandules* **(green pigeon peas), thawed**
  2 **quarts chicken stock or water**
  2 **tablespoons light olive oil**
  ½ **medium red onion, chopped**
  ½ **red bell pepper, seeded and chopped**
  2 **sweet chili peppers, seeded and diced**
  3 *recao* **leaves, minced, or 2 tablespoons chopped cilantro**
  2 **garlic cloves, peeled and minced**
  1 **cup tomato sauce**
  2 **cups short-grain rice**
  1 **pound West Indian pumpkin, peeled and diced**
  ½ **tablespoon salt, or to taste**
  ⅓ **cup chopped cilantro**

In a large pot or soup kettle, combine the *gandules* and 2 cups of the stock. Cook until tender, about 20 minutes. Drain and set aside. Heat the oil in a skillet. Add the onion, bell pepper, chili pepper, *recao*, garlic, and tomato sauce. Sauté over medium heat for 5 minutes.

Combine the *gandules*, tomato mixture, rice, pumpkin, salt, and the remaining stock in a soup pot. Bring to a boil; lower the heat and simmer for 25 minutes, or until the rice is cooked and the soup has thickened. Add the cilantro just before serving.

Serves 6

Chicken Broth with Plantain "Dumplings"
(Caldo de Pollo con Bolitas de Plátano)

Green bok choy leaves make an unexpected garnish for this everyday peasant dish.

1 large green plantain, peeled and shredded through the next-to-finest side of the grater
10 cups chicken stock
½ tablespoon salt
½ tablespoon black pepper
1 cup bok choy leaves cut in very thin strips

Form dumplings from ½ tablespoonfuls of shredded plantain and set aside. Bring the chicken broth to a boil in a large pot. Add the salt, pepper, and dumplings. Reduce the heat to medium-low and cook for 15 minutes. Add the bok choy and cook for another 5 minutes.

Serves 6 to 8

Plantain Soup Creole Style
(Sopa de Plátanos Estilo Criollísimo)

I had this soup at Criollísimo, one of the finest restaurants in San Juan. Giovanna Huyke, island cooking teacher and television personality, arranged a tasting menu for me. We both agreed that this soup, although very easy to prepare, is packed with flavor.

    6 cups chicken stock
    2 green plantains, peeled and coarsely grated
    1 small yellow onion, chopped
    1 tablespoon annatto oil (see page 8)
    3 garlic cloves, minced
       Salt and black pepper to taste

Combine all of the ingredients in a large soup pot and bring to a simmer. Reduce the heat to low and cook, stirring occasionally, until the plantain is tender, about 20 minutes.

Serves 6

Gallician Soup
(Caldo Gallego)

This soup from Spain has become as much a part of our culinary tradition as roast suckling pig.

- 8 cups chicken stock or water
- ½ pound white navy beans, cooked
- ½ pound smoked ham, diced
- 2 *chorizos* (red Spanish sausages), sliced
- 1 medium yellow onion, sliced
- 3 garlic cloves, peeled and chopped
- 1 pound potatoes, peeled and diced
- 1 10-ounce box frozen collard greens, thawed
  Salt and black pepper to taste

Combine all of the ingredients in a large soup pot and bring to a boil. Lower the heat and simmer for 30 minutes.

Serves 6 to 8

White Bean Soup
(Sopa de Habichuelas Blancas)

I had a nanny, Delfa, who used to make this delicious soup. At lunch-time I would run home from school and find her waiting for me with a steaming bowl of bright red soup filled with white beans and chunks of salami.

1 tablespoon annatto oil (see page 8)
4 ounces fresh bacon, diced
4 ounces Genoa salami, diced
¼ cup Basic *Recaíto* (see page 16)
½ cup manzanilla olives, chopped
1 cup tomato sauce
½ pound white navy beans, cooked
8 cups water
¼ cup short-grain rice
2 ounces angel hair pasta or fidellini
½ tablespoon salt
1 teaspoon black pepper

Heat the oil in a heavy skillet and sauté the bacon and salami. Add the *recaíto*, olives, and tomato sauce. Cook over medium heat for 3 minutes.

In a soup kettle, combine the beans and water. Add the bacon mixture, rice, noodles, and salt and pepper. Bring the soup to a boil, then reduce the heat and simmer for 20 minutes, or until the rice is cooked.

Serves 6 to 8

Tripe Soup
(Mondongo)

A soup to cure anything! Adela Fargas of Casa Adela in New York is famous for her mondongo.

    2 pounds honeycomb tripe, cut into small pieces
    4 cups lemon juice combined with 8 cups cold water
    3 quarts cold water mixed with 1 tablespoon salt
    1 tablespoon annatto oil (see page 8)
    1 tablespoon corn oil
    ¼ pound smoked ham, diced
    ½ cup Basic *Recaíto* (see page 16)
    1 cup tomato sauce
    1 cup *alcaparrado*
    ½ pound each *yautía* (taro root), *yuca* (cassava), and
        calabaza (West Indian pumpkin), all peeled and diced
    1 green plantain, peeled and sliced
    4 bay leaves
    ½ tablespoon black pepper
      Salt to taste

Soak the tripe in the lemon water for 30 minutes. Rinse and put in a large soup pot with the 3 quarts of cold salted water. Bring to a boil. Lower the heat, cover, and simmer for about 2½ hours, or until the tripe is tender. Drain and rinse.

In a clean pot, heat the oils. Add the ham, *recaíto*, tomato sauce, and *alcaparrado*. Sauté over medium heat for 5 minutes. Add the tripe, root vegetables, plantain, bay leaves, and enough cold water to cover. Add pepper and salt. Bring to a boil, reduce the heat, and simmer for 40 minutes, or until the root vegetables are cooked.

Serves 10 to 15

NOTE: You can also add 1 cup drained canned garbanzos (chick-peas) to taste. Add them 5 minutes before serving.

Assorted Root-Vegetable Soup
(Sancocho)

Sancocho, *a classic stew, is like a tropical still life. It is a combination of root vegetables, tubers, plantains, and meats. Meats can vary from beef and pork to chicken. Traditionally served with white rice, sancocho is a meal in itself. It is ideal for cold days of winter. Serve it with garlic bread and a tossed salad.*

- 2 **pounds short ribs of beef**
- ¼ **pound smoked ham, diced**
- 4 **quarts chicken stock or water**
- ½ **cup Basic *Recaíto* (see page 16)**
- 1 **cup tomato sauce**
- 1 **pound each *calabaza* (West Indian pumpkin), *yautía* (taro root), *apio*, *ñame* (yam), and *yuca* (cassava), peeled and diced in 1-inch cubes**
- 2 **medium green plantains, peeled and cut in 2-inch pieces**
- 3 **ears fresh corn, cut into 1-inch pieces**
- 1 **tablespoon salt**
- 1 **tablespoon black pepper**
- 1 **quart water**

In a big soup pot, combine the first 6 ingredients, including all the root vegetables. Cover and bring to a boil. Reduce the heat to medium, cover, and simmer for 30 minutes.

Add the remaining ingredients and bring to another boil. Lower the heat and simmer, covered, for 45 minutes, or until the vegetables are cooked. Adjust the seasonings.

Serves 10 to 12

Caldo Santo

This soup is typical of Loíza Aldea, a town located on the east coast, where our African heritage is predominant. A lot of coconut-based dishes originated here.

Caldo Santo *is eaten during Holy Week. My friend Evelyn Collazo described this soup to me while we were viewing an art exhibit at the Museo del Barrio in New York City. We daydreamed about an open fire near the beach and the sweet fragrance of coconut milk and root vegetables on the breeze.*

7   cups coconut milk
½   cup annatto seeds
1   cup Basic *Recaíto* (see page 16)
3   quarts water
1   cup *alcaparrado* or manzanilla olives
1   pound each *yuca* (cassava), *yautía* (taro root), *batata* (Puerto Rican sweet potato), *calabaza* (West Indian pumpkin), and *ñame* (yam), peeled and cut into 1-inch cubes
2   green plantains, peeled and shredded, shaped into 1-inch balls (12 to 14 balls)
    Salt to taste
1   pound medium shrimp, peeled and cleaned
1   pound *bacalao* (salt codfish), cooked and shredded (see page 8)
8   blue crabs
1   pound boneless fillet of red snapper, cut into pieces

Heat 1 cup of the coconut milk with the annatto seeds. When the milk turns bright red, remove it from the heat and strain. Set the milk aside and discard the seeds. In a big soup pot, combine the annatto-colored milk, the remaining coconut milk, and the *recaíto*. Bring to a simmer. Add the water, *alcaparrado*, root vegetables, and plantain balls. Add the salt and bring to a boil. Add all the seafood and simmer for 30 minutes, or until the root vegetables are cooked. Let the soup cool a little before serving.

Serves 8 to 10

Chayote Seafood Chowder
(Sopa de Chayote y Mariscos)

Chayote, *a tropical squash shaped like a pear, has a mild flavor and a firm, crunchy texture.* Chayote *is low in calories and is a good source of potassium. Combined with seafood, it produces a delicate chowder with a tropical touch.*

> 2 medium *chayotes,* peeled and diced
> 2 celery stalks, cut into small pieces
> 2 carrots, peeled and diced
> 5 cups chicken stock or water
> 1 cup fresh, frozen, or canned corn kernels
> 1 cup light cream
> ½ pound medium shrimp, peeled and cleaned
> 12 clams, in shells, cleaned
> 12 mussels, in shells, cleaned
> ½ cup golden rum (optional)
> 3 cups water
> 3 sprigs cilantro
> 1 teaspoon salt
> White pepper to taste
> Pimiento strips for garnish

In a large soup pot, combine the *chayote,* celery, carrot, and chicken stock. Bring to a boil, reduce the heat, and simmer for 30 minutes. Let cool a little, then purée in a blender. Add the corn and cream and set aside.

Combine the seafood, rum, water, and cilantro in a large pot. Cover and cook briefly until the shrimp turn pink and the shellfish open up. Drain and combine with the *chayote* mixture. Return to the stove, add the salt and pepper, and simmer until hot, but do not boil. Garnish with pimiento strips.

Serves 6

Cold Taro Root Soup
(Sopa Fría de Yautía)

While doing my culinary apprenticeship with Joe Kugler, a French chef, I learned to prepare cold leek-and-potato soup. I grew up eating viandas (root vegetables), so I immediately adapted this classic dish using yautía *(taro root).*

2½   pounds *yautía* (taro root), peeled and diced
2   medium yellow onions, sliced
4   cups chicken stock or canned broth
1   cup light cream
1   teaspoon salt
1   teaspoon white pepper
   Pinch ground nutmeg

Cook the *yautía* with the yellow onion in the chicken stock for 30 minutes, or until tender. Drain. Purée the mixture in a blender or food processor and strain through a sieve. Add the remaining ingredients.

Refrigerate for 2 hours before serving.

Serves 6

NOTE: This soup is also good hot or at room temperature.

Cold Avocado Soup La Fortaleza

(Sopa Fría de Aguacate Estilo La Fortaleza)

Although we have summer weather throughout the year in Puerto Rico, cold soups are not an everyday food. When the former governor, Carlos Romero Barceló, took over La Fortaleza (the Governor's mansion) in 1981, he served a cold avocado soup at the opening-ceremony lunch. The soup became an instant hit in the best restaurants in San Juan.

    4 medium avocados, peeled and diced
   ½ cup plain yogurt
   ½ cup light cream
   2 cups chicken stock
      Juice of 3 lemons
      Salt and white pepper to taste
2 or 3 plum tomatoes, roughly chopped, for garnish
   2 tablespoons watercress, roughly chopped, for garnish

Combine all of the ingredients except the tomato and watercress in a blender or food processor and process until very smooth. Season to taste. Chill for at least 1 hour before serving. Garnish with tomato and watercress.

Serves 6 to 8

Papaya and Garlic Soup
(Sopa de Papaya y Ajo)

On a trip to the island, I discovered a papaya tree in my father's back-yard, full of beautifully ripe fruit. I had a great time figuring out ways to use all those papayas. Sipping some freshly squeezed orange juice, I came up with this simple and flavorful soup.

- 4 garlic cloves, peeled and sliced
- 1 cup fresh orange juice
- 3 cups chicken stock
- 4 papayas, peeled and cut into 1-inch dice
- 1 cup light cream
- 3 tablespoons sugar
  Fresh mint leaves for garnish

In a skillet, combine the garlic with the orange juice and chicken stock. Simmer until the garlic is tender, about 20 minutes. Let the mixture cool to room temperature. Purée the papaya with the orange-juice mixture in a blender or food processor and pass it through a sieve. Transfer the mixture to a bowl and whisk in the cream and sugar. Garnish with mint leaves.

Serves 6 to 8

NOTE: This soup can be served at room temperature or chilled.

Cold Mango and Rum Soup
(Sopa Fría de Mango y Ron)

On the island mangoes are in season from February until August. Here they are a real summer joy. This soup can be served as an appetizer or to end a Sunday brunch.

- 5 medium mangoes, peeled and cut into small pieces
- 1 cup coconut milk
- 1 cup milk
- ½ teaspoon ground cinnamon
- 3 tablespoons honey
- 3 tablespoons golden rum
  Freshly grated nutmeg for garnish

Purée the mango in a blender or food processor, then pass through a sieve. Combine the mango purée with the remaining ingredients except the nutmeg. Garnish with the nutmeg.

Serves 6

70

West Indian Pumpkin and Apple Soup
(Sopa de Calabaza y Manzana)

This is my Puerto Rican version of a delicious soup prepared by Waldy Malouf, chef at the Hudson River Club in New York.

3 pounds *calabaza* (West Indian pumpkin), peeled, seeded, and cubed
4 green apples, peeled, seeded, and coarsely chopped
1 medium yellow onion, diced
1 Italian frying pepper, seeded and diced
2 sweet chili peppers, seeded
6 cups chicken broth
½ tablespoon salt
   White pepper to taste
   Chopped cilantro and ground nutmeg for garnish

Combine all of the ingredients except the cilantro and nutmeg in a large soup pot and bring to a boil. Lower the heat and simmer for 20 minutes. Drain any excess liquid and purée in a blender. Adjust the seasonings. Rewarm the soup over medium heat. Garnish with cilantro and nutmeg.

Serves 8

6

SALADS AND VEGETABLE DISHES

(Ensaladas y Platos a Base de Vegetales)

Although we are not big salad eaters, some salads, such as *chayote* and potato, are basic to our traditional cooking.

There are also dishes resulting from the Puerto Rican New Cuisine. Beans, used traditionally in stews, are now combined with other vegetables. These new bean salads in some cases replace traditional rice and beans as side dishes.

Pasta salads have become very popular, too. Avocado is combined with seafood in light main-dish selections. Overall, salads and vegetable dishes have become a larger part of our daily diet than ever before.

Chayote Salad
(Ensalada de Chayote)

The firm, moist flesh of chayote is ideal for salads and vegetable dishes. Cubes of chayote are good with chicken, pork, or seafood. For a main-dish salad just toss chayote with avocado slices and a light vinaigrette. I also like to serve it with Ajilimójili Sauce (see page 19) or the dressings that follow.

4 medium *chayotes*
1 6-ounce jar pimientos, drained and diced

Peel the *chayotes* and cut each into 4 pieces. Boil in enough salted water to cover for 20 minutes, or until tender. Let cool at room temperature. Add a dressing and toss gently.

Serves 6

CILANTRO VINAIGRETTE
3 tablespoons olive oil
1 tablespoon vinegar
1 tablespoon chopped cilantro
Salt and black pepper to taste

SHERRY VINAIGRETTE
¼ cup sherry vinegar
1 tablespoon Dijon mustard
1 cup olive oil
Salt and black pepper to taste

CITRUS VINAIGRETTE
¼ cup fresh lemon juice
¼ cup fresh orange juice
2 tablespoons fresh orange peel
1 cup olive oil
Salt and black pepper to taste

TOMATO AND BASIL DRESSING
   2 tomatoes, chopped
   ¼ cup chopped fresh basil
   ¼ cup cider vinegar
   1 cup olive oil

Traditional Green Salad
(Ensalada Verde Tradicional)

No meal on the island is complete without a bowl of this salad. Red-tipped curly lettuce can be used instead of green. My mother used to drizzle on just a touch of oil, vinegar, and salt. You can use white-wine vinegar or a fruit vinegar such as raspberry.

- 3 cups curly green lettuce, cleaned and cut in thin strips
- 2 medium tomatoes, sliced
- 1 cucumber, peeled, seeded, and diced
- 1 cup cooked or canned corn kernels
- 1 cup green peas, cooked and chilled
- 1 6-ounce jar pimientos, drained and cut in strips, for garnish

Combine all of the ingredients except the pimientos in a serving bowl. Garnish with the pimientos.

Serves 6

Mom's Potato Salad
(Ensalada de Papa de Mami)

Summer vacations meant countless trips to the beach. The whole family would plan the menu, and my mom always prepared this potato salad.

3 pounds potatoes, peeled, diced, and cooked
1 cup mayonnaise
1 medium yellow onion, chopped
1 green bell pepper, seeded and chopped
4 eggs, hard-cooked and roughly chopped
2 medium apples, peeled, cored, and diced
1 6-ounce jar pimientos, drained and cut into strips
½ cup green peas, cooked, for garnish

Combine all of the ingredients except the peas in a serving bowl. Garnish with the peas.

Serves 8 to 10

Green Beans in Garlic Vinaigrette
(Habichuelas Tiernas con Vinagreta de Ajo)

While I was in college, Luis Loyola, a dear friend, prepared this salad for me and my roommate Mabel. You can use fresh green beans, so abundant in the summer months. I have added chopped black olives as a garnish.

1½	**pounds green beans, cleaned and cut into 2-inch pieces**
6	**garlic cloves, peeled**
3	**sweet chili peppers, seeded**
¼	**cup white vinegar**
¾	**cup olive oil**
1	**teaspoon salt**
1	**teaspoon black pepper**
⅓	**cup chopped black olives for garnish**

Blanch the green beans in boiling water for 3 to 5 minutes. Drain and cool. In a mortar, crush the garlic and sweet chili peppers. Transfer them to a bowl and add the vinegar, oil, salt, and pepper. Toss the beans with the dressing. Garnish with the olives.

Serves 6

Green Pigeon Pea and Carrot Salad
(Ensalada de Gandules y Zanahorias)

Edgar Sanchez, my son's godfather, is an excellent cook. He served this salad at Alex's christening party.

   2 **14-ounce bags frozen *gandules* (green pigeon peas) (or
      2 14-ounce cans, drained)**
   2 **quarts chicken stock or water**
   2 **pounds carrots, peeled and diced**
   ½ **cup cider vinegar**
  1½ **cups olive oil**
   1 **yellow onion, sliced**
   1 **yellow bell pepper, seeded and sliced**
   3 **bay leaves**
   1 **teaspoon salt**
   1 **teaspoon black pepper**
   ½ **teaspoon dried oregano**

Cook the *gandules* in the chicken stock for 20 minutes, or until tender. Drain and cool. Blanch the carrots in boiling water for about 5 minutes. Drain and cool. Combine the remaining ingredients and add the *gandules* and carrots. Let the salad marinate for at least 2 hours in the refrigerator, or better, overnight.

Serves 6 to 8

Green Pigeon Pea and Orzo Salad
(Ensalada de Gandules y Orzo)

Orzo (rice-shaped pasta) combined with gandules *(green pigeon peas) makes a pretty variation of the rice–and–gandules dish. Yellow peppers add the perfect touch.*

- **1 cup orzo, cooked according to package instructions**
- **1 16-ounce can *gandules* (green pigeon peas), drained**
- **1 medium yellow bell pepper, seeded and diced**
- **1 medium red onion, sliced**
- **¼ cup red wine vinegar**
- **1 cup sunflower oil**
- **2 teaspoons salt**
- **1 teaspoon black pepper**
- **3 tablespoons chopped cilantro**

Combine the orzo, *gandules*, yellow pepper, and onion in a large bowl. In another bowl, whisk the oil into the vinegar and add the salt and pepper. Pour the dressing over the salad. Add the cilantro and toss well. Refrigerate for at least 30 minutes before serving.

Serves 6 to 8

Avocado and Tomato Salad
(Ensalada de Aguacate y Tomate)

This simple salad is usually served with viandas *(root vegetables) and* bacalao *(salt cod).*

1 **large avocado, peeled and sliced**
1 **pound plum tomatoes, sliced**
1 **medium yellow onion, sliced**
   Cider vinegar and olive oil to taste
2 **teaspoons salt**
2 **teaspoons black pepper**
   Dash hot sauce (optional)

Combine all of the ingredients in a nonreactive bowl.

Serves 6

VARIATION: For an interesting twist add a papaya, peeled and diced. You can also substitute a red onion for the yellow.

Rice Salad
(Ensalada de Arroz)

During my last year in college a group of friends got together for Thanksgiving. It was my first potluck dinner. Lourdes Morales, a classmate, prepared a rice salad. She used bottled Italian dressing, but I prefer a fresh garlic-and-cilantro vinaigrette.

2 cups cooked rice
2 cups frozen mixed vegetables, cooked
2 tablespoons olive oil
1 medium yellow onion, chopped
1 medium red bell pepper, seeded and chopped
1 garlic clove, peeled and chopped
⅓ cup loosely packed cilantro
⅓ cup olive oil
1½ tablespoons cider vinegar
1 teaspoon salt

Combine the rice and mixed vegetables in a large bowl. Set aside. Heat the oil in a skillet and sauté the onion and pepper until golden brown. Let cool to room temperature. Combine the garlic, cilantro, oil, and vinegar in a blender or food processor; add the salt, and set aside. Add the onion and pepper to the rice mixture. Pour the dressing over the salad and toss.

Serves 6

Sautéed Chayotes
(Chayotes Salteados)

Get away from the meat-and-potatoes routine with this light and delicious side dish.

- **3 medium *chayotes*, peeled and sliced**
- **1 tablespoon butter**
- **1 tablespoon corn oil**
- **1 teaspoon salt**
- **Black pepper**

Blanch the *chayote* slices in boiling water for 2 minutes. Drain and set aside.

Heat the butter and oil. Add the *chayote* and sauté over high heat until it turns lightly golden. Sprinkle with salt and pepper.

Serves 6

NOTE: Sprinkle toasted pine nuts on top for a tasty garnish.

Chayote Hash
(Boronía de Chayote)

This hash can be served for brunch with breakfast sausages or ham.

    3 quarts water
    1 tablespoon salt
    4 medium *chayotes*, peeled and diced
    1 tablespoon annatto oil (see page 8)
    3 eggs, beaten
    2 tablespoons tomato sauce
    ½ tablespoon Basic *Recaíto* (see page 16)
       Salt and black pepper to taste

In a large pot, bring the water to a boil. Add the salt and the *chayote* and cook for 20 minutes. Drain and set aside. Heat the oil in a skillet. Add the eggs and cook over medium heat until they are slightly set. Add the tomato sauce, *recaíto*, and *chayote*. Cook for 5 more minutes, stirring constantly, or until the eggs are completely cooked.

Serves 6

Stuffed Chayotes
(Chayotes Rellenos)

This dish is a meal in itself. Serve it with a green salad.

- 3 large *chayotes*
- 1 tablespoon annatto oil (see page 8) or olive oil
- 4 ounces smoked ham, cut into small cubes
- ½ cup manzanilla olives, chopped
- ¼ cup Basic *Recaíto* (see page 16) combined with ¼ cup tomato sauce or 3 tablespoons tomato paste
- 1 pound ground beef
- 2 eggs, beaten
- ½ cup plain bread crumbs
- Parmesan cheese to taste (optional)

Cut the *chayotes* in half and cook them in a large pot of boiling water for 30 minutes. Drain and cool. Heat the oil in a heavy skillet. Sauté the ham, olives, *recaíto* or tomato paste, and ground beef over medium heat. Scoop the pulp out of the *chayotes*, chop, and add to the meat stuffing.

Preheat the oven to 375°F. Fill each *chayote* shell with the meat mixture. Top each shell with eggs and bread crumbs and sprinkle with cheese. Bake for 10 minutes, or until the egg has set.

Serves 6

NOTE: You can also use equal parts of ground beef and veal or veal and pork.

Stuffed Italian Frying Peppers
(Pimientos de Cocinar Rellenos)

This is an adaptation of the all-American dish, stuffed bell peppers.

- 1½ tablespoons annatto oil (see page 8)
- 2 tablespoons Basic *Recaíto* (see page 16)
- ½ cup *gandules* (green pigeon peas)
- ½ cup tomato sauce
- 1½ cups converted long-grain rice
- 2 cups boiling water or chicken stock
- ¼ cup dried currants
- 1 teaspoon salt
- 1 teaspoon black pepper
- 6 Italian frying peppers (if possible get them all the same size)
- 1 tablespoon olive oil

Heat the annatto oil in a saucepan. Add the *recaíto, gandules,* and tomato sauce and sauté over medium heat for 5 minutes. Add the rice, water, currants, and seasonings. Bring the mixture to a boil, and cook over medium-high heat until the liquid evaporates. Reduce the heat to low and stir. Cook, covered, for 20 minutes, stirring after 10 minutes.

Preheat the oven to 375°F. Cut the peppers on the top and remove any seeds. Stuff each with 3 tablespoons of the rice mixture. Grease a baking pan with the olive oil. Arrange the peppers in the pan and bake for 40 minutes. Serve each pepper with ½ cup of the remaining rice.

Serves 6

Stewed Okra
(Quimbombó Guisado)

Okra is my father's favorite vegetable. A gift from the African conti-
nent, it is a staple vegetable in traditional Puerto Rican cooking.

- ½ pound fatback, diced, or 6 slices bacon, chopped
- 1 cup sliced yellow onion
- 1 pound fresh plum tomatoes, seeded and chopped
- ½ cup Basic *Recaíto* (see page 16) combined with 1 cup tomato sauce
- 1½ pounds fresh okra, tips trimmed
- ½ cup chicken stock or water

Sauté the fatback or bacon in a Dutch oven over medium-high heat. Discard the excess fat. Add the onion, tomato, and *recaíto* mixture. Bring to a boil and cook for 5 minutes. Add the okra and chicken stock. Bring to another boil. Reduce the heat and simmer for 15 minutes, or until the okra is cooked.

Serves 4 to 6

VARIATION: You can add 2 fresh ears of corn, cut into 1-inch pieces, when you add the okra.

Puerto Rican Polenta
(Funche Puertorriqueño)

Funche, *a staple in the Taíno diet is known in Italy as polenta and in the American south as cornmeal mush. Funche can be sweet or savory. Cooked with milk and sugar, it is served for breakfast or dessert. As a side dish it is classically combined with beans.*

2 **tablespoons butter**
6 **cups water**
1 **tablespoon salt**
2 **cups yellow cornmeal**
Butter for greasing the baking pan

Bring the butter, water, and salt to a boil in a large pot. Whisk in the cornmeal, stirring constantly. Reduce the heat to medium-low and continue to cook, stirring constantly for 15 minutes, or until the *funche* is thick enough to hold its shape. Pour into a greased 9-inch square baking pan. Let it cool for 5 minutes before slicing.

Serves 6 to 8

88

Polenta Gnocchi
(Gnocchi de Funche)

A creative way to serve funche.

1 recipe Puerto Rican Polenta (see page 88)
1 tablespoon olive oil
½ recipe tomato sauce used for cannelloni (see page 180)
1 cup shredded mozzarella

Prepare the polenta as in Puerto Rican Polenta, but pour it into a sheet pan with sides (a jelly roll pan will work) and let cool.

Preheat the oven to 350°F. Cut the polenta into 1-inch circles with a cookie cutter. Grease a large shallow baking pan with olive oil. Arrange the polenta circles and cover them with the tomato sauce and mozzarella.

Bake for 30 minutes, or until the cheese has melted.

Serves 8

Puerto Rican Tamales
(Guanimes)

Corn tamales were another staple in the Taíno diet. In traditional cooking they were served with salt codfish stew. If banana leaves are not available, you can use parchment paper or aluminum foil. You'll also need butcher's twine, for tying.

1 pound	yellow cornmeal
¼ cup	all-purpose flour
2 cups	milk
2	cinnamon sticks
1 teaspoon	salt
10 to 12	plantain or banana leaves, or parchment paper
3 quarts	salted water

Combine the dry ingredients in a large bowl. In a small saucepan bring the milk, cinnamon sticks, and salt to a boil. Remove the cinnamon sticks and add the milk slowly to the dry ingredients. Mix until the liquid is absorbed.

Cut the plantain leaves in pieces large enough to wrap ¼ cup of the dough in each (about 8 × 8 inches). Put the dough in the center of a plantain leaf. Fold up the sides and ends and tie with butcher's twine. Repeat until all of the corn mixture has been used.

Bring the salted water to a boil in a very large pot. Add the *guanimes* and simmer for 1 hour. To serve, unwrap the *guanimes* and place on a platter. Serve with Salt Codfish Stew or *Mojito Isleño* (see pages 119 and 21).

Makes 10 to 12 guanimes

PLANTAINS, ROOT VEGETABLES, AND TUBERS
(Viandas)

All root vegetables can be cooked by steaming or boiling. In traditional dishes they are usually fried, however. New dishes include stuffed *mofongo* (plantain dumplings), *yuca* (cassava), vegetarian chili, and sautéed yellow plantain with Parmesan cheese.

Viandas are also eaten as a side dish instead of rice and beans. Since root vegetables are high in complex carbohydrates, they are healthy options in today's recommended diet.

Basic Fried Yellow Plantains
(Maduros Fritos)

Fried yellow plantains, like green ones, are staple everyday side dishes. They are also served for breakfast with eggs and Vienna sausages.

1 **cup corn oil**
3 **yellow plantains, peeled and cut into 2-inch slices**

Heat the oil in a skillet and fry the plantain slices until golden brown on all sides.

Serves 6

Baked Yellow Plantains
(*Maduros Asados*)

In the old days, cooks would roast plantains over el fogón (an open fire). You can do it in the oven. It is easier, although not as much fun as it used to be.

6 medium yellow plantains
4 tablespoons olive oil
Salt to taste

Preheat the oven to 400°F. Cut a 2-inch slit in each plantain and wrap with aluminum foil. Bake for 40 minutes. Peel the plantains and arrange them on a serving platter. Drizzle olive oil over all and season with salt.

Serves 6

Yellow Plantain and Meat Pie
(Pastelón de Amarillos)

The mozzarella cheese adds an Italian touch to this Puerto Rican version of lasagna.

FILLING
- 1 pound ground beef
- 5 plum tomatoes, seeded and diced
- ½ cup Basic *Recaíto* (see page 16)
- ½ cup manzanilla olives, chopped
- ½ cup golden raisins
- 1 cup tomato sauce
- 1 teaspoon salt
- 1 teaspoon dried oregano
- ½ tablespoon black pepper

"DOUGH"
- 2 cups corn oil
- 7 very ripe yellow plantains, peeled and cut into 3-inch slices
- ½ pound mozzarella cheese, shredded

TOPPING
- ½ pound green beans, cooked
- 6 eggs, beaten

Brown the meat in a large frying pan. Add the remaining filling ingredients and cook over medium heat for 5 minutes. Set aside.

Preheat the oven to 350°F. Heat the oil and fry the plantain until golden brown. Drain on paper towels.

Spread ½ cup of the filling in the bottom of a 9-inch square baking pan. Add a layer of half of the plantain slices and cover with the remaining filling. Add the mozzarella cheese. Top with the remaining plantain slices. Sprinkle the green beans on top and pour the eggs over all. Bake for 45 minutes, or until the eggs are set.

Serves 12 to 15

Yellow Plantain Boats Stuffed with Beef Picadillo

(Canoas de Plátano Relleno de Carne)

This was one of my favorite lunchtime dishes at Restaurante El Roble in Río Piedras. A whole plantain makes a main dish; pieces of stuffed plantain "boats" are lovely as a side dish.

- 2 cups corn oil
- 6 ripe but firm yellow plantains, peeled
- 1 recipe Beef *Picadillo* (see page 180)
- ¼ pound Cheddar cheese, shredded

Preheat the oven to 350°F. Heat the oil in a frying pan and fry the plantains until golden brown. Drain on paper towels. Make a slit in each plantain from top to bottom. Fill each with 2½ tablespoons of the *picadillo*. Sprinkle the cheese on top. Bake for 15 minutes, or until heated through.

Serves 6

Sautéed Yellow Plantains with Parmesan Cheese
(Amarillos con Queso Parmesano)

While looking for healthier ways to cook our staple root vegetables, I came across this simple recipe. It is good with fish or chicken.

2 tablespoons butter or margarine
2 tablespoons light olive oil
3 very ripe plantains, peeled and cut into ½-inch slices
¼ cup grated Parmesan cheese

Heat the butter and oil in a nonstick skillet. Sauté the plantain slices over medium heat until golden brown. Drain on paper towels and sprinkle the cheese on top.

Serves 6

Roasted Yellow Plantains with Balsamic Vinegar

(Amarillos con Vinagre Balsámico)

Balsamic vinegar combined with brown sugar gives sweet yellow plantains just the right touch. They go perfectly with a rice-and-bean stew.

3 **medium ripe plantains**
3 **tablespoons butter**
1 **tablespoon balsamic vinegar**
1 **tablespoon brown sugar**
   Ground cinnamon for garnish

Preheat the oven to 400°F. Make a slit in each plantain and place them on a cookie sheet. Bake for 40 minutes. Melt the butter in a saucepan and add the vinegar and sugar to it. Peel the plantains and arrange them on a platter. Drizzle with the butter mixture and garnish with cinnamon.

Serves 6

Traditional Mofongo
(Mofongo Tradicional)

*This superb dish combines green plantains with pork cracklings and
fresh garlic. It is served with chicken broth. I prefer to use bacon instead of cracklings.*

3 large green plantains
3 cups water mixed with ½ tablespoon salt
½ pound bacon, diced
3 garlic cloves, peeled and chopped
3 sweet chili peppers, seeded and minced
¼ cup extra virgin olive oil
   Salt and pepper to taste
¼ cup corn oil

Peel the plantains and cut them into ½-inch slices, dropping
them into the salted water. Sauté the bacon and drain and discard the fat. Chop coarsely and set aside. Combine the garlic,
chili peppers, and olive oil and season with salt and pepper.
Heat the corn oil and fry the plantain slices until golden
brown. Drain on paper towels. Put a few teaspoons of the
garlic-oil mix in a mortar. Add one-sixth of the bacon and 5 or
6 slices of plantain. Mash and press firmly into the mortar. Invert onto a plate. Repeat the process five more times.

Makes 6 mofongos

New Plantain Dumplings Stuffed with Shrimp

(Nuevo Mofongo Relleno de Camarones)

One of the new trends is mofongo *stuffed with seafood. This recipe was inspired by Tino's Restaurant on the west coast of Puerto Rico.*

STUFFING

    2 tablespoons extra virgin olive oil
    3 large garlic cloves, peeled and crushed
    ¼ pound smoked ham, diced
    ¼ cup sliced scallion
    ¼ cup roughly chopped cilantro
    ½ cup chopped manzanilla olives
      Juice of ½ lime
    1 cup tomato purée
    1 cup tomato sauce
    2 pounds medium shrimp, peeled, cleaned, and cut in
      half

MOFONGO

    3 large or 6 medium green plantains
    ¼ cup corn oil

Heat the olive oil in a large skillet. Add the remaining stuffing ingredients, except the shrimp, and sauté over medium heat for 5 minutes. Add the shrimp and cook until they turn pink. Set aside.

Peel the plantains and cut them into ½-inch slices. Heat the corn oil in a large skillet and fry the plantain slices until golden brown. Drain on paper towels.

Mash 5 or 6 plantain slices in a mortar with a little of the stuffing liquid. Fold in ½ cup of the shrimp mixture and shape into a ball with your hands. Repeat the process five more times.

Serves 6

Pasteles

Pasteles *are like a rainbow. Cubed pork and smoked ham mixed with raisins, alcaparrado, chick-peas, and other ingredients form the traditional stuffing. New stuffings include lobster and shrimp and vegetables like zucchini. (See the stuffing recipes that follow.)*

The dough is an intriguing combination of assorted shredded root vegetables and tubers. Traditionally, this mixture is wrapped in banana or plantain leaves. Parchment paper or aluminum foil can be used if these are unavailable.

Pasteles can be eaten year-round, but they are an essential Christmas dish on the island and for Puerto Ricans on the mainland.

1¼ pounds *yautía* (taro root)
3 pounds unripe (green) bananas
¾ pound potatoes
1 green plantain
2 tablespoons milk
¼ cup annatto oil, plus extra to grease the leaves or parchment paper (see page 8)
Salt to taste
Banana leaves, plantain leaves, parchment paper, or aluminum foil for wrapping
Traditional Pork Filling or Lobster Filling (see page 102)
Salted water to boil *pasteles*

Peel the vegetables and soak them in salted water for 5 minutes. Drain and grate on the finest side of the grater. Add the milk, oil, and salt. Let the dough rest for at least 1 hour in the refrigerator. (It is better if refrigerated overnight.) Brush the leaves or parchment paper with annatto oil. Spread ½ cup of the dough onto the center of an 8 × 10-inch wrapper. Place 2 tablespoons of the filling on the left side of the dough. Fold about 2½ inches from the left side of the wrapper. Fold twice more. Fold 2½ inches from the top and bottom. You should have a rectangle about 3½ inches wide and 6½ inches long. Tie with butcher's twine. Bring the water to a boil in a large soup pot. Add the *pasteles* and bring to a boil again. Reduce the heat and simmer, covered, for 45 minutes, turning the *pasteles* once.

Makes 16 pasteles

TRADITIONAL PORK FILLING

½ pound boneless pork shoulder, cut into small pieces
    Adobo to taste (see page 15)
2 tablespoons annatto oil (see page 8)
4 ounces ham, diced
½ cup Basic *Recaíto* (see page 16)
1 8-ounce can tomato sauce
¼ cup golden raisins
⅓ cup chick-peas
½ cup manzanilla olives
1 6-ounce jar pimientos, drained and chopped
1 teaspoon salt
1 teaspoon black pepper
1 tablespoon dried oregano
    Hot sauce to taste
2 tablespoons shredded unsweetened coconut

Season the pork with *adobo.* Heat the oil in a skillet and sauté the pork and ham for 5 minutes over medium heat. Add the remaining ingredients. Reduce the heat to medium-low and cook for 25 minutes, or until the pork is cooked through. Cool to room temperature before using.

Makes enough stuffing for 16 pasteles

LOBSTER FILLING
   1 tablespoon annatto oil (see page 8) combined with 1
      tablespoon light olive oil
   ¼ cup Basic *Recaíto* (see page 16)
   ¼ cup currants
   ½ cup sliced manzanilla olives
   ½ cup tomato sauce
   1 pound cooked lobster meat, diced
   2 teaspoons salt
   1 teaspoon black pepper

Heat the oil in a heavy skillet until hot but not smoking.
Add the *recaíto*, currants, and olives. Sauté for 2 minutes. Add
the tomato sauce, lobster, and salt and pepper. Cook over medium heat for 5 minutes. Cool to room temperature before using.

Makes enough stuffing for 16 pasteles.

Baked Puerto Rican Yam
(Batata Asada)

Simple yet packed with sweetness and flavor, baked batatas *can be used like baked potatoes.*

6 batatas (Puerto Rican yams), scrubbed
6 tablespoons (¾ stick) butter

Preheat the oven to 400°F. Rub 1 tablespoon of the butter on each *batata*. Set the *batatas* in a pan and bake for 1 hour.

Serves 6

Puerto Rican Yam Fries
(Batatas Fritas)

This traditional side dish for roasted chicken is sold along the roads on the island. You can also pan-fry the slices.

3 pounds *batatas* (Puerto Rican yams)
  Salted water for soaking
2 cups corn oil
1 teaspoon black pepper
  Ground nutmeg to taste (optional)

Peel the *batatas* and cut them into ¼-inch slices. Soak the slices in salted water to cover for 15 minutes. Drain and pat dry. Heat the oil in a skillet and fry the *batata* slices in a single layer until golden brown on both sides. Drain on paper towels and sprinkle with pepper and nutmeg to taste.

Serves 6

Cassava Fries in Garlic Oil
(Yuca con Mojo de Ajo)

Yuca (cassava) with garlic oil is a staple peasant side dish. It is usually eaten with bacalao (salt codfish), fried fish, or chicken.

- **4 large garlic cloves, peeled and chopped**
- **1 sprig fresh thyme**
- **½ cup sunflower or other vegetable oil**
- **3 pounds *yuca* (cassava)**
- **2 quarts water combined with 1 tablespoon salt**
- **1 cup corn oil**

Combine the garlic, thyme, and oil. Set aside. Peel the *yuca* and cut it in "steak fry" 3 × ½ × ½-inch strips. Boil the salted water in a large soup pot, add the *yuca*, and cook for 30 minutes. Do not overcook; the *yuca* should have a firm texture. Drain and pat dry with paper towels. Heat the oil in a heavy skillet. Sauté the *yuca* until golden brown. Drain on paper towels. Arrange the strips on a platter, and pour the garlic oil over the "fries."

Serves 6

Sweet-and-Sour Cassava
(Yuca Agridulce)

A simple and different way to serve yuca (cassava) as a side dish.

3 pounds *yuca* (cassava), cut into small dice (about 3 cups)
Salted water
2 tablespoons butter
2 tablespoons soy sauce
1½ tablespoons brown sugar

Cook the *yuca* in the salted water for 25 minutes. Drain and set aside.

Melt the butter in a frying pan. Add the soy sauce and sugar. When butter mixture starts to bubble, add the *yuca*. Sauté over medium-high heat for 5 minutes.

Serves 6

Cassava Chili
(Chili de Yuca)

Yuca *(cassava)* and white beans replace beef and red kidney beans in this vegetarian variation of the traditional chili con carne.

    3½ pounds *yuca* (cassava), peeled and cubed
        Salted water
     2 tablespoons annatto oil (see page 8) combined with 1
        tablespoon corn oil
     ¼ cup Basic *Recaíto* (see page 16)
     1 16-ounce can whole tomatoes, drained, seeded, and
        chopped
    1¼ cups tomato purée
     1 cup tomato sauce
    2½ cups white navy beans, cooked
    1½ teaspoons chili powder
     2 teaspoons salt
        Pinch ground nutmeg

Boil the *yuca* in the salted water for 25 minutes. Drain and set aside.

Heat the oil in a large skillet and add the *recaíto*, tomatoes, tomato purée, and tomato sauce. Cook the mixture for 5 minutes over medium-low heat. Add the beans, *yuca*, and seasonings. Cook for 10 more minutes.

Serves 6

Pickled Medallions of Taro Root
(Medallones de Yautía en Escabeche)

Try serving this as an alternative to yams on Thanksgiving Day!

- ½ cup white vinegar
- 1¼ cups plus 3 tablespoons olive oil
- ½ tablespoon salt
- ½ tablespoon black pepper
- ½ cup roughly chopped manzanilla olives
- 3 bay leaves
- 1 pound yellow onions, sliced
- 2½ pounds *yautía* (taro root), peeled

In a bowl, whisk the vinegar and the 1¼ cups olive oil. Add the salt, pepper, olives, and bay leaves. Set aside. Heat the 3 tablespoons olive oil, and sauté the onion slightly. Add the onion to the dressing.

In a large soup pot, cover the *yautía* with cold water and bring to a boil. Reduce the heat and simmer for 20 minutes, or until the *yautía* is tender. Drain and cool completely.

Cut the *yautía* into 1-inch-thick medallions and toss with the dressing.

Serves 4

FISH AND SHELLFISH
(Pescados y Mariscos)

Living on an island with the Caribbean Sea on one side and the
Atlantic Ocean on the other has allowed us access to a great
variety of fish and shellfish. Our typical seafood dishes display
our Spanish heritage clearly, as they are mostly prepared in a
sofrito-based sauce or *escabeche* style. *Bacalao* (salt cod) has been
an important staple for centuries. It is cheap, readily available,
and keeps without refrigeration.

One of our favorite fish has always been red snapper. Shellfish include shrimp, *langostinos* (saltwater crayfish), mussels,
and the spiny lobster characteristic of Caribbean Sea waters.
Conch and octopus are used mostly in salads.

The introduction of sophisticated herbs such as tarragon
has led to the evolution of delicate sauces to use over fish.
Poaching has been incorporated as a cooking method to keep
up with trends toward lower fat consumption.

Fish in Mojito Isleño Sauce
(Pescado en Salsa de Mojito Isleño)

This is a classic dish that is served throughout the island's coastal towns. Mojito isleño, a sauce that originated in Salinas, combined with red snapper is delicious evidence that simple cooking can also make a memorable meal.

> 3 whole red snappers (1 to 1½ pounds each), each split lengthwise into 2 pieces
> ½ tablespoon *Adobo* (see page 15)
> ¼ cup corn oil
> 1 recipe *Mojito Isleño* (see page 21)

Season the fish with the *adobo*. Heat the oil in a large skillet and sauté the fish until golden brown on both sides. Transfer the fish to another pan and add the sauce. Bring to a boil, then reduce the heat and simmer for 15 minutes, or until the fish is cooked through.

Serves 6

Pickled Fish
(Pescado en Escabeche)

My friend Miguelina serves this dish as a Lenten specialty. Traditionally sierra, Spanish mackerel, is used, but I prefer to use blue snapper.

1 lemon, cut in half
6 blue snapper steaks, 1 inch thick (about 3 pounds total)
1 cup all-purpose flour seasoned with 2 teaspoons each salt and black pepper
1 cup corn oil
1 recipe *Escabeche* Sauce (see page 17)

Squeeze the lemon over the fish steaks and dredge them in the seasoned flour. Heat the oil and fry the fish until golden brown on both sides. Drain on paper towels. Set the fish in a nonreactive bowl and pour the *escabeche* sauce over it. Let it marinate for at least 2 hours or overnight.

Serves 6

Swordfish Marinated in Recaíto
(Pez Espada Marinado en Recaíto)

Recaíto, a staple seasoning, highlights a marinade to make swordfish sweet and pungent.

MARINADE

- ½ cup **olive oil**
- ¼ cup **tomato sauce**
- ½ cup **Basic** *Recaíto* **(see page 16)**
- ¾ cup **fresh orange juice**
- 3 **bay leaves**

- 6 **swordfish steaks**

SAUCE

- ¼ cup **(½ stick) butter**
- ½ cup **fresh orange juice**
- ½ cup **frozen passion fruit juice concentrate, thawed**
- 2 **garlic cloves, peeled and chopped**
- 1 **tablespoon Dijon mustard**
  Zest of 1 small orange, or more to taste
- 2 **tablespoons olive oil**
- 1 **red bell pepper, seeded and diced, for garnish**
- ¼ cup **chopped cilantro for garnish**

Combine the marinade ingredients in a bowl. Add the fish, cover, and refrigerate for 2 hours. Turn the steaks every hour.

While the fish is marinating, prepare the sauce. Melt the butter and add the remaining ingredients, except the oil, bell pepper, and cilantro, and bring the mixture to a boil. Reduce the heat and simmer until the liquid is reduced to ⅔ cup. Set aside.

Drain the fish and discard the marinade. Heat the oil in a nonstick skillet and sauté the fish until lightly browned on both sides.

To serve, arrange the fish on a platter and pour the sauce over it. Sprinkle the bell pepper and cilantro on top.

Serves 6

Fish Sticks
(Palitos de Pescado)

These fish sticks are excellent party food. Serve with sofrito *dipping sauce.*

    2 pounds sea bass, trout, or tile fish fillets
    1 tablespoon *Adobo* (see page 15)
    3 cups corn oil
    1 egg, beaten
    1½ cups bread crumbs
    1½ cups all-purpose flour

Cut the fish in strips 2 inches long and ½ inch wide. Season with the *adobo*. Roll the strips gently to "round" them.

Heat the oil in a frying pan. While the oil is getting hot, dip the fish strips, one at a time, in the egg. Let any excess egg drip off. Dredge each strip in bread crumbs and then in flour. Shake off any excess. Fry the strips in small batches until golden brown.

Serves 4 to 6

NOTE: You can keep the fish sticks warm in a 250°F oven.

Scrambled Eggs with Salt Codfish
(Bacalao con Huevos Revueltos)

Bacalao *(salt codfish) has been a staple food for centuries in Puerto Rico. During the Depression years it was called "the steak of the poor." This is the simplest of our daily* bacalao *dishes.*

   3 tablespoons corn oil
   1 medium yellow onion, sliced
   1 red bell pepper, seeded and cut into strips
1½ pounds *bacalao* (salt codfish), cooked and shredded
      (see page 8)
   6 eggs, lightly beaten
   1 teaspoon black pepper, or to taste

Heat the oil in a skillet and sauté the onion and bell pepper over medium heat until the onion just browns. Add the codfish and eggs and cook until the eggs are set. Season with black pepper.

Serves 6

Salt Codfish with Spinach
(Bacalao con Espinacas)

*Fried codfish is one of my father's favorite dishes. I have added
sautéed spinach and prunes for a sweet touch.*

> 1½ pounds *bacalao* (salt codfish), cooked and drained but
>   not shredded (see page 8)
> 1 cup all-purpose flour
> 2 teaspoons black pepper
> 2 cups corn oil
> 3 tablespoons light olive oil
> ⅓ cup sliced almonds
> 10 prunes, pitted and chopped
> 1 10-ounce package frozen chopped spinach, thawed
>   and drained

Combine the flour and pepper on a plate. Cut the codfish
into 2- to 3-inch pieces and coat lightly with the flour.

Heat the corn oil in a skillet and fry the codfish until golden
brown on both sides. Drain on paper towels, set aside, and
keep warm. In another pan, heat the olive oil and sauté the almonds until lightly browned. Add the prunes and spinach and
cook over medium heat for 5 minutes. To serve, divide the codfish on serving plates, then top with the spinach mixture.

Serves 6

Salt Codfish Stew
(Bacalao Guisado)

This stew was served as everyday lunch food for centuries. Freshly harvested boiled root vegetables are the perfect side dish for this genuine peasant delicacy!

 2 **tablespoons annatto oil (see page 8)**
 ½ **cup Basic *Recaíto* (see page 16)**
 6 **plum tomatoes, diced**
 1 **cup tomato sauce**
 2 **pounds *bacalao* (salt codfish), cooked and shredded**
   (see page 8)
 2 **bay leaves**
 1 **teaspoon salt**
 1 **teaspoon black pepper**

Heat the oil in a skillet and add the *recaíto*, tomatoes, and tomato sauce. Cook over medium heat for 5 minutes. Add the remaining ingredients and cook over low heat for 15 minutes.

Serves 6

Salt Codfish Salad
(Ensalada de Bacalao)

I spent some time on a farm in Naguabo, located on Puerto Rico's east coast. I remember how Don Sabad would go to the field in the morning and get some yautías (taro roots), plátanos (plantains), and panapén (breadfruit). His wife, Doña Ana, an excellent cook, would put together three stones in the backyard, where a fire would be built. Over this open fire we would prepare a delicious lunch of bacalao (salt codfish) salad and boiled viandas (root vegetables). The yellow bell peppers add a colorful touch to this traditional dish.

- 1½ pounds *bacalao* (salt codfish), cooked and shredded (see page 8)
- 1 large potato, boiled, peeled and cut into chunks
- 1 medium Spanish onion, peeled and minced
- 1 avocado, peeled and cut into chunks
- 3 hard-boiled eggs, sliced
- 1 red and 1 yellow bell pepper, seeded and cut into strips
- 1 tomato, seeded and chopped
- ⅓ cup white vinegar
- 1 cup olive oil
- Salt and pepper to taste

In a serving bowl, combine the codfish with the potato, onion, avocado, egg, peppers, and tomato. In a separate bowl, combine the vinegar and oil and season to taste. Pour the dressing over the codfish mixture and toss well.

Serves 4 to 6

Coconut Shrimp
(*Camarones con Coco*)

This shrimp dish, crispy on the outside yet tender inside, is great party food. It is even better served over a bed of Coquí Rice (see page 163).

    2 cups coconut milk
    1 egg, beaten
   24 jumbo shrimp, peeled and cleaned
    ½ cup unsweetened shredded coconut
    ½ cup sweetened shredded coconut
    1 cup all-purpose flour
    1 tablespoon baking powder
    1 tablespoon *Adobo* (see page 15)
    ¼ cup corn oil

Combine the coconut milk and egg in a large bowl. Add the shrimp and marinate for 30 minutes. Blend the remaining ingredients, except the corn oil, by pulsing a few times in a food processor. Drain the shrimp and discard the marinade. Dredge the shrimp in the coconut-flour mixture. Heat the oil and fry the shrimp until golden brown on both sides. Drain on paper towels.

Serves 12 as an appetizer or 6 as a main dish

Shrimp, Papaya, and Avocado Platter

(Plato de Camarones, Papaya, y Aguacate)

Papayas and avocados are so abundant on the island that they are everyday foods. I created this recipe inspired by the bright colors of these fruits (yes, avocado is a fruit) during my days on Wall Street. It was served for a corporate Christmas lunch. Miriam and Nelson, my co-workers, had a lot of fun preparing it to serve 500 people!

Salted water or chicken stock to boil shrimp
Juice of 1 lemon
1 lemon, cut in half
1 Italian frying pepper (or bell pepper), seeded and diced
½ medium yellow onion, peeled and diced
2 pounds medium shrimp, peeled and cleaned
2 tablespoons brandy (optional)
⅓ cup fruit vinegar (my favorite is raspberry)
1 cup olive oil
¾ cup coarsely chopped cilantro
1 teaspoon salt
½ teaspoon white pepper
2 cups Boston lettuce leaves, cleaned
2 medium avocados
2 papayas

Combine the water, lemon juice, lemon, frying pepper, and onion in a pot large enough to hold the liquid and shrimp. Bring to a boil. Add the shrimp and cook for 5 minutes, or until they turn pink. Drain and cool.

In a bowl, whisk the brandy, vinegar, oil, cilantro, salt, and pepper. Reserve ⅓ cup. Pour the rest over the shrimp and let it marinate in the refrigerator for at least an hour or overnight.

Line a platter with the lettuce. Peel and slice the avocados and papayas and alternate slices of each. Brush with the reserved dressing. Drain the shrimp and put them in the middle of the platter.

Serves 6 to 8

Paella Río Mar

Paella, the national dish of Spain, has become a staple rice dish on the island. Traditional versions include meats, poultry, and seafood.

Accentuated by saffron, this is a simple combination of shellfish and rice. This recipe was inspired by the Río Mar resort located on the east coast of Puerto Rico. At Río Mar the breeze from El Yunque Rain Forest meets the sea, creating a peaceful and pleasant environment.

⅓ cup light olive oil
1 medium yellow onion, peeled and diced
1 yellow bell pepper, seeded and diced
4 garlic cloves, peeled and chopped
3 cups parboiled long-grain rice
4½ to 5 cups boiling chicken stock
Generous pinch saffron, soaked in an additional 1 cup boiling chicken stock
2 teaspoons salt
½ teaspoon black pepper
12 mussels, in shells, cleaned
12 clams, in shells, cleaned
½ cup water or white wine
1 pound medium shrimp, peeled and cleaned (save shells for broth)
4 lobster tails, shelled and cut into small pieces (save shells for broth)
1 cup frozen tiny green peas, thawed
1 6-ounce jar pimientos, drained and cut into strips

Heat the oil in a paella pan or Dutch oven. Sauté the onion, pepper, and garlic over medium heat for 5 minutes. Stir in the rice and mix well. Add stock to cover, then add the cup with saffron. Add the salt and pepper. Bring the rice to a boil.

In a large pot, steam the clams and mussels in water or

wine; drain and set aside. Add the shrimp, lobster, and peas to the rice and mix well. Reduce the heat and simmer for 20 minutes, or until the rice is cooked. Mix the clams and mussels into the rice just before serving. Transfer the paella to a platter. Garnish with pimiento strips.

Serves 10 to 12

Shrimp Stew
(Camarones a La Criolla)

Salinas, a town located on the south coast of the island, is best known for its seafood restaurants. For many years Ladi's was the most famous of these. Any special occasion would merit a trip to this beautiful part of the island.

I have sweet memories of walking along the beach and eating endless plates of tostones (fried green plantains) while waiting for a dish of succulent shrimp stew served on a bed of white rice with beans on the side.

- 1 tablespoon annatto oil (see page 8) combined with 2 tablespoons olive oil
- ¼ cup Basic Recaíto (see page 16)
- 3 bay leaves
- ½ cup alcaparrado or manzanilla olives
- 3 ounces smoked ham, cut into small dice
- 1 cup tomato sauce
- 1 16-ounce can whole tomatoes, drained and roughly chopped
- 2 pounds medium shrimp, peeled and cleaned
- 2 teaspoons salt
- 2 teaspoons black pepper

Heat the oil in a soup pot. Add the recaíto, bay leaves, alcaparrado, and ham. Sauté over medium-high heat for 3 minutes. Add the tomato sauce and canned tomato. Bring the mixture to a boil, reduce the heat to medium, and add the shrimp. Cook until the shrimp turn pink, about 5 minutes. Stir in salt and pepper and cook 2 minutes more.

Serves 6 to 8

Octopus Salad
(Ensalada de Pulpo)

The most popular beach on the west coast of Puerto Rico is Boquerón. There are kiosks on the beach that sell all kinds of traditional delicacies. Octopus salad served in a paper cone is a favorite for beachgoers.

Traditional ingredients include white vinegar and yellow onions. Red onions impart color and raspberry vinegar a subtle flavor.

- 3½ pounds fresh or precooked octopus
- 4 bay leaves
- ½ tablespoon black peppercorns
- 2 sprigs cilantro
- 1 teaspoon salt
- ¼ cup raspberry vinegar
- ¾ cup olive oil
- ½ cup manzanilla olives
- ½ medium red onion, finely chopped
- Black pepper to taste

If using fresh octopus, in a large pot combine the octopus, bay leaves, peppercorns, cilantro, and water to cover, and bring to a boil. Reduce the heat and simmer for 1 hour. Drain and cool. Clean the octopus by cutting out the eyes and cut it into small pieces.

Whisk the remaining ingredients in a bowl. Add to the cooked octopus and refrigerate for at least 1 hour before serving, although it's better if left overnight.

Serves 6

9

POULTRY
(Aves)

Poultry recipes, like those for seafood, exhibit our rich Spanish heritage. Chicken is eaten almost every day.

Turkey was once prepared only for the Thanksgiving holiday. Today, on the island as on the mainland, turkey parts are available year-round and are seasoned with ingredients like *adobo*. New dishes include chicken with fruit sauces, roasted chicken stuffed with *mofongo*, and various birds in *escabeche* sauce made with red onions.

Traditional Chicken with Rice
(*Arroz con Pollo Tradicional*)

On all Spanish Caribbean islands, arroz con pollo *is a classic preparation. It is an easy one-pot dish.*

   2 garlic cloves, peeled and chopped
   1 tablespoon cider vinegar
   1 tablespoon *Adobo* (see page 15)
   1 4-pound chicken, cut into pieces (you can also use
       thighs and legs combined)
   ⅓ cup corn oil or 2 tablespoons annatto oil (see page 8)
       combined with 3 tablespoons corn oil
   ⅓ cup olive oil
   1 medium yellow onion, sliced
   2 Italian frying peppers, seeded and cut into small dice
       (or 1 green bell pepper cut into strips)
   ¼ cup Basic *Recaíto* (see page 16)
   1 cup tomato sauce
   1 12-ounce can beer
   3 cups short-grain rice
   3½ cups boiling chicken stock
   ½ cup *alcaparrado*, or to taste
   2 teaspoons dried oregano
   2 teaspoons salt
   1 teaspoon black pepper
   1 cup cooked peas and carrots for garnish

Combine the garlic, vinegar, and *adobo* and season the chicken with the mixture. Let it rest in the refrigerator for 1 hour, or better yet, overnight.

Heat the corn oil in a large skillet and sauté the chicken over medium heat for 5 minutes. Drain and set aside. Heat the olive oil in a large skillet and sauté the onion and pepper until the onion is lightly browned. Add the *recaíto*, tomato sauce, beer, and chicken. Continue cooking over medium-low heat for 5 minutes.

Stir in all the remaining ingredients except the peas and carrots and bring to a boil. Reduce the heat to low, stir well, cover, and cook for 30 minutes or until all the liquid has evaporated. To serve, arrange the rice and chicken on a platter and sprinkle the peas and carrots on top.

Serves 8

Chicken and Rice with Asparagus and Tarragon

(Arroz con Pollo con Espárragos y Estragón)

Traditional arroz con pollo gets refined by substituting asparagus for green peas and chicken thigh strips for whole chicken pieces. Fresh tarragon, a natural with chicken, replaces cilantro, a staple in many chicken dishes. The bright annatto oil is omitted, giving this island dish a subtle and appetizing color.

- 2 **tablespoons corn oil**
- 2 **ounces ham, cut into small dice**
- 4 **chicken thighs, skinned, boned, and cut into strips**
- 1 **medium red bell pepper, seeded and sliced**
- 2 **tablespoons fresh tarragon leaves, minced, or 2 teaspoons dried**
- 1 **cup tomato sauce**
- 2½ **cups long-grain rice**
- 4 to 4½ **cups chicken stock or canned chicken broth**
- ½ **pound fresh asparagus spears, blanched, for garnish**

Heat the oil in a large saucepan. Add the ham and chicken and sauté until the chicken is browned, about 5 minutes. Add the bell pepper and sauté for another 2 minutes. Add the tarragon and tomato sauce and bring to a simmer. Add the rice and chicken stock and bring to a boil. Cover, reduce the heat, and simmer until the rice is tender, 20 to 25 minutes. Garnish with the asparagus and serve.

Serves 6

Chicken with Rice Aibonito
(*Arroz con Pollo a lo Aibonito*)

Aibonito, hometown of Dennis Rivera (president of Local 1199, New York City's hospital workers' union), produces the best chickens on the island. This small town also has an annual flower show. Inspired by the many colors of the fresh flowers, I created this dish. It is a variation of the classic arroz con pollo.

    2 whole bone-in chicken breasts with skin, cut into
       2-inch pieces
    1 recipe Traditional Garlic Dipping Sauce (see page
       20)
   ¼ cup olive oil
   ½ cup black olives, pitted and chopped
   ⅓ cup golden raisins
   ½ cup green peas
    1 6-ounce jar pimientos, drained and cut in strips
    4 cups long-grain rice
4 to 5 cups chicken stock
       Generous pinch saffron, soaked in an additional 1
       cup boiling chicken stock
    2 teaspoons salt
    1 teaspoon black pepper

Marinate the chicken pieces in the dipping sauce for 30 minutes. Drain and discard the liquid. In a skillet, heat 2 teaspoons oil, lightly sauté the chicken pieces, and set aside. Heat the remaining olive oil in a Dutch oven. Sauté the olives, raisins, peas, and pimientos for 5 minutes. Stir in the rice. Add enough chicken stock, including the cup with saffron, to cover the rice, and bring to a boil. Add salt and pepper. Reduce the heat and add the chicken. Simmer for 20 minutes, or until the rice and chicken are cooked.

Serves 10 to 12

Chicken with Macaroni
(Macarrones con Pollo)

This is a dish with an Italian influence, but the sofrito *definitely gives it a Puerto Rican touch.*

½ pound rigatoni, cooked according to package
    instructions
2 tablespoons annatto oil (see page 8)
¼ pound smoked ham, diced
¼ cup Basic *Recaíto* (see page 16)
2 pounds chicken pieces, seasoned with *Adobo* (see page
    15)
¼ cup manzanilla olives, chopped
1 tablespoon capers
1 cup tomato sauce
½ teaspoon black pepper
½ cup grated Parmesan cheese

Put the cooked pasta in a bowl. Heat the oil in a skillet and sauté the ham and *recaíto* over medium heat for 3 minutes. Add the chicken, olives, and capers and cook for 5 minutes. Add the tomato sauce and bring to a boil. Reduce the heat to medium-low and cook, covered, for 20 minutes. Add the pasta, pepper, and cheese and toss well.

Serves 6

Traditional Chicken Fricassee
(Fricasé de Pollo Tradicional)

Traditionally, this chicken stew dish was made with red wine. I prefer to use golden rum for a lighter touch.

1 4-pound chicken, cut into pieces
1 tablespoon salt
1 teaspoon black pepper
½ tablespoon dried oregano
3 tablespoons safflower oil
4 ounces smoked ham, diced
½ cup Basic *Recaíto* (see page 16)
1 Italian frying pepper, seeded and diced
½ cup *alcaparrado*
1 tablespoon white-wine vinegar
2 cups tomato sauce
2 cups water
½ cup golden rum
3 bay leaves

Season the chicken with salt, pepper, and oregano. Set aside. Heat the oil in a large skillet and sauté the ham, *recaíto*, frying pepper, and *alcaparrado* over medium heat for 5 minutes. Add the chicken and cook for 5 minutes more. Stir in the remaining ingredients. Bring to a boil, then reduce the heat and simmer for 25 minutes.

Serves 6

Chicken Stew with Cinnamon
(Pollo Guisado con Canela)

This was a specialty of my husband's grandmother. Serve it on a bed of white rice.

1 3- to 3½-pound chicken, cut into pieces
   Adobo to taste (see page 15)
3 tablespoons annatto oil (see page 8)
½ cup Basic *Recaíto* (see page 16)
8 ounces smoked ham, diced
1 cup tomato sauce
1 16-ounce can whole tomatoes, cut into pieces
1 cup water
½ tablespoon ground cinnamon
1 teaspoon salt
1 teaspoon black pepper

Season the chicken with the *adobo*. Refrigerate for 30 minutes. Heat the oil in a skillet and sauté the *recaíto* and ham over medium heat for 5 minutes. Add the tomato sauce, tomatoes, and water and bring to a boil. Add the chicken, cinnamon, salt, and pepper, and bring to a boil again. Reduce the heat to low and simmer for 30 minutes.

Serves 6

Pickled Chicken
(Pollo en Escabeche)

Red onions make this everyday dish a festive one!

3 pounds chicken pieces
   Adobo **to taste (see page 15)**
3 tablespoons corn oil
1 recipe *Escabeche* **Sauce using red onions (see page 17)**

Season the chicken with the *adobo*. Heat the oil in a large skillet and sauté the chicken until it is lightly browned. Remove from the pan and drain on paper towels.

Bring the *escabeche* sauce to a boil in a Dutch oven. Lower the heat, add the chicken pieces, and simmer for 35 minutes, or until the chicken is tender.

Serves 6

Ginger-Citrus Chicken

(Pollo en Salsa de Gengibre y Frutas Cítricas)

Ginger is not commonly used for savory dishes on the island. Here, combined with citrus fruits, it makes a spectacular sauce for chicken.

- **6 chicken thighs, boned and skinned**
- **4 teaspoons salt**
- **2 teaspoons black pepper**
  Juice of 2 large oranges
- **3 tablespoons butter**
- **1 2-inch piece fresh ginger, peeled and cut into strips**
- **1 orange, peeled and sectioned**
  Juice of 1 lemon

Season the chicken with the salt and pepper and marinate in ½ cup of the orange juice for 10 minutes. Drain and set aside. Heat the butter in a large skillet and sauté the ginger over medium-high heat until lightly browned. Add the chicken and cook until lightly browned on both sides. Add the orange sections, the remaining orange juice, and the lemon juice. Simmer for 10 more minutes.

Serves 6

Chicken in Citrus Escabeche Sauce
(*Pollo en Escabeche de Frutas Cítricas*)

Citrus fruits, brought to the New World by the Spanish settlers, are abundant throughout the island.

Inspired by traditional escabeche*-style dishes, I combined the fresh juice of my three favorite citrus fruits: oranges, lemons, and limes. The red onion and yellow pepper give the dish a colorful touch.*

- **2 pounds boneless chicken breast, cut into pieces and lightly flattened with a meat mallet**
  ***Adobo* to taste (see page 15)**
- **¾ cup olive oil**
- **1 medium red onion, sliced**
- **1 yellow bell pepper, seeded and cut into strips**
- **3 garlic cloves, peeled and chopped**
  Juice of 2 oranges, 2 limes, and 2 lemons
- **3 tablespoons honey**
- **3 tablespoons capers for garnish**

Season the chicken with the *adobo*. Heat ¼ cup of the oil in a large skillet and sauté the chicken over medium-high heat until lightly browned. Let it cool to room temperature on a serving platter. In another pan, heat ¼ cup of the oil and sauté the onion, pepper, and garlic until soft. Add the onion mixture to the chicken. Combine the juices, remaining ¼ cup oil, and honey. Pour over the chicken and toss. Garnish with capers.

Serves 6 to 8

Chicken with Papaya
(Pollo con Papaya)

Chicken and papaya is a dish representative of the island's new cuisine. Pieces of boneless chicken breasts are marinated in papaya juice. It is as perfect a combination as all-American ham and pineapple.

3 whole chicken breasts, skinned, boned, and split in half
2 teaspoons salt
2 teaspoons black pepper
1 tablespoon chopped fresh basil
2 cups papaya juice
1¼ cups light olive oil
1 fresh ripe papaya, peeled and cut into slices, for garnish

Season the chicken with the salt and pepper. Mix the basil and the juice with 1 cup of the oil and pour it over the chicken. Marinate for at least 1 hour.

Drain the meat and discard the marinade. Heat the remaining oil in a skillet over medium-high heat. Quickly sear the chicken on both sides. Lower the heat and cook, partially covered, for 15 minutes, turning the meat once.

To serve, arrange the chicken on a platter and garnish with fresh papaya slices.

Serves 6

Roasted Chicken with Honey-Rum Glaze

(Pollo Asado con Glaceado de Ron y Miel de Abejas)

Honey and rum make the perfect glaze for this simple roasted chicken dish. Serve over rice with green pigeon peas.

1   3- to 3½-pound chicken
    Adobo to taste (see page 15)
2   tablespoons golden rum or Spiced Rum (see page 226)
¼   cup honey

Preheat the oven to 400°F. Season the chicken with the *adobo* and set aside. Combine the rum and honey and brush the chicken with a light coat of the glaze. Sprinkle more *adobo* over the chicken. Place the chicken in a roasting pan and cover with aluminum foil.

Bake for 20 minutes. Remove the foil and brush the chicken again with the glaze. Bake, uncovered, for 30 minutes more, brushing the chicken with glaze every 10 minutes. Let the chicken cool a little before carving.

Serves 6

Roasted Chicken Stuffed with Mofongo

(Pollo Asado Relleno con Mofongo)

Mofongo *is an innovative stuffing for chicken. You can also prepare your Thanksgiving turkey with* mofongo *stuffing.*

- 1 **whole 3- to 3½-pound chicken**
- 2 **tablespoons *Adobo* (see page 15)**
- 2 **tablespoons corn oil**
- 1 **recipe Traditional *Mofongo* (see page 99)**
- ½ **cup chicken broth**

Preheat the oven to 350°F. Season the chicken with the *adobo* and brush with oil. Combine the chicken broth with the *mofongo* and mix until it is moist. (Add more stock if needed.) Stuff the chicken and loosely sew up the opening.

Bake for about 1½ hours, or until the meat is very tender.

Serves 6

Cornish Hens in Tamarind Sauce
(*Gallinitas en Salsa de Tamarindo*)

Tamarind combined with garlic and mushrooms creates a spectacular sauce for roasted Cornish hens.

3 **Cornish hens, seasoned with** *Adobo* **(see page 15)**
2 **tablespoons light olive oil**
4 **garlic cloves, peeled and chopped**
1 **cup sliced fresh mushrooms**
1 **cup tamarind pulp (see page 12)**
1 **cup chicken stock**
2 **tablespoons sugar**
1 **tablespoon cornstarch**
3 **tablespoons each chopped cilantro and scallion for garnish**

Preheat the oven to 350°F. Bake the Cornish hens for 30 minutes, or until the juices run clear when the breast is pricked with a fork. While the hens are baking, heat the oil in a skillet and sauté the garlic and mushrooms for 5 minutes over medium heat. Set aside. In a blender or food processor, combine the tamarind pulp, chicken stock, and sugar. Set ½ cup of the liquid aside and dissolve the cornstarch in it. Bring the remaining liquid to a boil. Remove the pan from the heat and mix a small amount with the reserved cornstarch mixture. Pour all liquid back into the pan, put the pan back on the stove, and cook over medium-low heat until the sauce is thick enough to coat the back of a spoon. Add the mushrooms and set aside.

When the hens are done, cut each in half and pour sauce over it. Garnish with cilantro and scallion.

Serves 6

10

BEEF AND PORK
(Carne de Res y Cerdo)

Traditionally, our diet has been rich in beef and pork. Roast suckling pig, a national dish, has always been a holiday preparation. Steak and onions is an everyday dish. Roast pork shoulder has become a favorite holiday dish for Puerto Ricans on the mainland who do not have access to a whole pig.

Stuffed pot roast is another favorite dish. Pork ribs are stewed or prepared with yellow rice and green pigeon peas.

Puerto Rican Steak and Onions
(Bistec Encebollado)

This is the traditional steak-and-onions dish. I remember, when I was growing up in Cayey, how my mother used to season the meat and let it marinate for a few days in the refrigerator. She used alcaparrado. I prefer to use manzanilla olives.

2 pounds beef top round, cut into thin slices
½ tablespoon salt
　Black pepper to taste
⅓ cup white vinegar
1 cup olive oil
½ cup manzanilla olives, sliced
3 cloves garlic, peeled and chopped
1 cup green bell pepper strips
2 cups Spanish yellow onion slices

Pound the meat to tenderize it. Season with salt and pepper. Combine the vinegar and ¾ cup of the olive oil. Add the olives and garlic; set aside. In a nonstick skillet, heat the remaining ¼ cup of oil and sauté the pepper and onion lightly. Remove the pepper and onion with a slotted spoon and set aside.

Reheat the oil remaining in the skillet until very hot and sear the beef on all sides. Return the pepper and onion to the skillet with the meat. Pour the oil-and-vinegar mixture over the meat. Cook over medium to low heat, partially covered, for 20 minutes, or until the meat is tender.

Serves 6

Traditional Corned Beef
(Carne Bif Tradicional)

This is one of my father's favorite dishes.

   2 **yellow plantains**
   1 **cup corn oil**
   1 **tablespoon olive oil**
   ¼ **cup Basic *Recaíto* (see page 16)**
   ½ **cup *alcaparrado***
1½ **cups tomato sauce**
   ¾ **cup water or beef stock**
   2 **12-ounce cans corned beef**
      Black pepper to taste

Peel the plantains and cut them into ½-inch slices. Heat the corn oil in a large skillet and fry until golden brown. Drain on paper towels and set aside.

Heat the olive oil in a separate skillet. Add the *recaíto*, *alcaparrado*, tomato sauce, and water or stock. Cook over medium heat for 5 minutes. Add the corned beef and black pepper. Cook over medium to low heat for 10 minutes. Add the plantain slices and cook for 5 minutes more.

Serves 6

NOTE: You can keep the plantain warm in a low oven. French fries, corn, or mixed vegetables can be substituted for fried plantains. For a more elegant dish, substitute 2 cups blanched broccoli florets and ¼ cup sliced almonds for the fried plantains.

Puerto Rican Pot Roast
(Carne Mechada al Estilo Puertorriqueño)

Pot roast is a dish enjoyed throughout Latin America. Our version is stuffed with smoked ham, olives, and chorizo. I have added currants for a sweet touch.

⅓ cup olive oil
3 tablespoons white-wine vinegar
1 tablespoon *Adobo* (see page 15)
½ tablespoon dried oregano
3 to 3½ pounds eye of round

STUFFING

⅓ cup dried currants, soaked in ⅓ cup sherry
½ cup manzanilla olives, chopped
¼ pound smoked ham, diced
1 *chorizo* (red Spanish sausage), chopped

BRAISING MIXTURE

2 cups tomato sauce
2 cups beef broth
⅓ cup sherry from the marinated currants
⅓ cup Basic *Recaíto* (see page 16)
Remaining stuffing

6 red potatoes, cut into pieces

Combine the olive oil, vinegar, *adobo*, and oregano. Season the meat with this mixture. With a sharp knife, cut a large incision through the center of the meat.

Combine all of the stuffing ingredients. Stuff the meat, cover, and let stand for 1 hour.

Sear the meat on all sides in a large pot or Dutch oven over medium-high heat. Combine all of the braising ingredients. Add to the meat and bring to a boil.

Reduce the heat to a simmer and cook for 1 hour. Slice the meat; return it to the liquid. Add the potatoes and cook for 10 minutes, or until the potatoes are done.

Serves 8 to 10

149

Puerto Rican Roasted Suckling Pig
(Lechón Asado Puertorriqueño)

Our national dish, roast suckling pig, is a festive presentation. Farmers usually pick one that has been specially fed to be prepared on Christmas Day.

These pigs can weigh from 75 to 100 pounds! At home the size of the pig will probably be determined by the size of your oven and the number of people you plan to feed. A 10- to 15-pound baby pig will feed a crowd of 15 to 20 people. Season the meat a few hours before cooking; keep it in the refrigerator overnight if you can.

½ cup garlic cloves or to taste, peeled and chopped
½ cup coarsely chopped onion
½ cup salt
   Black pepper to taste
3 tablespoons dried oregano
1 cup corn oil
1 10- to 15-pound suckling pig, cleaned and ready to
   cook
   Extra corn oil for basting
1 orange (optional)

Preheat the oven to 350°F. Combine the garlic, onion, salt, pepper, and oregano with the oil. Wash and dry the pig thoroughly. Marinate it in the garlic-and-oil mixture for a few hours or overnight.

Set the pig in a large roasting pan. Insert a ball made of aluminum foil into the pig's mouth. Fold the hind legs under the belly and tie them in place. Cover the ears with small pieces of foil. Bake for 3 to 3½ hours, basting occasionally with corn oil, until the leg juices run clear when pricked with a fork.

To serve, transfer the pig to a serving tray and insert the orange into its mouth. Let the pig rest for 10 to 20 minutes before you carve the meat.

Serves 12 to 15

Roasted Baby Suckling Pig with Guava Glaze

(Lechón Asado con Glaceado de Guayaba)

My father had a friend, Bonilla, whose roasted pig was well known in town. People on their way to Ponce would stop at his shop and buy lechón asado con guineitos (roast pork and boiled green bananas).

I have adapted the recipe by using a more manageable-size pig for the home cook. (Traditionally, a 40- to 50-pound pig is used.) When you go to the island you can see men turning pigs over an open fire in the countryside. The guava glaze gives an interesting touch.

1 10- to 12-pound baby pig, cleaned and ready to cook
   Adobo to taste (see page 15)
2 lemons, cut in half
6 garlic cloves, peeled and crushed
1 bunch cilantro, cleaned and chopped
¼ cup spicy brown mustard
¾ cup guava jelly or preserves
1 orange

Wash and dry the pig. Season it to taste with the *adobo*. Squeeze lemon all over the meat. Combine the garlic and cilantro, and rub the mixture over the pig. Let the pig marinate for several hours.

Preheat the oven to 350°F. Fold the hind legs underneath the belly and tie them in place. Place the pig in a large roasting pan. Combine the mustard with the jelly in a blender or food processor. Brush the entire surface of the pig with the glaze. Roast for 3 to 3½ hours, basting with the remaining glaze several times until the leg juices run clear when pricked with a fork.

To serve, transfer the pig to a serving tray and insert the orange into its mouth. Let the pig rest for 10 to 20 minutes before you carve the meat.

Serves 12 to 15

Roasted Pork Shoulder
(Pernil de Cerdo al Horno)

Puerto Ricans on the mainland have adapted the traditional roast pig to a pork shoulder for convenience and availability.

This recipe is a specialty of La Familia Restaurant in Jersey City, New Jersey.

8 **garlic cloves**
8 **black peppercorns (or assorted peppercorns)**
2 **teaspoons dried oregano**
2 **tablespoons corn oil**
2 **tablespoons cider vinegar**
2 **tablespoons salt**
1 **5½- to 6-pound pork shoulder**

Combine the first 6 ingredients in a mortar and crush. Rub the meat well with this "adobo." Let the meat rest for at least 3 hours in the refrigerator, or overnight if possible.

Preheat the oven to 350°F. Bake the pork shoulder in a roasting pan for 3 to 3½ hours, or until the skin is very crispy, turning it every hour.

Serves 6 to 8

Epi's Pork Pot Roast
(Pernil al Caldero al Estilo de Epi)

I spent a summer in New York's South Bronx, where the largest group of Puerto Ricans in the United States lives. There I met Epi, a wonderful home cook who became a dear friend. She showed me a different way of preparing the traditional pork shoulder. The recipe is especially good for the hot summer months when you don't want to use the oven.

        1 **4-pound pork shoulder or butt**
        1 **tablespoon salt**
        1 **tablespoon black pepper**
        2 **tablespoons dried oregano**
        4 **large garlic cloves, peeled**
       ⅓ **cup corn oil**
    2 to 3 **cups water or chicken stock**

Remove any excess fat and skin from the meat. Make small cuts all over. Wash and dry. In a mortar, combine the salt, pepper, oregano, garlic, and oil. Crush all of the ingredients to make a paste. Rub the meat with this mixture. Place it in a bowl and cover it with plastic wrap. Refrigerate for 2 hours.

In a large pot, brown the meat over high heat. Lower the heat and add the water or stock. Cook, covered, over medium-low heat for 3 hours. Add more liquid if necessary. The pot roast is done when the meat shreds easily. To serve, cut the meat off the bone.

Serves 6

Pork Loin in Tamarind Sauce
(Pernil de Cerdo en Salsa de Tamarindo)

Here pork gets a twist from the savory tamarind sauce. If fresh tamarind is unavailable, frozen pulp can be used.

1 cup tamarind pulp (from 10 shelled tamarind pods), or
    1 cup frozen tamarind pulp, thawed (see page 12)
2 cups beef stock or canned broth
3 tablespoons sugar
1 3- to 3½-pound boneless pork loin, tied crosswise at
    1-inch intervals
2 tablespoons corn oil
1 teaspoon dried oregano
½ tablespoon salt
½ tablespoon black pepper

Combine the tamarind pulp, stock, and sugar in a nonreactive saucepan. Bring to a boil, reduce the heat, and simmer for 5 minutes. Strain the sauce through a colander; discard the solids. Set aside.

Preheat the oven to 350°F. Rub the pork with oil, oregano, salt, and pepper. Transfer the meat to a roasting pan. Roast for 1½ hours, or until a meat thermometer inserted reads 150°F. Transfer to a carving board and let stand for 10 minutes. To serve, warm the sauce over medium heat. Remove and discard the string from the pork. Carve the meat into ¼-inch slices. Transfer a portion of the pork onto each dinner plate and spoon some sauce on top.

Serves 6 to 8

Pork and Eggplant Stew
(*Carne de Cerdo Guisada con Berenjena*)

Pork is enhanced by eggplant, a meaty-tasting vegetable.

    2 **tablespoons olive oil**
 2½ **pounds boneless pork roast, diced**
  ½ **cup Basic *Recaíto* (see page 16)**
    1 **cup tomato sauce**
2 to 2½ **cups water or beef stock**
    2 **bay leaves**
    1 **teaspoon salt**
  ½ **teaspoon black pepper**
    1 **1-pound eggplant, peeled and diced**

Heat the olive oil in a large skillet. Brown the pork. Add the *recaíto*, tomato sauce, liquid, and bay leaves, and bring to a boil. Reduce the heat to a simmer and cook, covered, for 40 minutes. Add the salt, pepper, and eggplant. Continue cooking, covered, for another 20 minutes.

Serves 6

Mom's Fried Pork Chops
(Chuletas Fritas al Estilo de Mami)

This is a traditional everyday main dish on the island. Mami likes to sprinkle the pork chops with white vinegar. Puerto Ricans usually serve them with white rice and bean stew. They can also be served with tostones and a mixed green salad.

    8 garlic cloves, peeled
    1 tablespoon *Adobo* (see page 15)
    ½ cup olive oil
       White vinegar to taste
    6 center-cut pork chops
    3 cups corn oil

In a mortar, crush the garlic. Add the *adobo*, olive oil, and vinegar. Use the mixture to season the pork chops. Heat the oil in a skillet. Drain any excess olive-oil mixture from the pork chops. Fry until golden brown.

Serves 6

NOTE: You can season the pork chops and let them marinate in the refrigerator overnight.

Pork Ribs Glazed with *Sofrito*
(*Costillas de Cerdo Glaceadas con Sofrito*)

Sofrito *makes a delicious marinade. Serve these ribs with rice and beans or tostones.*

SOFRITO MARINADE
- 1 tablespoon annatto oil (see page 8)
- 1 tablespoon olive oil
- 2 tablespoons cider vinegar
- ½ cup Basic *Recaíto* (see page 16)
- 2 cups tomato sauce
- 2 tablespoons tomato paste
- 1 teaspoon black pepper
- 1 tablespoon guava jelly
- ¼ cup coffee liqueur (such as Kahlúa or Tía Maria)

- 8 pounds pork ribs (preferably baby back)
- Additional coffee liqueur for basting

Heat the oils in a large skillet. Add the vinegar and sauté the *recaíto* over medium heat for 2 minutes. Add the remaining marinade ingredients and cook for 5 more minutes over medium to low heat. Cool the sauce completely.

In a bowl, combine the ribs with the marinade and let sit for at least 1 hour, or overnight.

Preheat the oven to 350°F. Drain the ribs and discard the marinade. Place the meat in a baking pan and bake for 40 minutes. Turn and bake for another 40 minutes, basting with the coffee liqueur every 15 minutes.

Serves 6

RICE, BEANS, AND PASTA
(Arroz, Habichuelas, y Pasta)

In Puerto Rico, rice and beans have been the base of our diet for more than 300 years. Today, Puerto Ricans of all socioeconomic levels still enjoy rice and bean dishes. If there is a dish that identifies us as Puerto Ricans, it is rice and beans.

Rice

Traditionally, rice is eaten twice daily. It is made into dishes that range from appetizers to desserts. Rice flour is used as a breakfast cereal, to make fritters, and in some desserts.

Most of the short-grain white rice we eat is grown in California and processed on the island. In recent years farmers have started to grow rice on Puerto Rican soil, but only on a small scale.

People who came to live on the mainland have adapted traditional dishes to long-grain rice. Most yellow-rice dishes are made with *sofrito*, annatto oil, smoked ham, and *alcaparrado*. (Annatto oil gives the rice its bright and distinctive yellow

159

color.) Brown rice is eaten mostly by vegetarians. Wild rice has become popular as part of the island's new cuisine.

The most distinctive characteristic of Puerto Rican rice dishes is the *pegao*, the crusty bottom of the rice that sticks to the *caldero*, the heavy iron pot rice is cooked in. (A Dutch oven also works well.) *Pegao* is formed by the way we cook the rice. Oil is heated and the rice is quickly sautéed before boiling water is added. Once the liquid is absorbed, the rice is stirred and covered. The rice is stirred several times as it cooks over low heat, and the *pegao* is formed.

Beans

On some parts of the island, beans are also known as *granos*. With the exception of chick-peas, our beans are all native to the New World, are harvested locally, and are usually eaten fresh. We also use dried and canned beans. *Gandules* (green pigeon peas) are our national bean, the only ones we also use frozen. Pink beans are favorites for daily meals. Other beans commonly used are lima, small white, chick-peas, and small red. Pinto and black beans have become part of our repertoire thanks to the growing number of Cuban and Dominican immigrants who have come to live on the island.

In New York I have come across new varieties of beans known as "boutique" beans. They can be used to prepare interesting versions of traditional Puerto Rican dishes. The Christmas lima, calypso, appaloosa, or Jacob's cattle can turn a peasant bean dish into an elegant presentation.

Beans are used mostly in stews and soups. Traditionally, beans were cooked with a piece of smoked ham, *recaíto*, and bay leaves. Many people like to prepare bean stews using the water in which the beans were cooked.

Dried beans are usually soaked overnight and prepared the following day. The cooking chart (see page 172) is based on beans that have been soaked.

All beans start cooking in cold water. Use 3 parts water to 1 part beans. Bring to a boil, then simmer for the recommended time. I grew up adding salt to the beans at the beginning of the cooking process, but after doing extensive research, I learned that beans should be cooked plain and seasoned when they are almost done. This keeps them from toughening. Some foam will form on the surface as beans cook. Remove it as it rises.

Pasta

Most of our Italian-influenced dishes include a combination of pasta, meat, and a tomato-based sauce prepared with *recaíto*. Smoked ham and *chorizo* are also often added. Beef *picadillo* is used to prepare spaghetti, lasagna, and cannelloni; stewed chicken pieces combined with rigatoni are a daily staple. This dish is a specialty at La Taza de Oro restaurant in New York.

Until recently only dry pasta was available. Now fresh pasta shops have opened throughout the San Juan metropolitan area. We can have fresh pasta every day if we want to.

Basic Puerto Rican White Rice
(Arroz Blanco Puertorriqueño Básico)

The crunchy bottom of the rice pan served with bean stew is the best part of the meal!

> **3 tablespoons corn oil**
> **2½ cups short-grain rice**
> **4 to 4½ cups boiling water**

Heat the oil in a medium saucepan with a tight-fitting lid. Add the rice and sauté quickly over medium-high heat for 2 minutes. Add the water and cook until almost all of the liquid has evaporated.

Stir well, reduce the heat to very low, and cover the rice. Cook for 20 more minutes, stirring after 10 minutes.

Serves 6

NOTE: Make sure you scrape the bottom of the pot!

Coquí Rice
(*Arroz Coquí*)

My friend John Haney and I created this tasty and visually exciting rice dish for his final project at the French Culinary Institute in New York. Coquí is a native rain-forest frog that hops on the bright green grass.

> 2 tablespoons corn oil
> 4 cups water or chicken stock
> 1 teaspoon salt
> 2½ cups parboiled long-grain rice
> 2 tablespoons butter
> ½ cup shredded carrot
> ½ cup chopped cilantro
> ¼ cup golden raisins (optional)

Bring the oil, water, and salt to a boil in a saucepan with a tight-fitting lid. Add the rice and reduce the heat to a simmer. Cook until the liquid evaporates. Turn the heat to low and cook, covered, for another 10 minutes. Stir the rice to make it fluffy.

Melt the butter in a saucepan. Add the rice, carrot, and cilantro. Cook over medium heat until the carrot and cilantro are slightly wilted. Add the raisins, if desired. Toss the mixture with the rice.

Serves 6

Rice with Coconut
(Arroz con Coco)

A savory coconut rice dish; serve it with Ginger-Citrus Chicken (see page 138).

2½ tablespoons corn oil
2 cups parboiled long-grain rice
¼ cup raisins (optional)
¼ cup shredded coconut (preferably unsweetened)
5 cups boiling water or chicken stock
2 teaspoons salt
1 teaspoon white pepper

Heat the oil in a saucepan with a tight-fitting lid. Add the rice, raisins, if desired, and coconut. Sauté lightly. Add the boiling liquid, salt, and pepper. Cook on high heat until the liquid is absorbed. Reduce the heat to very low and cook, covered, stirring every 10 minutes, for 25 minutes.

Serves 6

Rice with Vienna Sausages
(Arroz con Salchichas)

This is a typical fonda *dish. Served with bean stew, tostones, and a salad, it makes a hearty meal.*

> 1 **9-ounce can Vienna sausages, drained and cut into pieces**
> 1 **tablespoon annatto oil**
> 2 **tablespoons corn oil**
> 2 **tablespoons Basic *Recaíto* (see page 16)**
> 1 **cup tomato sauce**
> ½ **cup manzanilla olives, chopped**
> 2 **cups short-grain rice**
> 4 to 4½ **cups boiling water or chicken stock**
> **Salt and pepper to taste**

Combine the sausages, oil, and *recaíto* in a large pot. Sauté quickly over medium-high heat; reduce the heat and add the tomato sauce and the olives. Cook for 5 minutes.

Add the rice and the water and season to taste. Turn the heat back to medium-high and cook ·until the water is absorbed. Stir the rice well, reduce the heat to low, and cover the pot. Cook for another 20 to 25 minutes.

Serves 4

Rice with Squid
(Arroz con Calamares)

This is the only combined rice dish in our cuisine that is not yellow!

- 1 **tablespoon olive oil**
- 2 **6-ounce cans** *calamares en su tinta* **(cuttlefish in its ink)**
- ½ **cup** *alcaparrado*
- 2½ **cups short-grain rice**
- 4½ to 5 **cups boiling water or chicken stock**
- 2 **teaspoons salt**
- 1 **teaspoon black pepper**

Heat the oil in a saucepan with a tight-fitting lid and sauté the *calamares* over medium heat for 5 minutes. Add the remaining ingredients. Bring the liquid to a boil. Reduce the heat to a simmer and cook until the liquid has evaporated.

Stir the rice, cover, and cook over very low heat for 30 minutes, stirring every 10 minutes.

Serves 6

Basic Yellow Rice
(*Arroz Amarillo Básico*)

The bright yellow color of this rice reminds me of a beautiful sunny day on the island. This is an everyday rice dish.

> **2 tablespoons annatto oil combined with 1 tablespoon corn oil**
> **2½ cups rice**
> **4 to 4½ cups boiling water or chicken stock**
> **2 teaspoons salt**

Heat the oil in a saucepan with a tight-fitting lid. Add the rice and stir to combine. Stir in the boiling liquid and salt. Bring to a boil, reduce the heat to a simmer, and cook until the liquid evaporates. Cover and cook over very low heat for 20 minutes, stirring after 10 minutes.

Serves 6.

Puerto Rican Fried Rice
(Arroz Frito al Estilo Puertorriqueño)

When I was growing up, the Chinese restaurants in my hometown, Cayey, used to serve fried rice made with iceberg lettuce. I have added annatto oil to make it more like our yellow rice dishes.

- 4 tablespoons annatto oil (see page 8)
- ¼ cup chopped scallion
- ½ cup chopped Italian frying pepper
- 1 cup bean sprouts
- ¼ cup shredded iceberg lettuce
- 2 eggs, beaten
- 2½ cups cooked rice
- ½ teaspoon salt
- ½ teaspoon black pepper

Heat 2 tablespoons of the annatto oil in a large skillet. Sauté the scallion, Italian pepper, bean sprouts, and lettuce over medium-high heat for 2 minutes. Add the eggs and cook until scrambled soft. Set aside.

In another pan, heat the remaining annatto oil. Add the rice and cook over high heat, stirring constantly, until the rice has become completely yellow. Add the egg mixture, salt, and pepper, turn the heat to medium, and cook for another 2 minutes.

Serves 6

Yellow Rice with Shrimp and Mixed Vegetables

(Arroz Amarillo con Camarones y Vegetales Mixtos)

Elsa Ayala from the Commonwealth of Puerto Rico office in New York has a relative of Pakistani background. She has developed what she calls "Paquirican" cuisine. This delicious shrimp with yellow rice is one of her favorite holiday dishes.

>   2 tablespoons annatto oil (see page 8)
>   1 tablespoon corn oil
>   1 pound medium shrimp, peeled and cleaned
>   1 cup frozen mixed vegetables, thawed
>   2½ cups short-grain rice
>   4 cups boiling water or chicken stock
>   2 teaspoons salt
>   ½ teaspoon black pepper
>   ½ teaspoon curry powder

Heat the oils in a large pot with a tight-fitting lid. Sauté the shrimp over medium-high heat for 2 minutes. Add the mixed vegetables and rice. Toss well and continue cooking for 1 more minute. Add the boiling liquid and seasonings. Cook until the water has evaporated. Stir, lower the heat, and cook for 20 more minutes, stirring after 10 minutes.

Serves 8 to 10

NOTE: If you want rice with a spicier touch, increase the amount of curry powder.

Yellow Rice with Crab
(Arroz con Jueyes)

I originally prepared this rice using crabs I had just caught on a fishing trip with my friend Pablo Baez. If fresh crabs are unavailable, use lump crabmeat. It works just fine.

> 4 tablespoons annatto oil (see page 8)
> 12 crabs, cooked, or 1 pound lump crabmeat
> ½ cup Basic *Recaíto* (see page 16)
> ½ cup manzanilla olives, chopped
> 1 cup tomato sauce
> 3 cups parboiled long-grain rice
> 4 to 4½ cups boiling water (you can use the same water used to cook the crabs)

Heat the oil in a large pot with a tight-fitting lid. Add the crabs or crabmeat, *recaíto*, olives, and tomato sauce. Sauté over medium heat for 2 to 3 minutes. Add the rice and water; bring to a boil. Reduce the heat, cover, and simmer for 20 minutes, or until the rice is cooked.

Serves 10 to 12

Yellow Rice with Green Pigeon Peas
(Arroz con Gandules)

This is our national rice-and-bean dish. It is a must during the Christmas season!

> 2 tablespoons annatto oil (see page 8)
> ¼ cup sliced *chorizo* (red Spanish sausage)
> ¼ cup diced smoked ham
> ¾ cup Basic *Recaíto* (see page 16)
> 1 can (about 16 ounces) *gandules* (green pigeon peas), or 1 14-ounce bag frozen
> 2 cups tomato sauce
> 2 cups short-grain rice
> 4 to 4½ cups water
> Salt and black pepper to taste

Heat the oil in a large pot with a tight-fitting lid. Add the *chorizo* and smoked ham and fry lightly. Add the *recaíto*, *gandules*, and tomato sauce. Mix well and cook over medium heat for 5 minutes. Add the rice and water to cover. Turn the heat to medium-high and cook until the water is entirely absorbed. Add salt and pepper, stir, and turn the heat to low. Cover and cook for 30 to 45 minutes.

To serve, turn the rice out onto a platter. Scrape off the crusty layer that will have formed at the bottom of the pan, and top the rice with it.

Serves 4

TRADITIONAL DRIED BEANS

Type of Bean (1 Cup Dry)	Approximate Cooking Time	Yield (in Cups)
Black	45 min.	2⅓
Black-eyed peas	25 to 30 min.	2½
Cannellini (white)	45 min.	2½
Garbanzo (chick-peas)	55 min.	2½
Great Northern (white)	1 hour	2½
Green peas	1 hour, 15 min.	2½
Lentils	15 to 20 min.	3
Lima (small)	25 to 30 min.	2½
Lima (large)	1 hour	2½
Lowfield peas	30 min.	3
Navy (small white)	45 min.	2½
Pigeon peas (gandules)	1 hour	2½
Pink	50 to 55 min.	2½
Pinto	45 to 50 min.	2½
Red kidney (small)	1 hour	2⅓
Red kidney (large)	45 min.	2
Roman	35 to 40 min.	2⅓

BOUTIQUE DRIED BEANS

Type of Bean (1 Cup Dry)	Approximate Cooking Time	Yield (in Cups)
Adzuki	30 to 45 min.	3
Appaloosa	50 min.	4
Black soybeans	2 hours	2½
Calypso	1 hour, 40 min.	3½
Cargamanto	1 hour, 50 min.	3
Christmas lima	1 hour	4
Cranberry	1½ to 2 hours	2½
European soldier	1½ hours	4
Jacob's cattle	1¼ hours	3½
Low's champion	1½ hours	3
Rice	½ hour	3
Snow cap	45 min. to 1 hour	5½
Tongues of fire	45 min.	3½

NOTE: Packages of these beans can vary from ½ pound to 1 pound. These beans, except for black soybeans and adzukis, do not require soaking.

Black soybeans need at least 12 hours of soaking. Start with boiling hot water and change it once or twice to prevent the beans from beginning to ferment (sour).

Traditional Dried Bean Stew
(Habichuelas Secas Guisadas Tradicionales)

You can use any of the beans used in traditional Puerto Rican cookery in this tasty stew.

1 tablespoon annatto oil (see page 8) combined with 1
   tablespoon olive oil
½ pound smoked ham, diced
1 *chorizo* (red Spanish sausage), sliced
¼ cup Basic *Recaíto* (see page 16)
1½ cups tomato sauce
1½ cups water or chicken stock
¼ pound *calabaza* (West Indian pumpkin) or potatoes,
   peeled and diced
¼ cup *alcaparrado*
3 cups cooked beans (see page 160)
½ teaspoon black pepper

Heat the oil in a large pot. Add the ham and *chorizo* and sauté over medium heat for 2 to 3 minutes. Add the *recaíto* and tomato sauce. Cook for 5 minutes. Add the water, *calabaza*, and *alcaparrado*. Bring the mixture to a boil.

Reduce the heat to a simmer and cook for 10 minutes. Add the beans and black pepper and turn the heat to medium-low. Cook for 10 minutes more.

Serves 6

NOTE: To make a bean stew that combines Cuban and Puerto Rican cookery, use 1½ cups cooked *gandules* (green pigeon peas) and 1½ cups cooked black beans.

Quick Bean Stew
(*Habichuelas Guisadas Rapiditas*)

Traditional flavor is combined with the modern convenience of canned beans.

2 tablespoons olive oil
¼ pound smoked ham, diced
¼ cup Basic *Recaíto* (see page 16)
1 cup tomato sauce
2 cups water or chicken stock
¼ pound *calabaza* (West Indian pumpkin), peeled and diced
1 cup *alcaparrado*
2 16-ounce cans beans, drained and rinsed
1 teaspoon black pepper

Heat the oil in a large pot. Sauté the ham for 3 minutes. Add the *recaíto* and tomato sauce, and cook over medium heat for 5 minutes. Add the water and *calabaza*. Bring to a boil, and add the *alcaparrado*, beans, and black pepper. Bring to a boil again. Reduce the heat and simmer, uncovered, for 15 minutes.

Serves 6

Five-Bean Stew
(Cinco Habichuelas Guisadas)

All the beans that are used daily on the island are combined here, in case you can't decide which ones you like best!

> **1 recipe Traditional Dried Bean Stew (see page 174) using:**
> ½ **cup cooked** *gandules* **(green pigeon peas)**
> 1 **cup cooked pink beans**
> ½ **cup cooked small white beans**
> ½ **cup cooked small red beans**
> ½ **cup cooked chick-peas**

Serves 6

Mamposteao Rice
(Arroz Mamposteao)

In the old days, mamposteao *rice was leftover white rice and bean stew combined with fresh herbs and spices. Today it is made from scratch and served at fine dining establishments on the island.*

2 tablespoons corn oil
¼ cup diced green bell pepper
2 garlic cloves, peeled and chopped
1 tablespoon chopped cilantro
1 cup any bean stew (see recipes, pages 174–176)
3 tablespoons tomato sauce
3 cups cooked rice

Heat the oil in a large pot. Sauté the green pepper, garlic, and cilantro over medium heat for 3 minutes. Add the beans and tomato sauce. Cook for 2 more minutes. Add the rice and cook, stirring constantly, for 5 more minutes.

Serves 6

177

Calypso Beans and Rice
(Arroz y Habichuelas Calipso)

This is a variation of Mamposteao *Rice (see page 177) with a touch of curry.*

- **1 tablespoon butter**
- **2 tablespoons olive oil**
- **3 cups cooked rice**
- **3 cups cooked calypso beans**
  Salt to taste
  Curry powder to taste

Heat the butter and oil in a large skillet. Add the rice and beans. Sauté over medium-high heat for 5 minutes. Season to taste.

Serves 6 to 8

NOTE: If calypso beans are unavailable use pink, black, or your favorite bean.

Orzo and Barley Pilaf
(Pilaf de Orzo y Cebada)

Orzo (Greek pasta) and barley combined make an excellent substitute for everyday white rice.

- **2 tablespoons butter**
- **1 tablespoon olive oil**
- **1½ cups cooked orzo**
- **1½ cups cooked barley**
- **Salt and pepper to taste**

Heat the butter and oil in a large skillet. Sauté the orzo and barley over medium heat for 5 minutes. Season with salt and pepper.

Serves 6

NOTE: For a dramatic presentation, prepare a bean stew with a boutique bean like calypso and serve it with this simple but flavorful pilaf.

Puerto Rican Cannelloni Minés Style
(Canelones Puertorriqueños al Estilo de Minés)

During my college years I lived in a boardinghouse where I received cooking lessons from Minés, the owner. She was an excellent cook and kept us well fed, especially during midterm days. This cannelloni dish was one of her specialties.

SAUCE

- 2 tablespoons olive oil
- 1 medium yellow onion, finely chopped
- 2 garlic cloves, peeled and finely chopped
- 1 medium Italian frying pepper, seeded and finely chopped
- 6 tablespoons tomato paste
- 4 cups tomato sauce
- 1 28-ounce can whole tomatoes, roughly chopped, with liquid
- 5 cups water
- 1 tablespoon salt
- ½ teaspoon black pepper
- ½ teaspoon sugar
- ½ teaspoon *Adobo* (see page 15)

BEEF PICADILLO STUFFING

- 3 pounds ground beef
- 1 cup manzanilla olives, chopped
- 1½ cups tomato paste
- ¾ cup Basic *Recaíto* (see page 16)
- ½ cup golden raisins
- 1 tablespoon salt
- 2 teaspoons black pepper

- 3 quarts water
- ¼ cup olive oil
- 18 pieces cannelloni
- 2 cups shredded mozzarella cheese

Heat the oil in a large pot. Sauté the onion, garlic, and Italian pepper until soft. Add the remaining sauce ingredients and bring to a boil. Reduce the heat to a simmer and cook for 2 hours, stirring occasionally and adding water as needed. Set aside.

Brown the ground beef in a skillet over medium heat. Drain any excess fat. Add the remaining stuffing ingredients and cook for 10 minutes. Set aside. In a big pot, bring the water and olive oil to a boil. Add the cannelloni and cook for 5 minutes. Drain and rinse in cold water.

Preheat the oven to 375°F. Stuff each cannelloni with 4 tablespoons of beef *picadillo*. Arrange them in a shallow baking pan. Pour the sauce over the pasta, and sprinkle the cheese on top. Bake for 30 to 45 minutes, or until the cheese is completely melted and slightly browned.

Serves 6

12

DESSERTS AND BREADS
(Postres y Panes)

Our national dessert is *flan*, the versatile caramel custard. Many other desserts are based on coconut. We also prepare bread pudding, *arroz con dulce* (rice pudding cooked with coconut and ginger), and fruit sherbets like tamarind and soursop.

New desserts use our tropical fruits in very creative ways. Now guava mousse and *piña colada* cake can be found on the menus in many restaurants.

Breads once were limited to Mallorca bread and banana bread. Baking was not a part of home cooking; bread was mostly purchased at a local bakery along with desserts like guava turnovers. Today, I love to experiment with many different breads, giving them all a Puerto Rican touch!

Note: *Flans* are often cooked in a *bain-marie*: The custard is poured into a mold and the mold is then set and cooked in a pan of very hot water. The water should come about halfway up the sides of the mold.

Basic Vanilla Custard
(Flan de Vainilla Básico)

Rosa Franco, who owns a flan manufacturing company in Connecticut, showed me how to make this exquisite yet simple custard.

½ cup sugar
4 eggs
1 14-ounce can sweetened condensed milk
1 12-ounce can evaporated milk
1 tablespoon vanilla extract
Fresh mixed berries for garnish

In a small heavy saucepan, cook the sugar over low heat until caramel forms. Pour it into an 8-inch round mold. Set aside. In a bowl, beat the eggs until frothy. Add the condensed milk, evaporated milk, and vanilla; mix well with the eggs.

Pour the mixture into the caramelized mold. Cook on top of the stove in a *bain-marie* on medium-high heat (see page 183), partially covered, for 35 minutes. The *flan* is done when a toothpick inserted near the center comes out clean. Let it cool at room temperature. Refrigerate for at least 2 hours (or better, overnight) before serving.

To serve, invert the *flan* on a platter. Garnish on top with fresh berries.

Serves 8

Irma's Stovetop Custard
(Natilla de Irma)

A dear friend, Irma Rosario, prepared this simple dessert for me many years ago. I've added fresh raspberries and whipped cream.

1 cup heavy cream
2 cups milk
1 cup sugar
3 eggs
½ cup cornstarch
2 pints fresh raspberries
Ground nutmeg for garnish

Whip the cream and set aside. Combine the milk, sugar, eggs, and cornstarch in a blender or food processor. Pour into a saucepan and cook over low heat, stirring constantly, until the mixture coats the back of a spoon (about 15 to 20 minutes).

Pour the custard into a 9-inch baking pan and let it cool at room temperature. Transfer to the refrigerator until completely chilled. Arrange layers of custard, whipped cream, and raspberries in 6 glasses. Sprinkle with nutmeg.

Serves 6

NOTE: You can substitute sliced papaya, mango, or kiwi for berries.

Pumpkin Custard
(Flan de Calabaza)

Flan, *a dessert of our Spanish heritage, made with* calabaza *(West Indian pumpkin), results in a sophisticated dessert.*

½ **cup sugar**
1½ **pounds** *calabaza* **(West Indian pumpkin), peeled and diced**
   Water for boiling pumpkin
4 **eggs**
1 **12-ounce can evaporated milk**
1 **14-ounce can sweetened condensed milk**
1 **tablespoon vanilla extract**
   Pinch ground cinnamon

Heat the sugar carefully in a heavy saucepan until it caramelizes. Pour the caramel into a round 8-inch pan; set aside. Boil the pumpkin in the water until tender, about 15 to 20 minutes. Drain and purée in a blender or food processor.

Beat the eggs lightly in a large bowl. Add the remaining ingredients and mix well. Pour the *flan* mixture into the caramelized saucepan. Cook on top of the stove in a *bain-marie* (see page 183), covered, for 30 minutes over medium heat. Let the *flan* cool at room temperature. Turn upside down onto a platter.

Serves 8

Stovetop Coffee Flan
(*Flan de Café Hecho en la Estufa*)

My cousin Osvaldo taught me how to make flan in a bain-marie on the stove. This coffee flan is one of my son Alex's favorites.

⅓ cup plus 2 tablespoons sugar
4 eggs
1 cup evaporated milk, undiluted
1 cup sweetened condensed milk
¼ teaspoon salt
½ cup strongly brewed black coffee

In a small heavy saucepan, cook the ⅓ cup of sugar over low heat until it caramelizes. Pour into a 2-quart mold; set aside. In a large bowl, beat the eggs until frothy. Add the remaining ingredients and strain through a fine sieve. Pour the custard mix into the caramelized mold. Cook on top of the stove in a *bain-marie* (see page 183), on medium-high heat, covered, for 25 minutes. Let the *flan* cool at room temperature. Refrigerate for 2 hours before transferring to a serving platter.

Serves 6 to 8

187

Coconut Custard
(Tembleque)

Called tembleque *(the word translates as "shaky"), this custard has a jellylike consistency. This recipe can also be prepared in a 1-quart mold. It can be made the day before it is served.*

3 cups fresh coconut milk, or unsweetened canned
    coconut milk
½ cup sugar
¼ cup cornstarch

Blend all of the ingredients well in a blender or food processor. Transfer to a saucepan. Bring to a boil, stirring constantly. Reduce the heat and simmer until the custard coats the back of a spoon, about 4 minutes.

Pour the custard into 6 glass custard cups. Cover with plastic wrap to prevent a skin from forming. Refrigerate until firm, about 4 hours or overnight.

Serves 6

Coconut Custard with Mango Sauce

(Tembleque con Salsa de Mango)

The mango sauce not only adds flavor to the tembleque; it also adds color.

- 1 recipe Coconut Custard (see page 188)
- 2 medium mangoes, peeled, seeded, puréed, and pressed through a strainer to remove fibers
- 2 tablespoons golden rum or spiced rum

Unmold the coconut custard onto a platter. Combine the mango and rum. Pour the sauce over the custard.

Serves 6

Coconut Kisses
(Besitos de Coco)

These delicious dessert "cookies," served on sea-grape leaves, are sold at the Luquillo Beach kioskos.

- **2 cups grated fresh coconut (the meat of 1 medium-size coconut)**
- **1 cup water**
- **1½ cups dark brown sugar**

Combine the coconut and water in a saucepan with a heavy bottom. Bring to a boil. Add the brown sugar. Reduce the heat to low and cook for 30 minutes, stirring occasionally, or until the mixture becomes thick and sticky. Drop the mixture by tablespoons onto a greased cookie sheet. Let the coconut kisses cool completely.

Makes 18 "kisses"

NOTE: Use a measuring spoon to keep the "kisses" uniform in size.

Coconut-Guava Cookies
(Galletitas de Coco y Guayaba)

These are a variation of the traditional polvorones. *You can replace the guava preserves with other jams such as raspberry, papaya, or mango.*

1 **cup (2 sticks) unsalted butter at room temperature**
½ **cup sugar**
½ **cup sweetened flaked coconut**
½ **teaspoon vanilla extract**
¾ **cup guava preserves**

In a large bowl, beat the butter and sugar until fluffy. Blend in the coconut and vanilla extract. Refrigerate until the dough is firm, about ½ hour.

Preheat the oven to 350°F. Shape each tablespoon of dough into a ball. Arrange them on an ungreased baking sheet, 1 inch apart. Make a small indentation in the center of each cookie with your thumb. Bake the cookies until they are lightly browned around the edges, about 15 minutes. Let them cool on a rack. Fill each indentation with guava preserves.

Makes 3½ dozen

Edgar's Bread Pudding with Fruit Cocktail

(Pudín Diplomático de Edgar)

This is bread pudding with fruit cocktail added, the dessert we serve on special occasions. Edgar, my son's godfather, always serves it at dinner parties.

1 pound sliced white bread, cut into small pieces
1 cup milk
½ cup coconut milk
3 eggs
½ cup sugar
1 tablespoon vanilla extract
2 cups fruit cocktail in light syrup, drained
  Butter to grease baking pan
  Ground cinnamon for garnish

Preheat the oven to 350°F. In a large bowl, combine the two milks and mix with the bread. Set aside. In a separate bowl, beat the eggs, sugar, and vanilla and mix in the fruit cocktail. Add the egg mixture to the bread.

Grease a 9-inch baking pan and pour in the bread mixture. Bake for 50 minutes, or until a toothpick inserted in the center comes out clean. Cool at room temperature. Sprinkle with cinnamon.

Serves 12 to 15

Passion Fruit Bread Pudding
(Budín de Pan con Parcha)

This is our traditional bread pudding, with a touch of passion fruit.

1 pound sliced white bread, cut into small cubes
½ cup golden raisins
4 eggs
½ cup sugar
¾ cup evaporated milk
¾ cup milk
¾ cup sweetened condensed milk
1 cup frozen passion fruit juice concentrate, thawed
   Butter to grease a 9-inch baking pan

Preheat the oven to 350°F. Combine the bread pieces and
raisins in a bowl; set aside. In a separate bowl, mix all of the
remaining ingredients well. Pour over the bread, making sure
everything is well combined.

Grease the baking pan and pour the bread mixture into it.
Bake for 50 minutes, or until a toothpick inserted in the center
comes out clean. Cool at room temperature. Refrigerate for at
least 1 hour before serving, or overnight if possible.

Serves 12 to 15

Puerto Rican Rice Pudding
(Arroz con Dulce)

This pudding is one of the traditional Christmas desserts. Fresh ginger and coconut distinguish it from the American version.

Islanders use regular brown raisins. I prefer currants for an elegant touch.

- 3 **cups water**
- 1 **teaspoon salt**
- 2 **cinnamon sticks**
- 6 **whole cloves**
- 1 **1-inch piece fresh ginger, peeled and sliced**
- 1 **14-ounce can coconut milk**
- 1 **cup water**
- 1 **cup short-grain rice**
- ⅓ **cup dried currants or raisins**
- 4 **tablespoons shredded sweetened coconut**
- ½ **cup sugar**
- **Ground cinnamon for garnish**

In a large saucepan, combine the 3 cups water, salt, cinnamon sticks, cloves, and ginger. Bring to a boil. Pour the liquid through a colander into a bowl; discard the spices.

Combine the spiced water with the coconut milk and 1 cup water in a large saucepan. Bring the liquid to a boil. Add all the remaining ingredients except the cinnamon. Reduce the heat, cover, and simmer for 20 minutes. Remove the lid from the pan, stir, and cook for 15 more minutes, or until the rice is cooked. (All the liquid should be absorbed.) Pour onto a platter and sprinkle with cinnamon.

Serves 6 to 8

NOTE: For a fruity variation, add 1 cup of diced mango during the last 5 minutes of cooking.

194

Ginger and Soursop Sorbet
(*Sorbete de Gengibre y Guanábana*)

I miss fresh soursop so much that I try to adapt every recipe to the frozen pulp available here in the States. This simple sorbet gets the right touch with the addition of fresh ginger. Sit back and enjoy a little piece of the Caribbean right here at home!

3 cups frozen soursop pulp, thawed
1 cup sugar
½ cup Spiced Rum (see page 226)
3½ teaspoons grated fresh ginger
2 tablespoons fresh lemon juice

Process the soursop pulp in a blender or food processor. Pass through a sieve and return it to the blender or food processor. Add the remaining ingredients and purée. Freeze in an ice cream maker according to the manufacturer's instructions. To serve, let the sorbet sit at room temperature until it begins to soften.

Makes 1 quart

NOTE: If you don't have an ice cream machine, pour the mixture into a metal baking pan. Cover with aluminum foil and freeze until firm.

Mango and Passion Fruit Frozen Yogurt

(Yogurt Congelado de Mango y Parcha)

A more refreshing and mouth-watering frozen dessert is hard to imagine!

- 4 medium mangoes, peeled and cubed
- 1 cup passion fruit pulp
- ⅓ cup sugar
- ½ teaspoon vanilla extract or more to taste
- 1½ cups plain yogurt

In a food processor or blender, purée the mango, then strain through a sieve. Add the remaining ingredients. Pour the mixture into a shallow square 9-inch baking pan. Cover with foil or plastic wrap. Freeze until solid (1 to 2 hours). Break the frozen mixture into pieces. Purée until soft but not completely melted. Repeat the freezing and processing once or twice more. Serve or return to the freezer for later use.

Makes 4½ cups

Guava Mousse
(Mousse de Guayaba)

This mousse can be served immediately or frozen for later use.

    6 egg whites
    1½ cups sugar
    1½ cups heavy cream
    1 cup frozen guava pulp, thawed

Beat the egg whites and sugar in a large bowl until stiff peaks form. In a separate bowl, whip the heavy cream until soft peaks form. Fold the whipped cream and guava into the egg whites, in alternating batches.

Serves 6 to 8

Piña Colada Cake
(Bizcocho de Piña Colada)

Coconut milk and pineapple, classic ingredients in the famous piña colada, are combined here to produce a delicate dessert. This cake can be accentuated with a raspberry sauce. It is best to let the cake soak overnight in the coconut syrup.

1½ cups coconut milk
½ cup coconut cream
3 tablespoons dark rum
¼ cup canned crushed pineapple, drained
1 cup confectioners' sugar
⅔ cup ground almonds (about 3 ounces)
⅓ cup all-purpose flour
4 egg whites
3 drops almond extract
3 drops vanilla extract
¼ pound (1 stick) unsalted butter or margarine
   Butter to grease the custard cups
   Shredded sweetened coconut for garnish

Combine the coconut milk and cream in a saucepan. Bring to a boil. Lower the heat and simmer until the liquid is reduced to 1 cup. Add the rum and set aside. Grease 4 custard cups and divide the pineapple evenly among them. Set aside.

Combine the sugar, almonds, and flour in a bowl. Add the egg whites and extracts and whisk until the mixture is smooth. Preheat the oven to 375°F. Melt the butter in a saucepan over medium heat until it turns brown, then add to the batter. Divide the batter evenly among the 4 custard cups, making sure to cover the pineapple.

Bake for 20 minutes, or until the cakes are golden brown. Pour the coconut syrup over the hot cakes. Let them soak for at least 2 hours or overnight.

To serve, run a small knife around the sides of the cups to loosen the cakes. Turn them out onto a plate. Garnish with shredded coconut.

Serves 4

Soursop Terrine
(Terina de Guanábana)

A simple dessert, ideal for a hot summer day!

- 2 cups frozen soursop pulp, thawed
- 2 envelopes plain gelatin
- 1 cup heavy cream, whipped
  Fresh kiwi slices for garnish

Purée the soursop pulp in a blender or food processor. Pass it through a sieve. Heat the pulp in a saucepan over medium heat and add the gelatin. Stir until it dissolves. Cool the pulp over iced water; fold in the whipped cream. Pour the mixture into an 8-inch round pan or a small bread pan. Refrigerate until the terrine is set. To serve, place the terrine briefly in a pan of hot water to loosen it. Turn it upside down on a platter and garnish with kiwi slices.

Serves 8

NOTE: You can serve this with a raspberry sauce.

White Cheese and Fruit Salad
with
Lemon-Honey Dressing
(Ensalada de Queso Blanco y Frutas con Salsa de Miel y Limón)

This light and refreshing salad is the perfect end to a summer brunch.

1 ripe papaya
2 medium ripe mangoes
1 small ripe pineapple
½ cup fresh lemon juice
4 tablespoons honey
1 pound Puerto Rican white cheese, cut into small pieces
   Fresh mint sprigs for garnish

Peel the fruit and cut it into chunks. Combine the lemon juice and honey; pour over the fruit. Toss well. Divide the fruit and cheese among 6 bowls. Garnish with mint.

Serves 6

Tropical Gazpacho Fruit Soup
(Gazpacho Tropical de Frutas)

This bubbly fruit gazpacho combines sparkling water with tropical fruits. It makes a refreshing cold dessert soup.

- 3 **cups fresh or frozen raspberries**
- 3 **cups sparkling water**
- ½ **cup sugar**
  Juice of 1 lemon
- 1 **papaya, peeled and cut into small pieces**
- 1 **medium mango, peeled, seeded, and diced**
- 2 **kiwis, peeled and diced**
- 1 **cup fresh pineapple pieces**
  Shredded fresh ginger to taste for garnish

Purée the raspberries in a blender or food processor. Pass through a sieve to remove the seeds. In a nonreactive bowl, combine the raspberry *purée* with the sparkling water and sugar. Add the remaining ingredients except the ginger. Refrigerate for 1 hour before serving. Garnish with the ginger.

Serves 6 to 8

Sautéed Bananas with Orange Liqueur
(Guineos Salteados con Licor de China)

Bananas cooked in butter, sugar, and orange liqueur make a delicious topping for vanilla ice cream.

3   tablespoons butter
1   tablespoon brown sugar
1   tablespoon orange liqueur
3   medium bananas, sliced in half and cut into 1-inch
    pieces
1   quart vanilla ice cream
    Shredded sweetened coconut and chopped walnuts for
    garnish

Melt the butter in a saucepan over medium heat. Add the brown sugar and orange liqueur. Sauté the bananas until lightly golden. Divide them among 6 dessert bowls. Put a scoop of ice cream in each bowl. Sprinkle with coconut and walnuts.

Serves 6

Honey-Rum Mousse
(Mousse de Miel y Ron)

This is a very rich and delicious dessert that is simple to make and perfect for warm weather.

- **6 egg yolks, at room temperature**
- **⅓ cup honey**
- **1 cup whipping cream, chilled**
- **2 tablespoons Spiced Rum (see page 226)**

Beat the yolks and honey in a bowl until they have the stiff texture of meringue (about 10 minutes). In another bowl, beat the cream and rum until the mixture forms soft peaks. Fold the two mixtures together. Spoon into 6 custard cups.

Serves 6

NOTE: You can also freeze this dessert and serve it later.

Guava Cheesecake
(Bizcocho de Crema con Guayaba)

This cheesecake is easy to make. The intense guava flavor makes it quite rich.

CRUST
   4 ounces vanilla wafers, crushed
   2 tablespoons butter, melted

FILLING
   1½ pounds cream cheese, softened
    6 eggs
    1 cup frozen guava juice concentrate, thawed
    3 tablespoons sugar
    4 tablespoons all-purpose flour
    1 18-ounce can guava shells, drained and cut into thin
       slices, for garnish (optional)
      Fresh mint leaves for garnish

Preheat the oven to 400°F. Combine the vanilla wafer crumbs with the melted butter. Press into a 10- or 12-inch springform pan. Refrigerate while you prepare the filling.

In a food processor or with an electric beater, beat the cream cheese until it is fluffy. Add the eggs one at a time. Continue beating until the eggs are well incorporated into the cream cheese and the mixture is light. Add the guava concentrate, sugar, and flour, and beat until well mixed.

Pour the batter into the pan. Bake for 1½ hours, or until a knife inserted in the center comes out clean. (If the top starts to brown too quickly, place a piece of aluminum foil loosely on top.) Cool at room temperature. Refrigerate for at least 1 hour before serving, or overnight. To serve, arrange the guava-shell slices and mint leaves on top of the cake.

Serves 8 to 10

Puerto Rican Jelly Roll
(Brazo Gitano al Estilo Puertorriqueño)

Jelly roll filled with guava preserves is a favorite traditional Puerto Rican dessert. You can use mango, papaya, or passion fruit jellies, jams, or preserves.

> 2 tablespoons vegetable shortening
> 1 9 × 15-inch piece of parchment paper
> ⅓ cup egg yolks (about 8 yolks)
> 1¼ cups egg whites
> 1¼ cups sugar
> 1 teaspoon salt
> ⅔ cup milk
> 1¼ cups cake flour
> ¾ tablespoon baking powder
> ¾ cup guava preserves
> Confectioners' sugar for garnish

Preheat the oven to 350°F. Grease a 9 × 15-inch sheet pan with vegetable shortening. Place the parchment paper on the baking sheet and grease well. Set aside.

Beat the egg yolks and whites, sugar, and salt at high speed until stiff peaks form. While the eggs are beating, scald the milk and cool briefly.

Fold the flour and baking powder into the egg mixture. Add the scalded milk and blend thoroughly. Spread the batter evenly onto the parchment-covered sheet pan. Bake for 8 minutes, or until lightly browned.

Remove the cake from the pan by lifting the paper. Let it cool on a rack for 5 minutes. Spread the marmalade evenly over the entire surface of the cake.

Gently loosen the cake from the parchment paper and roll it tightly from the short end. Sprinkle with confectioners' sugar.

Serves 4 to 6

Rum Cake
(Bizcocho de Ron)

Spiced rum and honey flavor this cake. Serve it with whipped cream and chopped nuts.

¼ **pound (1 stick) butter or margarine, at room temperature**
¼ **cup brown sugar**
¼ **cup honey**
2 **eggs**
¼ **cup water**
½ **cup Spiced Rum (see page 226)**
2 **cups cake flour, sifted**
2½ **teaspoons baking powder**
¼ **teaspoon salt**
   Butter to grease pan
   Confectioners' sugar for garnish

Preheat the oven to 350°F. Cream the butter and brown sugar in a large bowl. Add the honey, eggs, water, and rum. Mix well.

In another bowl, combine the cake flour, baking powder, and salt. Pour over the creamed mixture and beat until all of the ingredients are combined. Grease an 8-inch round pan and pour in the batter. Bake for 30 minutes, or until a knife inserted in the center comes out clean. Let the cake cool in the pan or on a cooling rack.

To serve, invert the cake onto a platter. (Trim the top if uneven.) Sift confectioners' sugar on top.

Serves 8

Orange and Papaya Tart
(Tarta de China y Papaya)

Papaya and orange are combined in this simple dessert.

1 **pound frozen puff pastry, thawed**
    Flour for dusting
    Grated peel of 1 orange
1 **1-pound bag beans (to prebake the tart pastry)**
1 **large papaya, peeled, seeded, and sliced**
¼ **cup apricot preserves**
1 **teaspoon honey**

Preheat the oven to 400°F. Roll out the puff pastry to ¼ inch thick. Dust with flour. Place the pastry in a 10-inch tart pan with a removable bottom; trim the edges. Prick the pastry all over with a fork, and sprinkle orange peel over the dough. Place a sheet of aluminum foil over the pastry. Distribute the beans evenly over the foil to create some weight. Bake for 15 minutes. Remove the beans and foil. Continue baking for another 30 minutes, or until the puff pastry is golden brown and completely cooked. Cool at room temperature.

Arrange the papaya slices on the pastry. In a saucepan over medium-low heat, warm the apricot preserves and honey. Strain and let cool. Brush the tart with the apricot mixture.

Serves 6 to 8

Almond Cookies
(*Polvorones*)

I first heard about these cookies during my junior-high-school years. They were a specialty of Lizzie Morales, one of my classmates. Serve them with tea or café con leche.

- **1 egg yolk**
- **½ cup sugar**
- **½ cup (1 stick) butter**
- **1 teaspoon almond extract**
- **1½ cups all-purpose flour**

Preheat the oven to 350°F. Beat the egg yolk, sugar, butter, and almond extract in a large bowl. Blend in the flour a little at a time. Shape a tablespoon of dough into a ball. Repeat with the remaining dough. Place the cookies on an ungreased cookie sheet. Bake for 20 minutes, or until light golden brown.

Makes 22 polvorones

Guava Turnovers
(Pastelillos de Guayaba)

These are eaten with café con leche *as an afternoon snack. They can also be served for dessert. I like to sprinkle cinnamon and nutmeg on the dough.*

> **All-purpose flour for dusting**
> 1 **pound frozen puff pastry, thawed and cut into 4-inch squares**
> **Ground cinnamon and nutmeg to taste**
> 1 **cup canned guava preserves (not guava paste)**
> 1 **egg, beaten**
> **Butter to grease cookie sheet**
> **Parchment paper**

Preheat the oven to 350°F. Dust your working surface with flour. Roll out the puff pastry to make a rectangle measuring 8 × 16 inches. Sprinkle cinnamon and nutmeg on the dough. Put 1½ tablespoons guava preserves in each piece of puff pastry. Brush the edges with beaten egg. Fold over to form a triangle.

Grease a cookie sheet and line with parchment paper. Place the pastries 2 inches apart. Refrigerate for 30 minutes. Bake for 25 to 30 minutes, or until light golden brown. Cool before serving.

Makes 8 to 10 pastries

Banana Bread
(Pan de Guineo)

A simple bread, packed with banana flavor.

  3 **very ripe bananas**
  ½ **cup sugar**
  ½ **cup (1 stick) butter**
  3 **eggs**
  ½ **teaspoon salt**
  2 **cups all-purpose flour**
  1 **teaspoon baking powder combined with 2 tablespoons
       sour cream**
       Butter to grease pan

Preheat the oven to 350°F. In a large bowl, mash the bananas. Add the sugar, butter, and eggs. Beat until well blended.
In a separate bowl, sift the salt and flour together. Combine
with the banana mixture. Add the baking powder–sour cream
mix.

Grease an 8-inch pan and pour the batter into it. Bake for 30
minutes, or until a toothpick inserted in the center comes out
clean.

Serves 6 to 8

Mallorca Bread
(Pan de Mallorca)

The perfect afternoon coffee break is a steaming hot cup of café con leche *and a* pan de mallorca.

The traditional bread is somewhat complicated and time-consuming to prepare. Through the years I have tried different ways to make this delicious bread in a reasonable amount of time and a less complicated fashion. Here is my final version.

       6 **tablespoons (¾ stick) butter**
       1 **package active dry yeast**
      ¼ **cup lukewarm water**
      ¼ **cup sugar**
      ¾ **teaspoon salt**
       3 **egg yolks**
      ½ **cup milk**
2½ to 3 **cups all-purpose flour**
         Flour for dusting work surface
         Butter to grease bowl and pan
         Confectioners' sugar for dusting

Melt the butter and let it cool slightly. In a large bowl, dissolve the yeast in the water. Add the sugar, salt, egg yolks, milk, 4 tablespoons of the cooled butter, and 2½ cups of the flour. Mix well. Lightly flour a work surface. Turn out the dough and knead for 5 minutes. Add enough of the remaining flour so that the dough is not sticky.

Grease a bowl with butter. Put the dough in it and cover with plastic wrap. Let the dough rise in a warm place for 45 minutes. Grease a 9-inch square baking pan. Set aside. Punch the dough down. Knead it on a lightly floured surface into a rectangle about 18 × 9 inches. Brush with the remaining melted butter. Roll up the dough from one short end and cut it into 9 slices; trim the ends to make them neat. Arrange the slices in the baking pan. Cover and let rise for 40 minutes.

Preheat the oven to 375°F. Bake the rolls for 30 minutes, or until lightly browned. Let the rolls cool in the pan for 5 minutes. Transfer to a platter and dust with confectioners' sugar.

Makes 9 rolls

Carnival Corn Bread
(Pan de Maíz de Carnaval)

Food festivals have become popular on the island over the past ten years. In 1991 I went to the mabí festival in Juana Díaz. Street vendors were offering different versions of the drink the town is most famous for: mabí, a drink made of fermented tree bark that tastes a bit like root beer. There were also tables with traditional and new dishes. A corn bread made with carrots caught my attention.

1 cup sifted all-purpose flour
1 cup yellow cornmeal
¼ cup sugar (or less to taste)
1 tablespoon baking powder
1 teaspoon salt
¼ cup (½ stick) butter or margarine, softened
1 egg
1 cup plain or vanilla yogurt
2 medium carrots, peeled and shredded
½ cup fresh, canned, or frozen corn kernels
Butter to grease pan

Preheat the oven to 425°F. Sift the flour, cornmeal, sugar, baking powder, and salt into a bowl. Cut in the butter until the mixture forms little balls the size of peas.

In a separate bowl, beat the egg until frothy. Add the yogurt, carrots, and corn. Combine with the dry ingredients. Pour into a greased loaf pan. Bake for 20 minutes, or until a toothpick inserted in the center comes out dry. Cool in the pan.

Serves 10 to 12

Campobello Bread
(Pan Campobello)

This semisweet corn-and-banana bread is ideal for brunches or pic-nics. Serve it with eggs and sausages.

2 **large bananas**
¼ **cup (½ stick) butter, melted**
2 **tablespoons honey**
1 **cup all-purpose flour**
1 **cup yellow cornmeal**
2 **teaspoons baking powder**
½ **teaspoon salt**
½ **cup fresh, canned, or frozen corn kernels**
   Butter to grease pan

Preheat the oven to 350°F. Purée the bananas in a blender or food processor. Add the butter and honey and process again. In a large bowl, sift together all of the dry ingredients. Stir in the banana purée. Pour into a greased 8-inch baking pan. Bake for 30 minutes, or until a toothpick inserted in the center comes out clean.

Serves 6 to 8

13

DRINKS AND BEVERAGES
Bebídas y Refrescos

As the main producer of rum in the world, we have very interesting drinks in addition to our famous *piña coladas*. Rum and (occasionally) flavored liqueurs are combined with traditional fruit juices. There are also some very good and festive nonalcoholic drinks—the tastes are so good you won't miss the liquor!

Piña Colada

There are as many recipes for this drink, created on the island by Ramón Marrero, bartender at the Caribe Hilton Hotel, as there are people living in Puerto Rico. My version gets a splash of vanilla extract and uses coconut milk instead of the very sweet cream of coconut.

- 2 cups coconut milk
- 3 cups pineapple juice
- 2 cups crushed pineapple
- ½ cup shredded sweetened coconut
- 1 cup golden rum
- ½ cup sugar
- ½ teaspoon vanilla extract or more to taste
- About 2 cups ice cubes
- Fresh mint leaves for garnish

In a bowl, combine all of the ingredients except the ice and mint leaves. Mix in batches with the ice in a blender. Garnish with mint leaves.

Serves 10 to 12

Rum and Banana Colada
(Guineo Colada con Ron)

This is a twist on the classic piña colada. *It is made with fresh bananas and banana liqueur.*

¼ **cup white rum**
1 **banana, peeled and sliced**
¼ **cup banana liqueur**
¼ **cup cream of coconut**
  About 2 cups ice cubes
  Fresh mint leaves for garnish

Combine all of the ingredients, except the mint leaves, in a blender. Garnish with mint leaves.

Serves 2 to 4

Rum Collins

Move over gin! Here comes white rum and fresh lime juice.

- ¼ cup golden rum (or more to taste)
- 2 tablespoons fresh lime juice
- 1 teaspoon sugar
- ½ cup club soda
- 1 orange slice for garnish

Mix all of the ingredients except the orange slice. Pour into a glass filled with ice cubes. Garnish with the orange slice.

Serves 1

Old San Juan Daiquiri
(Daiquiri al Estilo del Viejo San Juan)

This is a daiquiri à la Puerto Rico—white rum mixed with guava nectar.

¼ **cup white rum**
½ **cup guava nectar**
   Dash grenadine syrup
1 **lime wedge**

Pour all of the ingredients except the lime wedge into an iced-filled glass. Squeeze the lime wedge into the drink.

Serves 1

Puerto Rican Sangría
(Sangría Criolla)

The addition of rum and passion fruit makes this a very Puerto Rican sangría!

- 1½ cups frozen passion fruit pulp, thawed
- 2 cups pineapple juice
- ½ cup fresh lemon juice
- 2 cups lemon-lime soda
- 2 cups red wine
- 1 cup white rum
- 1 6-ounce can mandarin oranges
- Ice cubes

Combine all of the ingredients in a pitcher. Chill for at least 1 hour before serving.

Serves 10

Guava Hidden Treasure
(Tesoro de Guayaba Escondido)

Fresh guavas are available on the mainland for only a short time during the summer months, but guava nectar, with its perfumelike aroma, is available year-round. This drink will make you think guavas are made in heaven!

¼ **cup white rum**
¼ **cup guava nectar**
¼ **cup pineapple juice**
¼ **cup coconut cream**
About 2 cups ice cubes
Orange slices for garnish

Combine all of the ingredients except the orange slices in a blender. Pour into tall glasses. Garnish with orange slices.

Serves 2

Caribbean Kiss
(Beso Caribeño)

Strawberries, like a kiss from red lips, give the perfect touch to this inviting rum drink.

- ¼ **cup white rum**
- 1 **tablespoon grenadine syrup**
- 1 **tablespoon sugar**
- 5 **fresh strawberries, sliced**
- 4 **ice cubes**
  Juice of 1 lemon
- 2 **tablespoons light cream or evaporated milk**
  Grated coconut for garnish

Combine all of the ingredients except the coconut in a blender. Pour into a tall glass. Garnish with coconut.

Serves 1

Mango Magic
(Magia de Mango)

When I first came to New York in 1981, it was very hard to find fresh mangoes. But in recent years they have become more abundant, and we have been lucky enough to enjoy them as early as February.

1 cup fresh mango pulp
¼ cup Triple Sec (or any other orange liqueur)
   About 2 cups ice cubes
¼ cup golden rum
1 tablespoon sugar
   Juice of 1 lime

Mix all of the ingredients in a blender. Serve well chilled.

Serves 4 to 6

Spiced Rum
(Ron con Especias)

This fragrant spiced rum can be used to soak dried fruits and to make desserts. Or simply add it to your after-dinner coffee.

- **1 vanilla bean**
- **3 cinnamon sticks**
- **6 whole cloves**
- **4 whole allspice**
- **1 whole nutmeg, crushed**
- **3 star anise**
- **Pinch aniseed**
- **1 liter golden rum**

Make a slit along the vanilla bean. Scrape the pulp into a glass jar. Add the vanilla bean and the remaining ingredients and cover. Store the rum in a dry, cool place for at least 2 weeks. Strain and pour back into the rum bottle.

Makes 1 liter

Pineapple Liqueur
(Licor de Piña)

This is the perfect after-dinner drink to end a summer meal.

- **2½ cups fresh pineapple pieces**
- **1½ cups white rum**
- **1½ cups golden rum**
- **1 teaspoon vanilla extract**
- **½ cup simple sugar syrup (½ cup sugar with ¼ cup water, boiled)**

Combine the pineapple, rums, and vanilla in a glass jar. Cover and set aside in a dark place (inside a kitchen cabinet, for instance) for 3 weeks; stir the mixture every 3 days. Drain, reserving the liquid. Purée the pineapple in a blender or food processor. Pass through a sieve lined with a coffee filter. Discard the pulp. Drain the liquid again through a coffee filter–lined colander. Combine the remaining liquid and the rum-vanilla liquid with the sugar syrup. Pour into a glass jar.

Makes 3 cups

Papaya Shake Siglo Veinte
(Batida de Papaya a lo Siglo Veinte)

Through the years El Siglo Veinte, a restaurant located on Fortaleza Street in Old San Juan, has been known for the delicious papaya shakes it prepares. Sipping one after a play at the Tapia Theater is a cherished tradition among Puerto Ricans.

I have added a touch of coffee liqueur. It can also be served as an unusual dessert following a light meal.

- **2 ripe papayas, peeled, seeded, and diced**
- **4 cups ice-cold milk**
- **4 tablespoons coffee liqueur**
- **Freshly ground nutmeg for garnish**

Mix all of the ingredients except the nutmeg in a blender. Sprinkle with the nutmeg.

Serves 6 to 8

Passion Mimosa
(Parcha Mimosa)

Think of the patio of a parador (country inn) and a glass of champagne combined with passion fruit. It is also a splendid way to start the Sunday brunch at home.

- 1 **bottle champagne**
- 1 **quart passion fruit juice**
  Fresh fruit slices for garnish: oranges, strawberries, or kiwis

Fill 6 glasses two-thirds full with champagne. Add passion fruit juice and garnish with fresh fruit.

Serves 6

229

Rum Eggnog
(Coquito)

Coquito *is the traditional Christmas beverage in Puerto Rico. I learned to make it from my Aunt Celia. She would start preparing it at the beginning of December, and by the twenty-fifth the* coquito *would be what she called "cured." It is best if you use fresh coconut milk.*

1 cup coconut milk
1 cup sweetened condensed milk
1 cup evaporated milk
1 cup white rum, or to taste
1 cup water
3 cinnamon sticks
4 egg yolks, well beaten
  Ground cinnamon for garnish

Combine all of the milks and the rum in a blender or a food processor. Set aside. Boil the water with the cinnamon sticks. Cool to room temperature. Discard the cinnamon sticks.

Combine all of the ingredients except the ground cinnamon and beat well in a blender or food processor in batches. Pour the eggnog into glass bottles and refrigerate until ready to use. To serve, transfer the eggnog to a punch bowl and sprinkle the cinnamon on top.

Makes 5 cups

Arturo's Christmas Punch
(Bul de Navidad a lo Arturo)

*I prepared this recipe when Ralph Paniagua, publisher of the maga-
zine* Viva New York, *asked me to prepare a Christmas menu with a
"new twist." Arturo Fortún, president of La Carta Publications, gave
me this recipe.*

    4 cups pineapple juice
    4 cups orange juice (freshly squeezed, if possible)
    1 cup fresh lemon juice
    1 cup golden rum
    1 lime, cut into small pieces
    ½ cup each fresh mango and papaya chunks (if mango is
        not available, use 1 cup of papaya)
       Ice cubes
       Fresh mint leaves for garnish

Combine all of the liquids in a punch bowl. Add the fruit,
ice, and mint leaves. Serve well chilled.

Serves 10 to 12

Birthday Punch
(Bul de Cumpleaños)

On the island we celebrate a girl's fifteenth birthday much as main-land Americans celebrate the Sweet Sixteen. When the party takes place at home, a birthday punch is usually prepared.

> **2** cups each orange, grape, pineapple, and pear juice
> **3** cups beer
> **2** cups golden rum

Mix all of the ingredients. Serve icy cold in pitchers or a punch bowl.

Serves 12

NOTE: Some people like to add a can of fruit cocktail as a garnish.

Hot Rum Punch
(Bul de Ron Caliente)

This drink is a way of bringing island sunshine to your home on a cold winter night. This punch is perfect for holiday parties.

- 3 **cups apple cider**
- 2 **tablespoons sugar**
- 3 **cinnamon sticks**
- 2 **star anise**
- 5 **whole cloves**
  Pinch aniseed
- ¼ **cup fresh lemon juice**
- ¾ **cup golden rum (or to taste)**
  Lemon slices for garnish

Heat the cider, sugar, and spices in a nonreactive pan over low heat for 5 minutes. Strain through a sieve. Add the lemon juice and rum. Place a lemon slice in each serving cup before pouring in the hot punch.

Serves 6 to 8

NOTE: You can use Spiced Rum (see page 226) to make this punch.

Basic Tropical Fruit Drink
(Refresco Tropical Básico)

You can prepare this delicious beverage with any tropical fruit: mamey, soursop, passion fruit, or guava.

Equal parts fruit pulp and water
Sugar to taste
Ice cubes

Combine all of the ingredients in a pitcher. Serve well chilled.

Villa Puerto Rico Passion Fruit and Raspberry Ginger Ale Cooler

(*Villa Puerto Rico Parcha y Gingerale de Frambuesa*)

Inspired by the bright yellow color of passion fruit, I created this drink and named it after one of the casitas, *Villa Puerto Rico, which is painted bright yellow.*

4¼ cups raspberry ginger ale
1½ cups passion fruit pulp
    Ice cubes
    Strawberry slices for garnish

Combine all of the ingredients except the strawberries. Serve well chilled, garnished with the strawberry slices.

Serves 6 to 8

235

Soursop and Milk Drink
(Champola de Guanábana)

When I was growing up, almost every backyard in my neighborhood had a guanábana tree. My nanny, Delfa, used to give me this delicious drink as an after-school snack. The milk-and-cookie idea came to the island much later.

3 cups soursop pulp
4 cups milk
1 cup sugar, or to taste
Ice cubes
Ground nutmeg for garnish

Combine all of the ingredients except the nutmeg in a pitcher. Refrigerate for 1 hour before serving. Sprinkle each glass with the nutmeg.

Serves 6 to 8

Orange Wine
(Vino de Chinas)

My Aunt Aurea used to serve a liqueur that she called "orange wine" at Christmas. This makes a good after-dinner drink.

 2 cups white rum
   Juice of 10 oranges (save the oranges)
   Peel of 1 orange
 1 cup sugar
 3 cinnamon sticks
 2 star anise
 5 whole allspice
 2 whole cloves
 1 whole nutmeg, crushed
   Pinch aniseed
 1 vanilla bean, chopped

Combine all of the ingredients, including the oranges, in a glass jar. Cover and let the mixture settle for 2 days. Shake the jar every night. Drain the liquid; refrigerate before serving.

Makes 5 cups

White Nonalcoholic Sangría
(Sangría sin Alcohol Blanca)

The summer of 1974 was very special for me. My mother (seven months pregnant with my brother) completed her bachelor's degree and I graduated from high school. To celebrate I created this nonalcoholic white sangría for her.

4 cups white grape juice
3 cups sparkling water
1 cup orange juice
1 orange, cut in small pieces
4 to 5 fresh strawberries, sliced
Ice cubes

Combine all of the ingredients in a pitcher. Refrigerate for 1 hour before serving.

Serves 8 to 10

Pineapple Punch
(Bul de Piña)

This is my favorite Easter Sunday drink.

½ cup loosely packed mint leaves
3 cups pineapple juice
3 cups lemon-lime soda
1 orange, cut up in small pieces, for garnish

Combine all of the ingredients in a pitcher. Serve well chilled.

Serves 6 to 8

GLOSSARY

a caballo a folkloric expression that means a plate of rice and beans with a fried egg "mounted" on top.

aceite con achiote annatto oil. (See "The Basics," page 8.)

aceite de maíz corn oil. (See "The Basics," page 8.)

aceituna olive. The olive most used in Puerto Rico is the manzanilla, which is a pitted green olive stuffed with pimiento.

acelga Swiss chard. Used to make caldo Gallego (Galician soup).

acerola West Indian or Barbados cherry. This fruit is best known for its high vitamin C content. Traditionally it was used to make *refresco de acerola*, or **acerola** juice.

achiote or **achote** annatto seeds. (See "The Basics," page 8.)

achiotera a container used to store annatto oil with its seeds. The oil is heated every time it is needed so the seeds can release their yellow color.

adobo   The basic seasoning combination of Puerto Rican cooking. (See "The Basics," page 8.)

aguacate   avocado.

agua de azahar   orange blossom water. A distilled water made of orange blossoms, used to flavor traditional desserts like rice-flour stovetop custard.

ají caballero or **ají picante**   hot chili pepper. A hot pepper about 1 inch long. It is the only hot pepper used in traditional cooking. It is also used to make *pique*, a fermented vinegar used as a condiment.

ají dulce   sweet chili pepper. (See "The Basics," page 8.)

ajilimójili   a traditional sauce made with garlic, peppercorns, oil, vinegar, and lemon juice. It is served with boiled root vegetables or over grilled meats.

ajo   garlic.

ajonjolí   sesame seeds.

alboronía de chayote   chayote salad.

alcaparra   caper. Most frequently used in **alcaparrado**.

alcaparrado   a mixture of green olives, capers, and pimientos. (See "The Basics," page 8.)

alcapurría   a traditional fritter made of grated **yautía** (taro root) and green bananas, stuffed with **picadillo**. It can also be stuffed with crabmeat or chicken.

almojábana   rice-flour fritter.

amarillo   ripe yellow plantain.

anafre   portable burner. Used in the old days in place of a stove. It was usually made of a cracker-tin can, with holes added to improve the ventilation. **Anafres** were also made of iron and placed on top of the **fogón**.

aní en semilla   aniseed. Used mostly to prepare desserts.

annatto (See "The Basics," p. 8.)

apio a root vegetable with brown skin, yellow flesh, and a very strong starchy taste. It is used mostly to make heavy soups like **sancocho** and tripe soup.

arroz rice.

arroz amarillo basic yellow rice made with annatto oil, which can also be combined with meat, seafood, or vegetables.

arroz con dulce Puerto Rican rice pudding. A traditional dessert made with rice, coconut milk, ginger, and spices.

arroz con gandules yellow rice with green pigeon peas. This is our national rice dish.

arroz con pollo yellow rice with chicken.

arroz y habichuelas rice and beans.

asalto Navideño Christmas caroling. Traditionally, a group of people get together and surprise a neighbor in the middle of the night with Christmas songs. They go from house to house, and at the last stop they prepare a chicken **asopao**.

asopao one of our national soups. It has a thick consistency and is derived from the Spanish **paella**. It is a mixture of rice, chicken, **alcaparrado** and **recaíto**. **Asopao** can also be made with seafood, green pigeon peas, or salt codfish.

avellana hazelnut. Hazelnuts and walnuts are traditional Christmas nuts on the island.

bacalao salt codfish. (See "The Basics," page 8.)

bacalaíto salt codfish fritter.

barrilito a type of Puerto Rican rum that is 86 proof.

batata, batata blanca Puerto Rican yam or sweet potato. A root vegetable with a skin that varies from pink to purple. It has a gray-white flesh and a very sweet taste. **Batatas** are eaten boiled, baked, or fried.

berenjena eggplant.

besito de coco coconut kiss. A traditional dessert made with fresh-grated coconut, sugar, and spices.

bilí a mix of rum and **quenepas** that gets fermented. The rum is then drained and served. This is a typical drink of Vieques, an island located on the east coast of the island.

bistec cubed steak. Used to prepare Puerto Rican pepper steak.

bodega Spanish grocery store.

bollo de pan a loaf of bakery bread.

boronia de chayote Chayote stew.

buñuelo beignet a fritter made with flour, eggs, butter, and sugar. It can be sweet or savory (made with Parmesan cheese).

burén flat griddle. This was traditionally made of clay and used by the Taíno natives to cook **casabe**.

butifarra pork sausage seasoned with spices like cinnamon and anise, usually eaten for breakfast.

cabrito young goat. Usually prepared in a stew.

café coffee.

café con leche strong black coffee with steamed milk.

café negro black coffee.

café puya unsweetened black coffee.

café tinta espresso.

calabaza West Indian pumpkin. (See "The Basics," page 8.)

calamar en su tinta squid in its ink. Sold canned, it is used to make rice with squid.

caldero cauldron or cooking pot. This traditional pot, made of iron or thick aluminum, is used to make Puerto Rican rice dishes.

camarón shrimp.

canela cinnamon.

caña de azucar sugar cane.

caramelo caramel. Made of granulated sugar; used to coat the pan in which **flan** is cooked.

carne vieja dry salted beef, sold in small slabs covered with a layer of lard. It is usually prepared with scrambled eggs and onions.

casabe cassava bread. A flat bread made with grated cassava.

cascos de guayaba guava shells. They are usually cooked in a sugar syrup and are readily available canned.

cazuela a dessert casserole made of **calabaza** and yam.

champola a soursop drink made with milk.

chayote a vegetable of the squash family, also known as mirliton, vegetable pear, or christophine. It has a white or green skin and cream-colored flesh, with a somewhat bland taste. **Chayotes** can be stored at room temperature and are available year-round.

chicharrón pork crackling. Deep-fried pieces of pork skin or cut-up pieces of boneless pork shoulder. Small pieces of deep-fried chicken are also called **chicharrón**. (See recipe, page 51.)

chillo red snapper.

china orange.

chironja a cross between an orange and a grapefruit.

chorizo Spanish sausage. Used to make yellow rice and found in braised meat dishes like **carne mechada** (pot roast).

cilantro leaves of coriander. (See "The Basics," page 9.)

clavo clove.

coco rallado shredded coconut.

coco seco dry, mature coconut with a brown, hairy shell and firm white flesh. (See "The Basics," page 9.)

coco verde green coconut, usually sold refrigerated at road-side stands. The flesh is soft and the water, which is usually sweet, can be drunk straight from the coconut shell.

codito elbow macaroni.

colador de café cloth colander used in the old days to pre-pare coffee.

conejo rabbit. Stewed rabbit meat is eaten on holidays and special occasions like weddings or christenings.

coquito rum eggnog. This is a traditional Christmas drink.

crema de coco coconut cream. (See "The Basics," page 9.)

criolla creole. This term is used to denote traditional Puerto Rican cooking.

cuchifrito deep-fried pork pieces sold at roadside stands. These usually consist of pig's ears, tails, stomach, etc. **Cuchifrito** is also the name given to the fast-food establish-ments on the island that serve traditional fritters to go.

culantro is another name for **recao**. (See "The Basics," page 11.)

dita a bowl carved from the *higuera* tree. In the old days it was used to wash rice and measure beans.

domplín dumpling.

dulce a sweet, usually eaten as a dessert, made with yam, pineapple, or coconut.

dulce de plátano a dessert dish made with very ripe yellow plantains cooked in red wine, sugar, and spices.

empanada turnover. A fritter made of dough stuffed with **picadillo**, crab stew, or chicken.

empanadilla small turnover.

escabeche a pickling marinade traditionally prepared during the Lent season. Foods prepared **escabeche** style include salt codfish, chicken, green bananas, and fish.

fideo noodle.

filete beef tenderloin.

flan custard. A national dessert of Spanish heritage made of milk, eggs, sugar, and spices.

fogón a hearth made of three stones arranged in a triangle, with pieces of wood placed within.

fritura fritter.

funche Puerto Rican polenta. This has been a staple dish since the Taínos lived on the island. It used to be made with lard, but today corn or olive oil is used instead.

galleta por soda soda cracker. Eaten as an afternoon snack with **café con leche**. Crushed soda crackers, known as **galleta molida** (cracker meal), are used for breading.

gallina hen.

gandinza pork liver.

gandul green pigeon pea. (See "The Basics," page 9.)

garbanzo chick-pea.

granada pomegranate.

grano dialect term for rice-flour fritter on Puerto Rico's east coast, and the word for beans on some parts of the island.

greca de café Italian coffee pot used to make strong black coffee.

grosella gooseberry. Cooked in water and sugar to make a compote.

guanime Puerto Rican *tamal*. **Guanimes** have been a staple food since the Taíno days. They are made plain, without stuffing, and are wrapped in banana leaves. Served with salt codfish stew, **guanimes** are an everyday peasant lunch.

guarapo de caña sugar cane juice. Sold freshly squeezed at roadside stands.

guayaba guava. A fruit with a green skin, pink flesh, and small seeds. Fresh guavas are hard to find and can be expensive. Frozen pulp and juice concentrate are easily found year-round. On the island, where they are abundant, guavas are made into a paste and the shells are cooked in sugar syrup. Both are served as desserts with white cheese.

guayo grater. Used to shred root vegetables.

guineo banana.

guineo maduro ripe yellow banana. Eaten as a fruit.

guineo manzano apple banana. Eaten green as a **vianda** (root vegetable), or ripe, as a fruit.

guineo niño lady-finger banana. Eaten only when ripe. Dipped in flour and deep-fried, it is served as a side dish.

guineo verde green banana. Eaten as a side-dish starch. Green bananas are a part of the **viandas** family. The leaves are used to wrap **guanimes, pasteles,** and arroz apastelado.

guingambó okra.

guisado stewed.

haba lima bean.

habichuela bean. (See "The Basics," page 9.)

habichuela blanca white bean.

habichuela colorada small red kidney bean.

habichuela marca diablo red kidney bean.

habichuela rosada or **rosita** pink bean.

hoja de guineo banana leaf. Used to wrap **pasteles** and **guanimes**.

hojaldre puff pastry.

horchata de ajonjolí a drink made of ground sesame seeds, water, and sugar.

horno de microonda microwave oven.

jamón de cocinar smoked cooking ham. (See "The Basics," page 10.)

jíbaro envuelto lady-finger banana dipped in flour, fried, and served as a side dish.

juey Caribbean land crab.

langosta lobster. The lobster commonly found in the Caribbean Sea is the spiny or rock lobster. It is very hard to find on the mainland, but American (Maine) lobster can be substituted.

leche de coco coconut milk. (See "The Basics," page 9.)

lechón pig.

lechón asado a la varita a whole pig seasoned with **adobo** and cooked slowly over a charcoal pit.

lechón de mechar beef round cut, used on the island to make pot roast.

lechonera a stand where pit-roasted pig is sold by the pound or by the portion.

lechosa papaya. (See "The Basics," page 10.)

lerén a plant similar to a water chestnut, cultivated by the Taínos.

limber fruit juice frozen into ice cubes and eaten as a snack. The most famous **limbers** are sold in Old San Juan.

limón lemon.

limón verde a lime with very acidic juice, known on the mainland as key lime.

lima lime.

longaniza Spanish pork sausage, seasoned with **cilantro**, spices, and bay leaves. Used to make yellow rice.

mabí a fermented drink made from the bark of the **mabí** tree. On the island this is a daily drink. On the mainland, especially in the New York area, it is available only from April to September.

maicena cornstarch. Cornstarch is prepared as a hot breakfast cereal on the island, with milk and egg yolks. It is also used in the preparation of many custard desserts.

majarete a rice-flour dessert made during the Christmas season, especially on Three Kings Day (Epiphany).

malanga a root vegetable with brown skin and white or purple flesh. It is used to make **sancocho** and tripe soup. It is also boiled and served with salt codfish salad.

mamey a fruit with a rough brown skin and bright red flesh. It is mostly eaten in preserves and compotes. Fresh **mamey** is very hard to find, but the frozen pulp is available year-round in Hispanic markets.

mandarina mandarin orange.

mero red grouper. This fish is traditionally used to prepare **escabeche** during the Lent season.

mofongo fried green plantain mashed in a mortar and shaped into a ball. Traditionally it was seasoned with fresh garlic and pork cracklings. New versions are stuffed with seafood, chicken, or vegetables.

mojo a classic sauce that originated in the coastal town of Salinas, made with olives, tomato sauce, and vinegar.

mojo de ajo a garlic dipping sauce served with **tostones** or boiled cassava.

molleja   chicken gizzard stewed in tomato sauce; usually served as an appetizer.

mondongo   a thick soup made with beef tripe, assorted root vegetables, and seasonings.

morcilla   blood sausage. A black sausage made from fresh pork blood and cooked rice. This is a traditional Christmas food.

naranja   orange.

naranja agría   sour orange, used mainly to prepare marinades. The white shell of the fruit is cooked in sugar and served as a dessert.

nuez moscada   nutmeg.

ñame   yam. A root vegetable with brown skin and white flesh. It is used in **sancocho** and eaten boiled.

olla   soup pot. Usually made of aluminum.

oregano brujo   Puerto Rican wild oregano. This oregano, with its distinctive pungent aroma, grows wild on the island. It is mostly used to make **sofrito**. It is very hard to find on the mainland.

paella   a Spanish dish that consists of rice, saffron, **chorizo** and meat or seafood.

paellera   a round, shallow iron pot with two handles, used to cook **paella**.

pana or **panapén**   breadfruit. A round fruit with green skin and white flesh that came to the island from Tahiti. When green, it is eaten as a **vianda** or made into chips and **tostones**. When ripe, it is made into a dessert custard or boiled and mashed like potatoes. Breadfruit is available only during August and September. It can be stored in the refrigerator for a day or two and can also be frozen. Peel and remove the middle seed before cooking.

pana de pepita breadfruit nut. A chestnutlike seed that is generally eaten boiled.

papa potato.

parcha passion fruit. (See "The Basics," page 10.)

pasteles dumplings made from shredded root vegetables, stuffed with **picadillo** and boiled in banana or plantain leaves.

pasta de guayaba guava paste. This is found in most *bodegas* and many supermarkets. It is used in many desserts, and as a jam.

pastel de masa grated assorted root vegetables stuffed with pork, olives, and raisins and wrapped in banana leaves. A traditional Christmas food.

pastelón de plátano yellow plantain pie made of fried slices of yellow plantain, beef **picadillo**, and green beans.

patas de cerdo pig's feet. Usually prepared as a stew with chick-peas.

pegao the crusty bottom of the rice that sticks to the pot. It is scraped and served with bean stew.

pernil de cerdo pork shoulder.

picadillo a basic beef stuffing mix made of ground beef, **sofrito**, raisins, and olives.

pique vinegar seasoned with hot peppers, spices, and sour orange. Mostly used as a condiment.

pilón mortar and pestle. A cooking utensil traditionally used to prepare **recaíto**. Taíno **pilónes** were made of stone. More recently they were made of wood; nowadays they are usually made of aluminum or plastic.

pimiento bell pepper.

pimiento de cocinar Italian frying pepper. (See "The Basics," page 11.)

pimiento morrón   roasted red pepper. Usually sold in cans or jars, preserved in water and salt. This is a classic garnish for rice dishes like **arroz con pollo**, potato salad, and **asopaos**.

pincho   skewered beef cubes.

piña   pineapple. The best pineapples grown on the island are from the Lajas Valley on the southwest coast. Puerto Rican pineapples are rarely available on the mainland, but the Hawaian pineapples available there can be used instead.

pinón de amarillo   yellow plantain pie.

piónono   a fritter made with yellow plantain. The plantain is cut lengthwise and fried. It is then shaped into a cup, stuffed with beef, chicken, or crab, sealed with eggs, and pan-fried.

plátano   plantain. (See "The Basics," page 11.)

plátano maduro   yellow plantain. (See "The Basics," page 11.)

plátano verde   green plantain. (See "The Basics," page 11.)

platanutre   plantain chip.

polvo de galleta   soda-cracker meal.

pote   an empty metal can, used in the old days as a cup to drink black coffee.

presa de pollo   chicken pieces.

punto de nieve   egg whites beaten until very stiff (literally, "snow peak").

quenepa   the fruit of a Caribbean tree, with green skin, pink flesh, and a large pit. The best ones are grown in Ponce, a town on the south coast of Puerto Rico. **Quenepas** are available fresh mostly during August. They are sold in bunches or packed in small plastic bags, and can be stored at room temperature.

queso blanco, queso de hoja or **queso del país**   Puerto Rican white cheese. A lightly salted white cheese made of cow's milk.

A distinctive characteristic of this cheese is that it does not melt.

queso de papa   Cheddar cheese.

quimbombó   okra.

recaíto   a key seasoning in Puerto Rican cooking. It is a combination of onions, garlic, peppers, and **recao** or **cilantro.** (See "The Basics," page 11.)

recao   green spiny leaf. (See "The Basics," page 11.)

relleno   a fritter màde of mashed potatoes stuffed with **picadillo**, shaped into a ball, and deep-fried. Canned corn beef is also used as a filling.

repollo   cabbage.

salchicha   Vienna sausage. (See "The Basics," page 11.)

salchichón   salami. The salami used in Puerto Rico is similar to Genoa salami. **Salchichón** is widely available in *bodegas* and supermarkets.

salmorejo de jueyes   crabmeat stew.

salsa de tomate   tomato sauce. (See "The Basics," page 11.)

sancocho   a thick soup made of assorted meats, root vegetables, **sofrito**, and corn on the cob, and traditionally served with plain white rice.

sangría   Spanish wine punch.

sartén   frying pan.

serenata de bacalao   salt codfish salad. Made with salt codfish, potatoes, eggs, tomato, and avocado.

sirop   syrup.

sofrito   **recaíto** cooked with ham, **alcaparrado,** and tomato sauce. **Sofrito** is the base for many stews and sauces. (See "The Basics," page 11.)

sopón another name for **asopao**.

sorullo de maíz or **sorullito** a fritter made of cornmeal and shaped like a cigar, stuffed with cheese, and deep-fried. The most famous ones are made in Lajas, on Phosphorescent Bay (the same town where the island's best pineapples are grown). They are served with a sauce made of mayonnaise and ketchup.

sorbete sorbet.

tamarindo tamarind. (See "The Basics," page 12.)

tasajo Puerto Rican dry cured beef.

tayote another name for **chayote**.

tembleque a stirred custard made of coconut milk and sugar (literally "shaky").

tocino fatback. (See "The Basics," page 12.)

tomate tomato.

toronja grapefruit.

tostón a slice of green plantain fried, smashed flat, and refried.

tostonera the utensil traditionally used to prepare **tostones**. It is made of two flat pieces of wood screwed together. **Tostoneras** can be found in *bodegas* and supermarkets. If they are not available, smash the plantain between two pieces of plastic wrap or parchment paper.

turrón almond nougat. A sweet eaten during the Christmas season.

uva de playa sea grape.

verduras root vegetables.

viandas root vegetables. (See "The Basics," page 12.)

vinagre de manzana cider vinegar. (See "The Basics," page 12.)

yautía   taro root. (See "The Basics," page 12)

yuca   cassava, a root vegetable with hard white flesh and a rough brown skin. (See "The Basics," page 12.)

Mail Order Sources

Canada

Toronto Caribbean Corner
57 Kensington Avenue
Toronto, Ontario
(416) 593-0008
Caribbean foods

Tropical Harvest Food Market
57 Kensington Avenue
Toronto, Ontario
(416) 593-9279

North Central

La Preferida, Inc.
3400 West 35th Street
Chicago, IL 60632
(312) 254-7200

Middle Atlantic

Balducci's
424 Avenue of the Americas
New York, NY 10011
(212) 673-2600
Beans, cilantro, tropical fruits

Casa Hispanica International Food Market
P.O. Box 587
73 Poningo Street
Port Chester, NY 10578
(914) 939-9333
Caribbean foods

Dean and Deluca
560 Broadway
New York, NY 10012
(800) 221-7714
*Boutique and regular beans, cilantro, annatto seeds,
tropical fruits*

Latin American Products
142 West 46th Street
New York, NY 10036
(212) 302-4323
Beans, Caribbean foods

Mountain

Earthstar Herb Gardens
P.O. Box 1022
Chino Valley, AZ 86323
(602) 636-4910
Fresh herbs

Pacific

Bean Bag
818 Jefferson Street
Oakland, CA 94607
1-800-845-BEANS

Caribbean Delites
1057 East Artesia Boulevard
Long Beach, CA 90805
(213) 427-5594
Caribbean foods

La Preferida, Inc.
4615 Alameda Street
Los Angeles, CA 90056
(213) 232-4322

Paradise Farms
1101 Eugenia, Suite B
Carpinteria, CA 93013
(805) 684-9468
Fresh herbs

Rosado's International Foods
1711 Little Orchard, Suite B
San Jose, CA 95125
(408) 298-2326

South Atlantic

Continental Trading Co.
7826 Easter Avenue, N.W.
Suite 500
Washington, D.C.
(202) 829-5620
Caribbean foods

Dekalb World Farmers Market
3000 East Ponce de León
Decatur, GA 30034
(404) 377-6401
Caribbean foods

Jamaica Groceries and Spices
9628 S.W. 160th Street
Colonial Shopping Center
Miami, FL 33157
(305) 252-1197
Caribbean foods

J. R. Brooks and Son, Inc.
P.O. Drawer 9
18400 S.W. 256th Street
Homestead, FL 33090-0009
(800) 327-4833
Tropical fruits

La Preferida, Inc.
9108 N.W. 105th Way
Medley, FL 33178
(305) 883-8444
Caribbean foods

West North Central

Herb Gathering, Inc.
5742 Kenwood Avenue
Kansas, City, MO 64110
(816) 523-2653
Fresh herbs

West South Central

La Preferida, Inc.
4000 Telephone Road
Houston, TX 77087
(713) 643-7128
Caribbean foods

Index

Index

Index

Index

Index

Index

Index

The Aquarian Dictionary

The Aquarian
Dictionary
of Festivals

J.C. Cooper

THE AQUARIAN PRESS

First published 1990

© J.C. COOPER 1990

British Library Cataloguing in Publication Data

Cooper, J. C. (Jean Campbell)
The Aquarian dictionary of festivals.
1. Festivals
I. Title
394.2

ISBN 0-85030-848-8

The Aquarian Press is part of the Thorsons Publishing Group, Wellingborough, Northamptonshire, NN8 2RQ, England

Typeset by Harper Phototypesetters Limited, Northampton
Printed in Great Britain by Woolnough Bookbinding Limited, Irthlingborough, Northamptonshire

1 3 5 7 9 10 8 6 4 2

Acknowledgements

I am glad to have the opportunity for expressing my thanks and appreciation to the Embassies of the United States of America, Sweden, Ireland, Japan and Malaysia; to the Australia High Commission and the Hong Kong Tourist Association for their kindness in offering research facilities or supplying information; also to the Buddhist Society of London and Rashad Ahmad Chaudhri of the London Mosque. I am also greatly indebted to Anne Holden for the photographs of Morris dancing taken by the late W. Fisher Cassie, CBE, former Squire of the Morris Ring. Once again, my sincere thanks to the County Library Service, especially to the Ulverston and Barrow-in-Furness Branches, for their efficiency, patience and courtesy in tracing and supplying rare and otherwise unobtainable books for reference.

Introduction

Most traditional festivals had their origins in religion, if not in the worship of actual deities then in the religious awe inspired by the phenomena of nature. Early beliefs were inevitably influenced by nature in all her manifestations which defied human control and which were first associated with general pastoral and agricultural needs and customs rather than with particular divinities. Later, these manifestations were represented by deities whose behaviour was, or could be, as erratic and unpredictable as the powers they represented and personified, and who required special rites of propitiation on the one hand and of avoidance and aversion on the other. Added to the natural unpredictability, the deity might be away from home on a journey, or asleep, or in a bad temper; this could necessitate reproaches and remind him or her not only of the needs of the people but of the fact that, without the devotion of the people, the deities would be deprived of the sacrifices and worship they demanded. Festivals were the occasions for the most important of these services. But, as Theodor Gaster said, festivals have also been 'a symphony of religious overtones with popular undertones — done not only out of piety but also for fun'.

Festivals were times of contact with the higher powers and the rhythms of nature. It is almost impossible for modern, urbanized people to appreciate the total dependence of early civilizations, or, for that matter, of present-day tribal communities, on seasonal changes, with the death of vegetation in winter, the end of the supply of food, and then the eager and traumatic waiting for the renewal of life in spring, coupled with the ever-present fear that it might not come again. Even when spring came there was still a long wait before there was anything grown enough to eat and, in the mean time, any sort of disaster might interfere with the growing crops or the herds and so bring famine and death: a threat and disaster not confined to ancient times.

The great death-and-rebirth drama was thus a vital part of life, in fact its chief preoccupation, from which the early myths and festivals were born and many of the festivals were simply a ritual imitation of

Nature's courses, being closely associated with her cycles, so it is not surprising that the instinctive appeal of the people was to the powers which controlled these cyclic rhythms and the vagaries of the seasons. It is also difficult for people living in temperate climates to realize the sudden, magical, transformation of arid desert into luxuriant growth, teeming with life, at the coming of the rains in tropical lands, or for the people of those lands to understand the almost agonizing longing for the sun in Northern regions after the cold and darkness of winter. Seasonal festivals and rites are the acting out of these myths and the emotional responses are presented as ritual drama in them.

The rituals fall largely into two divisions, first those of preparation in rites of 'emptying', such as fasts, purifications, austerities, abstinences, wailing and lamentations, then in 'fillings', that is feastings, making offerings and sacrifices, rejoicings and the use of magic to combat any adverse powers or influences. To this branch belong the universal dramatizations of the struggle between good and evil, summer and winter, plenty and want. Rites of emptying are accompanied by purifications in preparation for the coming life and are followed by rites of encouragement, urging on the new life, feeding it with vitality by sympathetic magic, such as lighting bonfires to encourage the heat of the sun, or pouring water to bring rain, leaping high to make the crops grow tall, and the sacred marriage, or mating in the fields and orchards, to promote fertility, though in some cases this was forbidden as offensive to the earth. Then, when life reappeared, there were rituals of welcoming and rejoicing which were repeated later in the year, after the safe-gathering of the harvest, with feasts and merry-making; times of anxiety were followed by times of celebration, all with their appropriate festivals, which, while conforming to the rhythmic patterns of life, both in the cosmos and the every-day world, also allowed for individual and national freedom of expression within the set pattern of ritual; they became a combination of austerity and conviviality, fasting and feasting, asceticism and buffoonery, sexual abstinence and orgy.

There is a similarity in festivals the world over. Faced with similar situations people are likely to make the same practical and emotional responses to them, especially in the all-important seasonal changes and phenomena of nature. Geography and climate may make the names of deities different, though for the most part they are remarkably alike, but the underlying idea is that of being in tune with the workings of nature and co-operating with them, noting these powers with awe and celebrating them with rituals and rites and so entering into these rhythms and powers. While it was obvious that unpredictable forces were at work it was also felt that these divinities and powers could be influenced by prayers, sacrifices and gifts, or by the persuasions of magic. Nature was clearly alive and akin to all forms

of life and the relationship with her was one of mixed familiarity and fear. Nor was the co-operation with nature merely a pastoral and agricultural preoccupation. Cities and towns were small, everyone knew everyone else and the countryside was on the doorstep with its influence constantly felt; also most people owned land in the environs or cultivated some plot.

Early rituals of sympathetic magic simply mimed nature's cycles in dying and being reborn. As has been said, mankind had the mimetic instinct, splashing water to bring rain and lighting fires to create warmth and 'lept high that the crops might grow high'. People essayed to bind the potency to themselves by physical contact, making a solemn ceremony of eating and drinking at critical seasons, dressing in green leaves or skins of slaughtered animals. Later, gods and goddesses were added to account for the simple earlier rites. Of these the Earth Mother and her son, or lover, the Dying God of Vegetation, are the most significant; she associated with the moon and its time-keeping phases, he with the sun which died in winter and was reborn at the solstice to vanquish the powers of darkness.

The festivals of the solstice, of the rebirth of light, follow the myth-pattern of the contest between the two great powers of light and darkness, good and evil, summer and winter, the old and new year, etc., such as is also seen in all trials of the hero winning through to the goal. Grimm and Frazer both show that the passing of the old year and the triumph of the new were celebrated yearly as a festival of ritual combat. The contest was later dramatized in the plays which were a characteristic of festivals from those of Dionysos to the later, and still performed, dramas of the Christmas and Whitsuntide Mummers. The Mystery and Morality plays have now degenerated into the Christmas pantomime.

Most festivals included some form of drama, depicting sacred stories, myths, or events in the lives of deities and heroes and teaching various morals and virtues. As Cumont says, festivals are often myth dramatized, brought to the level of the people. Early religions relied on myth rather than on dogma and were more concerned with action than rigid belief. Festivals were a vital part of that action, but they also involved the emotions. Aristotle maintained that the gain from the Mysteries was not from definite instructions so much as from the emotions and impressions. This was even more the case in respect of the esoteric and orgiastic rites which were performed with dedication, verve and total commitment.

For the most part, solar festivals are associated with blood sacrifice, lunar festivals with sexual licence and intercalary celebrations with the time of chaos and hence the reversal of the normal order and the return to the beginning with time started again after the *nunc stans*; the re-enactment of the original act of creation and the turning over of a new leaf. Barriers are broken down between the worlds of the

dead and the living and of all classes of people; the supernatural and the natural meet and life and death go hand in hand. It is also a time of 'mischief and confusion' and for the recounting of myths, sagas and legends which also help to take the reciter and listener out of time, back to the more glorious, emotive situations with which all can identify; obliterating the present while suggesting the possibility of renewal and future splendour.

Many of the most important festivals are associated with the dead; those of the All Souls group occurring universally, but the attention to the dead is ambivalent, in some cases they are welcomed and regarded as beneficent and appealed to for help, at other times they are feared and regarded as potentially dangerous, if not actively malignant, or, again, at some festivals they are first welcomed then driven off at the end of the rites. Also, people who may have been harmless in life can turn vengeful and hostile in death if they are not properly buried or given due attention and offerings in the next world, so the rituals connected with such festivals are often 'rites of aversion', apotropaic in character. The dead are powerful and able to interfere with events in this world, both for good or evil, and they appear to require the attentions and considerations they enjoyed in this life, hence, for example, the almost universal prejudice against the remarriage of widows for fear of incurring the jealousy and wrath of the dead husband.

Festivals arising from the cult and rites of the dead also include the important class of those held in honour of a dead cult-hero, such as Achilles or Heracles, at which games were the main feature, giving rise to the great athletic festivals, the best known of such being the Olympiad, where the rites were a mixture of reverence paid to heroes and sacrifices made to the gods. From local events they expanded into major festivals and, as they did so, attracted large audiences, became international and gradually changed from amateur to professional. Degeneration set in and athletes were held in exaggerated esteem. Great artists and poets were employed, at equally great expense, to carve statues and write laudatory verse which had previously been tributes reserved for the gods alone.

Such imbalance naturally brought protests from the philosophers who could see the dangers. Euripides denounced the class of professional athletes which had arisen and warned against the one-sided and false ideal produced. Xenophanes, founder of the Eleatic school of philosophy, wrote of the athlete: 'This is a foolish custom, nor is it right to honour strength more than excellent wisdom' and he goes on to say that it would be 'small joy for a city to be governed by a man good at boxing or swift of foot'. He also castigates those who gather to watch instead of performing themselves. Hippocrates, the 'father of medicine', said that the excessive training produced 'a dangerous and unstable condition of the body', while Plato, himself a noted

athlete, condemned the over-development and advocated individual exercises such as dancing, gymnastics and riding. Galen, physician and philosopher, lampoons the worship of bodily strength and compares it with animals: in an Olympiad in which all animals were summoned to compete man would not win a single event.

The study of festivals, which reflect ancient beliefs and customs, provides a veritable mine of information on the ways and life of the people, past and present, both of the ruling class and of the populace. As festivals were religious before they became civic, they involved the whole community, since, in early times there was no dichotomy between the sacred and the secular, and they served a dual purpose in uniting both. As Aristotle said: 'They hold sacrifices and meetings, paying rites of worship to the gods while providing rest and recreation for themselves.' Festivals became a medley of religious rituals, athletic games and amusements and provided not only a much-needed break from the hard grind of daily work, but also complete relaxation and enjoyment combined with a breakdown of social barriers. They involved the complete interruption of all ordinary civic life: everything closed down for the duration. They also furnished occasions for feasting and eating meat, normally in short supply, so that although the festival would be religious in origin it became associated by the people with the luxury of meat-eating. The sacrificial animals were first offered to the deity, who absorbed the essence, while the flesh was distributed to the populace. An old Chinese proverb said: 'Rustics feast only twice a year; after the New Year feast they look for the Harvest Home.'

The large gatherings of people at festivals presented problems of catering for their needs, both during the actual festivities and in the free time between rites, so whenever there was a great festival trade followed. There were caterers providing food and drink, pedlars for souvenirs, and professional amusements such as acrobats and jugglers and, later, even a judiciary to deal with disputes and offences. This, from the time of the Olympiad and Delos, was the birth of the great fairs. On the serious side the ancient festivals also drew philosophers and mathematicians for learned discussions, and poets came to write hymns to laud the gods and victors. Festivals and their attendant fairs were also meeting places for family reunions and for meeting friends from a distance. The events were also encouraged by rulers, who saw in them a means of keeping the people united and contented and therefore easier to rule.

Later, many festivals degenerated into fairs and fairs became markets, thus losing their original spontaneous religious and entertainment aspects and becoming merely commercial; only the market cross remained to call to mind the earlier religious associations. In Europe the decline in festivals began with Protestantism and, in England particularly, with the Puritans who frowned upon merry-

making and prohibited the celebrations, and, although some events were restored later, the initial total participation by the populace was never fully recovered and the decline continued until now we see increasing secularization and the one-time festivals becoming spectacles, performed by a self-conscious few and watched by many. Easter and Whitsuntide carols have practically died out and, symptomatically, Whit Monday, once a great festival, is now replaced in England by a Spring Bank Holiday; the Bank having taken over from the Church.

*   *   *   *   *   *   *   *

In the present work, festivals have been taken to include only those occasions in which the entire community is involved. Such ceremonies as accompany birth, marriage and death are personal and of importance to individuals only. Primitive societies are more concerned with these day-to-day rites, with purifications, taboos and fending off the powers about them than with actual festivals which are more related to religions which have specific deities. The 'festivals' of tribal communities are thus mainly concerned with fertility rites and with first-fruits; they are treated here under national headings, as a whole, since customs and rites vary from one tribe to another in the same country, or, as in the case of the Amerindians under imported Catholicism, the traditional and superimposed become inextricably mixed, saints and heroes exist side by side.

As every tribe, city or land had its own spirits or divinities, each with its own special allegiance and each concerned with the appropriate rituals and festivals, it is obviously impossible to cover every aspect and the vast medley of rites involved. Any country or religion could provide a volume of its own festivals; for example, Nepal is said to have a festival for every day of the year and there are literally thousands of fiestas in Catholic countries, Christian saints' days are innumerable and every country in Europe has its own national events outside its religion. It is, then, only possible to include the major festivals which have been established and recognized down the ages and whose influence, in many cases, remains felt today.

Tense has been used to indicate past or extant practices and the emphasis throughout is on myth, tradition and custom rather than on history since most festivals had their origin in myth, and even the 'historical' religions are heavily influenced by the mythological and conform to its patterns, with the result that myth and history often become indistinguishable. Festivals are symbolic, embodying the psychological or spiritual feelings of the people and should be interpreted as such. Taken as literal or historical they lose their deeper significance. As Joseph Campbell says. 'The festival is an extension into the present of the world-creating mythological event . . . the

whole purpose of entering a sanctuary or participating in a festival is that one should be overtaken by that state known in India as ''the other mind'', where one is ''beside oneself'', spell bound, set apart from one's logic of self-possession . . . we enter the play sphere in the festival, acquiescing in a game of belief, where fun, joy and rapture rule and the laws of life in time and space dissolve.'

A

Ablutions. Ritual washing or ablutions appear universally in connection with religious festivals, either in purification of the person or in the washing of images of the deities or saints. In the case of the images the washing has the additional import of giving vigour to them; this is seen in the rites of the Phrygian Cybele, the Hindu Bhavani, the Greek Mysteries, the Roman Bona Dea, the Teutonic cult of Nerthus, and is still seen in Catholic fiestas such as that of Les-Saintes-Maries-de-la-Mer and in modern Caribbean festivals. Ritual ablutions of the person are a particular feature of Zoroastrianism, Judaism and Islam. Rain-making ceremonies involve bathing images or dropping objects in water. The waters are universally associated with creation, fertility and regeneration. In fertility cults the magic of water in making crops grow is of the first importance. Bathing, sprinkling or splashing water about is a fertility rite of sympathetic magic to ensure rain. Immersion in water is used in rites of initiation, regeneration and rebirth and symbolizes the return to the womb to be born again.

Adonia (Ancient Greek). The Adonia was a summer festival held at Athens and Alexandria. The feast lasted two days and symbolized the death and resurrection of Adonis, a Dying God. There were lamentations, beating of breasts and tearing of hair, as in the Tammuz/Dumuzi and Osiris cults. Images of Adonis and Aphrodite were made and laid on a silver couch and on the second day they were cast into the sea by women, together with Adonis Gardens, which were pots of earth stuck with flowers, symbolizing the revival of vegetation with the coming of the rains. There were votive boxes of myrrh, the tree of Adonis, incense was burned and pigs were sacrificed.

African. The calendar as understood in the West does not exist in tribal cultures, their time being reckoned by events of significance, largely seasonal and lunar, or by natural and personal phenomena. Months are generally named according to weather conditions or occupations, e.g. hunting, harvest, etc., with the year also composed

of a cycle of seasons and their particular events. Some tribes have a four-day week. In many communities there are festivals and ceremonies of first-fruits, harvesting, fertility, the beginning of the hunting or fishing seasons and rain-making, rain being regarded as sacred, and there are also thanksgiving ceremonies for sufficient rain. Such ceremonies are conducted by priests, priestesses, mediums, medicine-men or the head of the family, each community having its own leaders in rituals. Rites are accompanied by prayers, offerings and sacrifices, or rituals involving fire in order to send the smoke up and bring the rain down, or by rites of the sprinkling, spraying or pouring of waters which form a link between the human and the divine.

Feasts, generally annual, can be held and conducted by mediums in order to pay tribute and offer thanks to particular controlling spirits or divinities. The dead can be offered food and libations of remembrance and communion, the rites being performed by the oldest member of the family. There are also fire ceremonies with the lighting of the sacred fire for purifying the crops and from which burning twigs are taken to rekindle domestic fires which have been ritually extinguished — a death and resurrection symbol.

Sacrifices are made as gifts of propitiation, as offerings of thanks, or as a means of communication either for the gods or the dead. Sacrificial animals must be of one colour. Priests taking part in rites must fast, abstain from sex and certain foods, wear special clothing and not be touched. Most ceremonies are accompanied by music, singing and dancing which, performed together, strengthens the bond in the community. For the African the universe, and particularly the firmament, is permeated by a deeply religious sense of divine influence.

In most tribes there is a festival and feast of the **First Fruits**. This marks the beginning of a new year and depends on the locally cultivated crops, thus there can be several such festivals and new years. In some cases the wife of the chief grinds the first grain and offers some to the ancestors with the words: 'Here is the New Year corn' and prays for fruitfulness. At the ripening of fruits a drink may be poured onto graves saying: 'This is the New Year, let us not fight, let us eat in peace'. This can be called 'eating the New Year'. When yams are cultivated the feast of yams ends the year and heralds the new one with the beginning of work in the fields again.

The New Year is equated with the new harvest and fresh food supply and there are rites of cleaning away the old and beginning anew.

As an example of the general type of festival the Lower Niger agricultural cycle may be quoted. There are: 1) Sacrifices and devotions to the Great Creative Spirit with prayers for a good crop; 2) first fruit offerings and devotion to household gods; 3) feast of the

new yam; 4) feast of the hunters; 5) celebration for the God of Justice and public appearance of the Ruler; 6) the *crumbo*, or remnants of the yam for the Ruler only; 7) feast of the yam at the end of the year and public notification of the recommencement of work with a festival in honour of the God of the Crops and gratitude for a good year.

Today there exists an intermingling of Hindu, Christian and Islamic influences with the original cultures. Diwali (see **Hindu**) becomes a festival of light triumphing over darkness and good over evil; Christian festivals are kept together with older customs, and African Muslims keep three of the major Muslim festivals: 1) New Year **Muharram**; 2) **Eid-ul-Fitr** at the end of **Ramadan**; 3) **Id el Azha** or **Id el Kabir**, the great feast in the pilgrimage month which ends the year.

Agrionia (Ancient Greek). The Agrionia was a women's festival in which they searched for Dionysos, the lost Dying God, in rites similar to those of Tammuz, Osiris, etc. The fertility-whipping of women was a feature of this festival as in the Roman **Lupercalia**.

Akitu (Babylonian & Assyrian). Akitu or Zag-mug, was the great New Year festival held on the first to the tenth of *Nisan*, at the spring equinox, in honour of the sun god Marduk or Meridach and celebrating his triumph over Tiamat, Chaos. In Assyria the national god Ashur took the place of Marduk. The festival was essentially one of the marriage between heaven and earth, associated with the rising of the waters. It started with the priestly ritual bathing in the waters 'two hours before the end of night', a process repeated throughout the festival. A procession accompanied the magnificently equipped ship-car of the God from his temple to the place of the festivities and back to the temple. The gods were believed to sit in conference with Marduk at this time to decide the fates for the people in the coming year — the 'Fixing of Lots'.

The Epic of Creation was recited and the death and rebirth of the God and his victory over Chaos were celebrated first with mourning and wailing, then with rejoicing. Images were veiled in the temples (as in Catholic Churches as Passiontide) and later light was brought to symbolize the return of life. Chaos was depicted by ritual contests between powers of light and darkness, Marduk and Tiamat. The order of the days was: 1) mortification and abstinence; 2) reversal of normal roles, slaves being waited on by their masters, and general licence; 3) ceremonies of purification at temples, cleansing with water and incense and with the blood of sheep. In this process the priest-slaughterer and exorcist priest became ritually unclean and had to leave the city until the festival was over. The head and carcass of the sacrifice were thrown into the river as a scapegoat, taking the uncleanness and sins of the people with them; 4) the use of a human scapegoat, a criminal, who was paraded, beaten and driven out of

the city; 5) mimed combat between good and evil, light and darkness, symbolized by Marduk vs Tiamat, Ninarta vs Zu, etc. 6) the King was taken to the temple and degraded before the God, first making a confession and protesting innocence and then reinstated; 7) the Sacred Marriage between the King and Queen or Priestess; 8) festival banquet; the king inviting the gods to the feast; 9) the return of the dead to this world, with funerary offerings made; 10) the sacred miming of the God who, having descended to the underworld, now returns to the earth amidst universal rejoicing.

All Saints & All Souls (Christian) 1 and 2 November. Celebrated from the third century. November is associated with the cult of the dead, the death of summer and the beginning of winter. In Celtic and other pagan ceremonies fires were carried over the fields as a fertility rite; Christianity adapted these so they became fires to light the soul of the dead heavenwards. In earlier times there was a midnight vigil with cakes and wine prepared for the return of the dead, soul cakes were eaten by all and lights burned to guide the dead to their earthly homes, an almost universal custom at festivals of the dead. Children — Soulers — went round to houses a-souling and soul cakes were given to them. They sang:

Soul, soul, for a soul cake.
I pray, good mistress, a soul cake,
An apple, or pear, a plum, or a cherry,
Any good thing to make us merry.
One for Peter, two for Paul,
Three for Him who made us all.
Up with the kettle, down with the pan,
Give us good cheer and we'll be gone.

There are many local variations of the song.

Libations of milk were offered at graves in Brittany. In Latvia, Estonia and Slav countries a banquet was held at the Feast of All Souls at graves, and torches lit the feast for the souls. In England, in some cases, the cakes were eaten hot while prayers were said for souls in Purgatory. Originally money was collected to pay for masses for the souls of the dead, but it degenerated into largess for the singers or Soulers. The fire element now appears to have been transferred in England to Guy Fawkes Night commemorating a political event, but is now the occasion for bonfires, fireworks and effigy-burning. See also **Dead**.

Ambarvalia (Ancient Roman). Held about 29 May, the Ambarvalia was a movable feast, a spring rural festival of Mars in his agricultural aspect. There were prayers to Mars and lustrations for the purpose of averting disease and inclement weather, to prosper the flocks and give health to the farmer and his household. The prayer was:

'Father Mars, I pray and beseech thee that thou mayest be propitious and of good will to me, our house and household, for which course I have offered the offering of a pig, sheep and ox to be led round my farm, that thou mayest prevent, ward off and avert disease, visible and invisible, barrenness and waste, accidents and bad weather, that thou wouldst suffer the crops and fruits of the earth, the vines and shrubs, to wax and prosper, that thou wouldst preserve the shepherds and their flocks in safety and give prosperity and health to me and our house and household.'

The sacrificial victims were driven three times round the boundaries before being killed. Other offerings could include food, wine, honey, milk, cheese, cakes, fruit, and also flowers, wreaths and garlands. Prayers were also offered to Ceres. This rural ceremony was later followed by the *Amburbium* which ceremonially defined the sacred boundaries of the city. The Ambarvalia was taken over by the Christian Church as **Rogationtide**.

Amerindian North. For the most part Amerindian time and their festivals are controlled by the moon, the calendar varying from 12, 12½, to 13 moons in a year. Those having 12 moons allow a supernumerary 'lost moon' every 30 moons. Some tribes rely only on the change of the seasons for fixing their festivals, others compute time by knotted thongs.

Regular festivals are held in connection with the ripening of crops and fruit, or with the migration of game. Festivals are usually elaborate in nature, being preceded by a fast, followed by ceremonial and symbolic dances, heroic songs, magical rituals and purifications, ending in great feasting. Dancing, music and dramatized history are essential features. The drama has much in common with Mummers' Plays, with a Witch Doctor, the Old Man, the Old Woman and the Fool.

Some tribes begin the year at the spring equinox, others in autumn or at snowfall, or the rutting season, or with the migration of animals, or with a 'new fire' ceremony. The basic factor is living in harmony with nature, the ceremonies and festivities following the seasons: spring, planting, germination and growth; summer, rain-making and protecting the crops; autumn, harvest thanksgiving and hope for future fertility; winter, prayers for snow and full rivers, but also protection from blizzards and the cold. Added to these are rites of the hunt, fishing, etc.

Many of the ceremonies are now intermixed with Christian customs, such as **Christmas**, saints' days and fiestas imposed on the pueblos and largely artificial and staged for tourists. In a few cases the ceremonies are reserved for the Indians only, such as the Plains Indians' Sun Dance. Originally festivals varied from small family gatherings to large feasts with each tribe having its own communal

rites. One of the most famous of the large gatherings is the **Potlatch**, a festival of the Pacific Coast tribes, especially the Kwakiutl and Haida, usually held in winter at a time when food has been stocked during the summer and autumn. The essence of the festival is giving away quantities of goods, usually blankets and food, but an important occasion could include such things as canoes. The donor is subsequently the recipient of goods from other potlatches and gifts should be returned with interest. The value and quantity of things distributed is a prestige symbol, reflecting the status of the giver. The first and largest gifts go to the most important guests and distribution then continues downwards in social order. During the festival carved poles are erected; children are initiated into the tribe and secret societies and into the use of titles and privileges of the clan; noses or lips can be tattooed, pierced or ornamented. There is dancing, feasting and singing with shamans giving mythological displays involving ancestors and creatures; these precede the distribution. The festival lasts several days and there can be potlaches for other occasions such as name-giving, marriage, or in honour of the dead. A potlatch for the dead is usually presided over by an effigy.

There can also be a display of lineage as well as wealth. The Iroquois New Year Festival of Dreams (see **Dream Festivals**) takes place at a time varying from January to March and is virtually a **Saturnalia** and general chaos, with people supposed to be out of their minds and therefore permitted complete license, attacking others and their property, holding a ceremony of driving out evil spirits, making a general confession of sins, dressing in disguises, skins and masks, and making fearful sounds. The only escape from the attackers is to guess what they dreamed. The Hurons hold a similar festival on special occasions, they also have four religious festivals each year: singing feasts, farewell feasts, thanksgiving feasts and prayer feasts for deliverance from sickness. These rites last for anything from one to 15 days. Medicine-men play an important part at them — controlling the weather to bring rain or sun as needed, to cure the sick, to find lost objects and exorcize ghosts.

The **Buffalo Dance** is a typical hunting festival. The Mandans of Dakota mark the return of the migrating buffalo at a time when the willows are in full leaf. Eight dancers, wearing buffalo skins and painted black, red or white, mime the actions of the animals, each carrying a rattle in his right hand and a six-foot-long rod in his left and wearing a bunch of green willow on his back. The dancers take up positions at the four points of the compass round a canoe. Two men dressed as grizzly bears stand by the canoe and growl and threaten anyone approaching; they are placed by the onlookers who throw them food which they carry off into the prairie, symbolizing the wild animals which might deflect or rob them of the buffalo and therefore must be appeased. The elders of the tribe beat

Amerindian Dog Dance (*Mary Evans Picture Library*)

on sacks and chant prayers for the success of the hunt. On the fourth
day a man dressed as an evil spirit enters the camp but is driven out
with curses and stones — a typical **scapegoat** ritual. This is followed
by general fasting.

Feasts of the Dead are held by some tribes at the end of the
summer, in honour of the Ancestors. Some are held every 8 to 10
years in a festival of great importance and ceremony when the dead

are removed from their local graves and placed in a common grave, with food, weapons and ornaments. A widow then fasts for 10 days and goes into mourning for a year. Alaska holds a feast for the dead about every two years, the ceremonies being conducted by a shaman who is responsible for teaching the traditional dances. There is feasting and an exchange of gifts and dancing round a fire into which food, money and other articles were thrown. In California it became a New Year festival when all debts are wiped out.

First Fruits, a summer festival at the ripening of the corn, bears great similarity to the Greek and Roman rites. The new corn must not be eaten or touched before the celebrations. New clothes and utensils are first distributed and the old, with all rubbish and left-over food, is carefully burned and dwellings are ritually swept. It is also a New Fire ceremony (see **Fire**), with fires being put out and ashes swept away. There is a three-day fast before the new corn is eaten sacramentally and the new fire kindled; it is then announced that the new fire has purged the sins of the old year.

There is also a Creek *Busk* or *Pushkita* festival of new fire and ripening of the corn at which the whole tribe watches the kindling of the fire by a shaman after a three-day fast. Four logs are placed in the form of a cross, indicating the four quarters of the world, and are burnt as an offering to the four winds. Feasting, dancing and singing follow the distribution of the new fire. Columbian tribes have an important festival and ceremonies associated with the first salmon and there are other rites of the first caribou, moose, bears, first roots and berries. There are whaling rites in Alaska and first salmon festivals among the Chinooks. These rituals include guardian spirit dances.

Important festivals and ceremonies centre round increasing the numbers of game animals, in a man-and-animal partnership and conflict. Alaskan tribes have a special 14 night *Animal Ceremony* with mask-dances representing the clan ancestors — wolf, owl, coyote, etc. and there are masked spirit dances. These were also used in initiation rites. The American Indian dances for almost every reason are in accord with the rhythms of nature — joy, thanksgiving, propitiation, protection, petition, fertility, rain and prowess in hunting and fishing. The dances also dramatize myth.

Amerindian South. It is said of many of the tribes that their knowledge of the calendar derives from the festivals rather than according to days and weeks. Festivals and feasts are largely concerned with the dead and purificatory rites, and with ploughing and tending crops and harvesting. In the cult of the dead disembodied spirits are regarded as dangerous or malignant, seeking to harm the living. Those unable to find a home in any other form, either human or animal, turn into wandering ghosts and live in dark

places. Spirits of enemies or strangers are particularly prone to be vengeful or malevolent. These are unlucky days on which spirits are at large and such days are holy. No work may be done, no business undertaken, no battles fought; they are 'days of pollution' and require ceremonies of purification, either by immersion in water or by sacrifice and the use of a scapegoat.

Confession or 'speaking out' was widely used among Incas. In festivals of the dead the deceased can be represented in the procession by ostriches and men eat ostrich meat, while the armadillo is the feminine animal. The dead are supposed to appear in great numbers, especially during the drinking feasts. The festival lasts four days with special lamentations on the fourth day. The ostrich dance is performed and is totemistic, aiming at influencing the dead and preventing them from doing harm.

Agricultural festivals have much in common with such ceremonies in other lands. The Corn Maiden, or Mother, appears as the Old Woman, the Maize Spirit. Planting, tending and harvesting are accompanied by great ceremony and much invocation of the Corn Spirit. The same applies to tobacco and manioc feasts. The Earth Mother is appealed to for abundant crops. Maize and tobacco are masculine plants; manioc and sweet potatoes those of women. The festivals and feasts are not only infused with the spirit of the plant, but in turn they help to strengthen the spirit. Among South American Indians tobacco and its narcotic properties play a similar part to the ancient intoxication of the Bacchante. Tobacco can also be offered to a demon to propitiate it or prevent it from interfering at a festival; plates of food are thrown out at a feast for the same purpose.

The South American feast *citua*, described by the invading Spanish, has much in common with rites of purification in other countries. The **Incas** expelled all deformed people from festivals, as did the Greeks.

Anna Perenna (Ancient Roman). The Anna Perenna, on 15 March, was in commemoration of the old woman who, in disguise, had married Mars instead of Neria, the maiden he loved; it was also a New Year festival. On the 23rd of the month the Feast of Mars and Neria was celebrated with great enthusiasm and Mamurius Veturius and Anna Perenna (the Anna Purna of the Hindus), who symbolized the Old Year and winter, were driven out and the youthful Mars and Neria were welcomed as the coming of spring. It was a plebeian festival and the people streamed out of town, going about in pairs, drinking in arbours and tents toasting Anna Perenna and Mamurius Veturius, who also represented the lunar and solar years. It was a year-in, year-out festival.

AN.TAH.SUM (Hittite). A spring festival lasting for more than a

month. The king and queen left their winter quarters to go to Tahurpa, and other sacred places, in a chariot; they were enthroned and 'great assemblies' were held with sacrifices of sheep and oxen to rain and storm deities. A fleece was brought to the temple of the Sun deity and hung on an evergreen tree, with offerings made of corn, wine and fat. There were separate ceremonies performed by the king and queen at different places. During the rites there were processions with music, dance and jesters, races, ritual ablutions, carrying the 'Year' to the House of the Dead, opening the grain store of the storm gods, making meat offerings and setting the cups before the storm gods. There were lamentations for Ishtar and meat offerings were made to her, followed by a 'great assembly' and feasting. Reference is also made to visits to the House of the Boxwood Tree, the evergreen, where sacrifice was made to the Storm Gods.

Anthesteria (Ancient Greek). The Anthesteria in February, the first spring month, was in honour of Dionysos and was held on the 11th to 13th of Anthesterion. It was a festival of ghosts, overlaid by that of Dionysos; both a placation and a purification. February, connected with the dead, was an unlucky month. Lucian said:

> 'There were among the Greeks certain days which brought with them complete idleness and cessation of business and which were called unlucky. On these days no one would accost anyone else and friends would positively have no dealings with each other and even sanctuaries were not used. These times were on account of the analogy of the month of February, when also it was the custom to sacrifice to those below, and all that month was dedicated to the dead and accompanied by gloom.'

This gloom was relieved by the Dionysian element of the wine-tasting ceremonies. On the first day they 'broached the new wine at Athens', according to Plutarch, 'an ancient custom to offer some of it as a libation before they drank it, praying at the same time that the use of the drug might be harmless and beneficial to them'. The festival was ancestral and household servants and slaves were included in the drinking. The second day of Cups, or wine jars, was one of feasting, revelry and drunkenness, with a drinking contest: the first to drain his cup was rewarded with a cake. 'Cups' were garlanded and wreaths were left with the priestess of the sanctuary of Dionysos. There was a solemn wedding of the wife of the King Archon (a magistrate who represented a past monarchy) to the God Dionysos, this being the only day of the year that his temple was opened.

The third day, of the Pots, was mainly a festival of ghosts, though there was also a dramatic contest, as Dionysos was also a god of poetry and drama. It was an unlucky day when precautions had to be taken. Dionysos also had a darker side as Lord of Souls, and the

pots were also associated with the jars used for storage and as burial urns. At the close of the festival the dead, who had been present and feasted, were dismissed with the words: 'Out of doors ye Keres (spirits). It is no longer Anthesteria.' The festival was also a special occasion for children, who were given presents of miniature wine-jars and three-year-old children were garlanded.

April Fool. Customary all over Europe, except Spain. A 'gowk' or 'cuckoo' in Scotland; a *Poisson d'Avril* in France. It is said to have originated as a feature of the festival of Venus on the first of the month of April when practical jokes were played. See also **Fool**.

Arrephoria (Ancient Greek). The Arrephoria was a mystery festival of underworld and fertility significance. Four girls of noble birth, between the ages of 7 and 11, dressed in white, with golden ornaments, carried special cakes and other unknown *sacra* to an underground sanctuary at night, left their gifts there and were given something wrapped up to bring back with them; this carrying was a sacred 'mystery'. The girls were called *arrephoroi*.

Ascension Day (Christian). Occurs 40 days after Easter and was established in the fourth century, but claimed by St Augustine to have been celebrated by the Apostles in commemoration of Christ's ascension to heaven. The Pascal Candle of Easter is extinguished, symbolizing the Light of the World having departed. Ceremonies performed involve processions of torches and banners and, in the Church, first fruits of beans, grapes, etc., are blessed. In Britain it was, and in some places still is, a time of decorating and blessing wells: a relic of the Roman **Fontinalia**.

Ash Wednesday (Christian). The first day of Lent is a penetential day; those attending mass are marked with ashes from the burnt palms of the previous year's Palm Sunday. It is not observed in the Eastern Orthodox Church, in which Great Lent starts on a Monday.

Assyria. See **Babylon**.

Astrology. In early societies the original consulting of oracles gave place to astrology as an exact science and, although omens were still taken into account, after the advent of astrology nothing was done without reference to astrologers, from undertaking a campaign, finding the right season for festivals, founding a city or a building, to setting out on a journey or contracting a marriage; all depended on the stars. The sun, moon and stars all controlled the seasonal festivals associated with climatic changes which were heralded by the heavenly bodies. Spreading from Babylonia to Greece and Rome, it was regarded by the Romans as the highest of the arts and exercised complete authority over the life of the state and the people and the days of the week were named after the stars.

In China the Grand Astrologer held an important place at Court, he and his 37 assistants were responsible for making the calendar. Astrology determined all fortunate or unfortunate influences in the seasons and hence the festivals concerned with them. The function of the astrologers was to watch the sun, moon and stars in the seasons and to keep the state in harmony with their rhythms and the powers of heaven and to avoid all adverse conditions. In the process of this careful watching and recording the celestial movements the Chinese and other ancient civilizations provided valuable and interesting information for succeeding generations.

The appointment of Court Astrologers was not confined to China or the East but was in vogue in medieval Europe. Cumont says that all cults based on astrology held the belief that the souls of the faithful and virtuous would ascend to heaven, from whence they came, to become one with the powers of light. In early Western civilizations planets were associated with divinities and thus with their festivals.

Australian Aboriginal. Time is reckoned by 'sleeps' and moons. The aboriginal, being ignorant of calendar time, is told by the moon when to hold ceremonies and festivals. To a people of tribal boundaries fixed by sacred myth and supernatural beings, the world is full of signs and symbols which must be translated into mystical meaning and ceremonies, the sacred dominating the profane. All is controlled by nature, her signs, portents and phenomena; a genuinely religious if non-theistic approach, though among some tribes a sky god is important. Totemism is the dominant characteristic of the culture and most of the rites are concerned with the ceremonies of birth, initiation, marriage and death, rather than typical festivals. Initiation is the most important and initiates recreate the original journey made by the Sky Heroes. There are magical rites of increase and fertility concerned with the renewal of life — human, animal and plant, with a deep sense of participation, somewhat akin to the early Mysteries. There are also rain ceremonies and culture hero commemorations with accounts of mythological supermen and supernatural peoples.

Groups perpetuate their own totemistic myth and heritage, singing it as sacred history. Rites are accompanied by ritual dance and song which keep the link between man and the cosmos and keep the people in touch with their own ancestral and spiritual heritage. Rites and their meaning vary locally and regionally, but all are highly symbolic. The totem may not be spoken ill of; in some parts it may not be eaten, in others it is allowable as food or eaten ritually. The dead are feared for the most part, as they can raise storms, but can also send rain and procure good hunting and food gathering if correctly appealed to.

A corroboree at Bagot Aboriginal Reserve, near Darwin, in Australia's Northern Territory (*Australian Overseas Information Service, London*)

Festivals which involve more than the normal ceremonies are held at sacred sites at suitable seasons, depending on the weather, as some places cannot be reached during droughts. These sacred rituals vary according to the place and prevailing conditions so are fluid and spontaneous rather than following any set formula, while other rites, such as initiation, conform to more fixed rules. Large assemblies gather at the centre and celebrations can last from four to six months for the completion of the compulsory full rituals.

Corroborees are such large gatherings together of members of a tribe and its divisions in the totem group in a dancing, singing and chanting festival combined with initiation ceremonies which pass on to the younger men the traditions and accumulated knowledge of the past history of the tribe and everything concerned with the totem. Preparations are elaborate and are made by men directed by an old man of special standing, and arrangements are discussed in whispers by a 'committee'. The rites take place at a chosen ground, the *Engwura*, but the rituals differ for different totem groups. A totemic pole is made and used in the sacred ceremonies, but is employed only once. Its form, again, varies from tribe to tribe but it is always elaborately decorated and may be of a considerable height; some are made of twigs, grass stalks and human hair-string, and decorated

with feathers and down, this pole is called the *Nurtunja* or *Waninga*.

A special mound, the *Parra*, may be made and decorated with small gum-tree boughs. The men have elaborate head-dressings and bodies are decorated with patterns, incised on the skin, with down fixed on these lines with blood and coloured yellow and red with ochre, charcoal and white pipe-clay. There are blood-drawing ceremonies and sacred objects, the *Churinga*, are displayed to the initiated and examined; these are usually made of wood or flat stone and carved with the sacred tracks of the Sky Heroes. They contain *kurumba* or *djang* — spiritual power or life essence. These festivals

A Kangaroo Dance at a corroboree staged at the Alice Springs district of Central Australia (*Australian Overseas Information Service, London*)

appear to circulate from tribe to tribe, but there are other sacred ceremonies which are not passed on and are held only by certain individuals by right of inheritance; these are associated with totems. In addition to *Nurtunja* and *Waninga* there is the *Kauaua*, which is regarded as common to all totemic groups and represents them collectively: it is a sacred pole made from young gum-trees, ritually cut down and not allowed to touch the ground until it reaches the ceremonial site or *Engwura* ground.

The Dream Journey, or Walkabout, is a yearly ritual renewal of union with the land, the country they inhabit; it is a visiting of places of power and the maintaining of contact with nature. It is at one and the same time a physical and spiritual, personal and social, renewal; a search for both food and places of spiritual power. The journey is seasonal and involves returning to a sacred place each year, but the seasonal cycle, being dependent on natural and food-growing situations, varies from one part of the country to another so the festival is movable.

In the North there are six seasons, in other parts four, or even two. In the dreaming 'big ritual' the sacred place often has to be made. The men then sit in two ceremonial rings and sing a series of chants, evoking the Sky Heroes, to the rhythm of sticks beaten hard on the ground, while two performers disappear to paint and decorate themselves. At the climax of the chanting they reappear and enact the myth of the Dream Time, the Sky Heroes and the First Animals. Only initiates take part in the dreaming rites.

Autumn Festival (Ancient Egyptian). An autumn festival was held at the beginning of winter, on the first day of the month of *Khoiak*, during the time when the waters of the Nile were falling; it commemorated the death of Osiris, slain by his brother Set. There were mourning ceremonies with Osiris bewailed by Isis and Nephthys. The trial and killing of Set was dramatized in ritual combat between the two forces of light and darkness and Osiris was brought back to life and taken in triumphant procession back to his palace. On the twentieth day barley was planted in flower pots and water from the Nile poured on, symbolizing the resurrection of Osiris. A variation of the ceremony was to put barley and sand in a statue of Osiris, cover it with rushes, and bury it ceremoniously, disinterring it nine days later. The barley and sand were then removed and incense put in and, after adornment, the image was put in the sun. The removed grain was also exposed to the sun but did not sprout as did the beds of barley dedicated to the god; the image-grain was sent down the Nile accompanying images of gods and 365 candles.

All this was associated with ploughing and sowing ceremonies when the floods subsided. When the actual sowing began the image

The Tet of Osiris, with the plumes, horns, disk, breast-plate and pectoral of the god (*from a bas-relief at Abydos*)

of Osiris was buried in a lunar-crescent shaped coffin of mulberry wood and the previous year's image was placed in the branches of the sacred sycamore tree. There were two chief shrines of Osiris, at Abydos in the south and Busiris in the north. As his dismembered body had been widely scattered at his death it was natural that there should be many places dedicated to his cult, all with varying rites. Another ceremony at his festival was the drama of a boat carrying the image of Osiris accompanied by his son Horus, who was followed by priests and the crowd, being attacked by Set and his accomplices. Horus then fought them off and the procession continued to the temple, taking the dead Osiris to his tomb amid intense wailing and beating of breasts. Again there is a ritual fight between the opposing forces with the body of Osiris lost, searched for and found then returned to his palace as a living god, triumphant over death. His festivals brought pilgrims from all over the country to obtain his blessing.

These Mysteries of Osiris were also performed annually at Denderah where models of the dismembered parts of the body were made of paste and grain and were watered and tended for 21 days, after which they were tied together, dried in the sun, then embalmed and buried. Although the processions and offerings were public affairs, the essential rites were performed out of sight in the inner sanctuaries of the temples. Osiris took great pleasure in dancing, music and 'watching buffoons', so these were included in his festivals and in acts of worship. There was a 'dance of the gods' in which a pygmy was a prized possession for this performance. The conclusion of the festival was marked by the dedication of a new statue of Osiris and great quantities of offerings. The *Tet*, the backbone of Osiris, being raised into an upright position, was one of the most solemn rituals; it was the oldest symbol of Osiris and it is suggested that it was the sacrum, i.e. the seed of Osiris.

Aztec and Toltec. The year was of 18 20-day periods with five intercalary days. The 20th days were feast days. Beginning in what is now February each successive festival was associated with seasonal aspects and the appropriate deity. The first festival was a rain festival; poles were set up, with painted emblems fluttering from paper streamers, at sacred places such as springs, caves and mountains. Young children were sacrificed, decked and garlanded and carried in litters to the temples, accompanied by crowds and loud music and shouting to drown their cries; their tears were a good rain omen.

There were 13 principal and more than 200 minor deities, each with a festival, so that each month was consecrated to some divinity, with minor festivals almost every week. Sacrificial festivals were celebrated on each of the 18 months in which countless men, women and children were ritually slaughtered to supply the sun god with the blood and hearts he required to sustain his life.

The chief god was Huitzilopochtli, the Aztec Mars, identified sometimes with the sun, sometimes with lightning, and symbolized by the serpent and clothed in a mantle of humming-bird feathers. His chief festival took place at the winter solstice when an image of the god was shot through with an arrow, emblematic of the death of the old year. Numbers of captives were sacrificed to him, also shot with arrows; there were gladiatorial contests in which a captive fought Mexicans in succession, if he defeated them he went free, if killed his body was ritually eaten at a feast.

Next in importance was Tezcatlipoca, Creator and sky god, whose festival was in April. He was represented by a handsome, blemish-free young male captive who was kept in luxury for a year, with every wish fulfilled and extravagant homage paid to him as the representative of the god. A month before the festival he was given four beautiful girls, representing the chief goddesses, as his consorts. At the ceremony he was stripped of his robes and garlands and his musical instruments were broken, then, at the summit of the pyramid-temple, he was met by six priests and ritually sacrificed, his heart being torn out, held up to the sun, then cast at the foot of the god.

Other ceremonies were of a less gruesome nature, consisting of songs, dances and processions of men, women and children, carrying garlands and censers and bearing offerings of fruit and maize.

At festival banquets, attended by both men and women, a ritual ablution took place with ewers and cotton napkins provided. Halls were perfumed and strewn with scented herbs and flowers which were also given to guests on arrival. Tobacco was then offered in the form of pipes, cigars or snuff. Game was served, particularly the ritual turkey, but there was also cannibalism if the festival were of a religious nature, when sacrificed slaves or a slain gladiator was eaten.

Fermented juices were drunk and the banquet was followed by dancing; minstrels played and sang while buffoons and jugglers provided entertainment. Guests were given rich dresses and ornamanets on leaving.

Human sacrifices were regarded as incarnations of the deity. Paste images of the gods were also made and ritually eaten.

B

Babylonian and Assyrian. The Ancient Babylonian calendar is much disputed and the experts often contradict each other while the names of the months show a variability and multiplicity, many of them taken from festivals and bearing the name of the feast of a divinity and all being regulated by the priesthood. It is, however, accepted that the Babylonian year was first lunar, with 354 days in periods of 29 to 30 days alternating, with an intercalary month as appropriate; but this being inexact a solar calendar was adopted about 1000 BC with a 19 year cycle, the 19 solar years being equivalent to 235 lunar months. There is no complete calendar of Babylonian festivals; each city varied its months according to the period and locality, and the methods of determining dates are uncertain just as the intercalation of months adjusting the lunar and solar years were irregular and different cities had different calendars.

But there were two chief divisions of the year, the first in the spring, when the rains came, since the Tigris and Euphrates had none of the stability of the seasonal Nile, and were unreliable in their rise and fall, the Tigris flooding from the Northern snows at the end of March or early April (the month of *Nisan*) and the Euphrates flooding when the Tigris subsided. Thus the rains were all-important after the scorching heat and drought of summer, bringing relief and new life and giving rise to the great spring festival, **Akitu**. The second division of the year was in *Tishri* — September–October — when the harvest was gathered in and celebrated with a festival. During the year each deity had a day in the calendar and there were lucky and unlucky days. Minor festivals were held every month dedicated to the various divinities associated with the lunar calendar.

Festivals:
Akita or Zagmug.
Harvest.
The Feast of **Ishtar**.
Midsummer.
The **Sacaea**.

Bakr-id (Islam). Among Muslims in India Bakr-id commemorates the sacrifice of a goat or ram by Abraham instead of his son. It is an occasion for blood sacrifice of rams and goats and is also called the *Feast of Sacrifice* or the *Feast of Daylight*.

Beltane (Celtic). 1 May. A widespread festival celebrating the beginning of the Celtic summer. It has been suggested that Beltane was originally a pastoral festival, with midsummer as the agricultural; both are similar in their rites. Some suggest that the festival was presided over by the Celtic god Bilé; others deny that such a god existed, while yet another tradition links the name with Baal, the Semitic sun god, or the Celtic Belus; on the other hand Ramsey of Ochtertyre, a friend of Sir Walter Scott, said it was 'a Druidic festival of Biel or Baal'. The Beal-tane fire was usually lit on the tops of hills. Like all other Celtic festivals it started on the previous eve.

All fires were extinguished and the next day the 'need-fire' or 'force-fire' was kindled by friction from oak, pine, or other specified woods in different countries, or from flint. Fire was then carried off to rekindle domestic fires. The bonfires were sometimes lit under a sacred tree, or round a tree dressed with greenery, this pole surviving as the **Maypole** and representing the vegetative spirit. The kindling of the fire was the central ritual, fire having divine qualities and preserving from disease. The people danced and sang round the tree-fire or bonfire, moving in a clockwise direction as sun magic, they then jumped through the fire, or between two fires, and drove the cattle and flocks through it and ran over the fields with burning brands. It was propitious to run or jump three times; in jumping, the higher one jumped the higher the crops would grow.

The Beltane cake was eaten and one special portion doomed its partaker to being the 'carline', a term of opprobrium, and he was 'sacrificed' by various ritual gestures such as pretending to throw him in the fire, or making him jump over it, pelting him with eggshells and making him assume the attitude of one dead. He was spoken of as dead. This was almost certainly a relic of human sacrifice, known to have been practised by the earlier Celts. Sometimes a straw man or a large wicker effigy was burned. Beltane cakes were also rolled downhill.

Like **Samhain**, Beltane was a time of danger and power with contact with the dead and fairies; the latter came out on 2 May to dance and roam at large until Samhain or Hallowe'en. Animals were sacrificed, among them horses, notably in Ireland where a horse's skull and bones were placed in the fire, or a man wearing a horse's skull or head leapt through the fire. Again, there were ritual combats between the powers of light and darkness, such as were found all over Europe at seasonal festivals; these struggles also stimulated growth. Beltane and Lugnasad or **Lammas** were favoured times for visiting

sacred wells, moisture being necessary for the crops; on these visits no word was to be spoken and no looking back was allowed.

Blood represents the life principle, the soul and the red solar power, the vital fluid; hence blood sacrifice at festivals. Blood is always interchangeable with wine in sacrificial rites and both appear as chief ingredients in sacrifice. Blood was used almost universally in early festivals, in tribal ceremonies and eucharistic sacraments; widely prohibited as food but on the other hand also drunk in some ceremonies as absorbing the life-force and as assimilating the power of a slain enemy. It was used in rites of atonement; to seal covenants and to establish kinship or friendship in the mingling of blood. Blood smeared on doorposts or writing in blood is apotropaic and has magical qualities. It was also used in the baptism of initiates, the blood of the bull being used in Mithraism; similarly the blood of the lamb is spoken of in Christianity in the context of salvation and sacrifice; the blood of the bull is sacred in Zoroastrianism.

Blood is both a power and a peril, hence the shedding of blood releases a dangerous force which requires careful rituals. The dead are able to renew their strength and revive life through the drinking of blood and the spirit world may be approached through blood offerings which also open the way to the world of the supernatural and can establish a vital link and communion with gods. A widespread custom existed of founding new buildings, particularly those of a sacred nature, on a blood sacrifice. See also **Sacrifice**.

Bon or O-Bon (Japanese). A festival of the dead, held in July, preceded by rigorous cleaning of houses, tombs and ancestral tablets; it has both Buddhist and pre-Buddhist characteristics. Priests and nuns visit houses and graves to recite Buddhist sutras and pray for the souls of the dead. New mats are spread at altars and shrines and vases are filled with flowers; presents of raw fish are given. It is the **Tama Matsuri**, 'All Souls', at which each family invites the dead back. The spirits are welcomed on the 13th and bidden farewell on the 16th of the month. They are welcomed at the graves and accompanied back to the house with lanterns; a meal is in readiness for them at home. Torches are lit and lights are set at doors. The spirits return to wander in the gardens among the flowers and it is especially a time for poets to return to the beauties of the world. On the last day the spirits are bidden farewell and they take gifts away with them. Spirits of those who have no relatives are given little boats with paper lanterns and set adrift on the Tide of the Returning Ghosts. No sailor will go to sea at this time as it belongs to the dead. There are special *bon-odori* dances of the souls performed by young women by moonlight.

Bona Dea (Ancient Roman). May began with the purely feminine

festival the Bona Dea, the Good Goddess. The actual deity honoured is not known but it is suggested as Fauna, Damia or Vesta, in any case some guardian of women. All men were excluded. The temple housed the sacred snakes of the Earth Mother and various healing herbs, but myrtle was taboo, as was wine. Sows were sacrificed. The goddess had another festival in December, with similar rites. The Christian Church adopted the May festival to that of the Virgin Mary, making it one of purity and chastity; hence the embargo on marriages in May, as well as its funereal associations.

Booths, Feast of (Hebrew). See **Tabernacles**.

Boundaries. At a time of no maps and an illiterate people it was important to define boundaries for crops and stock in order to protect them from any encroachment; this also applied to tribal hunting and fishing rights. The marking and upkeep of boundaries were occasions of many festivals such as the Roman **Ambervalia** and **Terminalia** and the Christian **Rogationtide**. The Teutonic and Scandinavian Holda, Thor and Freya were all guardians of boundaries, while the Graeco-Roman Hermes, the most famous of all, was also associated with merchants, markets and fairs which often functioned on boundaries and were the occasion of feasting and merriment. The word 'landmark' was probably connected with the boundary markers or termini set up as pillars or stones which were ritually placed and regarded as sacred and could represent deities; they were frequently a place of sacrifice. In addition to pillars and stones, markers could be earth mounds, grave mounds, ditches, stakes, cairns, altars, crosses or images of Hermes.

Natural features were also used such as rivers, the sea, trees, mountains, hedges, tracks through a forest or branches hung up on trees, or tracks of wasteland. In some cases holy fire was carried round boundaries; they could also be ridden — 'riding the marches'. The custom of whipping the young at boundary markers fixed the position in their memories. The removal of boundary markers was a serious offence which incurred retribution from both gods and men. In Babylon boundary stones were sacred to certain divinities who imposed curses if any boundary laws were transgressed.

A boundary, like a threshold, is also a dangerous place, stepping over into the unknown, and often protected by ghosts, as in Indian and Chinese beliefs; like crossroads they could also be the haunt of evil spirits and witches. Of the fairs set up at boundaries, that which was established between the Etruscan and Sabine lands was one of the first and most important fairs of Europe. In London various parishes were defined in an urban ceremony, e.g. the Savoy Liberty. Willow wands were carried by choir boys accompanied by the Stewards of the Duchy of Lancaster, eight jurymen, the Beadle and Bailiff. In the case of parishes which had a coastal or river boundary

ceremonies could include beating the waters and blessing the waters and ships. These ceremonies still take place in some parishes.

Boxing Day (Christian). The day following Christmas Day was said to be called Boxing Day either from the opening of the Church Alms Box for the poor of the parish, or the box which apprentices took round with them to collect largess from the houses of clients.

Boys' Festival (Japanese). *Tango no Sekku*. Also known as the Fifth of the Fifth, derived from an Ancient Chinese festival, the Feast of the Flags and Carp Banners. In China and Japan the carp symbolizes courage and persistence, swimming upstream against the current. Flags in the shape of carp which inflate are flown everywhere and the Sweet Flag, the Iris, is displayed and put in the ritual bath for health and strength. Balls of flowers or herbs may be hung on five-coloured cords as apotropaic. There is also an element of encouragement of military arts in the warrior or hero dolls being presented with an invocation for the health of the male offspring and in the traditional weapons being handed down as heirlooms, this being of a more recent Japanese origin rather than Chinese, who traditionally despised warfare. Young men gather at Shinto shrines for contests of strength and there is a battle of kites.

Bread and Wine. These are the sacramental foods representing the corn and vine, food and drink, the sum of man's agricultural labours. Bread is the food of the body with wine as the spirit, they also represent the feminine and masculine powers as the bread of the earth and the wine of inspiration. The breaking, or eating of bread can symbolize the death of the body of the sacrificial victim, with the drinking of wine as the blood, giving communion with the divinity and imparting spiritual power. Both are frequently used at festival rituals connected with the dead, giving food for the departed and for communion with them.

Buddhism. Festivals are universally lunar in character following the Vedic custom of keeping the times of the new and full moons as sacred; later the quarter moons were also held sacred. Buddhist calendars combine the lunar with the solar, with 12 months in the year and an occasional intercalary month, but Tibetan and Chinese Buddhism follow the 60 year cycle, thus their New Year's Day is not fixed and remains lunar.

In ancient India there were three seasons celebrated at the full moon: summer, the rainy season, and winter, but Buddhism is now world-wide and though everywhere is tied to lunar phases, ceremonies and festivals vary greatly from one land to another, influenced by Theravada and Mahayana Buddhism and by local beliefs. Others are influenced by Taoism, Hinduism and Islam, such as the Hindu-Buddhist syncretism of Nepal, the Taoist-Buddhism of

China, now in Taiwan and Hong Kong, and the folk-religion and animistic fusion in Oceania together with the Islamic influence in Malaysia. It is thus impossible to itemize the innumerable festivals involved (Nepal is said to have one every day of the year), but as a general rule all temples or pagodas have some form of festival on the first and 15th days of the month of the lunar calendar, often with feasts of local Bodhisattvas added. Special sermons are preached on full moon days and much value is placed on pilgrimages.

In popular Buddhism the liturgical year of festivals and ceremonies is largely concerned with the rites of the dead, of averting natural disasters and the ceremonies attached to birth, marriage, death and house-warming. By and large, Buddhist festivals are more the concern of the priesthood than the people, as compared with other religions, while some festivals are for monks only.

Festivals:
Festival of **Lights**.
Gunia.
Kathina.
Pavarana.
The **Tooth** or Asala Perahara.
Ullambana, Yu-lan-p'en or **Urabon**.
Uposatha Days.
Vassa or Rains Retreat.
Vesakha, Wesak, Waicaka or **Purmina**.

Buffalo Dance. See **Amerindian North**.

Bull. One of the chief sacrificial animals, sacred to all sky gods and symbolizing the powers of fertility and generation; it can also, especially when white, represent the lunar goddesses. The sacrifice of the bull at New Year festivals signifies the death of winter and the rebirth of the creative force. Bull symbolism and sacrifice were prevalent among all Sumerian and Semitic religions and were the focal points of Mithraism. In Egypt the bull was worshipped under the form of Menves or Menwer; in India it was the vehicle of Siva and an attribute to Agni. In Crete it played a central part and was sacrificed to the earth and the Earthquake God. Celtic bull gods represented divine power and the white bull was sacrificed by the Druids.

Vestigial remains of the ancient sacrifice are seen in the Spanish bull ring, in which the bull is killed, and in other parts, such as Portugal, Pamplona and the Camargue, where the Cretan bull games are echoed in the bull-running and playing with bulls in the arena, pitting skills against the bull but not killing it, at the spring festivals. These games are followed by dancing, drinking and roasting an ox, in the manner of ancient times.

Busk or **Pushkita** (Ameridian, North). See **New Fire**.

C

Cakes. Loaves. These were frequently made from the first fruits, being offered at festivals and sacramentally eaten by the priest or, on other occasions, by the people in general. In eating, the spirit of the corn, maize, rice, etc., is sacramentally absorbed. The custom is universal: among countless examples are the cakes or buns of Artemis, shaped like the moon and marked with the cross of the four quarters; the first loaf of the **Thargelia** at Athens; the Roman cakes made from the *mola salsa* by the **Vestal Virgins**; the Inca Virgins of the Sun making cakes from the first maize, to be eaten by the Inca and his nobles; at Delos there was an altar of the pious on which only cakes of barley or wheat were offered; in Egypt cakes of different shapes were offered to the deities then given to the sacred crocodiles; there are the loaves of the Hebrew **Pentecost** and the Shewbread; among rice-eating peoples a cake is prepared from the first sheaf; rice cakes are offered at Japanese festivals and the Ainus make a sacred cake of millet.

Cakes can be made of leavened or unleavened flour, mixed with oil, blood, milk, honey, cheese or butter or other agricultural or pastoral products; they can also be sprinkled with seeds and made of all shapes from the lunar round of the moon goddesses to the triangles and ovals of Egyptian offerings, to symbolic shapes such as the lyre of Apollo. Fig cakes were given to the *pharmakos*, the scapegoat victim in Greece. Offerings of cakes and bread were often hung in trees, on the head of the October Horse and on the horns of cattle. In Hindu festivals the horns are decorated with cakes which are scrambled for as good omens. Cakes were carried in ritual procession and were cast into chasms for the underworld deities and into the sea to propitiate its powers.

It was usually the custom that the new harvest might not be used for food until the first fruit cake or loaf had been ritually eaten. Vestigial remains of such customs are seen in the loaf shaped like a sheaf which appears at harvest festivals in churches and the Hot Cross Bun at the lunar **Easter** festival. Cakes were also used as a means of selection of a sacrificial victim or a leader of festivities, as,

for instance, the Celtic carline cake at **Beltane** and the **Twelfth Night** bean-and-pea cake. There were also, in Europe, Soul cakes and Yule cakes and in Christian festivals there were, and still are, Christmas cakes, **Mothering Sunday** or Simnel cakes, and the pancakes of **Shrove Tuesday**.

Calendar. The existence of a calendar, or continuous time-reckoning, denotes a stage of civilization. Primitive people having no knowledge of time other than natural manifestations, such as the waxing and waning of the moon, the recurrence of night and day and the seasons, had no fixed 'year'. Many tribes do not know how many moons there are to a year, so they have no yearly calculations.

The early calendar was roughly empirical, influenced by natural phases, and was religious before it was civil, being largely the preoccupation of the priesthood, among whom was formed a special class whose duty it was to observe the heavens and all seasonal phenomena. Festivals were tied to the calendar, the word being derived from the Roman *Kalends* or *Calends* which occurred on the first of each month and 'proclaimed' the coming of the new moon.

There was a sense of an ordered universe and powers in control, with which humanity could co-operate and communicate and the seasons were watched, welcomed and celebrated with festivals. The calendar controlled the lives of the people, their religion and social traditions, their civic, agricultural and pastoral pursuits, their sports and pastimes; it also dictated lucky and unlucky days, periods and times suitable for magic and divination. Time was of the utmost importance in determining the correct performance of all observances and festivals.

The moon provided a natural monthly time-keeper with its phases (see **Moon**), the months in a year varying from 12 to 13, the number being fixed in most civilizations by the religious authorities who not only decided how many months there should be but also when an intercalary month should be inserted. There was a wide divergence in practices and rules in these calculations.

The sun, on the other hand, does not wax and wane as the moon does, but is concerned with the seasons in the increase or decrease of heat. There are no definite rules for the beginning of a season-year; it began with the season, which varied from one land to another, and the year could be divided in a number of ways, in some cases into two halves, giving a New Year festival twice in a year, as in Babylon.

The other time-controller was the helical rising of stars. The lunar calendar was efficient for the religious and civic year, but the agricultural year required, and was fixed by, the change of the seasons, the solstices and equinoxes, the signs of the zodiac and the position of the fixed stars.

In early cultures, to adjust the lunar and solar years and bring them

into working agreement, months were moved forwards or back-wards, added to or left out, according to circumstances. For example, the Rabbi Gamaliel II, in the first century AD said: 'We make known to you that the lambs are small and the young birds are tender and the time of the corn harvest has not yet come, so that it seems right to me and my brothers to add to this year 30 days.' This was the intercalary month, the last month of the year *Adar*. In Babylon the month *Nisan* was 'forgotten' and the term 'lost' or 'forgotten' was, and is, used for these months among certain tribes both in North America and Africa.

The Egyptians developed the earliest solar calendar in 4236 BC. It was vital to know the time of the rising of the Nile floods which came at the helical rising of **Sirius**. Reckoning on an arrangement of 36 decades gave 360 days; five days were added as a special feast time and one day was added every four years. This was the first recog-nition of the year as a unit of time.

Most peoples reckon time by nights rather than days, e.g. sennight, fortnight, a custom found in the *Avesta*, in Sanskrit, Celtic, Amer-indian, Polynesian, Australian, Arabic and many other cultures. The day is broken up by activities, but the night is solid in sleep and thus an undivided unit.

In the West the Julian solar calendar was introduced to rectify the difficulties experienced under the lunar year; it corrected the inac-curacies of earlier reckonings and gave the year 365¼ days. While the Ancient Egyptian solar year had 12 months of 30 days and five intercalary days of festival at the end of the year, the Julian calendar distributed the five days through the year and instituted a leap year every fourth year; this gave an error of eight days in 1000 years. To rectify this the Gregorian calendar of Pope Gregory XIII, in 1582, abolished 10 days and revised the calendar of leap years, thus harmonizing the calendar with the seasons, from which it had strayed.

The Julian New Year was on 1 March; the Gregorian calendar put it on 1 January and Christmas was changed from 6 January to 25 December. (See **Christmas**.) This calendar is now used in the West, though most Protestant countries did not adopt it until the eight-eenth century: 1700 in Germany, 1752 in Britain and the American colonies and 1753 in Sweden and Denmark. Japan adopted it in 1873, China in 1912 and the Eastern Orthodox Church in 1924 and 1927. It is used in most parts of the world now as a civic calendar.

The solar calendar starts the year in midwinter. Other religious calendars vary; the Islamic lunar calendar varies the new year from year to year, going through the seasons and returning to its original position after 33 years; the Jewish begins at the autumnal equinox.

In many cases there could be more than one new year, as in ancient Babylon. In Japan there is a Greater New Year and a Lesser New Year,

the former, derived from the Ancient Chinese lunar calendar, occurs on the first of the first month and the latter on the 15th of the first month, influenced by agricultural observances.

Throughout this work the influence of the calendar is noted at the beginning of each account of a country's festivals.

Calends or Kalends (Ancient Roman). The New Year festival of the Calends had the same freedom as the **Saturnalia**; presents were exchanged and food and drink indulged in to excess to symbolize plenty for the coming year. Men, dressed as animals, ran capering through the streets, a habit still seen at carnivals and in the hobby-horse, and there was a general air of festivity and abandon.

Canaanite. The new year began with the coming of the rains after the heat of summer. The land varied from the hills of Judea to below sea-level in Jordan. A long, rainless summer gave fruit and crops ideal conditions for ripening; rains, coming in the autumn, were vital for life. Baal, god of rain and fertility, was opposed to Mat, god of drought, sterility and death. At the autumn festival of Baal the windows of his temples were opened to symbolize the opening of the heavens. He was a dying god associated with the rhythms of the seasons.

The spring festival of **First Fruits** of the sun god Shamash was the prototype of the Hebrew **Pentecost** or Feast of Weeks; the agricultural festivals of the Canaanites were largely taken over by the Jews and Yaveh shows many of the characteristics of Baal and other storm gods whose voice is manifest in thunder and lightning and who wars with the monsters of the deep who, like the Babylonian Tiamat, symbolize chaos.

Worship was mostly in 'high places', but there were also cults of trees, caves and springs. At festivals animals were sacrificed and offered to the gods either by burning or being thrown into a pit. First-born children were sacrificed and there was also adult sacrifice, though this was less frequent. Later a lamp, symbol of light and life, was buried instead of infant sacrifice. Incense was also offered to the gods.

Candlemas (Christian). 2 February. A spring festival of light when candles or torches were lit from the Yule Log then carried in procession. It was also a feast of purification when Christmas decorations were removed and burned. Decorations are now usually dismantled at the end of the Twelve Days, on 6 January, but in earlier times celebrations lasted from Christmas to Candlemas. When the decorations were discarded it was also a time of purification and spring cleaning. Herrick wrote:

Down with the Rosemary, and so
Down with the bays, and mistletoe,
Down with the holly, ivy, all
Wherewith ye decked the Christmas Hall.

The festival of the Roman goddess Februa, Mother of Mars, was on 2 February and the festival also had affinities with the **Lupercalia** and the festival of Juno; it also follows the pattern of the Eleusinian Mysteries when there were torchlight and candle processions in honour of Demeter when she searched for her lost daughter Persephone and light came back to the world when she was found.

Rites of purification were part of the ceremonies. The Celtic festival of Brigit, or Bride, on that date was adopted by Christianity as St Brigit, and had fertility rites similar to the Dionysian Mysteries. Women dressed a sheaf of corn or oats in female clothes and set it in a basket, with a club, paralleling the Dionysian *liknon* and phallic club, and called it Bride's Bed; or a bed was made of hay and corn, with candles burning round it, and Bride was invited to come as her bed was ready. Like the Roman Vesta, she was also a goddess of fire and fertility.

In the sixth century the festival was adopted as that of the Purification of the Virgin Mary (Luke 2.22). Pope Sergius decreed that the people should 'offer up a candle brenning at the worship that they did to this woman Februa and do worship Our Lady'. Mary became the Theotokos, Mother of God, the Light bearer. In the Eastern Orthodox Church the **Hypante** is celebrated when Simeon and Anna met Christ in the Temple as the Light of the World.

At the festival candles are blessed, sprinkled with holy water, and carried in procession. In Ireland, St Brigit's Day, Candlemas Eve, is the beginning of spring, with preparations for the sowing of crops. A feast is held and St Brigit visits houses where cakes, butter and food are laid out for her. Elaborate crosses used to be made, and in some places still are, of twigs, straw and rushes and hung in the houses, byres and stables to protect against storms, fire, disease or evil powers, with many local variations of the ceremonies.

Cannibalism. Authorities suggest that cannibalism was established in Palaeolithic times. There are various reasons for the practice, the first probably being the need for food, but later its purpose was to absorb the life-qualities and power of the person consumed, thus a relative could be eaten out of affection or an enemy to acquire his strength and cunning, hence the priority given to taking the vital organs such as the heart, brain and liver first. In religious ceremonies and at festivals cannibalism could also provide communion with the dead or the divinities to whom the victims were sacrificed. There is also the sacramental eating of the body and blood of the deity to effect communion.

Another reason for cannibalism is to gain magical powers in absorbing the life-force or soul. In some cases cannibalism was entirely ritualistic and religious when a human sacrifice was eaten as a meal shared between men and gods at festivals. Myth also speaks of cannibalism in such instances as Cronos swallowing his children; the Lamia as childeaters; Dionysos eaten by the Titans and the Russian Baba-Yaga, the cannibalistic witch. There are similar myths of cannibalism among most animistic tribes.

Carnival. Carnivals represent the re-entry into chaos, a reversal of all natural order, celebrated especially at the time of the winter solstice and the new year, as with the 12 days of chaos in Babylon and the Roman Saturnalia; they are also a feature of the spring and May Day fertility cults and of Mardi Gras in Christian countries. Orgies at these times symbolized the union of the Sky God with the Earth Mother, encouraging the forces of nature by sympathetic magic.

The origin of the word 'carnival' is disputed. Some say it is from *carne vale*, 'farewell meat' before the fast of Lent, others maintain that it derives from *currus navalis* or *car navale*, the ship-cart. The floats of modern carnivals point to the earlier ship-carts of the Greek Dionysian processions and the Roman ship-car of the Isis festival, while the Italian *carne vale* could well indicate the festivities which took place before the rigours of the Lenten fast and the eating-up of

Carnival in the port of Spain, Trinidad (*Mary Evans Picture Library*)

all meat and animal products on **Shrove Tuesday** or Mardi Gras. The ship-carts bore images and symbols of the deity, as did the later wooden ship in medieval Germany, and were accompanied by orgiastic dancing, burlesque, ribaldry, transvestism, masks and effigies. These ship festivals, like the Roman **Saturnalia** and **Lupercalia**, were times of unbridled license.

At such times of license and disorder the **Trickster** element is prominent as archetypal chaos. As Joseph Campbell says:

'In the carnival customs of Europe this figure survives in the numerous clowns, buffoons, devils, Pulcinellas and imps who play the roles, precisely, of the clowns in the rites of the Indian Pueblos and give the character of topsy-turvy to the feast.'

Carols. Originally a secular ring-dance with song, danced in streets, castles and palaces in medieval times, carols were not hymns so much as emotional and devotional poetry. W. Howitt, in *The Rural Life of England*, wrote: 'These ditties, which now enliven the industrious maid-servant, and the humble labourer, gladdened the festivity of royalty in ancient times.' They were prohibited in England in the Cromwellian period and were looked down on as 'rioting, chauntering and wantonness', but were revived at the Restoration and remained secular for another 200 years, after which they were in danger of dying out. However, they were rescued by the revival of interest in music in the nineteenth century and were heard in churches and became seasonal hymns. Christmas is now the main season of carols, Easter and Whitsun carols having almost died out.

Waits were originally kept as a civic body and paid by the Town and City as 'a small body of wind instrumentalists maintained at public charge'. They ceased to exist at the end of the eighteenth century and their place was taken by groups of private people, church choirs or children.

Many carols are pagan, such as 'The Holly and the Ivy' of Greek and Roman symbolism, and the 'Running of the Deer' of the Horned God of the Celts and the ancient King-Sacrifice.

Ccapac Rymi. See **Inca**.

Ccoya Rymi. See **Inca**.

Celtic. A predominantly lunar calendar, reckoned by nights, not days, with seven months of 30 nights and five of 29 nights, giving a year of 355 nights with 12 intercalary days in the year. The Calendar of Coligny had 62 consecutive lunar months with two intercalary months and was divided into half-months, reckoned by nights and noting lucky and unlucky days. All festivities began on the previous night, hence the prevalent 'eve' of festivals. The chief divisions of the

year were made by the festivals held on 1 February, 1 May, 1 August, and 1 November, though dates varied in Gaul and the Isle of Man. The year was tied to the seasons and agriculture.

There is some evidence that attempts were made to synchronize lunar and solar time. **Samhain** and **Beltane**, the two great solar festivals, divided the year into two. They heralded the coming of winter with food scarce and cattle slaughtered for winter meat, and the coming of summer and the growing season, while Brigit's Night and **Lammas** divided winter and summer, making quarter days. The Celtic year began at Samhain.

Festivals:
Beltane. 1 May.
Brigit's Day, Coming of Light; 1 February.
Lugnasad (Celtic); **Lammas** (Anglo-Saxon); Lughnasa (Irish); 1 August.
Samhain or Samhuinn; 31 October, the eve of 1 November.

Chanting. See Music.

Chinese. Festivals were tied to the old lunar calendar, the oldest lunar calendar in the world, and to the agricultural year, controlling the times of sowing and reaping. The year was one of 12 months of 29½ days with an intercalary month every two and a half years — a lunar leap year. A solar calendar was used in official matters and was divided into four seasons, corresponding to the four cardinal points. Later it was discovered how to calculate the divisions of the elliptic directly. New and full moons, as times of spiritual power, had their own festivals, many of which were celebrated out of doors in a garden or pavillion.

Chinese beliefs and practices have been consistently concerned with the dead and the two major festivals of spring and autumn, the **Ching Ming** and **Chung Yang**, were commemorations of the dead. Graves were visited and presents taken for the departed, all gifts being sent to the next world by means of burning them in paper effigies. They might also be sent such things as they had desired in this life but were denied. Spells and charms having occult powers were on sale at all festivals.

Various festivals are still celebrated and are concerned with some particular season or aspect of life. China adopted the Gregorian calendar in 1912.

In earlier times there were various festivals associated with archery and games, weight-lifting, foot shuttle-cock, quail-fighting, kite-flying and chess or gambling games. There were also children's games aimed at developing strength, quickness and skill. As at fairs, there were theatricals, strolling players, peep-shows, conjurers, acrobats and fortune-tellers, together with vendors of food and drink.

Festivals accompanied by music often had huge orchestras. In the T'ang dynasty one such had 120 harpists alone. The music had to harmonize with the seasons, the time and the signs of the zodiac in order to preserve the harmony between heaven and earth.

Festivals:
The Chung Yang Festival.
Dragon Boat Festival.
Feast of Lanterns.
Festivals of the **Dead**.
Festival of Kitchen God.
Festival of Tin Hau.
Moon Festival.
New Year or spring, early February.
Oxherd and Weaving Maiden Festival.
Tam Kung.

Ching Ming (Chinese). The Ching Ming and **Chung Yeung** were spring and autumn commemorations of the dead. Graves were visited and gifts taken for the departed and the offerings were burned in effigy to send them to the next world. The dead might also be sent such things as they had desired, but been denied, in this life.

Christian. The Christian calendar was originally based on the Julian calendar of the Romans, the year beginning on 25 March, the ancient pagan spring festival, until 1582 when Pope Gregory XIII reformed the calendar, introducing the calculations now used in the West and starting the year from 1 January. Most Protestant countries, however, did not adopt the Gregorian calendar until later — 1700 in Germany, 1752 in Britain and 1753 in Sweden. It is now used almost universally as a civic calendar.

Most Christian festivals, though based on scriptural sources, are of ancient lineage, some growing naturally out of pagan rites, some being a mixture of the historical and mythical, while others were deliberately adopted and adapted by the Church on the grounds stated by the Venerable Bede that: 'It is doubtless impossible for men being so rooted in evil customs to cut off all their abuses.' Gregory the Great also wrote, with regard to Christianity in England:

'I have, upon mature deliberation . . . determined that the temples and idols in that nation ought not to be destroyed. Let holy water be made and sprinkled in the said temples; let altars be erected and relics placed, that seeing their temples are not destroyed, the people may the more familiarly resort to the place in which they have been accustomed. And because they have been used to slaughter many oxen in the sacrifice to devils, some solemnity must be exchanged for them on this account, as that on

the day of dedication of the nativities of holy martyrs whose relics are there deposited. They may build themselves huts of boughs of trees about those churches, which have been turned to that use from temples and celebrate the solemnity with religious fasting and no more offer beasts to the devil, but kill cattle to the praise of their God in eating.'

In this building of booths, common to most pagan and other festivals, we have the origin of many of the great fairs which began in the church precincts. As has been said, 'paganism served as old stock on which the vigorous branch, capable indeed of fairer fruit, but owing its vitality to alien sap, might be engrafted'.

In countries under Protestant influence the main festivals appear to have suffered a dichotomy, they seem either to have remained church occasions, celebrated by members of the religion, or, on the other hand, to have become almost wholly secularized, with holy days becoming holidays. In Catholic countries, either Roman or Eastern Orthodox, the continuity has been better maintained by keeping the sacred from being taken over by the profane, by the expedience of Bede and Gregory in incorporating ancient pagan customs with Christian worship and festivals, re-enacting many of the rites and scenes from pre-Christian times.

To combat polytheism Saints' Days were substituted for many festivals and people could pray to the saints as they had to the lesser deities, as witness St Dionysus who grew a vine at Naxos and made wine, while St Elias took over the hill-top shrines of the sun god Helios as well as his chariot as an emblem, and the cult of Isis gave all its qualities to that of the Virgin Queen of Heaven. Mary took on the role of Theotokos and acquired the characteristics of the Magna Mater, depicted with the child on her knee in the style of Isis with Horus. The consular processions of Constantinople and those of the vegetation festivals of Rome were changed to ceremonies which had the liturgy as a counterpart of the sacrifice of Jupiter. A procession to St Peters was substituted for the **Robigalia**, while the **Ambarvalia** became **Rogationtide**.

The language of baptism is that of Mithraism, with the lamb substituted for the bull, 'washed in the blood . . . sacrificed from the beginning of the world'. The Pope took the title and geographical situation of the Pontifex Maximus and the Cardinals were the successors of the *flamens* and their functions; St Peter held the keys of Janus and the 'birthday of the unconquerable sun' became Christmas Day. The Church Militant goes back further than Mithraism to the Mysteries of Isis and the Sacred Cohorts; the Twelve Days of Christmas were paralleled in Babylon and had similar rites to the **Saturnalia**. Norse, Teutonic, Celtic, Danish, Norman and Anglo-Saxon traces are also evident throughout.

The early Christian festivals were occasions for both solemn services in church or cathedral and times of excess in feasting, the suspension of normal roles and much buffoonery, as with the Saturnalia and other pagan customs. Originally, Christianity, with its other-world and monastic traditions, contained a considerable element of world-negation and pessimism and the early church endeavoured to suppress the merry-making of the Roman **Calends**, but as time went on revelry crept in increasingly until by the Middle Ages it was so far invaded by paganism that we have the spectacle of 'both monks and nuns indulging in masquerades directly connected with the heathen festivals . . . monks mumming as wolves, foxes and bears and other diabolical masquerades'.

In the year 1198, at the Feast of Circumcision in Notre Dame, Paris, 'so many abominations and shameful deeds were committed that the place was desecrated not only by foul jokes but the shedding of blood'. At the election of the Fools' Pope 'in the very midst of divine service masqueraders with grotesque faces, disguised as women, lions and mummers, performed their dances, sang indecent songs in the choir, ate their greasy food from the corner of the altar near the priest celebrating mass, got out their games and dice, burned stinking incense made of old shoe leather and ran and hopped all over the church'. Such licentious buffoonery is a direct parallel with the customs and caricatures of the Roman Calends of January when people exchanged gifts, dressed as animals or old women and danced through the streets singing indecent songs to the applause of the populace.

In Catholic, and notably the Eastern Orthodox Churches, there are festivals associated with miracles wrought by relics and icons.

Ember Days were originally fasts for the four seasons of sowing, reaping, vintage and winter. They are celebrated on the Wednesday, Friday and Saturday following the first Sunday in Lent; Whitsunday; Holy Cross Day, 14 September; St Lucia's Day, 13 December.

Festivals:
All Saints and **All Souls**; 1 & 2 November.
Ascension Day.
Ash Wednesday.
Candlemas; 2 February.
Christmas; 25 December.
Corpus Christi.
Easter.
Epiphany; 6 January.
Festivals of the Virgin Mary.
Good Friday.
Harvest Festival, **Lammas**, 2 August.
Holy Week.

Lady Day; 25 March.
Lent.
Midsummer. St John the Baptist. 24 June.
Mothering Sunday.
Palm Sunday.
Plough Monday, first Monday after Twelfth Night.
Rogationtide.
Saints' Days.
Shrove Tuesday. (See **Shrove-tide**).
St Valentine's Day; 14 February.
Whitsuntide.

Christmas (Christian). 25 December. The Christ Mass from the Old English *Cristes maesse*; an adaptation of the ancient and almost universal festival of the winter solstice (see **Solstices**); it was not celebrated until AD 353 and then was on 6 January, the **Epiphany**, until the fourth century when it was moved to 25 December, the time when the dying sun has reached its lowest point and will then be born again to conquer the powers of darkness. It is the date of the birth of numerous dying gods of vegetation such as Tammuz, Osiris, Attis, Dionysos and Mithra and the ancient solar festival of the *dies natalis solis invicti*, the Birthday of the Unconquerable Sun.

It is essentially the festival of the birth of the Sun God from the Virgin Queen of Heaven when the Light of the World was born. Egyptian and Syrian priests emerged symbolically from underground cave-shrines at midnight announcing: 'The Virgin has brought forth: the light increases.' Mexican, Peruvian and other Indians also celebrated the birth of the Child of the Celestial Queen and in Scandinavia, at Yule-tide, Freya was born on 25 December and the dying god Baldur appeared on Yule-tide eve. The typical festivities of the Roman **Calends** and **Saturnalia** and the Scandinavian Yule were incorporated into those of Christmas, with the ancient Twelve Days of Chaos, found in Vedic, Chinese, European and pagan symbolism. St Augustine admitted that Christmas was neither derived from apostolic usage nor sanctioned by the General Council. It is now the most generally celebrated of the Christian festivals, in both sacred and secular aspects.

In England, in medieval times, the Lord of Misrule, or the King of the Bean with the Queen of the Pea, chosen by getting the bean and pea in the slice of the Christmas cake, presided over the Twelve Days of festivities and over the Shrove-tide celebrations at universities and Inns of Court. Frazer suggests that the King of the Bean was originally a scapegoat to be sacrificed and analogous with the selection of the 'carline' of the Celtic Beltane cake. Student festivities, though boisterous, were apparently not objected to by the authorities as they maintained that they learned more about the students' characters in

these 12 days than in any other 12 months.

Another festivity was the election of a Boy Bishop at the Choir Boy Feast; he was dressed as a Bishop, went in procession with his peers, received presents and preached a sermon on Holy Innocents' Day. There was also an Abbot of Unreason, but the practice died out under Puritan rule and was not revived. Burlesque and buffoonery were less widespread and uninhibited in England than in Europe. In France, for example, priests, sub-deacons and choir boys had special days in the Twelve Days of Christmas. That of the sub-deacons fell on the Circumcision and Epiphany and started at Vespers with 'He hath put down the mighty from their seats and hath exalted the humble and weak.' The elected sub-deacon then took over and became the Pope or Bishop of Fools and turned the higher clergy out of their stalls and burlesqued their functions. Sometimes an ass was brought in and there were brays in place of responses. French law students set up a separate mock kingdom of their own. These practices were at first tolerated as a Doctor of Auxerre said that wine broke its barrels unless air was occasionally let in, the clergy being 'nothing but old wine casks, badly put together and would certainly burst if the wine of reason were allowed to boil by continued devotion to the Divine Service'. On the other hand the Pope castigated 'the shameless frenzy of their play-acting' and the revelry gradually ceased.

Santa Claus is derived from St Nicholas and the American corruption of San Nicolaas, after Dutch colonists had established the festival in the New World. He was said to have been fond of children and given them surprise presents. His festival is on 6 December, but the custom of giving children presents was transferred later to Christmas Day, or Christmas Eve. In Germany children have their gifts round the tree on Christmas Eve; in Holland St Nicholas brings them by ship from Spain; French and Swiss children put out *sabots* on the hearth, but in Spain and Italy the festival is not of such importance and children do not get their presents until 6 January, the old Christmas date, when they are brought by the Three Kings and grass or hay should be left for their camels.

Puritan Scotland and Wales laid more stress on New Year celebrations. Stockings were not mentioned before 1854, but in Europe there was a custom for nuns to hang their stockings on the door of the Abbess's room and she filled them with sweets and little gifts. But Father Christmas was also the German/Scandinavian Woden/Odin who gave presents to his devotees from his tree and rode through the sky on his sleigh, drawn by reindeer. The tradition of Father Christmas coming down the chimney arises from his being a magical person who must therefore never touch the ground; the chimney is open to the sky from which he comes.

Before the advent of the Christmas tree, boughs of evergreen were

bound together, often in a circle or wreath or globe, and decorated with ribbons, glittering objects, apples and presents, and hung from the ceiling; these were known as Kissing Boughs. Candles were lit on Christmas Eve and every evening of the Twelve Days. The tree was introduced into Britain from Germany. Although Prince Albert is credited with its introduction at Windsor it had, in fact, appeared some years earlier in the household of Queen Charlotte and in the homes of German merchant settlers in Manchester. The origin of the tree is to be found in the pine of Attis and the fir of Woden/Odin. The sacred pine, under which the dying god Attis was killed, was festooned with streamers at festivals and hung with gold and silver ornaments and bells and had a bird in its branches. Votive gifts were placed under it by the devotees, as also in the case of the trees of Dionysos, Cybele and Atargatis, but the tree of Woden bestowed gifts on his worshippers. Lights on trees symbolize the sun, moon and stars on the branches of the Cosmic Tree, but Christianity adopted them as a symbol of Christ as the Light of the World and the gifts as those of the Magi to the Christ Child. Lights also represent souls of the dead. The star on the top of the tree is the Star of Bethlehem.

The Yule Log was a focal point of the festival among Scandinavians, Slavs and in Celtic Britain. It was brought home ceremoniously, decorated with bright ribbons and evergreens, most usually ivy. The log was anciently an aniconic form of Dionysos and the ivy the Crown of Dionysos; the Druids had the oak log of their Cosmic Tree as the masculine counterpart of the feminine mistletoe; the pine log was used in other countries. In many places the ashes were scattered in gardens, fields and orchards for fertility and as the regenerative power of fire. Holly was sacred to Saturn and decorated his temples, but the Christian Church called the red berries the blood of Christ and one tradition had it that holly was the wood of the cross. Evergreen decorations are also a relic of Celtic practices, signifying that life has not died out in winter.

Carols were originally singing round-dances and only later became church hymns. (See **Carols**).

During the **Twelve Days** there were traditional Mummers' Plays, varying in character but always following the theme of birth-death-resurrection and the triumph of light over darkness, good over evil; also symbolizing the death of the old year and birth of the new. Vestigial remains of these plays are now seen in the Christmas pantomime.

Waits went from house to house wassailing and were given hot spiced ale or punch to drink healths (*was haile*, Anglo-Saxon 'to be whole' — good luck).

Foods eaten at Christmas are puddings, pies and cakes, the pudding being originally a fruit and spice porridge; mince pies were formerly of minced meat, usually mutton, and for the festival they

were made in the shape of a cradle for the infant Jesus, one being eaten on each of the Twelve Days. Cakes were from the Yule *doos* — probably dough — and were flat, human-shaped, with facial features picked out in raisins, said to represent the infant Christ, but cakes and customs varied from one region to another. A poem, or Christmas song, of 1695 said:

Now thrice welcome Christmas,
Which brings us good cheer,
Minc'd pies and plum-porridge,
Good ale and strong beer;
With boar, goose and capon,
The best that may be,
So well doth the weather
And our stomachs agree.

The Scandinavian, Teutonic and Celtic boar's head, served as the main dish, with an apple in its mouth and decorated with evergreens, symbolized the life-force, vitality, abundance and protection. The goose, a solar bird, was eaten at Michaelmas and Christmas. The turkey, the sacred bird of the Toltecs, and the food for their ritual occasions, was only later introduced from America.

In Europe the Christmas festivities generally take place on Christmas Eve. At midnight on Christmas Eve animals traditionally have the power of speech and water turns into wine. Animals are represented in the cribs set up in churches. Other European names for Christmas, such as *Calends* (Provencal), the Polish *Kolenda*, Lithuanian *Kallendas*, Czech *Koleda*, would suggest that the festival was closely associated with the Roman **Calends** or Kalends, while New Year's Day, on 1 January, which followed as a festival, was a continuation of the **Saturnalia**, of which the Greek sophist Libanius wrote: 'Everywhere may be seen carousels and well-laden tables. The impulse to spend seizes everyone . . . people are not only generous to themselves, but also towards their fellow men. A stream of presents pours itself out on all sides.' See also **Yule-tide**.

Chrysanthemum Festival *Kiku no Sekku* (Japanese). A late summer festival on 9 September; a flower and first fruits celebration. The chrysanthemum, a flower emblem of Japan, symbolizes autumn, harvest, joviality, wealth, longevity and happiness.

Chung Yang (Chinese). The Chung Yang festival commemorates the warning received by a scholar, Huan Ching, that a terrible calamity was impending and told him to escape to a high place. The festival occurs on the ninth day of the ninth moon and is celebrated by going to as high a place as possible and flying kites which are of every possible design such as dragons, butterflies, birds and centipedes, all ingeniously contrived to move limbs, roll eyes and make sounds.

Citua. See **Amerindian South**.

Corn Dolly or Maiden, represents the Corn Goddess, Mother and Maiden, and is also the child of the future growth, the seed. She is also called the Old Woman and thus symbolizes the corn spirit, the old year and the coming year. Usually in the form of a doll, but sometimes only an elaborate knot, it was made from the last sheaf of corn gathered at harvest time. The figure was often dressed in female clothes and was carried back to the farm in procession, with great ceremony. Sometimes she was lowered to the ground with wailing and then raised high with shouts of joy to signify the death and rebirth of the corn divinity. The Dolly, kept until the next harvest, is also apotropaic and wards off witches and fairies and all evil influences. There are close analogies with the ceremonies of Demeter and Kore in the early Greek agricultural rites which were feminine in organization, men being excluded, since agriculture was then in the hands of women as priestesses of vegetation and fertility. Later both men and women took part. See also **Harvest**.

Corpus Christi (Christian). Occurs on the Tuesday after Trinity Sunday and was instituted in 1264 but dropped by Protestants at the Reformation. It is one of the highlights of the Catholic year as a special commemoration of the Eucharist; a day of gladness untinged by the gloom of Holy Week. The Host is carried in procession, under a canopy, preceded by girls in white and followed by clergy, choirs, guilds and fraternities wearing their insignia. It is a time of First Communion; also an occasion for fairs.

Corroboree. See **Australian Aboriginal**.

Cronia (Ancient Greek). The Cronia was one of the festivals of the gods; it was in honour of Cronos/Saturn and had all the characteristics of the Roman **Saturnalia** but was conducted in a more restrained mode. Later, under the influence of the Roman conquest, it developed a more Saturnalian character. The festival was held on the 12th of the month of *Hecatombaion*. Cronos was originally an agricultural deity and the month was previously called *Kronion*; it was the end of the farming year and a kind of harvest festival. It was also a time of the reversal of order and slaves and masters feasted together.

Cybele, *The Rites of* (Ancient Roman). A festival imported from Phrygia in honour of the Great Goddess Cybele, whose consort was Attis, a dying god. Her cult was well-established in Rome and her spring festival, from 15 to 17 March was a re-enactment of the drama of the finding of Attis by Cybele. A pine, the tree of Attis, and the origin of the Christmas tree, was felled and taken to the Palatine. The tree was swathed like a corpse and bound with fillets of wool and garlanded with violets, symbolizing both Attis, as his flower, and the

spirit of the vegetative world. The next day was one of grief and mourning for the dead god, the devotees and initiates mingling their wild cries with the shrill notes of flutes and lashing themselves and gashing their bodies; they were followed by neophytes in a frenzy of lamentation. At the finding of Attis the scene changed abruptly to a delirium of joy, this was the **Hilaria**, in which the Mother Goddess was united with her lover.

D

Dance. Dancing, which can be any expressive movement of the body, varying from the stately and controlled to the wild and ecstatic whirling of the dervishes and the orgiastic Bacchanalian frenzy, has always been associated with religion and ritual, and hence with festivals, as cosmic creative energy. It is religion dramatized, as Lucian said: 'You cannot find a single ancient Mystery in which there is not dancing . . . as all men know, many people say of those who reveal the Mysteries that they dance them out.' The rhythms of the dance are the natural means of producing euphoric and ecstatic states; they are an instant and instinctive expression of emotions, ranging from delight to fury.

Dancing both creates and releases energy. Movement also suggests life and vigour, it has always been believed to encourage growth and fertility; the livelier and more energetic, not to say frenzied, the dance, the greater the effect. The vigour of the dance as fertility is made clear by the Ancient Egyptian dances celebrating the death of Osiris and his resurrection; there was first the Dance of Lamentation of Isis and Nephthys, then the Dance of Armed Men, protecting the God, and finally the Dance of Fertility in which both sexes took part 'who by their vigorous movements sought to give vitality and strength to the newly arisen Osiris and through him to the people, their crops and lands'. This is also shown in the Cretan hymn in which the devotees of Greatest Kuros are exhorted to 'leap for full jars, and leap for the fleecy flocks, and leap for our fields and crops, and for the hives that bring full increase . . .' There was a widespread belief that the higher the leaping the greater the fertility and height of the crops.

Dancing also has magic powers and the gods were held to have taught their worshippers the sacred dances. Zeus, Apollo, Ares, Dionysos, Pan, Baal, Artemis and Hathor were all dancers and Hathor was also goddess of music and dancing and her priests are represented as 'dancing and clattering castanets'. Apuleius said there was also a sacred dance in the Rites of Isis. In this context dances were often performed in the disguise of some attribute of the divinity; this

gave the dance the appearance of power and helped to bring down that power from the deity to the worshipper. The movement of the dance also moves the deity, while dancing to trance or to exhaustion also leaves the body free for the entrance of the divinity invoked.

Ritual dancing is associated with all fertility festivals and war dancing had the same significance since war gods were usually also gods of agriculture, such as Ares/Mars, and part of the magic of ritual dancing was that the movement and jumping woke the earth and frightened away the powers of darkness; for this reason the dancers were mostly male, as solar and virility, and the heavy dancing of men in armour would be even more rousing. In other cases the sexes were paired as fertility in such well-known dances as the Helston Furry Dance and Les Treilles at Languedoc. Women's dances occur in the rites of the Earth Mother or, later, on the festival of some female saint. The former were frequently orgiastic.

Dancers must be anonymous, as protection against evil powers, hence the disguises, masks, blackened faces or long paper or woollen ribbons covering the mummers' faces. Silence must also be maintained. This anonymity also subordinates the individual to society,

Ritual dancers protect themselves against evil powers by maintaining their anonymity with disguises, masks and blackened faces

becoming one with the whole. Also in the frenzy of the dance the mundane personality is transcended, taking the participant into another state of consciousness to become one with the deity, in some cases the dancer taking the actual name of the divinity, such as the Bacchoi and Bacchai. This applies particularly to orgiastic dancing which produces ecstasy, there being an age-old and universal belief that the soul is able to leave the body in ecstasy, trance or sleep, to visit other realms, bringing back either divine or prophetic information.

Exceptions to the otherwise universal employment of dancing at festivals are the Babylonian and Assyrian rites which were restrained and austere, while Chinese festivals also lacked an uninhibited or ecstatic element, and dancing is generally forbidden in Islam, though it survives in the whirling dervishes, members of a Mohammedan brotherhood founded by the Sufi mystic Rumi (c. 1273). They are religious mendicants and practise a whirling dance which produces ecstasy.

Examples of the widespread dancing rituals, and their variety, are the fire dances in which torches were carried over the fields and through the orchards. The Tarahumara Indians of Central America had a man dancing the whole time that others were working in the fields. The snake dance of the Pueblos of New Mexico was a fertility rite to make the crops grow. Among hunting people the mimetic dance gives power over the animals represented, such as the kangaroo dance of Central Australian tribes and the Ainu ring dances imitating sacred birds such as the crane and heron, much of tribal dancing being pantomimic.

The Korybantes were orgiastic dancers in the worship of the Phrygian Cybele and Attis in sacrificial festivals. The Kouretes of Crete and the Orphic Mysteries were dancing, armed youths regarded as semi-divine fertility spirits. The Pyrrhic dance was in full armour and imitated all the movements of war and was danced at the Panathenia. In many cases special dancers were, and still are, kept in association with temple festivals, such as the Nautch Girls of Hindu temples and the Bali dancing girls. Ritual dancing is also prominent in Tibetan Buddhist festivals. In ancient Rome the Salii were a dancing brotherhood and had 12 dancers and a leader who performed in honour of Mars, originally a vegetation god, on his birthday on 1 March; they also accompanied the festival of Mamurius Veturius on the 14th, the feast of Anna Perenna on the 15th, and the Feast of Mars and Neria on the 25th.

Chain dances are of great antiquity, being depicted on rocks at Luxor in Egypt from before 3400 BC and occurring in ceremonies in the Iron and Bronze Ages, in early Mediterranean cultures and on tombs at Languedoc. They symbolize the linking of heaven and earth, male and female, and also form the magic circle which en-

closes sacred space. They are solar, following the sun's course and, in sympathetic magic, ensuring that it remained on that course.

Round dances. Dancing round encircles some sacred object, or protects it by the magic circle. The hearth is frequently such an object, being the meeting place and point of communion between the three worlds, the lower, earthly and heavenly. Round dances also imitate the movement of the firmament; they are particularly prevalent in primitive cultures. In monotheistic religions they represent the dance of angels round the throne of God. Circular dances are performed round the **maypole**. In medieval times in England dancing round the hearth took place at festivals celebrated by the Inns of Court when 'the Master of the Revels took the Chancellor by the hand, and he took Mr Page, whereupon Judges, Sergeants and Benchers danced round the fire, according to the old ceremony, three times, during which an ancient song with music was sung by a man in a Bar Gown'.

Sword dances. Sword and Morris dances are survivals of seasonal festivals using sympathetic magic. The earliest records of sword-dancing are of the Indian Maruts, attendants of the god Indra, dressed in shining armour, carrying gleaming swords or golden axes. They were picked young men of the same caste who helped Indra in his fight against evil adversaries; they were 'bringers of rain and fertility, shedding water, augmenting food. They leap and dance also at the sacrificial feasts of men'. Sword-dances are associated with agriculture rather than with war, though here, again, we have the close connection between the two in that the war and agricultural gods are the same. Though sword-dances were performed at agricultural festivals, it is possible that, like the gods, they represented both elements and were combined agricultural, fertility, hunting and war rites. Another suggestion is the possibility that the dance represented the death of the old year and the birth of the new.

The clashing of the swords is also apotropaic, frightening off evil powers and providing protection as did the Cretan Kouretes with the infant Zeus, and the Korybantes danced on Mount Ida. The same applied to the Pyrrhic dance and the dance of the Roman Salii. But the agricultural significance was shown in the Kouretes leaping 'for full jars, for thick fleeces and growth of the harvest'. There were, and still are, two forms of the dance, one with long swords of metal, the other with a short sword, usually of wood, the Rapper, or a sword with a wooden handle. The dance is performed in a snake-like weaving about with frequent clashing of swords, the noise of which, like the bells of the morris dancers, acts as a potent means of frightening off supernatural or evil forces. A circle is formed of locked swords and held up by the leader while the others dance round, with the Fool in the middle; each dancer then snatches his own sword and the Fool falls dead. Another variation is for the sword to be pointed

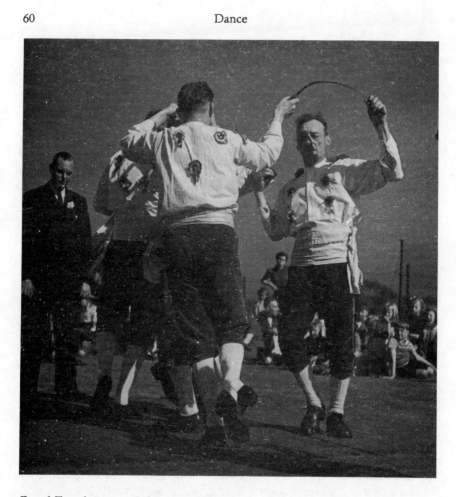

Royal Earsdon sword dancers, Northumberland (*W. Fisher Cassie*)

at the throat of the leader, or the swords are woven round his neck, and he sinks to the ground.

These 'deaths' suggest original human sacrifice. The Ten-Pound-Doctor is called for and arrives, wearing a top hat and carrying a black bag, and he restores the Fool or the leader back to life. Again, there are variations and a Boy King may be beheaded and revived by the Fool using a sword, or by Besom Bessy, Betty, or Dirty Bet, who is a hermaphrodite carrying a broom. She is said to be the last vestiges of Freya, the Great Mother and fertility goddess of Northern Europe. She also appears in **Plough Monday** Plays. Sword-dances are performed mostly at **Shrove-tide** and winter festivals and are associated with Mummers' Plays at **Yule-tide**, with Father Christmas as compere and stage manager.

Morris dances. The spring festival on 1 May was the beginning of the season for Morris dances; they appeared again at **Whitsuntide**, but

'The Queen's Delight', danced in Bedfordshire by the Greensleeves Morris Club (*W. Fisher Cassie*)

their dancing is not now confined to these festivals and they are performed on other civic occasions, such as the London Lord Mayor's Show. 'Morris' is suggested as 'Moorish' or 'Morisca', introduced from Moorish Spain by John of Gaunt, and this is one possible explanation for the blackened faces of the dancers, though these appear in other ceremonies and are also symbolic of loss of individual identity, or disguise to prevent recognition by evil powers; they are also adopted by Guisers who represent the souls of the dead and wear shrouds. Blackened faces are also a substitute for a mask as a disguise. The Moorish connection is strengthened by the presence of a Turkish knight, but this could well be the influence of the Crusades.

The Troupe consists of eight: six dancers, the Fool and the Musician, the Fool dresses conventionally in fool's garb and carries a fool's bladder or stick; he also functions as a barrier between the onlookers and the dancers, keeping the crowds back. Bells worn on the dancers' costumes are apotropaic, like the clashing swords of the sword dance.

Abbots Bromley horn dance, September 1950 (*W. Fisher Cassie*)

Horn dance. The dance is of obvious antiquity as the dancers use reindeer horns which were not found in England in Norman times. A hobby-horse is ridden by a man carrying a bow and arrow, leading 6 men with reindeer horns painted white and red. The dance can be varied with 12 dancers, 6 of them horned and the others as Robin Hood, Maid Marian, a Fool and two Musicians dressed in red and green. There is a horn dance at Abbots Bromley in England, on 1 September. Six men wearing stag horns have four attendants, with Robin Hood (the Green Man), Maid Marian — a man dressed as a woman — and the 'obby 'oss (one-legged, like Odin) and the Fool. It is an autumn festival of the turn of summer into winter.

Bean dance. The dancers wield staves with which they make clashing noises and thump the earth, possibly making symbolic holes for planting the seeds and at the same time employing the ancient rites of waking the dormant earth.

Country dance. The name is taken from a mis-application of the 'contra' dance, the French *contre-dance*, in which the partners stand face-to-face or 'counter'; an ancient fertility rite involving both sexes. During Christian holy days, or holidays, these dances often took place in the churchyard, usually on the north side since it was left unused for burial as long as possible, being the unlucky side. Later, all dancing and the plays with which it was associated, were forbidden during the Puritan Commonwealth. The Puritan Stubbs inveighed against them, writing:

'Then marche these companies towards the Churche or Church-yarde, their piping, Drummers thundering, their strumppes danc-ing, their Belles jyngling, their handker chiefs swinging about their heades, like madmen, their Hobbie Horses and other monsters skyrmishing among the throng, and in this sorte they goe to the Churche . . .'

Though revived at the Restoration, much was lost and church danc-ing fell into disuse. Such dancing is now a purely civic celebration.

Dance of the Little Bulls. See **Mayan.**

Day of Atonement (Hebrew). See **Yom Kippur.**

Day of the Bearers of the Year. See **Mayan.**

Day of the Caves. See **Mayan.**

Dead. Two contradictory attitudes are apparent in relationships with the dead; either they are objects of fear to be propitiated and warded off, or they are welcomed home and re-established in family life and feasted at festivals of the dead. But even in cultures where they are ritually welcomed and feasted they are dismissed at the end of the festival with ceremonies which either request them to leave and make provision for the journey back, or where they are actually driven away. The Greek **Anthesteria** and the Roman **Lemuria** rituals told them to begone, while Chinese and Japanese rites bid them farewell, providing them with lights for the journey.

It is usually believed that the dead are powerful and can be either benign or malignant. They require proper burial or disposal of ashes, otherwise their ghosts haunt the living and cause trouble until the omission is righted. This also applies to those who suffer from violent death or are murdered; they demand justice, for an unavenged victim cannot enter the next world until there has been retribution, so, in the meantime, the ghost becomes a threat and must be propitiated. While the dead resent being ignored, it is nevertheless unlucky to speak of them in any but complimentary terms — *de mortuis nil nisi bonum.*

The dead can also be applied to for help and advice; this applies particularly to dead heroes, saints or benefactors of humanity. Such people take on semi-divine qualities, if not actually becoming gods in the course of history, and prayers and offerings are made to them at their shrines and festivals. Ancestral spirits, on the other hand, are a family cult; they require constant remembrance and are given food and drink offerings on the occasion of their return at festivals of the dead.

Many of the ancient festivals rose from the cult of the dead and the funeral games instituted in their honour, such as the Greek athletic events, when prizes were sometimes given to every competitor,

illustrating the generosity of the dead hero.

Ritual observance was not only given for the purpose of propitiating or welcoming the dead, but their festivities involved the
deities who also took part and received offerings. It was an occasion
for communication between gods and mortals, and, as an added
benefit, these preoccupations with the next world assured the living
of continued life after death, while the well-being of one's ancestors
was clearly bound up with the future welcome of one's own soul into
the world beyond the grave. There was a constant need for reassur-
ance that death was not a dissolution but a change of form of life.
Attention was also given to the needs of the departed to assure merit
for the living: it was to 'lay up treasures in heaven'.

The mystery of death gave rise to the **Mysteries** in religious life.
'Just as truly as Osiris lives we also live; as truly as Osiris is not
destroyed, we will not be destroyed.' The great ceremonies of
initiation in the Mysteries involved a ritual death encounter and
assured the neophyte that death could be overcome and the fear of
death was destroyed in the light of the knowledge of immortality.

All vegetative divinities and dying gods are associated with the
dead and resurrection; they go underground in winter and return in
spring, such as the Corn Goddess Demeter and the Vine God
Dionysos. They belong to both worlds, the lower regions from which
all plant life springs and the upper world in which they flourish and
provide nourishment — their festivals constitute the Mysteries.

Since festivals of the dead include both deities and mortals they can
be known, as in Babylon, as Feasts of the Gods. Pindar speaks of
feasts at which the gods entertain the departed heroes.

In Egypt lamps were lit for the dead on the first and last days of the
year. In Persia the dead returned at the Feast of Tirajam. Greece had
the **Anthesteria** and soul feasts were made on the third and ninth
days after death and annually thereafter. In Rome the **Lemuria**,
Parentalia and **Feralia** were festivals of the dead. In Hebrew folklore
the Patriarchs of Israel visit their descendants at the **Feast of Booths**
and Jews visit the graves of parents between the first and tenth of
Tishri, the new year Day of Atonement. Christianity adopted the
Celtic **Samhain** as the Feast of **All Souls** — **Hallowe'en** — in
November.

In China gifts could be sent to the dead by burning them in paper
effigies by the grave at festivals of the dead, the custom of gifts for
the dead being widespread. In China and Oceania the festival of the
dead coincides with New Year's Day and there are four festivals of
the dead throughout the year. In Japan the **Bon Festival** involves the
visiting of graves and ancestral rites. The Tibetan Festival of the Dead
occurs in autumn with the tolling of bells, the sounding of gongs,
conches and drums and the reciting of mantras. The Zuni Indians
celebrate the return of the dead at the sacred lake at the summer

solstice with dancing, and the South American Indians of Equador lay out food for the souls who consume the essence while the living later consume the material of the offerings. At harvest festivals in the Transvaal spirits of royalty return in disguise, but only partially human, having only one leg, arm or eye; they join in the festivities. Such customs and rites are typical of the universal festivals of the dead.

Dead, Festivals of (Ancient Egyptian). Egypt celebrated frequent minor festivals in honour of the dead, which were carried out on an average of every fifth day at the tombs of the great kings. Offerings were made to the spirits of the ancestors to obtain their help and protection and to provide them with the necessities of life in the next world. This was also an insurance for the living, for when they joined the ancestors their offerings would be there, ready and waiting for them, as 'treasures laid up in heaven'. Offerings also brought the ancestors' spirits back to earth to celebrate with the living and to take an active interest in their present lives. Eating and drinking with the spirits also elevated the nature of the living and helped to make their souls divine.

Dedication of Lights (Hebrew). The Feast of the Dedication of Lights (Hanukah or Chanukah) is an eight-day festival of lights and rededication, on the 25th day of the month of *Kislev* (November-December) which celebrates the Maccabean rededication of the Temple and commemorates the miracle of a small one-day jar of oil lasting for eight days at the rededication. On the first day of the festival one light, either a candle or, more traditionally, an oil wick, is set in the window or door for all to see and another light is lit on each successive day, with recitations and blessings, and on the eighth day with the singing of a traditional hymn. It is also a festival of identity and liberty of the Jewish people.

Deer Dance. See **Mayan**.

Delos. The Delian festival, on the Island of Apollo and Artemis, mentioned in the Homeric 'Hymn to Apollo', was well-established as an international festival in the days when the **Olympics** were merely a local gathering. It was celebrated in spring, having a lesser festival each year with the great festival every third year of the Olympiad. During the Peloponnesian War it was changed to every fourth year. It appears that the festival concentrated more on art than athletics and was a completely joyous occasion in which choirs and people from distant lands competed. 'There, when the games are ordered, they rejoice to honour Apollo with boxing, dance and song.' A golden crown was offered to Apollo. The scene would appear to be one of gaiety, banquets and festivity, with ships anchored in the then great harbour, bringing richly-dressed spectators, men, women,

poets, musicians and dancers. It was more an artistic and convivial festival than the highly competitive sports of the Olympics. It also brought to Delos one of the largest and most famous fairs in history; not only providing food, drink and amusement for the crowds, but acting as a trading centre and a great slave market.

Diasia (Ancient Greek). The Diasia was a festival of Zeus Meilichios, in the month of *Anthesterion*, about mid-March; though a spring festival it was somewhat gloomy as an occasion of appeasement and penitence, at variance with the sky god aspect of the Homeric Zeus of the Olympiads. Zeus Meilichios was a god of wealth and thus associated with Pluto and underworld divinities. It has been suggested that he was probably the chthonic snake god Meilichios. Cakes in the form of pigs and other animals were offered to him, as to underworld deities. The festival was held outside Athens and was a general affair for the people.

Dionysia (Ancient Greek). In addition to his involvement in other festivals, such as the **Agrionia**, **Haloa** and **Anthesteria**, Dionysos, as the Dying God of Vegetation, had his own festival, the Dionysia, at Athens, in the month of *Elaphebolion*, as also a god of drama, inspiration, poetry and music. Plays of tragedy and comedy were performed and there was a procession at which baskets of fruit, special leaves, bread and phalli were carried. Bulls were sacrificed. The festival was held in the daytime, but carried on over into the night in contrast to the nocturnal orgies of the other side of the Dionysian festivals such as the **Tristeria**, a biennial winter festival on Mount Parnassus. Festivals celebrating his resurrection were nocturnal and conducted by women, in the depth of the mountains, with wild orgies. Dionysos also shared the shrine at Delphi with Apollo and took over for the three winter months, when Apollo was away visiting the Hyperboreans, and lead the 'dance of the fiery stars' and was associated with the cult of souls which was later assimilated into festivals of propitiation of the dead and an All Souls' Day. There was a city **Dionysia** in the month of *Elaphebolion* and a country **Dionysia** in Poseideon.

Divination. This was an ancient and widespread practice which was used extensively at festivals as a method of ascertaining what the gods desired or needed to appease them. It developed into a science controlled by priests, priestesses, professional soothsayers and oracles, either attached to a temple or cult or operating at some oracular shrine such as Delphi.

Divination was the means of obtaining information, by magical practices, foretelling future events and discovering what was hidden or obscure. There were many branches of the science: reading omens from the entrails — especially the liver, heart and blood — of

sacrificial animals; the movement of birds; unusual behaviour of animals; flights of arrows; astrology; dreams; presentiments; by ordeal; divine possession of an oracle, seer, shaman, prophet or spirit of a dead person; in trance or hypnosis; bodily actions such as sneezing; heavenly or climatic conditions, particularly eclipses, storms, comets or climatic changes; mechanical means such as a pendulum, throwing dice, taking odd and even numbers and so on. Any monstrosity or abnormality in nature was significant.

The neglect of a festival caused divine wrath which was manifested in the appearance of unfavourable omens which were reported and interpreted by oracles, priests and priestesses. Rites of divination were particularly prominent in Babylonian, Chaldean, Greek, Roman and Celtic festivals. Though present, they were not so important in Ancient Egypt. Divination plays a highly significant part in all primitive cultures and is used especially at all festivals involved in making a fresh start, such as the turn of the seasons and festivals of the dead.

Diwali, Dewali, Dipavali, or **Tihar** (in Nepal — Hindu and Sikh). Meaning 'a garland of lights' it is an autumn festival and probably the most universal and popular. It is both a festival of lights and fire, dedicated to Lakshmi, Goddess of Prosperity and Fortune. Prayers are offered to her in thanks for the past and hopes for the future. Lights are lit in all houses and temples, and children run about the streets with lighted sticks, torches and fireworks. Where there are waterways little boats made of leaves or coconut shells carry small lights down the river and out to sea, symbolizing *Ananta* or eternity. Houses are spring-cleaned and decorated, old clothes and rubbish are thrown out, new clothes are worn and the time is generally one of a fresh start. The business year closes, accounts are settled, and it is an auspicious time to start a new venture. It is an occasion for feasting and dancing, visiting and making matches between couples since one of the origins of the festival was said to be the marriage between Lakshmi and Vishnu. In rural areas it is a time of harvesting with processions to the fields where prayers, sacrifices and flowers are offered. In addition, in Nepal, Yama, God of Death, is propitiated and his messengers, crows and dogs (the latter as faithful to man and guardians of the gate), are venerated, as well as the cow; they are garlanded and feasted. It is also a brother-and-sister day commemorating the sister saving her brother from Yama. See also **Sikh**.

Dolls Festival, *Hina Matsuri* (Japanese). This festival, also known as the Girls' Festival and the Peach Blossom Festival, takes place on 3 March. Dolls are placed in rows on shelves with offerings of peach blossom and *saké*. Girls are dressed in their best with little girls playing the chief role. The urban festival is not ancient but derives

from a simpler rural ceremony of making coloured paper figures which, at the end of the festival, are set adrift on the waters, taking any sickness or evil influences with them; a scapegoat rite also seen in the Greek **Adonia** and elsewhere.

Dragon. The slaying or snaring of the dragon myth appears in all world literature: in the *Rig Veda*, the Babylonian *Epic of Creation*, the Caananite *Poem of the Gracious Gods*, the Hittite *Snaring of the Dragon*, in Eastern folklore, in Greek drama, the Scandinavian *Edda*, and it descends into popular drama in the Christian Mystery Plays, Mummers' Plays and in folk songs. In the West it is part of the drama between good and evil, summer and winter, plenty and want. These representations also incorporate the ancient rite of the ritual sacrifice and the shedding of blood to ensure the fertility of the soil. In the Far East the dragon symbolizes supernatural powers of the air, land and waters. In China there were a number of dragon festivals, occurring mainly in the southern regions. Now the Great **Dragon Festival** is still celebrated in Hong Kong, Taiwan and among Chinese communities abroad. It is both a cult hero festival and associated with a good harvest.

Dragon Boat Festival (Chinese). An ancient summer festival which takes place mainly in south China and especially in Hong Kong,

To the urgent beat of drums and the cheers of thousands of spectators, dragon boat rowers race towards the finish line (*Hong Kong Tourist Association*)

and also in Malaysia. Celebrated on the fifth day of the fifth moon, it is a cult-hero commemoration of the poet-philosopher Qu Yuan who drowned himself in protest at official corruption. It also has the objective of ensuring a good harvest and has been suggested as a vestigial sun-boat festival, or a rain festival of the dragon sky power. It is celebrated by racing long, narrow, dragon-shaped boats with scores of rowers. During the festival spells, charms and herbs are pasted or hung on doors and a special rice cake and liquor are eaten and drunk. The rice cakes commemorate those thrown in the water to prevent the fish eating the body; the boats kept the dragon away.

Dream Festivals. These occur in Amerindian culture at the time of the New Year, which varies considerably, or the festivals can take place on special occasions. They have the characteristics of a **Saturnalia**, a time of chaos, license and reversal of the normal, with the wearing of disguises and masks. People and property are attacked, often with old scores paid off, and the only escape is to know what has been dreamed. It is also a time of expelling evil spirits and confessing sins (see Amerindian, North). Australian Aborigines lay great stress on dreaming and dream time; the **Dream Journey** is an annual ritual renewal of union with their land. (See **Australian Aboriginal**.)

Dream Journey or **Walkabout**. See **Australian Aboriginal**.

Durga Puja or **Dassehra** (Hindu). A festival of northern India which takes place in September-October and is preceded by purification and abstinence. Decorated images of Durga (the feminine *shakti* energy) are made from any suitable material in any size and are consecrated with holy water and oblations, offered flowers, green leaves and incense. Women put on all their finery. There are sacrifices of goats and sheep; fires are lit and there is music and dancing and unrestrained revelry. Finally the images are broken up and cast into the waters.

In earlier times the festival marked the beginning of military activities after the rainy season. In Nepal the festival **Dassehra** lasts for 15 days with all work abandoned. Families meet at the parental homes. There is ritual bathing and sacrifices are made. The festival commemorates the slaying of the demon buffalo Mahishasura by Durga; and also the victory of Rama over Ravana.

Dying Gods. The disappearance of vegetation in the winter, brought about by the death of the Sun God, and the suspension of life during the infertile season, gave rise to some of the most important festivals. There are various myths of the dead or missing Sun God, the most usual being his disappearance underground, or he may be killed by the powers of darkness. Yet another is that he goes off in high dudgeon, in such haste that he puts his right boot on his left foot and

his left boot on his right foot, and in his absence everything dries up and withers. He is also the temporarily defeated god, power, or hero of the Slaying of the Dragon myths and dramas. He has to be searched for and found before fertility is restored; his return is the occasion for a great festival of rejoicing.

The myth is similar to those of the cults of Tammuz/Dumuzi, Osiris, Adonis, Attis, Baal, Orpheus, Mithra, Balder, Woden/Odin, etc. The Dying God is always young and beautiful, the personification of spring, its freshness and beauty. He is the son and lover of the Earth Mother Goddess and symbolizes cyclic death and rebirth in nature. There is also a variant with a girl who goes underground in the Kore/Persephone myth: while picking spring flowers, she was abducted by Hades/Pluto and taken to the underworld, she was searched for by her mother Demeter/Ceres and when found was allowed to spend half the year in the world of light — summer — but had to return to the underworld gloom for the other six months — winter.

E

Easter (Christian). The *Pascha* from the Hebrew *pesach*; French *Paques*; Dutch *Paach*; Italian *Pasqua*; Spanish *Pasena*. The first recorded (second century) and the greatest annual festival of the Christian year. Corresponding to the Hebrew sacrifice of the Paschal Lamb, it commemorates the resurrection of Christ. It is a lunar festival, occurring on the first Sunday after the 14th day of the calendar moon, on, or next after, 21 March, so can fall between 22 March and 25 April.

Gregory XIII tried to fix it on a set Sunday so that it fell on the same date each year, but this was not adopted and is still a point of controversy. The Council of Nicea (325) fixed Easter by the present rule and so dissociated it from the **Passover**, while the disciples and converts, being Jews, naturally carried over their own religious legacy and associated it with the festival of the **Passover**, and St Paul refers to Christ as 'our Pasche' or Paschal sacrifice. The lamb, being a widespread sacrificial animal, naturally has pagan associations as the lamb offered on the altar. Early church calendars, of 448, also listed pagan festivals, such as the **Lupercalia**, with only a few Christian festivals.

There was some confusion and controversy in early times as to the nature of the Easter commemoration; some kept it as a fast, others as a feast. It is now kept as a feast after the preparatory Lenten fast. It was the great baptismal festival of the early Church, bringing initiates into membership. The Eastern Orthodox Church celebrates Easter a week later, according to the Julian calendar, and regards it as the most solemn festival of the year.

The Paschal Taper or candle is lit at Easter and burns until **Ascension**, for the 40 days of Christ's presence after the resurrection; it also represents the light of the risen Christ.

The Venerable Bede said that the name 'Easter' was derived from the Teutonic goddess of spring, Eostre or Ostra; Grimm calls her 'the rising light'. The time is one of universal spring festivals. The Christian midnight mass parallels the timing of the Eleusinian rites and in the Eastern Orthodox Church there is a similar torchlight

procession. The ancient custom of wearing new clothes at the spring festival is also shown in the wearing of the new Easter bonnet at church on Easter Sunday. It is a time of renewal, throwing out the old and **spring cleaning**. In Ireland houses, byres and stables are also cleaned and whitewashed.

Earlier, it was the custom to rise before the sun on Easter morning to see the sun 'dance' as it rose on the horizon; vestiges of this are carried over into the United States of America where there are outdoor dawn services held, a custom brought over by the Moravian settlers.

Ball games, associated with Easter festivities, were played in and around the church with the Dean 'taking the ball in his left hand, then commenced to dance to the tune of the antiphon, the others dancing round hand-in-hand. At intervals the ball was bandied and passed to each of the choristers. The organ played according to dance or sport'.

The Easter Egg has become an important feature of the festival. Eggs, forbidden in the fast of **Lent**, were eaten again at Easter for the first time; they are also known as pasche, paschal or pace eggs and there are many varied customs associated with them in contests, either rolling them downhill or competing against each other — an egg is held by one person and struck by another, the unbroken egg being the victor, until all but one are broken. Eggs are also elaborately decorated or dyed.

Distribution of symbolically-coloured eggs takes place at the Eastern Orthodox mass on Easter Sunday, which, again, is a week later than the Roman Catholic and Episcopal date. Egg symbolism is universal as life and resurrection and the Easter Egg, or Hare (sometimes incorrectly called Rabbit or Bunny) is pre-Christian. In Teutonic myth it was the Hare which laid the Easter Egg and it was the emblem and sacrificial victim animal of Eostre. Eggs were dyed and eaten at spring festivals in Ancient Egypt, Persia, Greece and Rome and at the Jewish **Passover**, as symbols of immortality and resurrection. In this context they were also eaten at New Year festivals and feasts of the dead and used in agricultural rites. Burying or throwing eggs on fields signified the rebirth of life in spring.

Egg. Universally a symbol of creation, renewed life, resurrection, fertility and the mystery of existence, the egg was, and still is, used in festivals to express these qualities which are also connected with spring renewal and fertility rites. From earliest times eggs have been dyed, decorated and eaten at spring festivals. See also **Easter**.

Egyptian (Ancient). Depending entirely upon the Nile, the Egyptian festivals were tied to its rhythms. Melting snow in Abyssinia and spring rains caused flooding from which the Nile waters spread over the flat lowlands, leaving a deposit of fertile silt. Surplus water,

conserved in canals, tided over from the fall of the waters in October to the next floods; by June the river was reduced to a trickle. Flooding began in July with the morning rising of Sirius. The year was divided into three seasons: Inundation, Coming Forth, and Drought; it had 365 days and 12 months of 30 days with an intercalary five days. There were 'small years' of 360 days and 'large years' of 365 days.

Neither the solstices nor the equinoxes were used, though the calendar was solar, and the sun and the waters of paramount importance. Sirius, the Dog Star, appeared before the sun on the day the floods began. Rain was infrequent and seasonal and there were none of the vagaries of weather as in temperate climates. The agricultural year began in August with the opening of the canals and there is some evidence that a virgin was thrown into the river as a bride of the Nile God, Hapi. Grain was sown in November, and April was the harvest month and the time of the festival of Min. There were festivals based on the seasons, the heliacal rising of Sirius, national feast days, the lives of the gods, royal life and numerous local gods.

Festivals:
The Autumn Festival.
The Entry of Osiris into the Moon.
The Feast of Opet.
Festival of Isis.
The Festival of Min.
The **Sed** Festival.

Eid-Milad-an-Nabi, or **Mawlid** (Islam), commemorates the birth of the Prophet and is celebrated on the 12th of *Rabi-ul-Awwal*, a date of the greatest importance in the history of Islam. It is also that of the death of the Prophet, so that festivities are restricted. Leaders speak of all aspects of his life and teachings and there are salutations and songs of praise. In some regions mosques are decorated and public buildings may be decorated and illuminated. There is feasting and food is also distributed to the poor. In some large cities there are processions and chanting and praise while in other cases these celebrations of birth and death are not regarded as appropriate and, instead, there are simply addresses on aspects of the Prophet's life.

Eid-ul-Adha (Islam), the Feast of Sacrifice, is celebrated on the 10th of *Dhil-Hijjah*, the last month of the Muslim year and the day of the close of the *Hajj*, the pilgrimage to the *Ka'aba*, which occurs during the eighth to 13th of *Dhil-Hijjah*. There are seven ceremonies:

1) The putting on of *Ihram* which, for men, is a robe of two seamless white sheets, one covering from the waist down, the other being slung over the left shoulder with the right shoulder remaining bare. Women dress simply, but do not have to cover their faces;

2) The circuit of the *Ka'aba* anti-clockwise in the Grand Mosque, uttering ritual phrases;

3) The *Sa'ee*, in which pilgrims walk or run seven times between Safa and Marwah, two small hillocks near the *Ka'aba*, dramatizing Hagar's search for water for the infant Ishmael;

4) Visiting Mina, Arafat and Muzdalifa, having left Mecca for Mina on the eighth of *Dhil-Hijjah*, the night is spent in prayer and meditation. The following day, after *Fajr* prayer, they reach the plain of Arafat and encamp there, arriving after midday, and offer *Zuhr* and *Asr* prayers together and occupy the rest of the day with remembrance of Allah. This time at Arafat from midday to sunset is an important part of the Hajj ritual. To have arrived before sunset on the ninth day is accepted as participation in that Hajj. From Arafat the journey is to Muzdalifa, where *Maghrib* and *Isha* prayers are said and the night is spent in praising God and in meditation. After *Fajr* prayer the following morning, before sunrise, the pilgrims travel back to Mina;

5) Performing the *Rami*. On the 10th, pilgrims throw seven stones at Jumrat-ul-Aqba, one of the three pillars representing Satan. The pillars stand on the site of Abraham's temptation by Satan against the offering of Ishmael as a sacrifice according to the vision. *Rami* may be repeated on the 11th, 12th and 13th of *Dhil Hijjah* on each of the three pillars named Jumrat-ul-Oola, Jumrat-ul-Wasta and Jumrat-ul-Aqba;

6) On the 10th, pilgrims at Mina sacrifice an animal: camel, cow, sheep or goat, or a part of such an animal, according to what they can afford. This is a ritual sacrifice commemorating the sacrifice of the animal instead of Ishmael and showing submission to the will of Allah;

7) After the sacrifice heads are shaven or hair cut short. Those who cannot take part in the pilgrimage perform the Eid-ul-Adha ceremonies in their own surroundings. The festival is lunar; at the sighting of the new moon preparations begin and continue until the 10th of the month. Again, there is the early morning bathing and putting on of new or best clothes and assembly for prayer, but the ritual breakfast is not eaten until after the animal sacrifice. After prayer the Imam delivers a sermon giving the significance of the festival and the stories of Abraham, Hagar and Ishmael. The return home is by a different route and the praises of God are sung and the animals slaughtered.

Eid-ul-Fitr (Islam), occurs at the end of the fast month of **Ramadan**, at the new moon. It is a time of pleasurable excitement and rejoicing. On the eve of the festival streets and buildings are decorated and illuminated and preparatory trading is carried on until late into the night. The *Eid* day starts early in the morning with bathing and the donning of new or best clothes. Both men and women wear perfume. After a meal of a specially prepared dish of

Sheer Khurma, all assemble at some large meeting place, such as a mosque, hall, or in the open, where there are special prayers offered in congregation with the worshippers in rows, facing the Ka'aba in Mecca, and the Imam in front.

Following the ritual prayers the Imam delivers a sermon of edification on the significance of the festival. After the service people greet each other with '*Eid mubarak*' and embrace. There must be reconciliation and forgiveness among all. The congregation returns home for feasts, with special foods, shared by relatives and friends. Gifts, cards and greetings are exchanged and children receive special presents called *Eidi*. The poor should be fed and the needy and sick looked after and there are special contributions called *Fitrana* made on the occasion and paid by the head of the family on behalf of all members. The festival should be restrained with no overeating or indulgence.

Eleusinia (Ancient Greek). The Eleusinia was a local Athenian festival held yearly on the 13th of *Boedromion*, about harvest time, in honour of Demeter. The festival is said to be older than the Olympiad. Though originally local, it later spread to the colonies, and, as in the case of the Olympics, a truce was declared for 55 days to allow safe travel to and from the festival. Sacred objects, or *sacra*, were escorted to Eleusis by the *epheboi* (adolescent youths) who wore garlands of myrtle. The *sacra* were carried by priestesses.

The next day was one of initiation of novices; this was followed by rites of purification, heralded by the cry 'To the sea ye mystes'. Sacrificial pigs were carried to the sea and purified by immersion and the *sacra* were also escorted to the sea and back to Eleusis in procession, accompanied by music, chiefly of cymbals, the instrument of the Great Mother rites. The theme of Persephone and Demeter was central to the rituals in the solemn revelation to the mystics of an ear of grain.

The festival ended with the rite of looking up to the sky and crying 'rain', then looking down to the earth crying 'be fruitful'. It was both a religious and civic occasion, the rites being those of a mystery religion but in the hands of public officials under the king-archon. It was also a first fruits festival as these were ritually eaten after the purification ceremonies.

Epiphany (Christian). Occurring on 6 January, the Epiphany commemorates the manifestation of Christ to the world and the visit of the Magi to Bethlehem. The earlier date of the Nativity was 6 January and is still kept as such by Armenian and Syrian Christians. In the Eastern Orthodox Church the Epiphany is the time of baptism, the Feast of Jordan and the Feast of Lights. It celebrates not only the birth of Christ but also his baptism and his first miracle at Cana. The gifts brought by the Magi, gold, frankincense and myrrh,

are, in the words of the carol, symbolic of the God and King and Sacrifice. In Spain and Italy presents are exchanged at Epiphany instead of Christmas and the Magi bring the gifts to the children.

The period between Epiphany and Christmas is the ancient time of chaos, celebrated by the festivities of the **Twelve Days of Christmas**. During the Cromwellian reign of puritanism in England Christmas and all such festivities were abolished and officers were sent to dismantle decorations and break up any festivities. Though the festivals returned with the Restoration, much was lost. The seventeenth century thus saw a unique event in the history of festivals: neither before nor since have any been officially abolished and officially restored.

Eskimo. The year is divided into 13 months, counting the moons from the winter solstice, looking for the return of the sun. The winter solstice is marked by the position of the sun and from this the moons are counted until the moon can be seen no longer in the brightness of the summer nights. The period of unnamed months brings the lunar and solar year into harmony. The central Eskimos have a 'sunless month' of indeterminate length, then, after a few years, that month is left out. The moon is male and feared; the sun is his sister. There is a New Moon Feast conducted by a shaman. On the longest night of the year a ceremony is carried out by two shamans, one disguised as a woman, who go from hut to hut extinguishing all lights then rekindling them from a vestal flame, saying: 'From the new sun comes light.' The festival welcomes the return of the sun and good hunting weather; there is feasting, playing and dancing.

At an *autumn festival* there is a tug-of-war, using a seal-skin rope, between the Ducks, those born in summer, and the Ptarmigans, those born in winter. If the Ducks win it will be a good winter season, but it will be bad if the Ptarmigans are victorious. This represents the age-old and universal contest between summer and winter, light and darkness.

The importance of man against the elements plays a vital part in the Eskimo world and there are taboos against offending these powers or disturbing their balance. Also as man kills to eat and live, the souls of the slain must be propitiated. This is the reason for the autumn *Festival of the Bearded Seal*. After the killing of the seal the harpoon must stand by the blubber lamp during the first night, the soul, which is still in the head of the harpoon, can thus be warmed; no work may be done for three days and the festival, which has required a month's preparation, ends with the sinking, through a hole in the ice, of the bladders of all the bearded seals caught in the past year. This has affinities with the *Mask Festivals* (see **Masks**) which show belief in reincarnation and respect for the souls of slain animals. For example, the head of a bear is left with the nose turned inland

towards the mountains to become another bear. Fish intestines are thrown back into the waters, or else the soul would die.

Whaling Festivals vary from place to place, but Kund Rasmussen describes how the Bering Strait people wear new clothing with a brow-band of white skin ornamented with the picture of a whale. The people gather at the dance house of *qazge*, which has been painted outside to represent the sky with its stars, and equipped with cleverly-made mechanical figures of dolls. In ritual succession special spirit songs are sung or mumbled, until a man suddenly jumps up, with a feathered wooden ring in his mouth, and begins to dance. At first his movements are watched until all the mechanical images come to life and evoke a whole range of emotions from fear to delight and laughter. A mechanical bird under the roof flaps its wings and beats drums rhythmically and a feathered top is set spinning with a cord of sinew, all the feathers and down flying out and floating about like living birds, but the eagle's down at the top continues to spin and spread out with the buzzing speed.

Men who man the skin-boat are dressed as if embarking on a long journey in bad weather and wield their paddles vigorously, guided by the helmsman. At the entrance to the festival house there stands a man who has no lower body visible; he nods and waves to everybody as if they were his. The climax of the marvels comes with the appearance of the marten, not yet seen, who first seems to hesitate by jumping in and out of a den in the wall then springs out and runs across the room to the opposite wall with a galloping movement, propelled by a cord; it disappears into the opposite den, emerges again but this time, midway across the room, it seizes a bladder which has a rattle below it which has been suspended on a cord, then rushes back with the rattling bladder to its original den. This is a tense moment for if the marten fails to get the bladder into its den it presages the death of one of those present before the year is out.

The Hudson Bay ceremonies are comparatively simple. After the kill the men and old women collect in an open space in a circle of stones and eat a meal of whale meat while all work is stopped for three days.

Other groups have their own ceremonies connected with their own animals. Among central tribes festivals are held during which shamans travel in spirit to the bottom of the sea to 'harpoon' the Mother of the Sea, *Imap-ukua*, to persuade her to release the animals of the sea, which she keeps away from the land, for the benefit of the hunters.

There are trading fairs combined with festivals with rituals and drum-beating, and these take place round good hunting localities. At feasts presents are distributed to guests as they are at the North West Coast Indians ceremony of **Potlatch**. These feasts are also held in

connection with birth, marriage and death. There are special festival houses built of snow, sometimes large enough to hold 100 people; or an annex to a dwelling house can be built. Death feasts often have the distribution of valuable presents as a feature as well, since they prepare a happy existence in the next world.

Dancing, which is an important feature, is largely a knee-bending, body-swaying movement; the feet rarely move. Dancing is accompanied by a drum — a tambour with a handle, beaten with a drumstick — and rattles made of puffin beaks are also used. The drumming starts slowly but accelerates to a frenzied beating which continues to breaking point; a women's chorus accompanies it.

There appear to be taboos and regulations which prevent the merging of activities concerned with the land animals with those of the sea, for example there are such taboos as not eating fish and animal meat on the same day. Also, before seal hunting begins, the weapons must be smoked over seaweed to remove 'the smell of the land'.

Mask festivals, associated with Alaskan customs, are not of importance in Greenland or away from the central groups. In Alaska they are a feature of the great dance festivals (see **Dance**) which tell of the experiences of the shaman in the land of the spirit. Masks represent the spirit which possesses the shaman at festivals associated with divination.

The sea is of greater importance to the Eskimo than the land and winter is the dominant season by fact of its length, the summer being short and its warmth feeble. Ice in October is safe enough for transport, but later increasing darkness makes hunting difficult until it ceases almost entirely in December and January, so these months become a time of holiday, relaxation, visits and feasts, lasting until the increasing light makes breathing-hole hunting, and the long journeys for bear hunting, possible again. Caribou hunting takes place chiefly in autumn.

Killing animals for food, e.g. bears, caribou, seals and whales, exposes man to the danger of anger and revenge from the souls of those killed, hence ritual precautions must be taken — usually by the hunter's wife — against these threatening dangers. No work may be undertaken for a time after the kill of a bearded seal and, as said, the discarded parts must be returned to their native habitats.

Among Eskimos amulets have a fetish quality and help to form a mystic alliance between the wearer and the power symbolized; it being desirable to have as many amulets representing different powers as possible.

Esther. The Fast of Esther (Hebrew), Precedes **Purim** or the Feast of Lots (ref. Esther 4:15f.) The Book of Esther is read and special prayers are said. The Fast of Esther is commemorated after which,

at Purim, there is feasting and drinking to the point of over-indulgence by way of contrast. The festival is said to be older than Esther and derived from the Babylonian New Year festival; there are also similarities with the pagan rites of selection of a new ruler or monarch; the parade of the substitute king, the fast, the execution of a felon and the distribution of gifts.

Eves of Festivals. The prevalence of 'eves' in festivals is noteworthy since they are often given more significance than the actual day, for example, Christmas Eve in Europe, New Year's Eve and Hallowe'en. These appear to be a heritage from the lunar calendar and Celtic and Teutonic reckoning of time by nights and not by days, a custom also prevalent in tribal societies and still seen in such expressions as fortnight and sennight.

F

Fairs. The word 'fair' is derived from *feria*, a festival, since wherever a festival was held there was a large gathering of people whose needs were met by the fairs which developed to supply them with food and drink on the one hand and with entertainment and pleasure on the other. Traders and entertainers were quick to seize these opportunities from the earliest times and were found at all fairs in antiquity, in Delos, Egypt, China, India, Arabia, Africa and among the Aztecs. The oldest and largest of all fairs was the Kumbh Mela in India, held three-yearly, alternating between four holy places, the holiest being Allahabad on the Ganges where literally millions still assemble.

Fairs also hark back to the funerary rites, games and festivals, held at the tomb or burial mound of a cult-hero or royalty, such as the Olympics and Isthmean Games. Many of these festivals and fairs spread to Rome and from there followed the Roman conquests into Europe.

Of the ancient fairs Delos was probably the most important and famous. Situated at the meeting-point between the Middle East and the West, it was established long before the Olympics, and provided not only the necessary food and entertainment for the vast crowds, but was a great trading centre and slave market.

Other fairs were held at smaller festivals associated with some particular cult or temple, as, for example, the fairs held three times a year in the deltic region of Egypt. These had both a religious and a commercial aspect and sometimes the trading went on actually in the temple. The priests of Jupiter, in Rome, encouraged fairs and merchants at their temples and the Jews also traded in the outer court of the temple at Jerusalem. This custom was perpetuated later, under Christianity, when fairs were held in churchyards and trading actually invaded the church in some cases.

Not all fairs were associated with festivals, some being more in the nature of markets, such as the Roman *mundinae*, held at nine-day intervals. The country people worked for eight days then went to town with their wares on the ninth. These market-fairs were often held in streets, in booths, tents and stalls which were set up and from

Revel held just outside a churchyard (*from an old drawing*)

which every possible commodity was sold, including dogs —
especially greyhounds. The latest decrees were proclaimed at fairs
and markets and any important announcements were made. As
Roman conquests spread and colonies were esablished with
increasing populations, fairs were licenced on private land away from
the towns, giving rise to the great fairs all over Europe. Courts were
instituted to deal with the disputes which inevitably arose and there
was no appeal from the verdict of the Forum.

With the spread of the Roman conquests, fairs were established at
such places as Aix-la-Chapelle and Troyes (from which came the Troy
weight for bullion). Paris had a fair at St Denis, lasting for 10 days
from 10 October; it was associated with, and opened by, the monks
of St Denis, patron saint of France. Later, in England, Roman fairs
were inaugurated at Helston, Barnwell and along Hadrian's Wall.
The Normans also founded fairs and many were established at places
of pilgrimage. Other fairs were held on hill-tops, the traditional
ancient 'high places', or at boundaries or the intersection of roads,
following the old cattle, horse or sheep tracks used by traders.

Stringent rules were laid down for the protection of travellers and
merchants to fairs and their safe conduct. Lurking places for
criminals, such as woods, bushes and ditches, had to be cleared.

There were immense riches on the roads in the Middle Ages: gold, silver, furs, jewels, spices, horses, camels, sheep and goats were all transported along caravan routes in the Middle East, on the Silk Road of China and the trade routes of Europe.

Fairs required a licence since they could be the source of much strife, dishonesty and trickery. Licences were granted to such people as sheriffs and abbots and were limited to a nine-day duration for a certain number of years. William the Conqueror made laws, in England, controlling fairs and stipulating conditions under which they could be held. Anyone continuing to sell after the official closing could be fined 'double the value of that which is sold'. Later, many fairs were abolished as being 'the cause of grievous immorality and very injurious to the inhabitants of Towns'.

Following the pattern of the old Roman fairs, courts were set up to deal with the many disputes which resulted and with unruly conduct. They were known as Pie Powder, or Pie Poudre Courts, thought to be derived from *Pied Poudre* or *pieds poudres* — the dusty feet of the itinerant vendors, chapmen and entertainers; another suggestion was that these courts gave judgement so rapidly that the dust was still on the feet of the litigants. These courts were a feature of the English and Continental fairs. A statute of Edward IV stated that they 'should have lawful remedy of all manner of contracts, trespasses, convenants, debts and other deeds made or done within any of the same fairs'.

Fairs were trading centres for merchants from home and abroad, so normal guild regulations, which excluded strangers, were suspended for the duration. In many places a glove, or wooden hand, was hoisted and displayed as a symbol of openness of trading, and was removed on the closing date. Fairs were often named after the chief item of trading: horse or pony fairs, cheese, sheep, goose, mop or hiring fairs for engaging servants, the last usually at Michaelmas. The symbol of the trade was displayed — mop, whip, crook, etc. Certain fairs specialized in goods: Birmingham for gingerbread, Chertsey for onions, Nottingham for the Goose Fair.

The majority of licences for fairs were in the hands of the Church, which also benefited from the large numbers of travellers going to and from the numerous fairs since the monasteries not only held the licences but were also the hotels of the Middle Ages. In *Piers Plowman*, Avarice says he went to the Fayre at Winchester 'held on a high place, near a long barrow, which brought great wealth to both the Cathedral and the City'. Fairs were also focal points for preaching friars and monks who collected the tolls.

Of the famous fairs, Stourbridge, or Sturbridge, was said to be the largest in the West. It was originally given a charter by King John in 1211 for the Hospital of Lepers of St Mary Magdalene: 'the keepers of this Hospital hold 24 acres and a half of land in Cambridge Field,

Plan of Stourbridge Fair, 1767 — note the relatively small area devoted to shows and games *(compiled from a sketch and description by an eye-witness)*

for the support of the lepers therein dwelling according to the ancient right and custom'. The control of the revenues from the fair were a constant source of dispute between Town and University, a typical Town-and-Gown situation, such as also occurred between Oxford University and St Frideswide's Priory. Defoe, writing on Stourbridge in 1723, said:

'This fair is not only the greatest in the whole Nation but in the World; nor, if I may believe those who have seen them all, is the

fair at Leipsick in Saxony, the mart at Frankfort on the Main, or the fairs of Nuremberg or Ausburg, any way to compare with this fare at Stourbridge . . . The shops are placed in rows like streets, whereof one is called Cheapside, and here, as in several other streets, are all sorts of Traders, who sell by Retale and who come principally from London with their goods. Scarce any traders are omitted, Goldsmiths, Toyshops, Brasiers, Turners, Milliners, Haberdashers, Hatters, Mercers, Drapers, Pewterers, China-warehouse, Taverners, Bread-shops and Eating Houses innumerable, and all in Tents or Boothes . . . in another street, parallel with the Road, are like rows of Boothes, but larger, and more intermingled with wholesale Dealers.'

A square, formed by the largest booths and spacious enough for wagons to come in to load and unload, was called the Duddery (from Dulde — cloth) and Defoe continues: 'in this Duddery as I have been informed there have been sold £100,000 worth of Wollen Manufactures in less than a week's time. Wholesale men carry back orders from their Dealers for £10,000 worth of goods a Man and some much more.'

At the fair towns were represented from all over the country: Halifax, Leeds, Wakefield, Huddersfield, Rochdale, Bury, Manchester; wool from Lincolnshire; stuffs from Norwich and Chelmsford; Birmingham sent iron- and brass-ware and Edg'd Tools; knives from Sheffield; glass-ware and stockings from Nottingham and Leicester; hops from Kent and goods from abroad from Bristol, Exeter and Taunton. Heavy goods could be brought up-river in barges.

'As for the People of the Fair, they universally Eat, Drink and Sleep in Boothes and Tents and the said Boothes are so intermingled with Taverns, Coffee Houses, Drinking Houses, Eating Houses, Cook Shops etc. and all in Tents too; so many Butchers and Hagglers from all Neighbouring Centres come to the Fair every day with Beef, Mutton, Fowls, Butter, Bread, Cheese, Eggs and such things and go with them from Tent to Tent and Door to Door, that there's no want of any Provision of any kind, either dress'd or undress'd.'

Students from the university could buy and sell books and let off high spirits. It was at Stourbridge that Newton bought his first book on astronomy and, later, the very prism that appears on Roubillac's statue.

The Gentry, apparently, did not attend the fair until the end, when they came in and 'spent much money with the Retailers of Toys, Goldsmiths, Brasiers, Turners Milliners and Mercers, and also amused themselves with the Puppet Shows, Drolls, Rope-dancers

and the like'. The last day was the Horse Fair, at which there was both horse and foot racing. 'This ends the whole Fair, and in less than a week or more, there is scarce any sign left that there has been such a thing there.' Defoe adds: 'I should have mentioned that there is a Court of Justice always open, and held every day in a shed built on purpose . . . the Magistrates of the Town of Cambridge are Judges in this Court . . . they have final authority without Appeal.' There were cages, pillories, stocks and a whipping post for the punishment of offenders.

Many traders came from abroad, the Venetian and Genoese with wares from the East, Italians with silks and velvets and delicate glass,

A scene in *St Bartholomew's Fair*, 1721 (*drawn from a painting on a lady's fan*)

linens from Liège and Ghent, Spanish iron, Norwegian tar and pitch, Gascon wines, Hanse-towns furs, amber and eastern jewels, the last being channelled through Moscow and Novgorod, and so on.

St Bartholomew's Fair, in London, held on the patronal festival, started as a semi-religious centre for pilgrimage, with a reputation for miracles, and there were miracle plays performed; it ended in 1840 as one of the most famous places of riotous merry-making for the populace. Founded in the twelfth century by Rahere, Henry I's jester turned monk, it was satirized by Ben Jonson in his comedy *St Bartholomew's Fair*, but in spite of all the follies he derided, it was also the centre of considerable musical and dramatic talent as most of the stars of Covent Garden, Drury Lane and the Haymarket performed there. Ballet dancing was also a feature of the entertainment as well as the usual acrobatic, tight-rope walking and juggling feats, such as 'a Young Woman that dances with Fourteen Glasses on the Backs and Palms of her hands and turns around with them above a Hundred Times, as fast as a Windmill'. There were also menageries and dancing bears and 'Fripperies and Mercers of the Best; Chattels and Phantasies, Fairings for young and old'. There was also a slave market.

The diarist Evelyn gives an account of Southwark Fair in 1660, he says:

> 'I saw in Southwark, at St Margaret's Fair, monkies and asses dance and do other feats of activity on ye tight rope; they were gallantly clad à la mode, went upright, saluted the company, bowing and pulling off their hats; they saluted one another with as good a grace as if instructed by a dancing master. They turned heels over head with a basket of eggs without breaking any, also with lighted candles in their hands or on their heads without extinguishing them, with vessels of water without spilling a drop. I also saw an Italian wench dance and perform all ye tricks on ye tight rope to admiration; all the Court went to see her. Likewise there was a man who took up a piece of iron cannon about 400lbs weight, with the hairs of his head only.'

At the May Fair there were 'mountebacks, merry-go-rounds, fire-eaters, ass racing, sausage tables, dice tables, ups-and-down, grinning for a hat, running for a shrift, hasty-pudding eaters, eel-divers, and an infinite variety of similar passtimes.'

Royalty sent officers of the Great Wardrobe to the fairs to buy rich cloths and robes, spices, wax and other commodities for the royal family, its knights, clerks and servants of the household.

When a fair, or neighbouring taverns, could not supply enough beer, certain houses or cottages were allowed to sell it and green oak boughs were fixed above the doors to signify their rights; these became known as Bough Houses.

Though many fairs were spread by the Romans, there were other ancient fairs already established, such as the Fair of Uppsala, the *disting*, which was a direct continuation of the great pagan festival at the temple of Uppsala, held on the full moon after **Epiphany**, and the Irish Carman Fair, one of the most famous, and an example of a fair originating from funeral games and rites of the dead for mythical beings or cult heroes. Such fairs were usually held on burial mounds or cemetries, and later in churchyards. At Carman there were games, athletic contests, feats of horsemanship and racing, accompanied by the usual markets for food, drink, clothing and livestock.

Night Fairs. Some fairs began, or took place, at night, notably in Ancient Egypt, but also elsewhere, there having been one in Scotland in Aberdeenshire and at Croydon in England. Such fairs became known as Sleepy Markets. For the most part night fairs were presided over by women, which suggests that their origin may have been in the lunar festivals of the Great Mother Goddess.

Sunday Fairs were a cessation of work but not of trading, amusement and relaxation. They were suppressed in Britain by the Church and state in the fifteenth century, but were allowed to continue for the Sundays of Harvest.

Vestiges of the ancient fairs now remain in market days in towns, agricultural shows, and, in the modern age, in motor shows, boat shows, book fairs, antique dealers fairs and numerous local or international music and arts festivals.

Fasts, **Fasting**. Fasting as a preparation for feasts and festivals is a universal custom, with the exception of Zoroastrians (the Parsees) whose conception of the Good Life deprecates austerities and maintains that true fasting lies in abstinence from sin. Fasting occurs at all stages of culture and in all rites of purification and emptying, which precede festivities, as a negative form of purification. It can also be used in magic as a cleansing of the body to make the power more effective. It is employed as a preparation for sacramental meals or for initiation; as a spiritual discipline in penitence and penance in the expiation of sins and a ritual act of purification; in inducing ecstatic psychic states and obtaining visions and revelations from the deity, and in some cults it was, and still is, believed that the divinity can be influenced by fasting, in which case it can be used in the face of impending calamity.

The idea of abstinence arises from the belief that food may introduce impurities into the body, hence the total abstinence on important occasions, or partial abstinence in respect of certain foods, especially meat and strong drink. This is called 'reverential abstinence' by Apuleius in connection with the Egyptian initiatory rites of Isis. Babylonian and Assryian fasting, described in the Book of Jonah, tells of whole communities, with their animals, covered in

sackcloth, fasting and praying for forgiveness. The Hebrews also practised public fasting on occasions of calamity and on the Day of Catharsis (Lev. 16: 29–31), the **Yom Kippur** and the expelling of the scapegoat preceded the Feast of the Ingathering. Greek and Roman rituals had a period of cleansing and mortification before festivals; there was a fast at the **Eleusinian Mysteries** before taking the sacramental food and drink; the Roman *februare* meant to purify and in Mithraism there was a fast before the sacramental meal, while the fast for the mourning of Attis was followed by the rejoicing of the **Hilaria**. The Incas fasted for three days before the **Festival of Rymi**.

Taoism speaks of the 'fasting of the mind' as superior to material abstinence for spiritual progress. Buddhists fast at the new and full moons, at the anniversary of the Buddha's death and on various other occasions, though the Buddha preached moderation rather than excessive asceticism. Christianity had no direct rules laid down by its founder, but the Church took over the pagan rites of fasting before feasting and instituted fasts of **Lent**, **Ember Days**, **Rogation Days**, Fridays and the Vigils of Festivals and before the mass. Islam regards fasting as a physical, moral and spiritual discipline and has the Fast of **Ramadan**, while the Koran recommends fasting as a penance before pilgrimages.

Priests fast before performing ceremonies, often with prayer and austerities. Shamans and medicine men fast in training and fasting plays an important part in tribal ceremonies and initiations; in many cultures such as those of the Amerindians, Moroccans, and Malaysians, these rites still continue.

Fasting usually implies and accompanies other types of abstinence such as sex.

Fathers' Day. See **United States of America**.

Feasts. The banquet associated with most festivals had its origin in the idea of the followers of a deity gathering together as one large family and sharing a communal meal. In many early societies family meals were not customary and it was only at tribal or religious feasts that they ate together; the sacrificial feast was thus a public and social occasion.

Feasts naturally play a prominent part in celebrations of birth, naming, initiation, marriage and death, the last to honour the dead. It was also believed that the dead returned to their native haunts at certain times of the year, occasions which became festivals at which it was only natural that the revenants should be feasted. Memorial feasts were also held for the dead on anniversaries and ritual festivals of the dead; such feasts were often held at tombs, as in Roman and Chinese customs. The entertaining to a feast at funeral rites was, and still is, a widespread custom.

In tribal societies feasting takes place on any appropriate occasion

as a sign of plenty and the gathering of a harvest is usually a time for feasts and festivals. The 'harvest' may be grain crops, fruit, yams, or the results of hunting, fishing, or any in-gathering or first fruits. In tribal cultures such feasting may go on for weeks or months, as at the Yoruba Festival of Oro and the central Australian Corroborees. Feasts can also be seasonal, at the change of the year, the equinoxes, or the rising of some significant star or constellation such as Sirius and the Pleiades.

At ritual feasts connected with festivals, where animals were sacrificed, the animals provided the main food. It was assumed that the deities to whom the sacrifices were offered joined with their devotees in the feasting, the deities consuming the essence while their worshippers ate the substance.

From the most primitive to the most advanced religions feasting was, and still is, an essential part of a festival.

Feralia (Ancient Roman). The Feralia ended the festival of the dead, the **Parentalia**, with the rites performed at the tombs on 21 and 22 February, the latter being an occasion for family reunions and the worship of the *Lares*, probably originally family ancestral spirits who guarded the home.

Fire. In view of the importance of fire for humanity it is not surprising that it has been the subject of myth and ritual from the earliest times. As a symbol of the generative power of the sun the two are intimately connected and fire and sun gods are inextricably mixed; they appear universally in widely different cultures. In Vedic India, Egypt, Mesopotamia and Persia fire was a symbol of the divine and, as representing illumination and power, it could be divinity itself. There were fire and sun gods such as Agni, while Krishna called himself the fire of life. **Zoroastrians** have the Sacred Fire, with Ormuzd as god of light and Atar as solar and fire power. There were also the Egyptian Ra; the Grecian Helios and Apollo, with Hestia as goddess of the hearth; Hephaestos controlled the underworld fires, as did the Roman Vulcan, with Vesta as the counterpart of Hestia and the Vestal Virgins responsible for the sacred fire. The Incas also had a sacred flame attended by Vestal Virgins; the Chinese have a God of the Stove; the Scandinavian and Teutonic Woden/Odin symbolized light and fire, and Loki 'the fire that burns'; children were sacrificed in the fires of the Canaanite Moloch, while Prometheus was the cult-hero of fire.

Fire is ambivalent: it produces warmth, comfort, purification and defence, but it also produces destruction and fear; it can be creative and destructive, divine and demonic, Woden or Loki, or, as in Islam, divinity or hell and it is also symbolic of Pentecostal inspiration or the fires of hell in Christianity.

The idea of purification by fire is universal. Burnt offerings and

sacrifices are purified and there are numerous ceremonies connected with festivals in which both humans and their animals pass through fire which also fumigates and expels evil powers. Fumigation also imparts strength since smoke represents the energy of fire and it is also a preservative.

There was a world-wide custom of extinguishing and rekindling fires at certain ceremonies, notably New Year rites, as a symbol of death and rebirth. All fires were put out and then relit from the sacred fire at the festival, thus doing away with the old, outworn and sinful, and providing a fresh start.

As purification, fire was used 'to burn or repel the noxious things, whether conceived as material or spiritual' and was employed not only in the pastoral rites of driving flocks through or between fires, but in agricultural communities crops were purified by carrying torches or faggots over the fields and into orchards and vineyards, or throwing burning brands, or by lighting bonfires in the fields. The fire was then taken home to rekindle the domestic hearth fire. The custom still prevails in tribal communities.

The rites are not only purificatory but the divine power of fire and light expels evil influences. There are Arab customs of extinguishing old and lighting new fires at the New Year, with ceremonies of beating off evil spirits, and Frazer found evidence of fire purification in North Africa, notably among the Berbers of Morocco, where they were associated with the Islamic New Year. The Kikuyu and other African communities have a crop-purifying ceremony of lighting a holy fire from which domestic fires are rekindled.

Europe had a large number of fire ceremonies associated with seasonal festivals, these were **Lent**, **Easter** Eve, **May Day**, **Midsummer**, **Hallowe'en**, and **Yule**, largely taken over from the earlier Celtic fire festivals, the two most important being the summer and winter solstices — the turning point in the sun's course. Lenten fires were lit in Europe on the first Sunday in Lent and people danced round them; the more vigorous the dance the better the crops would grow. (See **Dance**.) When the flames died down boys and girls leaped over the embers and anyone not singed would be married within the year. Lighted torches were carried through the fields, orchards and vineyards. That the fires were not only for purification and fumigation but also for the expulsion of evil powers is shown by the cry 'Fire, burn the witches' which was chanted. At Easter Eve lights were extinguished (now perpetuated in the Christian service of Tenebrae.)

In the Church the Paschal Candle was, and is, lit from a freshly kindled fire. In some parts of Europe effigies of Judas were burned, a custom which has passed into Mexican and South American Catholicism. In Protestant countries the effigy could be that of Judas, or the Pope, while Catholics burned either Judas or Luther. The

'It was, and still is, a widespread custom to light bonfires at any public celebration or festival . . .'

burning of Judas and Easter kindling of fire also occurred in the Eastern Orthodox Church.

Need Fires, sometimes called Wild-fire, Living-fire, or Force-fire, were kindled at times of plague and pestilence and cattle, sheep, pigs and even geese, were driven through them. All domestic fires had to be extinguished and rekindled from the Need Fire which could not be started while any other fire was still alight. Need Fires were also lit as protection against witches. Such rites are known in Europe, Asia and Africa.

Epiphany by fire is common to many traditions, for example, the Burning Bush, Pentecostal tongues of fire, burning mountains, and shamanistic rites.

It was, and still is, a widespread custom to light bonfires at any public celebration or festival, such fires being frequently placed on

hilltops as were the pagan Sun God sacrificial fires, the Celtic **Beltane**, the *Walpurgisnacht* in Germany and the large hilltop fires in Sweden. These bonfires were also associated with the New Year festivals and the time of the new fire, from which domestic fires were lit. Bonfires were also lit at festivals of the dead, when the departed were warmed and feasted. Again, the fires were danced round, a universal practice, or jumped through; omens were read and it was a time of divination as well as warning off evil influences and witches.

Midsummer bonfires, lit at the turning of the sun, acted as sympathetic magic to encourage its power, while midwinter fires encouraged its rising strength. In early times human sacrifice was part of the fire rituals; later effigies were substituted or some scapegoat person was selected, such as the 'carline' of the Beltane fires, and made the subject of mock sacrifice. At these hilltop ceremonies flaming wheels were rolled downhill or torches thrown

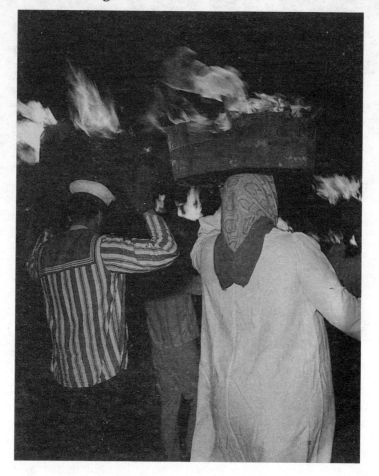

The flaming wheels taken to be rolled downhill

into the air; these carried away evil but were also concerned with divination and prophecy.

Fire-walking was also practised at festivals, often by the public as well as special classes of people such as the priestesses of Artemis who walked bare-foot over hot embers. Virgil and Pliny said that the rite of fire-walking was undertaken by the 'Soranian Wolves', drawn from special families who were exempt from military service, and was in honour of the God of the Greeks called Apollo, but whose name was really Soranus. Fire-walking was, and still is, widely practised in Japan, Fiji, in the West Indies, Central and North America, Southern Europe, among the Zulus, Hottentots and Maoris, in India and Sri Lanka. The passage across the fire symbolizes the sun's transit across the sky, but to be able to walk on fire is also the attribute of a supernatural person, such as Sita in Indian mythology.

It is debated whether fire-walking and bonfires are sympathetic magic to encourage the sun, or merely purification rituals. Against the sun-rite theory is the fact that sun rituals are performed in many parts of the world where the sun is too powerful and needs no encouragement but rather an abatement, but for the theory is the evidence that most of the fire festivals took place at the solstices, but there is little doubt about the purificatory significance of fire and it seems likely that both the influences and beliefs were at work.

There is no doubt about the power of fire to ward off evil since witches, warlocks and other evil forces were burned in effigy at May Day and midsummer festivals, though Frazer suggests that the effigies which were merely passed through the fire and not burned could be vegetative spirits going through the light and heat necessary for growth. This passing over the fire might possibly be the origin of being 'hauled over the coals'.

The universal rites of extinguishing fires and lights symbolizes darkness and chaos, in which identity is lost; the rekindling is re-creation, the bringing of form into being again.

First-Footing. A New Year custom of wassailing, prevalent from Scotland to Macedonia. At midnight on New Year's Eve the first-footer crosses the threshold, often bringing a sprig of mistletoe or some gift such as bread, salt, coal or kindling and is received in silence, while wishing all a happy New Year, and then being regaled with food and drink. The first-footer varies from one place to another, he is most usually a dark man, though a fair man is preferred in some parts, but red hair is never acceptable. In rare instances a woman may be a first-footer, but generally it must be a man for luck, with a redhead or woman, especially a fair woman, as bad luck. The custom now remains largely in Scotland, northern England and Ireland. In earlier times the wassail-bowl of spiced ale was carried round and the family went outside at midnight to wish all living

things well and to eat 'God cakes', a form of mince pie, shaped like a triangle, to represent the Trinity.

First Fruits. Festivals of first fruits are universal, not only geographically but also in every form of society from the most primitive tribal customs to advanced religions. Any first-time carries with it an element of the unknown and of chance and is therefore dangerous, so that all first occasions are accompanied by rites of warding off danger. First fruits were thus offered, for sanctification and as propitiation, to deities and nature spirits, sometimes to the dead, or to the spirit of the particular crop or animal sacrificed; they could also be offered to the emperor, king or chief, frequently regarded as divine. These divinities or spirits first ritually tasted the first fruits before they became safe for general consumption. In this ritual tasting the whole is present in the part.

All cultivated crops — grains, roots, fruits of the orchard, vine and olive tree — were, and in many places still are, the subject of these rites. Also included were wild plants and roots gathered, animals of the herds and flocks and those of the hunters and fishers. The first fruits were ritually gathered, sometimes a special crop being sown, or animals specially reared for the purpose. In tribal cultures where the plant or animal concerned is believed to be animated by a spirit, it is that spirit which must be propitiated before the food can be eaten. This is called 'eating the soul of the crop'. Sometimes special foods were made from the crops, such as the *mola salsa* prepared by the Roman **Vestal Virgins**.

The festivals of first fruits were, and are, solemn occasions and originally associated with strict taboos and elaborate rites, while the feasts connected with them were usually of a ceremonial order, requiring preparation by fasting, abstinence and, in some instances, notably among the Amerindians, emetics could be taken as a completion of the bodily cleansing.

After the solemnity of the first rituals, the feast which followed could turn into a **Saturnalia**, representing a time of chaos, the festival being regarded as both an end and a beginning and therefore equated with the New Year.

The deities or ancestors or the spirits of the crop itself were, and are, believed to join in the feast which then becomes a communion between divinities and mortals. Deities could be offended if first fruits were not offered. Artemis, Great Mother and Lady of the Beasts, expected to receive the heads and hides of hunted animals. First fruits were also sent to special shrines such as Delos and Delphi. The Semitic races, especially the Canaanites and Hebrews, attached particular sacredness to all first fruits. Such festivals still flourish in tribal communities.

Vestigial remains are seen in the West in **Harvest festivals**, Harvest

Homes and Suppers and in 'wishing' the first time anything new, or seasonal, is tasted.

Flagellation or **Whipping** is an ancient fertility rite; as an erotic stimulant it was believed to bring fertility and to rouse masculine virility and feminine fecundity. Flagellation was practised by the Ancient Egyptians at the **Festival of Isis**; the Galli, the eunuch priests of Attis flogged each other; Spartan youths were lashed until their blood spattered the altars of Artemis; at the Greek **Thargelia** the scapegoat or *pharmakos* was beaten on the genitals with wild fig branches and other purgative plants; Roman brides were whipped and the lashing of women with thongs from the skins of sacrificed animals was one of the main features of the **Lupercalia**. The Fool's

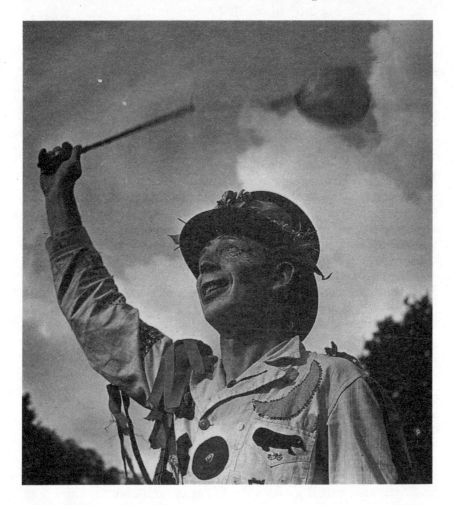

The Fool's bladder or 'whiffle'

bladder or 'whiffle', used in connection with Morris dancing, Mummers, etc., had the same origins. Whipping was also used to drive out demons and evil powers; in Tibet snake skins were used for this purpose. The thong or rod used was also believed to impart its qualities to the person whipped, hence the moral value of the birch, one of the straightest of trees. Whipping was also used at festivals concerned with the beating of the bounds, such as the Roman **Ambarvalia** and **Terminalia** and the Christian **Rogationtide**, when boys were beaten at certain points to impress them on their memories.

Floralia (Ancient Roman). The Floralia was a spring festival in honour of Flora, goddess of flowers and spring. She was said to have been originally a courtesan who left a fortune to the people of Rome to celebrate her memory, and was later elevated to a deity. Later, the festival largely lost its significance and became a time of games and license for the plebeians. It took place from 26 April to 3 May. Flora was later associated with Ceres and possibly also Venus. The prostitutes regarded it as their festival. Hares and goats, both symbolic of lasciviousness, were let loose; but as a goddess of plant life Flora had no associations with carnivores. Vetches, beans and lupins were thrown at people at the festival's circus. The Helston 'furry dance' or floral dance, is a vestigial relic of this type of festival.

Flower Festival, *Hana Matsuri* (Japanese). Celebration 8 April. This is largely a Buddhist festival celebrating the birth of the Buddha with gatherings at Buddhist temples and processions of gaily-dressed children carrying offerings of flowers and hydrangea tea. Minature shrines are also made. The date is also associated with an older hill climbing ritual when people go out to the hills to bring back wild flowers for the family shrine; the rites also have a close connection with ancestor worship since the spirits of the dead go to the mountains, which are considered sacred. Wooden grave markers are placed, symbolizing prayers for the dead.

Flowers and Plants. In addition to actual flower festivals, held in honour of flower divinities, such as the **Floralia**, flowers have always been an important feature of many festivals. No Hindu festival is without them and they are used extensively in Buddhism and in China and Japan where some of the most important festivals are associated with the times of the blossoming of flowers and trees. Scattering flowers in front of deities or heroes in their festival processions is almost universal and no spring festival is without flowers, garlands or the carrying of green boughs. Flowers are placed on altars, and **wreaths** adorn the heads of both divinities and their devotees, especially at the **Floralia** and the festivals of **Hera** at the **Sacred Marriage**.

Flower or plant arrangements or 'gardens' were made at festivals of Osiris in Egypt, for the **Adonia** in Greece, on graves at Roman rites of the dead and at midsummer festivals in many parts of Europe. Flower gardens are also connected with the Fields of the Blessed and Paradise. Zoroastrianism also has flower arrangements as a feature of festivals. Many of the plants and flowers used have apotropaic or medicinal qualities attributed to them and certain rites are associated with gathering them, such as the ritual gathering of flowers or plants for the May Day and midsummer festivals, with specific times laid down for their picking, or having to be picked in the dew.

Often flowers must be gathered in the dew, a sacred form of water, and in itself a symbol of fertility with seminal associations. Dew also represents blessings, invigoration and resurrection as a gift from heaven. All agricultural and pastoral peoples place the greatest importance on dew, especially in Eastern countries, as plant life grows more in the night than by day, so dew was, and is, looked upon as the moisture necessary for life and growth. As a fertility rite people also rolled in dew on midsummer morn and bathed the face in dew on May Day. The 'may' was either gathered in dew or dipped in it.

Alder. Associated with spring and fire festivals. Symbolized the feminine watery element to the masculine fire of the Ash. Sacred to Bran the Blessed; emblem of Pan. The Celtic fairy tree, representing divination and death and resurrection.

Apple. A magic fruit of the otherworld. The Celtic Silver Bough; the Hallowe'en fruit symbolic of immortality, fertility and marriage; the Tree of Avalon and sacred to Celtic divinities. When cut across the core it shows the pentagram or five-pointed star of magic. Sacred to Venus as love and a bridal symbol, the apple bough was awarded as a prize in the Sun Bridegroom race with the olive as the Moon-Virgin race award. It was also used in the rites of Artemis and Diana; and was an attribute of Nemesis. The apple tree is sacred to Apollo, and apple blossom is a Chinese symbol of peace and beauty.

Ash. The World Tree of Scandinavia, the Norse *Yggdrasil*, a world axis. Masculine fire to the alder feminine water element. The tree has healing properties and protects against snakes. It is sacred to Odin who hung nine nights and days on the tree; and also to Poseidon and Zeus/Jupiter. It is symbolic of modesty, adaptability and prudence.

Bay. As an evergreen it symbolizes resurrection, renewal and immortality; it is often used as a substitute for laurel as a victor's crown of glory and honour. Bay made the crown at the **Pythian Games**, and it is an emblem of Apollo.

Beans. They contain magic power, can transmogrify, they symbolize immortality and are closely associated with festivals of the dead. They are thrown at the Hindu *Holi* and scattered at the Japanese *Satsubun* as symbols of good health and good luck and, having magical properties, beans and peas are also used at Japanese festivals

of the dead. The Romans also used them at the **Lemuria** in ghost-expelling rites. Having chthonic nuances, the priests of Jupiter were not permitted to touch them or even mention them, but bean meal was used in sacrifice to Juno. Beans were sacred to the Roman god Silvanus. They were excluded from the Greek cults and festivals of Demeter, and Porphry said they were forbidden at the **Eleusinia**. The English Lord of Misrule who presided over the **Twelve Days of Christmas** was selected by finding the bean in his slice of Christmas cake and was then called the King of the Bean, with his feminine counterpart as Queen of the Pea. Frazer sees in this custom possible vestiges of earlier selection of human sacrifice.

Birch. A marker of boundaries, its silvery trunk made the limits or paths more visible at night. Because it was light and supple it was used to beat the boundaries and also used to beat those who overstepped them and to whip boys at boundary-marking festivals so that the points were impressed on their memories. It was also believed that the rod, or thong, used in whipping imparted its qualities to the person being beaten, thus the birch was used on account of its straightness. It represents the masculine and solar aspect to the Rowan's feminine and lunar. It is the Cosmic Tree of shamanism, and is sacred to Thor, Donar and Frigga.

Blackthorn. One of the four thorn spirit trees representing the winter spirit; said to be malignant and used as the black rod of magic.

Boughs. Boughs of evergreens or of other apotropaic plants were placed at the feet of statues of divinities or heroes and in front of houses, stables and byres at festivals, such as the **Thargelia** and **May Day**, to ward off evil powers. Boughs were placed in front of specially licensed houses permitted to sell beer at fairs in addition to the taverns. These became known as Bough Houses. (See **Fairs**.)

Box. The sacred tree of the Hittites, renewed yearly in the temples.

Buckthorn. An apotropaic plant chewed at the Roman **Lemuria**.

Cedar. The Babylonian Tree of Life, sacred to Tammuz. The sacred wood of the Temple of Solomon. It symbolizes strength, stateliness, uncorruptness.

Celery. A wreath of fresh celery was the victor's crown at the **Nemean Games** and a wreath of dried celery was that of the **Isthmean** Games.

Chrysanthemum. The flower emblem of Japan, where there is a **Chrysanthemum Festival**. Important in Chinese and Japanese symbolism as a symbol of harvest, autumn, happiness, longevity, wealth and ease.

Corn. See **Corn Dolly**.

Elder. A witch tree belonging to the Old Woman, whose permission must be sought before it is cut; she is the Scandinavian 'Elle', the Witch Mother. A lunar tree which, like the hawthorn and rowan, must not be brought indoors, nor should the wood be burned on

domestic fires. It is a death-and-rebirth symbol since it both dies and revives quickly.

Evergreens. Symbolize undying life in vegetation and therefore immortality. They are placed in temples, churches and homes at festivals, especially those of the winter solstice; they can also be placed on doors and windows of houses. An exception is mistletoe which is not placed in churches, being wholly pagan in associations. Wreaths of evergreens denote undying fame.

Fern and Fern Seeds. Gathered at midnight before Midsummer's Day or on St John the Baptist's Eve, to be used in magic rites. The seeds are associated with dew as evanescent.

Fig. A symbol of fertility and prosperity; figs are a 'pure food' of the Greeks and as such were worn in a necklace by the scapegoat at the **Thargelia**, and fig boughs were used to beat the scapegoat. Baskets of figs, carried in processions, represented the goddess as woman or mother. As a phallic symbol the fig is sacred to Dionysos/Bacchus, Jupiter, Silvanus and Priapus. It is the Islamic Tree of Heaven and, with the vine, a symbol of Israel.

Gorse. One of the four spirit thorn trees or bushes. Solar.

Hawthorn. One of the four thorn spirit trees on whose thorns spirits are speared and on whose spikes 'clooties' (pieces of cloth) are hung for magic, healing, or for the passing of souls. The flower is the garland for the May Queen. Old clothes were kept on until the May flower was out and new clothes donned at the festival. As it is associated with witches (the Old English *Hagg* the name for Hawthorn) it must not be brought into the house. It is feminine and lunar to the masculine yellow, solar Gorse.

Hazel. One of the five chief witch trees, used for divination and dowsing. A feminine tree of wisdom; hazel or willow was the shaft of the witches' broomstick. The hazel wand has magic powers. It is sacred to the Celtic groves and to Thor. Hermes carried a rod of hazel. It is also associated with the Mother Goddess.

Hemp. One of the apotropaic plants for the midsummer festival and the seeds were used for divination at **Hallowe'en**.

Holly. Sacred to Saturn, it decorated his temples and was used for decorations at the **Saturnalia**, which is now taken over by Christianity with other Saturnalian rites at **Christmas**. Christians also take the red berries and spikes as the blood and crown of thorns of Christ. As an evergreen it depicts eternal life; it also symbolizes good will, health and happiness. Holly protects against witches, who will not cross a threshold of hollywood.

Honeysuckle. Used with rowan as an apotropaic plant at **Beltane**.

Ivy. Sacred to Dionysos whose crown was of ivy, his thyrsus encircled with ivy and his cup the 'ivy cup'; also sacred to Osiris, Attis and Apollo. It takes on the symbolism of the evergreen. It is feminine to the masculine holly, but priests of the sacred temple fire could

neither touch nor mention ivy as its symbolism was also phallic.

Laurel. Symbolizes triumph, victory and as an evergreen also undying life and immortality; a Graeco-Roman emblem for victory and as such used for victors' crowns. Boughs were carried by boys at the **Panathenia** and laurel decorated the house of the *rex sacorum* in Rome and was renewed annually at the festival on 1 March. It is sacred to Apollo, Dionysos, Juno, Diana and Daphne.

Leek. A purgative plant like garlic and onion; it was used to beat the scapegoat at the **Thargelia**. It was a Celtic sacred plant, adopted for St David of Wales.

Lily. Statues of Hera, Goddess of Flowers as well as marriage, were adorned with lilies at the festival of the **Sacred Marriage**. It was sacred to all Virgin Goddesses and was a symbol of purity as it grew from the milk of Hera; sacred also to Diana as chastity.

Lotus. Both solar and lunar, appearing with Egyptian and Hindu sun gods and with Semitic moon gods and the Great Mother lunar goddess. It is also connected with both fire and water as growing from the waters and flowering in the sun, and also a symbol of divine birth as the sun emerging from the primeval waters. It is of particular significance in the East and Ancient Egypt; in the West it is often represented by the lily.

Lupins. With vetches and beans, lupins were thrown to the people at the **Floralia**.

Marsh-marigold or **King-cup**. An apotropaic plant; the yellow flower is solar. It is used at **May Day** festivals and is also known as the 'herb of **Beltane**'; and was spread on the floors of stables and byres in the Isle of Man as it has powers of warding off evil.

Mistletoe. As an evergreen it is a symbol of immortality; it is the life-essence, new life and rebirth at the winter solstice. It is the Golden Bough of Aeneas and of the Druids and is important in Norse and Celtic mythology where it represents the sacred feminine principle with the oak as the masculine. In Celtic ceremonies mistletoe had to be cut, left-handed, on the sixth day of the moon of a suitable month, at a suitable place, by a Druid fasting and wearing a white tunic and using a 'golden' sickle. The mistletoe was caught in a white cloth (it must never touch the ground or be touched by iron) and a white bull was sacrificed. It is associated with the Norse god Baldur and is an emblem of Frigg, his mother. It is the Scandinavian plant of peace; to meet under it is to form a truce. It is a magical plant, a charm against wounding in battle and protects against lightning and witches. In Sweden it was hung from the roof over a crib or stall to ward off trolls as it renders them powerless. In Brittany bunches of mistletoe were hung from the roofs of houses and stable doors to deter witches. In many places it was gathered with other magical plants at the winter solstice and midsummer festivals. It is an all-healing plant.

As neither a tree nor a shrub, neither being nor not-being, it

represents freedom from limitations, but equally freeedom from protection, hence anyone under the mistletoe has re-entered the realm of freedom, of the unrestricted and of chaos, and must accept responsibility for doing so as there is no longer any protection by normal laws. In such a position boons asked cannot be refused. Yuletide and Christmas kissing under the mistletoe also takes on this freedom from restriction or protection and is a fertility rite in which any liberty can be taken. Mistletoe is sometimes carried by first-footers. It is not used as a decoration in churches, except York Minster which has Norse associations, and has remained wholly pagan at festivals.

Mugwort. A magical plant used for divination on Midsummer's Eve.

Myrrh. A tree of Adonis, symbolizing sorrow and suffering, used at the Greek **Adonia**.

Myrtle. Symbolizes joy and tranquillity, and victory. Wreaths of myrtle were worn by the *epheboi* at the **Eleusinia**. It is sacred to Adonis, Artemis, Aphrodite, Poseidon and Europa, and is the sacred tree of the Hebrew **Tabernacle**; worn in rites by Mandean priests. Myrtle was taboo at the temple of the **Bona Dea**.

Oak. The sacred tree of the Celtic Druidical rites, the oak being the masculine principle with mistletoe as the feminine. It symbolizes strength, durability and the human body. It attracts lightning and is often associated with Thunder Gods such as the Scandinavian Thor and Zeus/Jupiter. The marriage of the Roman oak god Jupiter to the oak goddess Juno was celebrated annually in an oak grove, with devotees wearing oak garlands. A crown of oak leaves was often worn by a victor or hero. Oak groves were sacred places and the scene of Druidic and Teutonic ceremonies. Oak, rowan and yew were used to kindle festival fires, particularly among the Celts. The **Green Man** or Jack-in-the-Green was covered in oak sprays. Oaks were often planted as landmarks for the Beating of the Bounds ceremonies, and oak was the club of Heracles/Hercules and of Cu Chulainn. Sacred to Indra, Zeus/Jupiter, Thor, Dagda.

Olive. A sacred plant said to have been brought by Hercules from the land of the Hyperboreans; it symbolizes fruitfulness, immortality, peace, plenty and fertility. An olive branch was the harvest-home emblem at the **Thargelia** and was carried at the **Panathenia**. Crowns of wild olive were worn by the victors at the **Olympics** and by women victors at the **Heraea**. The olive tree on the Acropolis held the fate of the people. An olive branch is a symbol of peace. With the pine and savine, olive branches were thrown on the bonfires to purify the flocks at the **Paralia**. Sacred to Zeus/Jupiter, Athene/Minerva, Apollo and Cybele, an olive branch was also the prize at the Moon Virgin's Race.

Palm. A Tree of Life, its branches were carried in processions at

festivals of Isis and in triumphal processions it represented victory, fame and exaltation. Sacred to Baal-Tamar, Lord of the Palm, and to Ishtar and Astarte. It was an early Christian emblem of one who had made the pilgrimage to the Holy Land, hence a Palmer.

Parsley. A mystic plant representing the feminine principle; its seeds were supposed to come from the underworld. A crown of parsley was awarded to the victor at the Nemean Games. (See **Nemea**.)

Pine. Symbolizes uprightness, vitality and fertility (its cones containing many seeds), and as an evergreen, immortality. The Greek Isthmean (see **Isthmia**) festival took place in a pine grove. With the olive and savine it was put on purificatory bonfires at the **Paralia**. Sacred to Serapis, Zeus/Jupiter, Dionysos, Artemis, Diana, Attis and Cybele and associated with Mithras, Aesculapios and Confucius.

Reed. Associated with the waters. It was a symbol of royal authority in Egypt and, as the papyrus, a time-recorder. Reeds were strewn on floors in churches.

Rose. Roses were cultivated on Roman graves in 'gardens', or scattered on graves at the **Rosalia** as symbols of resurrection and eternal spring. They were used in the Egyptian mysteries of Isis and Osiris. It is a flower of paradise, and is sacred to Isis, Aphrodite/Venus, Adonis, Aurora, Helios, Dionysos and the Muses. It represents the Virgin Mary in Christianity and the Prophet in Islam. It is the emblem of England.

Rosemary. A funerary plant — represents remembrance and constancy. One of the apotropaic plants used at **May Day** ceremonies, it is sacred to Ares.

Rowan. The Gallic Tree of Life and the Gallic-Celtic sacred wood used for ritual fires, together with the oak and yew. A magic, fairy, witch tree which protects against all sorcerers and, tied to a cot, prevents 'taking' by fairies. The tree of the Celtic spring festival **Imbolc**; dedicated to the waters, holy wells and springs. It is used in **May Day** festivals and put on houses, stables and byres as apotropaic; it is sacred to Brigit, and also to Thor as attracting lightning.

Savine. Thrown on fires, with olive and pine, to purify the flocks at the **Paralia**.

St John's Wort. A midsummer festival flower representing the gold of the sun. It protected the eyes from the glare of the bonfires; and took its name from the change of the midsummer pagan festival to that of St John the Baptist.

Vervain or Verbena. A Celtic magic plant associated with the rising of Sirius when it was gathered by Druids for divination. Roman temples were swept with brushes of vervain and a twig was carried for luck and to ward off evil powers. A wreath of vervain was worn in marriage ceremonies, as it is sacred to Mars and Venus, the pair of lovers.

Willow. A witch tree of enchantments which can avert the evil eye; the wood must not be burned in the house nor used in building and must not be sawn. The willow wand is used in magic and it, or the hazel, is the wood of the shaft of the witch's broomstick. It was one of the boughs brought in on **May Day**. It was used for making the frame for the **Beltane** fire sacrifice to symbolize Baldur's pyre. It is associated with the Hebrew **Tabernacle** as the weeping willows of the Babylonian exile. Sacred to Tammuz, it is the Accadian Cosmic Tree and sacred to the Accadian Zeus; it is associated with Hecate, Persephone, Artemis and childbirth, with Kwan-yin, Europa and the Celtic Esus. Willow is used as a substitute for the palm on **Palm Sunday**.

Yarrow. Protects against witchcraft and prevents witches from crossing a threshold, but it is also used in spells and divination: especially associated with the *I Ching*.

Yew. Carries the symbolism of the evergreens. Used in **May Day** festivals together with the hawthorn, rowan and willow as apotropaic and used in kindling sacred fires. Like rowan it prevents 'taking' by fairies. It is associated with death and appears in churchyards, probably marking sacred places. Yew is a Celtic magic wood and is sacred to Hecate.

Fontinalia (Ancient Roman). On 13 October all wells and springs were garlanded at the festival of Fons, son of Janus, also in honour of the nymphs of springs. Such ceremonies survive today, having passed on to Christianity.

Fool. The Fool stands in contrast to the King as the lowest and highest in hierarchical powers. The fool, jester or clown occupies the humblest place in the court and symbolizes the forces of chaos and license while the king represents those of law and order. The fool often took the place of the king, as a scapegoat, in ritual sacrifice and later became ruler as the Lord of Misrule at Saturnalia-type festivals and at the **Calends** and all festivals associated with intercalary periods of chaos. He was carried over into Christianity in the Festival of Fools, or the Feast of Asses, as the Prince or Pope of Fools, or the Cardinal of Numbskulls, the Abbot of Unreason, or the Boy Bishop. In convents an elected nun could be dressed as a man and called the Little Abbess.

The revelries caricatured Baalam's Ass and the Flight into Egypt; there were processions in the streets with asses, or men dressed as asses, and asses were taken into the churches. There were coarse representations of Christian events and responses in the mock services were made by braying. The lower clergy were of the peasantry or petty bourgeois and more in touch with popular pagan beliefs and rites from the Roman, Celtic and Teutonic festivals than with the superimposed Christianity.

Most traditional festivals have a fool or clown — here the Fool is seen with
'Maid Marian' at the Abbots Bromley horn dance, 1950 (*W. Fisher Cassie*)

It was a time of reversal of the normal, chaos before rebirth, buffoonery and license, and therefore of fertility. The Boy Bishop conducted mock services and gave a sermon and sub-deacons took over the celebrations with riotous and crude conduct. The customs were abolished at the Reformation in England but revived in Mary Tudor's reign, to be revoked again under Cromwell; in France they lingered on until the eighteenth century. The early edict abolishing them said they were 'rather the unlawful superstition of gentilite (paganism) than the pure and sincere religion of Christe'.

Most traditional festivals had, and some still have, a fool or clown, often a 'natural' kept for the occasions; at other times it could be some citizen who dressed up as such and blackened his face. In earlier times the possessed and lunatics were regarded with reverence as being possessed by a divine power and having the gift of prophecy. In most places the fool was given considerable license and could mock and caricature the secret scandals and failings of local people, or he mocked and mimicked the performers of festival plays and dances. With the license of such occasions he was also taken as the putative father of any bastards born 'in forty weeks time . . . for if anything happens in forty weeks time the blame will be laid on the Clown'. The clown was garishly painted and disguised, which makes him impersonal, so he may break conventions and taboos in the freedom of the return to primordial chaos, which is also the return to the paradisal state of childish innocence before laws were imposed.

The fool often symbolizes the evils of winter, the time of cold and want which is killed by the coming of spring. This happens in Mummers' plays, sword, horn and Morris dances in which the fool is killed then revived to represent the resurrection of nature; he then greets the bride and dances with her to recommence the fertility cycle. He can also play the part of Beelzebub in such dramatizations. The fool's bladder or whip, with which he 'whiffles', takes the place of the fertility-whipping of the **Lupercalia** and other such ancient festivals with **flagellation** rites. The death of the fool probably originated in human sacrifice. The Ship of Fools at **carnivals** was originally the Ship of Nerthus, the Teutonic Earth Mother, at her spring festival.

G

Gahambars (Zoroastrian). The Six Gahambars are celebrations associated with the Six Holy Immortals evoked by Ahura Mazda, Lord of Wisdom. They are distributed through the **Zoroastrian** festival year and it is a sin not to celebrate them. Each occasion commemorates one of the Heptad. Originally one-day festivals, they now continue for five days and, in terms of relaxation, take the place of the weekly holiday of other traditions. The Service of All the Masters, lasting for about three hours from sunrise, is celebrated by priests at the Fire Temple and attended by the people who also celebrate with feasting in their own houses. The food eaten is consecrated and consists largely of bread, meat, dried fruit and nuts. Beggars are given unconsecrated food. It is a time of dignified merriment and joyful thanksgiving. Guests are welcomed and the sick and poor remembered. There is much visiting with singing and dancing combined with praying at the shrines. Only essential work is done but everything must be scrupulously clean.

First Gahambar — 30 April–4 May
Second Gahambar — 29 June–3 July
Third Gahambar — 12–16 September
Fourth Gahambar — 12–16 October
Fifth Gahambar — 31 December–4 January
Sixth Gahambar — 16–20 March

The Sixth Gahambar is of special significance, being part of the Holy Season, lasting 18 days and culminating in **No Ruz** which celebrated the end of the old year and the beginning of the new. The last night of the old year is an All Souls festival, the **Muktad**. The Sixth Gahambar is commemorated by the recitation and reading of texts and repetitions of prayers and with services at the fire temples. In some parts cakes are baked to symbolize the various forms of creation, or clay figures are made of animals, birds, people. The occasion can also be a time for rites of purification and confession for a new beginning.

Games. At large festivals and gatherings games are a natural social development. Games, dance and drama, closely related, all become part of the festivities, while rites, once performed as serious ritual acts, later degenerated into games; but all contain some inner meaning and symbolism, such as the death and resurrection theme, in which one player falls down and is revived, or in paired games and dances of fertility festivals, reminiscent of either personal courtship or the earlier marriage-by-capture. The demarcation between ritual and games is slight, especially in tribal cultures, where games are an essential feature of ceremonies. Like dancing, games give vigour to growth and to magic and are associated with both fertility and rain-making rites, or in imitative movement and guises when attracting game in the hunt.

Again, like dancing, games often form the magic circle, while ball games are found almost universally in connection with festivals from the earliest times to the present day, from tribal ceremonies to modern Shrove Tuesday football. In earlier cultures, when games had a largely magical purpose, they were still of ritual and religious significance. The Omaha ball games were between teams, thus introducing an element of masculine-feminine interplay and competition suggestive of fertility rites. The teams of the earth-people and the sky-people also symbolized the winds, the life-bringers. The Winnebago lacrosse was 'a contest between moieties'; in Sri Lanka ball games played with coconuts represented contending teams of gods and goddesses, the winning coconut being taken to the temple for dedication. Many of these games still continue.

Tug-o'-war is closely associated with festivals of driving away evil, either as disease or actual demons; it can also be part of rain-making magic.

Games of chance for divination or prediction at festivals were, and are still, widespread. The success of the harvest or of the hunt was foretold. Today omens are read at such festivals as **Hallowe'en**.

It was a belief in many cultures that festival and magic-making games were instituted by the gods and goddesses themselves. In Greece and Rome public games were held in connection with religious festivals and rites and were superintended by priests and priestesses and the magistracy.

Funeral games were a widespread custom. Though the most famous were the athletic festivals of Greece, these games occurred not only in classical history but in such widely different places as the Caucasus, Circassia, Siam, among Amerindian tribes and in Ireland. Often the games were founded as a memorial to some defunct prince, chieftain or hero, for example the Irish Carman Fair (see **Fairs**) which fulfilled the dying wish of the mythical hero that there should be established 'a fair of mourning to bear his name for ever'. Though called a fair it was, and is, chiefly famous for its games, races and

athletics, the fair having grown out of the games.

Pindar said that the **Olympics** were founded as funeral games, at the tomb of Pelops, by Hercules, son of Zeus, or by Zeus himself. Etruscan tombs depict chariot-racing, horse-racing and all athletics. Egyptian sports and games are pictured on tombs, and the festival of Heliea at Rhodes was said to have originated in the funeral games of Tlepolemus. Greek games were also held at famous shrines in honour of a god, such as Apollo at Delphi and at the sacred grove of Nemea. There was a belief that the dead hero also took pleasure in and derived satisfaction from watching the games in his honour and that the prizes were a reflection of his generosity rather than rewards for the competitors.

In Europe, ritual games were adapted by Christianity, were associated with the Church, and were played in churchyards; they were particularly connected with patronal festivals. They contained an element of ritual combat in their competitions and their rhythmic movements came close to dancing. Easter ball games, played in and around the church have been suggested as the origin of the opening of the cricket season. Cock-fighting, football matches, fives and other ball games also took place in churchyards and became associated with the **fairs** which were held there or nearby.

It will be seen, then, that the origin of many games was often more than play and was a ritual.

Geshi (Japanese). A summer solstice festival. Summer festivals are held throughout the country with varying ceremonies. Purification rites are carried out at Shinto shrines twice yearly; the summer festival is designed to get people safely through the heat and enervation of summer and to offer prayer for protection against disease for both people and crops. Rings of rushes are set up through which the people pass to reach the shrines, this sheds evil influences and ensures good health and fortune. Bathing is also part of the purification rites and in rural areas oxen and horses are driven through the waters. Wells, too, are cleansed. Dumplings, made from freshly harvested wheat flour, are eaten and offered to the gods. The first day of the sixth month is the traditional time for shedding old clothes and adopting summer wear; and in rural areas this was also associated with the belief that on this day snakes sloughed their old skins.

Gion Festivals (Japanese). These summer festivals are held over most of the country, but particularly at Kyoto. Respects should be paid at Shinto shrines to the god of the shrine, but since many people cannot get to the shrines the spirit of the god is transferred to a portable shrine which is taken in procession through the streets. There is a great procession of floats with tableaux and musicians; there is much competition among neighbouring associations in

producing the most colourful and ingenious designs. Shrines are later taken to the waters and twirled rapidly.

Good Friday (Christian). The Friday in Holy Week, Good Friday, Holy Friday, or Great Friday, is the most solemn occasion of the Christian year. In early times it was one of strict fasting and religious observances; it is preceded by the service of Tenebrae during which the Church is gradually darkened by extinguishing candles until only one is left; this is hidden for a time and then the lights are rekindled, representing death and resurrection. The funeral drama resembles the death rites of the Mysteries of Attis and other dying gods, with the death on the tree, the three days in the tomb and the final resurrection. Good Friday still depends on a lunar date. The hot cross buns eaten are associated with the sacred cakes or consecrated bread rites of Isis; cakes offered to Artemis were also marked with a cross and Friday was the day of the lunar Mother Goddess. Romans offered bread in honour of Diana and marked the loaves with a cross to signify the *quadra*.

Good Friday taboos were that no nails should be made or hammered on that day, no clothes washed or fishing done, the latter being a vestige of the sacred fish of Atargatis, whose day was Friday and to whom fish were sacred. Friday is also the day of Freya, wife of Odin, and in Scandinavia branches of the sacred ash were gathered and placed on door posts as protection against evil powers. In contrast to the solemnity of the Christian commemorations, Good Friday became a day for fairs which were recorded as being of a riotous nature with 'such rude sports that it was not considered proper for respectable folk to take part' and 'to the great scandal of religion there were near as many fairs held on Good Friday as any other day'.

Greek (Ancient). Ancient Greece was a land of small cultural urban populations within a land of peasants and herdsmen, hence the main festivals were largely agricultural and pastoral. As rain was a vital necessity it was natural that the supreme god, Zeus, should have been adopted from the Indo-European sky and rain gods and be enthroned on the high mountains from which the rain clouds came. The pattern of the climate was dry in summer with autumnal rains. The agricultural year had three main divisions: the autumn sowing, the *Pyanepsion*, followed by winter: the spring season with the blossoming of flowers and fruits in the *Anthesterion*: the early summer harvest, the gathering of fruits, figs and vines, the *Thargelion*.

The calendar, beginning in July-August, was lunar with 12 months of 29 or 30 days, totalling 354 days with an intercalary system of eight years with three leap years of 30 days; but this caused discrepancies between the actual agricultural lunar seasons and the solar calendar of the townspeople. The Athenian calendar adopted an intercalary

month at intervals to adapt the 354 days to the solar 365¼ days. Names of months varied from city to city, but all were connected with some festival. The festival calendar became the civic calendar. The Athenian year, officially starting at the summer solstice, had to wait for the coming of the new moon, celebrated by the great festival of the **Panathenia**.

Greece had local festivals, festivals in honour of deities, exclusively feminine festivals, and those that were primarily athletic, though these sources could overlap. Women's festivals were of great antiquity, certainly pre-Hellenic, associated with the Earth Mother and the dying god Dionysos. They were conducted by priestesses and celebrated by women only. Herodotus said the rites were imported from Egypt.

Festivals of the deities reflected the fact that all Greek life was pervaded by the presence of gods and goddesses, giving rise to festivals of propitiation and communion. The main festivals, nominally in honour of the Olympian deities, were overlaid with rites concerned with the dead, with purification and warding off evil powers. There were also many other local festivals of the gods which were more in the nature of patronal festivals. The Olympians were superimposed on an older religion of underworld divinities, so that the festivals combined both gloomy and joyous elements, fasting and feasting. There were rituals devoted to the Olympians coupled with rites of aversion and riddance against alien and threatening powers, together with the general fear of spirits. Religious festivals provided recreation and amusement for the ordinary citizen whose life was normally one of hard work. Homer said: 'Moreover we have provided for our spirit very many opportunities of recreation, by the celebration of games and sacrifices throughout the year.'

The origin of most of the athletic festivals is to be found in funeral games instituted in honour of some cult hero such as Heracles and Achilles. Before these athletics became popular they were largely aristocratic since they were held by chieftains and attended by neighbouring nobles and their families. The fact that the chariot-race was the most important feature placed the competition out of reach of all but the ruling class. The prizes were also lavish, for instance, the prizes provided by Achilles were: 1) A woman skilled in fair handiwork and a tripod. 2) A six-year old mare in foal. 3) A goodly cauldron untouched by fire. 4) Two talents of gold. 5) A two-handled urn. There were also horse races, foot races, boxing, wrestling, throwing the discus, spear throwing, and archery, the last two being indulged in by the ordinary soldier. Later, jumping, ball games and acrobatic feats, such as leaping from back to back of the racing horses, were added. These localized games gradually became popularized and general and thus developed into the great athletic festivals.

Athletics played an important part in the life of ancient Greece and they helped to unify the scattered communities and colonies. The Greek ideal was that of the whole man, the healthy mind in the healthy body, and athletics were not disdained by any citizen or class — philosophers, poets, townsmen, peasants and slaves all took part except when the event was beyond the means of the people, such as chariot-racing. This balance of mind and body continued until the age of Sparta, with its over-emphasis on bodily prowess, brought strictures from both philosophers and physicians such as Galen who said that:

'In the blessings of the mind the athletes have no share, beneath their mass of flesh and blood their souls are stifled in a sea of mud. Nor do they enjoy the best blessings even of the body. Neglecting the old rule of health, which prescribes moderation in all things, they spend their lives over-exercising, over-eating, over-sleeping, like pigs. Hence they seldom live to old age, or if they do are crippled and liable to all sorts of diseases. They have not health and they have not beauty.'

Socrates accused the athletes of his day of one-sided development and said their life was not compatible with the cultivation of the soul; but he also rebuked the unfit intellectual.

An important factor in athletic pursuits was that, being frequently at war, it was necessary for any Grecian to be ready and fit to defend his country, in this athletics developed the social side while gymnastics were individual. Originally athletes were not set aside to specialize in one thing only, nor was there a passion for record-breaking — grace of movement was of more importance, the union of strength and beauty.

Some athletic festivals remained local, while others developed into national events. Greek festivals survived the Roman conquest, took over the conquerors, and influenced their lives and customs.

Festivals:
Adonia.
Agrionia.
Anthesteria.
Arrephoria.
Coronia.
Diasia.
Dionysia.
Eleusinia.
Festival of Isis.
Haloa.
Panathenia.
Thargelia.
Thesmophoria.

Athletic festivals:
The Isthemia Games. (See **Isthemea**.)
The Nemean Games. (See **Nemea**.)
The Olympics.
The Pythian or Delphic Festival. (See **Pythia**.)

Green Man. At spring festivals the Green Man appears almost universally under different names and guises and can be traced back to a character who appeared in ancient times, in the Indus region of India, as the Green Thing. He also appears in the Tammuz and Ishtar myth in Babylon; as Al-Khidr; or as Elijah (Ilyas) in Islam, and in Europe in the St George and the Dragon plays and legends. He is Jack-in-the-Green, King of the May, The Garland, Robin Hood, or, in Germany, the Wild Man, the *pfingstl* in Sweden, and The Green George among the gypsies of southern Europe. He is the spirit of vegetation, the embodiment and emergence of spring, dressed from head to foot in green boughs, leaves or flowers, appearing at all spring festivals, dances, processions and mummers' plays.

Sometimes the Green Man is a chimney sweep, or he is accompanied by sweeps dressed in grotesque costumes; May Day, the great spring festival, being a sweeps' holiday.

As a symbol of spring the Green Man also represents the ancient initiatory emergence from death to rebirth. He is also suggested as vestigial tree worship and, to support this theory, there is the Slav and gypsy ceremony on St George's Day, or sometimes on Easter Monday, when a tree is cut and decked on the eve of the festival and carried in procession with singing and revelry. The tree is accompanied by a man clad entirely in green birch boughs and at the time of the festivities pretence is made of ducking him in water, but, in fact, an effigy is substituted at the last moment. See also **Gypsy**.

Gunia (Buddhist). In northern India and Nepal the Gunia occurs on the 15 days preceding the full moon of August-September and the following 15 days make up the sacred month of *Gunia*, a time of fasting, penance and pilgrimage which ends in feasting and rejoicing. The period is similar to the **Chaturmas** for the Hindus, **Lent** for Christians and **Ramadan** for Muslims. Priests recite prayers and visit houses; votive images are made and the **Festival of Lights** is held two days before the full moon. Lights are carried on pilgrimages in honour of the dead, and drums, cymbals and singing accompany the processions. There is also a **Festival of Lights** at the full moon of *Magh*, in February.

Gurpurbs (Sikh). Gurpurbs are three important anniversaries celebrating the birthdays of the first Guru Nanak and the last Guru Gobind Singh and the martyrdom of the fifth Guru Arjan. These are always celebrated as a holiday and usually commemorated by a

procession carrying the scriptures, *Guru Granth Sahib*, through the streets on a float with flowers and accompanied by an armed guard, five of them heading the procession to represent the *panj pyares*, the 'five beloved' original disciples. Bands play, speeches are made and prizes awarded in competitions. Other gurpurbs are local festivals celebrating some local event or martyrdom. There are numerous such *melas* during the year, mostly fixed by the lunar calendar. The *akhand path* is a feature of many gurpurbs, it is an unbroken reading of the *Guru Granth Sahib* and takes about 48 hours, during which readers take turns in relays; it commences in the morning two days before the festival in order to complete it before the dawn of the anniversary.

Guy Fawkes. Originally a political event in England when an attempt was made to burn down the Houses of Parliament, on 5 November 1605, the commemoration has taken on all the characteristics of a fire festival, with bonfires, fireworks and the burning of effigies. See **Fire**.

Gypsy. Gypsies in Slav countries celebrate the spring festival associated with the **Green Man** or Green George, of vegetation, later joined with the **Easter** and St George Day rites. A young willow is cut and set up on the eve of the festival and covered with garlands and leaves. Next morning the people gather round the willow and a boy, dressed as the Green Man, takes three nails, which have been immersed for three days in water, and knocks them into the willow, then pulls them out and throws them into running water. Finally the Green George goes through the pretence of being drowned, though actually a green-bough substitute is thrown into the river. These ceremonies propitiate the spirits of the waters just as the bonfire's sacrificial victim, burnt in effigy, does for the powers of fire; both have the same ritual significance.

There is also a ritual expulsion of evil at Eastertime, when a snake or lizard carcass is placed with herbs in a specially constructed wooden vessel, wrapped with red and white wool, and carried from tent to tent, spat on, exorcized, and finally thrown into running water. It is a **scapegoat** rite.

On 24 May, at Les-Saintes-Maries-de-la-Mer, a festival is held in which gypsy and Christian elements are combined and to which gypsies come from all over Europe. The saints venerated are the Three Marys and their Egyptian servant girl Sara who is taken over by the gypsies as a dark-skinned person of similar origins to their own. Some see in her the Indian Kali, with whom there are many similarities in her cult, and there is another tradition that she was Sara the Kali, of noble birth and chief of a tribe near the Rhône. She had a vision telling her of the arrival of the Marys and went to the shore to meet them. The sea was rough, but Sara threw her mantle

on the waters where it floated to bring the Marys safely to land.

Not being canonized, Sara remains in the crypt of the church and there the gypsies gather to keep a night vigil and perform ritual acts, the first of which is the dressing and veneration of the statue, with rites of touching it with items belonging to the absent sick in order to transmit healing. A procession is then formed, in traditional Egyptian and Eastern style, with the decorated figures carried through the streets on platforms in processions to the sea for the ritual bathing ceremony, as seen in all ancient cults of the Great Mother and of fertility. The usual festival candles are lit and there is dancing, singing, merry-making and drinking. At night the gypsies gather round fires for these festivities. The festival is a notable one in which outsiders are not excluded and the gypsies mix freely with the Christians and their rites. Gypsies also make pilgrimages to Lourdes, carrying a sky-blue banner bearing an effigy of Christ and the Madonna and a 16-pointed star.

H

Hahunga. See **Maori**.

Hajj. See **Eid-ul-Aida**.

Hakari. See **Maori**.

Hallowe'en. See **Samhain**.

Haloa (Ancient Greek). The Haloa was a threshing festival held on the 26th of the month of *Poseideon* (December-January) which, in addition to the mysteries of Demeter and Kore, included those of Dionysos at the time of the cutting of vines and tasting the wine. Threshing naturally took place as soon as possible after the grain was gathered in, not in winter, but here the new element of Dionysian worship took over and moved the festival to his date, 25 December, that of the Dying God, and produced the anomaly of a winter threshing festival. It was presided over by priestesses who presented bloodless offerings, the 'gentle foods' of Demeter, but Dionysos was associated with the bull, so *epheboi* were included in the ceremonies and in some sort of bull fight. The women carried the first fruits from Athens in procession and sported on the open, circular threshing floors.

A new element was also introduced in the wine of Dionysos, and Lucius said that the festival ended in a great banquet: 'Much wine was set out and the tables were full of all the foods that are yielded by land and sea, save only those prohibited in the mysteries, I mean pomegranate and apple and domestic fowls and eggs and red sea mullet and black-tailed crayfish and shark.' Men prepared the feast but then withdrew, leaving only women present. Cakes were made in the shape of sex symbols and obscenities, 'scurrilous jests' and mutual abuse were indulged in as fertility-making, it being predominently a fertility feast.

Harvest. Festivals and ritualistic ceremonies have been associated with the harvest from earliest times, deriving from the ancient worship of the Corn Spirit. They celebrate not only the completion of the

work for the year and security from want, but also the end of one season and the beginning of the next. The rites were usually concerned with offering the first-fruits to the deities, spirits, or ancestors, before they could be eaten in the feast which followed, establishing communion with those powers and propitiating them with appropriate rites.

In early times and in tribal societies animals and plants were believed to have spirits which required propitiation when the animal was killed or the plant cut. This is shown by the Ancient Egyptian custom of the reaper of the first sheaf stopping to lament and beat his breast; or the custom of the first stalks, whether wheat, maize or rice, being ritually cut by a chief, king or priest. The same applied to the plucking of fruit or the killing of the first game at the opening of the season. In earlier times propitiation could take the form of sacrifice, either human or animal, with the blood or ashes being sprinkled on the fields.

There was also particular significance attached to the cutting of the last sheaf; it was always ceremonious but the attitude to it was ambivalent. In some cases there was merit and good fortune attached to the act and there was a rush to be the cutter who was escorted home in triumph; in other societies it was a dangerous act and the reaper was regarded with opprobrium and became the target for rough treatment, if not an actual sacrificial victim.

There was, and in some places still is, a widespread custom of making a Corn Dolly from the last sheaf. The 'dolly' could take either human or animal form. In Germany animal forms used to be made, varying with the district; pigs, wolves, hares and goats were made and were called 'cocks' rather than 'dollies'. Among Slavs the last sheaf was the Wheat Mother, Rye Mother, etc., and in other parts of Europe the Mother of the Wheat, the Harvest Mother, Great Mother or Granny. In Britain she was also the Harvest Queen or Lady, the Wheat Bride, the Kern Baby or even the Old Woman. There are endless and world-wide variants. In some cases the Corn Dolly or Mother was burnt, or thrown into a river, suggesting earlier human sacrifice. More usually she was dressed in women's clothes and taken to the Harvest Home amid rejoicing and revelry; sometimes she was taken to the church instead of the farmhouse, making it a community affair. A relic of this is seen in the loaves baked in the form of a sheaf which are seen at Harvest Festival services.

The Corn Dolly was usually kept until the next harvest and mixing the seed from it with that of the next year carried the spirit of the corn over into the following crop. The Harvest Supper which ended the triumphal bringing home of the Dolly or last sheaf is the vestigial remains of the solemn feast of first fruits of earlier times. As in former feasts, dancing followed.

There is a universal belief in the virtue and significance of the last

remnant of anything, the last part being the repository of the power of the whole. That the remnants were sacred is shown by their being, in Scandinavia, the food for Odin's horses, or in Germany for the Good Mother, the Holzfrau or Wife of the Corn.

Today, decorating churches with flowers, fruit and the harvest loaf takes the place of the ancient Harvest Festivals and the Harvest Home. See also **Corn Dolly** and **First Fruits**.

Hearth. In early times the position of the hearth was central, as is seen by the Latin word *focus*. It was not only the central place in domestic life but was regarded as a spiritual centre, the meeting place of the upper and lower worlds, giving access to the underworld — an idea strengthened by the fact that the hearth was often a sunken hollow — and hence a focal point for the cult of the dead. In some places the dead were buried under the hearth. Food for the dead was left on the hearth at **Festivals of the Dead** and it is the place round which they gathered.

In Hinduism the domestic hearth has a religious significance, as does the sacred fire of Agni, denoting divine presence. In China it is closely associated with ancestor worship, the God of the Stove is equally the God of the Hearth. In most parts of Oceania the hearth is sacred to the spirits. Offerings to the hearth gods were customary in Greek, Roman, Hindu, Slav and Mexican rites. The Greek goddess Hestia and the Roman Vesta were the personification of the divine fire and libations to Hestia were made at the **Olympics**. With the multiple deities of the hearth worshipped in the household were the *penates*; later the *lares* were incorporated.

Hebrew. Jews, in any part of the world, preserve their religious traditions and festivals under different climates and conditions. The calendar is lunar, with 12 months beginning at the new moon and lasting 29 or 30 days, with 354 days and an intercalary month of 29 days, the *Second Adar*, but the ritual calendar is solar and based on agriculture. The Jewish festival year, greatly influenced by the captivity in Egypt and the Babylonian exile, has two points of commencement, either the religious year beginning with the first moon in *Nisan* (March-April), in the spring, with the **Passover**, or, more usually, the civil year starting on the first new moon of *Tishri* (September-October), with the **Rosh Hashanah**, a two-day festival for Orthodox and Conservative Jews and one day for the Reform and Israeli Jews. In earlier times, before accurate calculations could be made, the coming of the new moon was indicated by beacons being lit on the Mount of Olives and a chain of beacon-fires, or, for more remote districts, a messenger was sent.

Many of the Hebrew festivals are seasonal, such as the spring **Passover**, the autumnal and harvest **Tabernacles** and the winter **Hanukah**, a **Festival of Lights**.

Festivals are preceded by elaborate preparations such as lighting candles and ritual bathing and purification, both personal and throughout the household.

The Gregorian calendar is now used in civic life.

Festivals:
Dedication of Lights.
Fast of Ester.
Feast of Tabernacles.
Feast of Weeks.
Passover.
Purim.
Rosh Hashanah.
Sabbath.
Shevat.
Yom Kippur.

Heraea (Ancient Greek). As men competed naked at the **Olympics**, women could neither compete nor be present, but they had their own festival at Olympia, the Heraea, at which there were races for girls of different ages. The course was 500ft, one-sixth of the length of the men's stadium. Girls wore a short tunic with the right shoulder bare and hair loose down the back. The victors wore crowns of olives and had a share in a heifer sacrificed to Hera. The crown of wild olives as the Olympic prize was said to have been introduced on the advice of the Delphic Oracle. The branches were cut from the sacred olive trees by a boy whose parents were both living; he used a golden sickle.

Hilaria (Ancient Roman). At the conclusion of the Festival of Cybele, when the lost Attis was found, the mourning changed abruptly to wild joy, this was the Hilaria. The Mother Goddess was now reunited with her lover who had been cut off in his youth, like the flowers of the meadow and the crops, and was now resurrected from the winter death-sleep. The ecstatic rejoicing took the form of exuberant masquerades, lavish banquets and a general state of licence. The priests of Cybele, clothed in motley and loaded with jewels, processed through the streets to the music of tambourines, making house-to-house collections for temple expenses. After the wild elation there was a period of quiet, followed by the last day's long procession through the streets and countryside bearing a statue of Cybele, which was showered with flowers along the route, until the River Almo was reached. There the silver statue was ritually bathed and purified.

Hina Matsuri (Japanese). See **Dolls' Festival**.

Hindu. The year has six seasons: spring, summer, the rains,

autumn, winter and the season of dew and mist, and the calendar is closely associated with the seasonal religious festivals. The Vedic calendar, mentioned in the *Rig Veda*, was 12 months of 360 days and an intercalary month, the 'later-born month', to regulate the solar and lunar years. Festivals are associated with the moon rather than the sun since the moon 'determines the seasons'. The cycle of Hindu festivals has much in common with the pattern of those of the Greeks and Romans. Certain festivals, such as **Holi** in spring and the **Dassehra** (see **Durga Puja**) in autumn and the coming of the rains in June, are connected with the seasons; others, notably those associated with ceremonial bathing in sacred rivers, are tied to astronomical phenomena such as eclipses and the conjunction of stars and planets, so that not all festivals take place yearly; some occur at the eclipse of the sun and are celebrated at special holy centres. The new and full moons are observed as times of significance.

Apart from the major festivals every temple and district has its own festival days on which no work is done and people meet to lay on feasts for each other in turn; houses are decorated and fine clothes and jewels are worn. As at most festivals, religious processions are of the greatest importance. All festivals are greeted with flowers; all have local variations. The making of pilgrimages is an essential feature of Hindu life and festivals. Fairs also accompany festivals, not only for trading, but for every sort of amusement, supplying all the needs of the pilgrims and giving relief from the everyday grind of work as well as spontaneous release from normal sobriety and formalism.

Festivals:
Divali.
Durga Puja or **Dassehra**.
Holi.
Jagannath.
Makara-sankranti.
Naga Panchami.
Pongal.
Ramlila.
Vaisakhi.

Hittite. Knowledge of the Hittite civilization is fragmentary and meagre, but it is known that each city-state had its own deities and that the queen occupied the position of High Priestess with the king as High Priest. There were a large number of festivals of considerable variety, one tablet mentioning 18, some of which were tied to the seasons as there were instructions ensuring that they were performed at certain times only. Propitiation of the divinities appeared to be their main reason, but they were so important that in times of war

the king left the campaign to his generals and hastened back to the
capital to perform his part in the rites in his capacity of High Priest.
However, most festivals seem to have been confined to the winter
months when there would be no war and the king would be at home.
In all festivals he was attended by the queen and the crown prince.
There are monuments depicting him with hands raised, worshipping
in front of the bull, symbol of the weather god, Hatti, and pouring
libations before Hatti himself. The queen is depicted as conducting
the sacrifice to the Great Goddess of the Hittites, Fraktin, or
Ferahettin.

The Purulli appears to have been the chief festival, associated with
the earth and weather deities. It follows the familiar pattern of the
Snaring and Slaying of the Dragon spring festival with the death of
winter and the renewal of life; the triumph of good over evil. It
parallels the Babylonian *Epic of Creation* myth and appears in all
lands and ages, surviving to this day in the Mummers' Play (see
Plays), re-enacting the archetypal conflict between chaos and
creation. In the Hittite New Year festival it took the form of the duel
between Teshub, god of weather, and Iluyankash, serpent of chaos.
In the Hittite version the dragon is at first victorious over the weather
god, symbolizing the suspension of life in the earth, the god then
calls on all other gods for help. The Goddess Inaris calls up a hero-
figure who devises a ruse to snare the dragon, but makes it a condition that he should sleep with the Goddess. She consents and a
huge feast is prepared with unlimited food and drink. The dragon
and all his children come up from below, gorge themselves and
become so bloated that they cannot return to their holes and are
easily slain. The story is retold at the festival.

The AN.TAH.SUM was a spring festival lasting for more than a
month. The king and queen left their winter quarters to go to
Tahurpa, and other sacred places, in a chariot; they were enthroned
and 'great assemblies' were held with sacrifice of sheep and oxen to
rain and storm deities. A fleece was brought to the temple of the sun
deity and hung on an evergreen tree, with offerings made of corn,
wine and fat. There were separate ceremonies performed by the king
and queen at different palaces. During the rites there were
processions with music, dance and jesters, races, ritual ablutions,
carrying the 'year' to the House of the Dead, opening the grain store
of the storm gods, making meat offerings and setting the cups before
the storm gods. There were lamentations for **Ishtar** and meat
offerings made to her, followed by a 'great assembly' and feasting.
Reference is also made to visits to the House of the Boxwood Tree,
the evergreen where sacrifice was made to the storm god.

Hogmanay. See **New Year.**

Hola Mohalla (Sikh). Instituted by Guru Gobind Singh and first

celebrated in AD1700, Hola Mohalla takes place in the bright half of *Phalguna* (February-March) and is celebrated at the time of the Hindu **Holi** which gave a holiday period, but the Sikh festival was also designed to counteract the excesses of Holi, so it was made an occasion for military exercises, mock battles and manoeuvres and the two-day festival had its culminating point in a mock battle in which the Guru led the attack on a specially constructed fortification. There were also various contests in archery, wrestling, music and poetry. The festival ends in a procession of the flags of the *gurdwaras*. There is also a fair and pilgrims visit local shrines in the neighbourhood of Arandpur.

Holi (Hindu). Taking its name from *Holika* — half-ripe corn, the festival is held in *Phalgun* (February-March) in the two weeks before the full moon. It is a lunar festival of the vernal equinox; originally a spring festival of warding off disease from the growing crops and a celebration of the death of winter; also associated with Kama, God of Love and later with Krishna and Radha and the sporting with the *gopis*. Bonfires are lit and in some parts effigies of the winter demon are burnt. The festival also commemorates the destruction of the demon Holika who devoured children and who died when obscenities were shouted at her. A bonfire was made of her remains, so her effigies were also burnt.

Poles of the maypole type are erected and festooned with flags and topped with a sugar-cone, climbed for by boys. Red pigment is thrown at everyone (seen as vestigial remains of an original blood sacrifice) and beans are thrown. Bright clothes and jewels are worn. As in the Roman **Saturnalia** all restrictions and castes are abandoned and there is the uninhibited gaiety and license associated with fertility cults. Stories of the origin and meaning of the festival, and customs and rituals in its celebration, vary from one place to another, but the festival is of most importance in northern India.

Horns. As rising from the head, horns represent power and are a symbol of divinity, royalty and dignity, and also a natural symbol of strength. Most ancient religions had gods and goddesses with horns which appear with both the solar gods and lunar goddesses, the Sky God and Queen of Heaven. Horns also symbolize plenty. They had a widespread use in sacrificial rites as propitiatory offerings: votive horns were offered to Diana, and horns of oxen were gilded in Roman, Teutonic and Scandinavian sacrificial rites. At Hindu festivals, notably the **Pongal**, cattle have their horns painted and decorated with fruit and cakes. Horns frighten off evil powers and the blowing of horns drives off demons. The blowing of the *shofar* at Jewish festivals heralds the end of the fast and repels Satan. Horns are frequently used as musical instruments at festivals. Horn dances (see **Dance**), still performed, are of great antiquity.

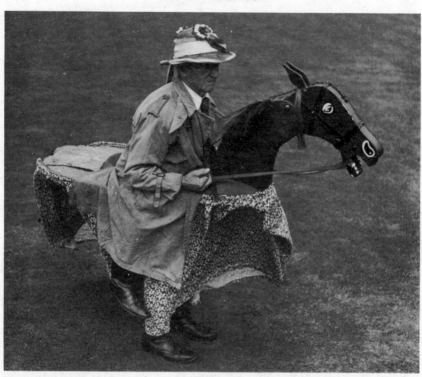

Sam Bennett, Fiddler of Ilmington, with his traditional hobby-horse (*W. Fisher Cassie*, 1950)

Horse. Associated with divinities and magic powers, the horse was one of the chief sacrificial animals and largely replaced the bull as such. The black horse symbolizes Death and Chaos and the sacrifice of the October Horse (see **Roman**) represented the death of Death and the conquest of Chaos. Horse festivals still continue in many places, such as at Arles, with the historic horse games of 'ring and lances' and 'scarves' and others. The Camargue Horse Festival is held about St George's Day, according to the weather. The Siena Palio festival has an ancient ritual horse-race. The hobby-horse, or Old Hob, appears in horn, sword and morris dances and is often ritually killed, as in the ancient sacrifice. The hobby-horse can also be a horse-head which cavorts about at festivals; it has snapping jaws and catches people who have to pay to be released, or it catches and threatens children who have not said their prayers.

Hsia Yuan (Chinese). One of the Festivals of the Dead, or Spirit Festivals, occurring on the first day of the tenth month and taking the form of a ghost-expelling festival of the **Hallowe'en** type. Masks are worn to imitate ghosts and monsters. There are Taoist services and spells to drive off ghosts, against whom the priest wields a magic

sword. Wandering ghosts are helped with spells and little paper boats bearing lights are set adrift on the waters while food and drink is offered. The Japanese **Bon** Festival has similar customs.

Hypante (Christian). In the Eastern Orthodox Church the Hypante is held in celebration of the time when Simeon and Anna met Christ in the Temple as the Light of the World. At the festival candles are blessed, sprinkled with holy water, and carried in procession. See also **Candlemas**.

I

Imbolc or **Oimele** (Celtic). A spring festival, on 1 February, associated with Brigit, Bridget or Bride, and the coming again of life and light. It was adopted by Christianity as St Bridget's Day. Corn Dollies were dressed and Bride Cakes baked, and straw cradles or baskets were made as Bride's Beds. A procession of girls preceded general dancing and feasting. In Ireland Bridget's Crosses were made of rushes and placed on houses, byres and stables to ward off evil powers. Bridget's Girdles, made of woven straw, and crosses were worn as protections.

Inca. The main function of the priesthood was to conduct the highly complex and elaborate rituals of the fasts and feasts. Each month had its festival, but the chief occasions took place at the new moon following a solstice or equinox. Inca worship was regulated by the progress of the sun through the year, but, although sun-orientated, the great festival of the sun was determined by the days of the lunar month. The three major festivals were the *Inti Rymi* (the Great Feast of the Sun) at the Peruvian winter solstice in June; the *Ccapac Rymi*, a New Year festival dedicated to the god Pachacamac and the *Ccoya Rymi*, the Feast of the Moon, at the beginning of September, the rainy season.

At the festivals nobles came from every quarter to the capital. There was first a three day fast and no fires were lit before the festival started. The Inca and his court, followed by the entire populace, dressed in lavish apparel and ornamented with jewels and brilliant feathers, also having canopies of these multi-coloured feathers, went at dawn to greet the rising sun and at the first rays there were shouts of joy and songs of triumph. There were ceremonies of adoration of the sun and the Inca offered a libation from a golden vase; he then tasted it himself before offering it to his nobles. A procession went to the temple for devotions and the sacrifice of a sacred white llama, from whose entrails auguries were taken. There were also offerings of grain and flowers. It is disputed as to whether the Incas practised human sacrifice, but it is accepted that they did not indulge in cannabalism as did the Aztecs.

At the Sun Festival fire was kindled from a mirror, or, if overcast (an unlucky omen), from sticks, and the sacred flame was tended by Virgins of the Sun, who, in the manner of the Roman **Vestal Virgins**, were segregrated and remained chaste, living in conventual conditions. Infringement of these rules led, again as in Rome, to being buried alive. They were known as the Brides of the Inca and later could be transferred to his seraglio. At the festival numbers of llamas were killed and burnt offerings were made, on which the people feasted. The feasting, drinking, dancing and revelry continued for several days.

The Situa, a September festival at the coming of the rains, aimed at warding off the sickness prevalent at that time of year. It was preceded by a fast on the first day of the moon of the autumnal equinox. Next day coarse pastes of maize were eaten, one plain and the other mixed with blood drawn from children. The blood-paste was used also to smear on the body after ablutions; this removed infirmities. The head of the family then applied the paste to the threshold of the house, while the High Priest carried out the same rituals at the Temple of the Sun. The people then worshipped the sun together with the Inca, who rode from his fortress to the capital, brandishing a feather-decked lance of many colours; there, four other Incas of the blood assisted him, waiting for him to touch them with his lance before running to the four quarters, driving out evil influences, and cheered on by the populace. There was ritual bathing, dancing and running with torches which were set up on boundaries to prevent the return of the evil spirits.

Incense. Used in homage to divinities. As agreeable to humans and used at banquets and in honour of important people, it was therefore assumed to be acceptable to deities and was used in honouring both them and spirits. Incense, as well as scented oils and flowers, caused them to smell a sweet odour; on the other hand such scents ward off evil powers and demons who dislike fragrant odours, hence they are also used in purification ceremonies in temples, churches and houses. Incense was also used to neutralize the unpleasant smells of blood and burnt sacrifices. The rising smoke of the incense symbolizes prayer rising to the heavens, it thus creates communion between humans and deities and can pass the 'subtle body' heavenwards. Incense could also be used as a substitute for burnt offerings. Resin, exuded from trees, represents the soul substance of the tree, while the trees from which it was obtained, the pine and cedar, were regarded as having great vitality and power to prevent corruption. Myrrh, sandalwood and other sweet-smelling woods were, and are, used, or incense is given flower scents.

Independence Day (United States of America). 4 July is the most significant political festival of the year, celebrating the birth of the

nation and the signing of the Declaration of Independence. It was first observed in 1777; it stated that 'all men are created equal, that they are endowed by their Creator with certain inalienable Rights; that among these are life, liberty and the pursuit of happiness' and that 'these Colonies are, and of right ought to be, free and independent states'. The initial celebration was one of bell-ringing, bonfires, fireworks displays and a gun salute, followed by a banquet. Elaborate fireworks displays are a feature of present-day celebrations. Philadelphia, home of the Declaration, elects a Miss Liberty Belle who reads from the Declaration and the Mayor gives an oration. There are parades, bands, pageants of flags and mummers, fountains and a terminating spectacular fireworks display of red, white and blue. There is also a *son et lumière* display at the Independence Hall.

Inoko or **Tokanya** (Japanese). A harvest festival. On the tenth of the tenth month the Rice God leaves the paddy fields and goes to the hills, having brought the crops to completion. He is given offerings and children visit houses, carrying straw guns, or bundles of straw, and are given rewards in return for which they wish the household prosperity. In some parts the scarecrows are ceremoniously brought out into the fields as guardian deities. There are also rites of beating the ground to drive away evil powers. The harvest is followed by the *Frost Month* ceremonies with offerings of *saké* in gratitude for the harvest.

Intercalation is 'the equalizing of the total number of moon months with the solar year' and it introduces the necessity for including an occasional month into the 12-month series, or omitting one from the 13-month series. It became customary to introduce the intercalary month at a definite time, thus giving the lunar-solar year. These months are called 'lost' or 'forgotten' months in many cultures. See **Calendar**.

Inti Rymi. See **Inca**.

Ishtar (Babylonian and Assyrian). The Feast of Ishtar, in the month of *Ab*, followed, and was associated with, the **Midsummer** and **Sirius** Festival of the previous month. It was also connected with the constellation Leo, the lion being the sacred animal of Ishtar. There was a great feast in her honour, continuing until the next month of *Elul*, 'the corn-bearer of Ishtar'.

Isis (Ancient Egypt). There were two major festivals of Isis: the first in winter when there was a commemoration of the slaying of Osiris by Set and the finding of the body. It started with great lamentation for his death and the singing of dirges. On the second day there was the search for the body, accompanied by wild grief, and on the third day there followed great rejoicing at the finding of the body; there was then a general air of festivity and license, with singing and

dancing to instruments. The second festival was in spring when Isis had 'lain to rest the storms of winter and stilled the tempestuous waves of the sea'. Its main feature was the ceremony of dedication to Isis of 'a barque that had never sailed the waves'. Apuleius, an initiate of the Egyptian cult of Isis, gives a full account of this festival as celebrated in Greece, at Corinth by the devotees of the goddess. (See **Isis**, Ancient Greek.)

Isis (Ancient Greek). The cult of Isis was carried from Egypt into Greece and Rome and her festival became an important occasion in both countries. Celebrated near Corinth, Apuleius tells us that there was a great procession headed by men dressed as a soldier, a hunts-man, a woman and a gladiator and there followed men dressed as magistrates, philosophers, fowlers and fishermen. Then came a tame bear, clad like a matron and borne in a litter; a monkey wearing a Phrygian plaited hat, a saffron robe and carrying a golden cup to represent Ganymede; and an ass with false wings glued to its back, walking beside an old man, representing Pegasus and Bellerophon. Women followed wearing white and bearing garlands of spring flowers, scattering flowers as they went; women with mirrors held behind their backs for the use of the Goddess; women with combs of ivory, imitating the combing and dressing of her hair and women who sprinkled the ground with scent and balsam as they walked. After them came a mixed multitude bearing lanterns and torches and tapers and all kinds of lights to depict the stars of heaven over which the Goddess presided. Then came musicians and a choir of boys magnificently dressed in festive apparel and singing to the sound of pipe and flute a beautiful hymn to Isis.

With these came the flute-players of Serapis/Osiris who 'through a reed held slantwise towards the right ear, repeated the hymn that the God and his Temple claim for their own'. A crowd of men and women of all ages and ranks followed, the men with shaven heads, the women with scented hair covered with gauze, representing the initiates of the Rites of Isis. Priests carried 'glorious emblems of the most potent gods', such as a golden bowl of fire, an altar, a golden palm tree, the staff of Mercury, a golden vessel shaped like the breasts from which a libation of milk flowed, a golden pitcher and a winnow-ing fan. Then came gods, such as Anubis, accompanied by priests carrying emblems and an ark full of objects of mysterious signifi-cance, and finally a small gold urn 'on which was set an asp with twisted coils, holding erect the stretched scales of its swelling neck'. The procession went to the shore where the High Priest arranged the images in order and made solemn supplication and dedicated them to the Goddess after the purification and the breaking of eggs.

A decorated ship was loaded with people who all vied in loading it with winnowing fans, spices and offerings; a libation of paste and

milk was poured on the waves and the ship was launched and watched out of sight before the procession, in the same order, returned to the temple. Prayers were offered for prosperity for all, then, after the 'safe landing of the ship' had been announced, there was general rejoicing and acclamation; people kissed the feet of the silver statue of Isis, which stood on the steps of the temple, and, in great joy, all went home bearing green branches, wands and wreaths.

Isis (Ancient Roman). The Festival of Isis was the first of the two great imported cults, those of Isis and Cybele. The reopening of navigation on the rivers after the winter was on 5 March and this day saw the Festival of Isis, protector of sailors. A magnificent procession wound its way to the river and a boat dedicated to Isis was launched. The procession was headed by a group of grotesque disguises, then came women dressed in white robes covered with flowers and carrying robes for the Goddess. A group followed carrying flaming torches, and hymns were sung to the music of the rattle of the sistrum of Isis. Priests in dazzling white followed, carrying images of the gods often in animal form. Initiates followed the priests to the street altar where the gods were offered for the veneration of the crowds who were entranced by the pomp and bizarre display.

Islam. The lunar calendar given to Muhammad on his last journey to Mecca consists of 12 lunar months of 29 (28 and 30) days each and the intercalary of *nasi* was forbidden, thus, about every 33 years the months passed through a circle of a whole solar year. 'Truly the number of months with God is 12 months in the book of God, on the day when He created the heavens and earth. Of these four are holy.' There are 354 days in a year and 355 in a leap year. Various means are employed for determining the leap years and their correspondence with the Gregorian calendar. The months are seasonal, depending on the sighting of the new moon so that the dates of festivals are approximate. Festivals and their forms of celebration differ from one sect or country to another, but all begin with prayer and devotions, and they are also times of festivity to be shared by all, with particular stress on the inclusion of the poor and lonely. Muslims are expected, if possible, to make the pilgrimage to Mecca, the **Hajj**, at least once in a lifetime. There are two main festivals in the year, the Eid, or Id (a day which returns often) — those of the **Eid-ul-Fitr** and **Eid-ul-Adha**.

Festivals:
Day of Assembly (Fridays).
Eid-ul-Adha.
Eid-ul-Fitr.
Eid Mawlid.
Lailat-ul-Qadr.

Muharram.
Rajeb.
Shab-i-Miraj.

Isthmia (Ancient Greek). The Isthmean athletic festival was reputed to be older than the **Olympics** in origin and was revived in 582 BC. It was probably associated with the worship of Poseidon, God of the Seas, and was held in a pine grove at the south east of the Isthmus of Corinth. One tradition has it that the festival was funereal, in honour of Melicertes, at the point where his dead body was carried ashore by a dolphin; another attributes it to games in honour of Theseus who rid the land of a notorious robber, or that Thesius himself founded the games in rivalry to Heracles and the Olympics.

Corinth and Athens were originally closely associated before intense commercial rivalry sprang up, and a special place was reserved for Athenians, the space being that of the size of the sail of the ship which brought them to the Isthmus. The festival had more of a carnival air than the other Games, with emphasis on luxury and entertainment, Corinth being the meeting point of East and West and influenced by the luxuries of the commercial world. It was also more cosmopolitan and therefore more tolerant of strangers and allowed Romans and other nations to take part. The prize was a crown of dried celery leaves. The festival was held in the 2nd and 4th years of the Olympiad. It is possible that a regatta was included in the contests. Under the Roman occupation the festival became decadent, lavish and brutal. Nero himself competed but resorted to intimidation and elimination in order to win.

J

Jagannath (Hindu). 'Lord of Creation' is one of the titles of Krishna as Eighth Avatar of Vishnu and is associated with the shrine at Puri in Orissa. Here there are two chief festivals, one in the May 'bathing' of the god, a baptism-type ceremony, which precedes the later celebrated fair-festival of the Great Car ritual. It is a time of pilgrimage with vast assemblies of people. Gaily decked images of the god are brought out of the temple by the Lion Gate and placed on a huge, specially made chariot, known as the *Jagannath* (or Juggernaut), being 45 feet high with 16 solid wood wheels of seven feet six inches in diameter. This is followed by other chariots only slightly smaller; all are drawn by ropes and there is great competition to seize them and draw the cars. The procession goes through the streets to the Jagannath's Garden House, where the figures are displayed and bowed to. Progress is slow and may take up to three days to cover the mile-and-a-half journey. The images are left for seven days before being taken back to the Great Temple by the same means. Dancing girls are seated round the god, fanning him with peacock-feather fans and fly whisks. The atmosphere is one of merry-making, dancing, great noise, chaos and license.

Jain. Jainas maintain that their religion is pre-historic and the original faith, but it emerges as historic at the time of Mahavira (528 BC). There are two principal sects, the *Shvetambara*, the white-clad, who wear a simple white cotton garment, and the *Digambara*, the sky-clad, that is to say naked. The calendar of festivals coincides with that of the **Hindus** and, while the chief Jaina festivals are restricted to their own religious practices, they now join in various major Hindu festivals such as **Diwali** and **Durga Puja** which are public holidays in India. Jaina festivals are largely organized by the monastic community; full moons are watched and four of the full moons are occasions for special fasts. The closing days of the religious year are considered the most sacred.

Festivals:
Karttika-purnima.

Mahavira-jayanti.
Paryushana-parva.
Shruta-pancami.
Vira-nirvana.

Japanese. Time is calculated in various ways. Based originally on the Chinese lunar calendar, it remained so until the Gregorian calendar was adopted in 1872. Some events are reckoned by the solar, others by the lunar calendar, though festivals were originally tied to the latter which was divided into 12 months of 29 or 30 days with an intercalary month in some years. A distinction is made between traditional festivals, *matsuri*, and other ceremonial occasions — *matsuri* being of **Shinto** origin and sacred in character. There are other seasonal festivals bearing Chinese origins.

The Shinto rites are based on propitiation of the gods, goddesses and spirits of the dead and on the agricultural seasons, particularly the cultivation of rice. The sense of need for communication between divinities and humanity is the essence of the *matsuri* but it also implies communication and communion among the people and involves symbolic acts through which such communion is maintained. As everywhere, there are included purificatory rites, offerings to deities or spirits, supplication for successful harvests and thanksgiving for achievement; combined with these sacred rituals are festive outlets, games and amusements. These two elements in festivals are recognized as *hare* and *ke*, the *hare* is the solemn and ritual aspect, setting the occasion aside from everyday life and tying it to the sacred; the *ke* is the everyday or profane festivity.

Matsuri were originally and traditionally associated with a rice-centred culture and revolved round the seasonal cycle of preparation, transplanting, weeding and harvesting, the spring festivals invoking the gods for a good harvest, autumn anticipating a time of plenty, with summer between taking on the rites of aversion and warding off any natural disasters. Winter festivals contain elements of both spring and autumn *matsuri*. Other rites are associated with lunar phases of the new and full moons and the first and last quarters. Traditionally the *matsuri* must be preceded by rites of purification and abstinence and the raising of a social fire to cook ritual food. Offerings of *mochi*, *saké* and special vegetables should be made; there are no sacrifices of living creatures and no broken bread offered. An essential element of the *matsuri* is also a communal participation of food offerings with the deities. The lunar and solar calendars, known as the 'old' and the 'new', give rise to some confusion in the times of festivals. There are also innumerable festivals with endless varieties in different geographical, urban and rural settings. The same rituals may be performed on different dates when the festival is controlled by the climate, e.g. the different times of flowering of the

cherry blossom from north to south for flower festivals.

Festivals:
Bon Festival.
Boys' Festival.
Chrysanthemum Festival.
Dolls Festival.
Flower Festival.
Gion Festivals.
Harvest Festival.
Jugoya.
New Year.
New Year's Eve. (See **New Year**.)
Rice Planting Festival.
Setsubun.
Seven-Five-Three.
Summer Solstice Festival. (See **Solstices**.)
Tanabata Festival.
Winter Solstice. (See **Solstices**.)
Yuki Matsuri. (**Snow Festival**.)

Jashans (Zoroastrian). Jashans are name-day festivals celebrating the particular divinities to whom the Zoroastrian months of the year are dedicated. The Souls of the Departed (the *Fravashis*) also have their jashan when they are remembered at the funerary towers and prayers are said for them. The chief of these occasions still observed are:

Mihr Jashan, 3 October. A five-day harvest festival with offerings of agricultural products made at the fire temple. It is also in honour of Mithra and celebrated mainly by the Iranis.

Aban Jashan, 26 October, commemorates the water deities. Hymns are recited by the waters and flowers and other offerings are cast in. It is celebrated mainly by the Parsis.

Adar Jashan, 24 November, commemorates the fire deities. Prayers and offerings are made and incense burned at the fire temples and there is no cooking on the domestic hearth during the day.

Jewish. See **Hebrew**.

Jugoya or *Tsukimi* (Japanese). The Moon-viewing Festival, it is held on the 15th night of the eighth moon of the old lunar calendar. It follows an Ancient Chinese custom. People assemble in gardens, at windows or on verandas to view the harvest moon. Scholars celebrate the occasion with poems while, for the populace, it is a time for feasting and music. Special dumplings or rice cakes are made and eaten and offerings are set out with pampas grass to symbolize the rice plant. Villages or teams divide for a ritual tug-of-war contest. The festival is also designed to produce a good harvest and prayers are addressed to the moon for protection from storms and for a good harvest.

K

Karttika-Purnima (Jain). Occurs at the full moon of *Karttika* (December) at the end of the rainy season when monks and nuns abandon their retreats and resume their wandering life. Before they leave they are thanked by their hosts for their company and religious instructions. The occasion is a festive one and the people celebrate it with a Car Festival. A lavishly decorated wooden vehicle, bearing the image of the Jina, is pulled by hand through the streets, in the manner of the **Jagannath**, accompanied by a procession of monks and nuns and the populace. A sermon is delivered in the park at the end of the journey and an appeal is made for gifts to support the temples, hospitals, etc. The procession then returns to the temple and merry-making follows.

Kathina (Buddhist). See **Vassa**.

Kiku No Sekku (Japanese). See **Chrysanthemum Festival**.

Kitchen God or Goddess (Chinese). More usually the God, but sometimes the Goddess of the Kitchen — or the God of the Stove of Chinese Alchemy — ascends the heaven, annually, to make a report to the Jade Emperor on the conduct of the family during the past year; it is therefore wise to feast him/her on honey or some other sticky substances before leaving so that the lips may be sealed or the report sweet. Doors are closed for the night then opened by the head of the house at dawn, in the ceremony of Opening the Gate of Good Fortune. The festival takes place at the end of the year, on New Year's Eve, in late January or early February, according to the lunar calendar, in preparation for the **New Year** celebrations.

L

Lady Day (Christian). 25 March, the beginning of the year before the adoption of the new calendar in 1752. It is the festival of Artemis, Great Mother and Queen of Heaven, and was adapted to the celebration of the Annunciation of the Virgin Mary in the seventh century, she had no festivals before that date when four were instituted: The Purification, 2 February, at **Candlemas**; The Annunciation, 25 March, or the Feast of Incarnation; the Assumption, or Sleep, 15 August — a Byzantine festival before being adopted by the Roman Catholic Church; The Nativity, 8 September.

Lailat-ul-Qadr (Islam). The Night of Decrees, also called the Night of Power, occurs in the month of **Ramadan** and commemorates the time when the Koran was first revealed to Muhammad; he was 40 years old at the time and the revelation continued until his death, about 25 years later; he said 'Look for the Night of Decrees among the odd nights of the last 10 nights of the month of Ramadan.' The whole of the month of Ramadan is a total fast from sunrise to sunset. Muslims gather in mosques and spend these nights in prayer and remembrance of Allah as it is related that the Prophet kept awake the whole night in worship.

Lamentations. Weeping, wailing, beating breasts and tearing hair are features of all festivals of Dying Gods of Vegetation, such as Osiris, Tammuz, Adonis, Attis and Dionysos. In Dionysian rites these lamentations were part of the ritual of a festival for women only which was held at night in the remote mountains; it was a wailing at the death and rejoicing at rebirth. It is suggested that the tears were also sympathetic rain magic, while Frazer suggests that the weeping was not only for the death of the god, gone underground, but also for the harsh treatment of the grain in flailing at harvest-time, all plant life being imbued with a spirit which required propitiation.

Lammas (Anglo-Saxon), **Lugnasad** (Celtic), **Lughnasa** (Irish). Held on 1 August, midway between **Beltane** and **Samhain**, in honour of Lug (Manx Lugus), a Celtic god, it was a pagan harvest

festival. Observing it ensured an abundance of corn, milk, fruit and fish; it was adopted by Christianity as Lammas-tide when bread was made from the first corn and was offered at mass. The festival was celebrated by sports and athletic contests which later gave rise to a fair at which men and women looked for marriage partners. In Ireland the festival of Lughnasa was associated with the death of a woman, Carman, who tried to blight the corn, or others say to the death of King Carman; in either case, the festival gave rise to one of the world's greatest fairs (see **Fairs**) where 'all Ireland met'. These were waterside gatherings at lakes, rivers and pools, with singing and dancing and driving the cattle, or racing horses, through the waters. The festival was also a favourite time for '**Patterns**' at wells and local shrines and was also an occasion for divination for the harvest and the coming weather.

Lanterns (Chinese). The New Year festival ends with the Feast of Lanterns which lasts for three days. Lanterns of all shapes, sizes and colours (except white which is the colour of mourning) are lit in front of both public and private buildings. Paper dragons, hundreds of yards long, supported by men with only the legs showing, wind through the streets. Lions and other creatures are featured and there are lion dances and singing. The lion dance has a gaily painted papier-maché lion teased by people in masks; the lion charges at them, snaps and rolls its eyes.

Lemuria (Ancient Roman). The Lemures or Larvae were spirits of the dead, dangerous to the living. The Lemuria was a three-day festival of the dead for the family, corresponding to the state occasions of the **Parentalia** and **Feralia**; it took place on 9, 11 and 12 May. At these times the passage between this world and the next opened up for the temporary return of the dead from the underworld. The places of the dead were at the same time both holy and unclean and required rites of purification and aversion. At these festivals all state affairs were in abeyance, no battles were fought, no business entered into and no marriage contracted.

May and February, associated with the dead, were both unlucky months and the superstition against marriage in them remains to this day. Ovid said that at the Lemuria the father of the house was responsible for laying its ghosts: he rose at midnight, in silence, and stood with bare feet, making an apotropaic sign with finger and thumb to keep off the ghosts. He washed his hands thrice in spring water then turned round and put black beans in his mouth, then, averting his face and going through the house, he spits them out and says: 'These I send forth, with these beans I redeem myself and mine.' This is repeated nine times without looking back. The ghost picks up the beans and follows behind if no one looks round. Again the father touches the water and then strikes a brass Temesa and begs the

ghosts to leave the house, saying nine times: 'Shades of my fathers depart.' He then looks back, the rite having been completed. Pitch was painted on the doors and buckthorn chewed, both apotropaic rituals. The rites follow the pattern and have the same significance as those of the Greek **Anthesteria**.

Les-Saintes-Maries-de-la-Mer. (See **Gypsy**).

Light (Celtic). 1 February marked the second half of the winter festival; the time of the coming of light. Little is recorded about it but it bears all the marks of the earlier pagan light festivals. The original Earth Mother Brigit was replaced by St Brigit's Day and **Candlemas**, but few traces of its origin are left.

Lights. Lights are an important feature of many festivals, for both the living and the dead. Light is regarded as a manifestation of divinity and creation and symbolizes new life from the divine source. Illumination also suggests supernatural powers and represents protection against the forces of darkness. Many cultures have feasts of light in which torches, lanterns or candles are carried in procession or lit in temples, churches and private dwellings. These festivals are mainly in February or at the coming of spring and the return of light after the winter darkness and new life coming to the earth. The Swedish celebration, however, occurs on 13 December with the Feast of St Lucia. The saint is represented by the oldest girl in the family who wears a crown of evergreens; a star and lighted candles represent the lengthening days and the melting of the winter ice. Lights are also used at festivals of the dead to light the departed back to the otherworld after being entertained in their old homes by the living. Lights were also carried at Mystery rites (see **Mysteries**), such as the **Eleusinia**, when Demeter searched for Kore and spring returned.

Lights, Feast of Dedication of Lights (Hebrew). Hanukah or Chanukah is an eight-day festival of lights and rededication, on the 25th day of the month of *Kislev* (November-December). It celebrates the Maccabean rededication of the Temple by the commemoration of a miracle of a small one-day jar of oil lasting for eight days at the rededication. On the first day of the festival one light, either a candle, or more traditionally an oil wick, is set in the window or door for all to see; another light is lit each successive day, with recitations and blessings, and, on the eighth day, with the singing of a traditional hymn. It is also a festival of identity and liberty of the Jewish people.

See also:
Divali — Hindu.
Diwali — Sikh.
Feast of Lanterns — Chinese. (See **Feasts**.)
Geshi — Japanese.
No Ruz — Zoroastrian.

Lights, Festival of (Buddhist). A Festival of Lights is held on the full moon of *Magh*, in February, when pilgrims to Buddhist shrines take part in prayer, chanting, ringing bells and distributing strips of scarlet cloth. After dark there is a procession of 1001 lights. Various festivals of light are spread through different Buddhist countries, taking many local forms but always celebrated with lamps, candles, torches or lanterns.

Lots, the Feast of (Hebrew). (See **Purim**.)

Lupercalia (Ancient Roman). The Lupercalia on 15 March was a spring fertility festival; it occurred between the **Parentalia** and the **Feralia**. It was said by Cicero to be so ancient in origin as to have been 'instituted before civilization and law existed'. People assembled at the cave, called the Lupercal, on the Palantine Hill, where Romulus and Remus were suckled by their wolf foster-mother. Goats and dogs were sacrificed and youths had their heads smeared with the blood of the victims, then washed it off with milk, as a death-and-rebirth symbol. The youths were naked except for the animal skins, from which thongs were also made and used to strike women rushing round through the streets. The women put themselves in the way to receive this fertility magic, regarded as also both purificatory and cathartic. The youths were called the Lupercai; they also made the rounds of the Palatine, thus putting it in the magic circle which both enclosed the sacred space and warded off evil spirits. The **Vestal Virgins** prepared the sacred *mola salsa* for the festival. Shakespeare uses this festival in 'Julius Caesar' when Mark Antony offers Caesar the crown: 'The barren, touched in this holy chase/ Shake off their sterile curse.' The purificatory ritual became, under Christianity, in the sixth century, the Purification of the Blessed Virgin Mary.

M

Magic. From earliest times to the present day it has been assumed that there are powers and entities superior to humanity and that these can control events, but they, in turn, could be influenced in favour of mortals by various rites, formulae and propitiations. Nature could be mastered by certain methods and rituals known only to certain people. It has been believed that the future could be foretold by these means and people, hence the seers of the offical priesthood and the famous oracles.

Embodied in these rites is a positive magic of sorcery and shamanism and a negative magic of taboo. Both enter into festivals to a considerable degree in the propitiation of supernatural powers, or the warding off of evil forces, and ascertaining the will and desires of divinities by divination.

Sympathetic magic played, and still plays in tribal communities, a large part in festivals aimed at influencing the elements, such as rain-making and encouraging the power of the sun; it can also be used for rites concerned with attracting game for hunters. Dancing, chanting, sexual orgies, mimetic gestures, spoken formulae and the use of numbers, all occupy an important place in seasonal magic which is intended to safeguard humans, animals and crops against dangerous times of the year and unlucky months and days. The obscene language used in Greek and Roman festivals by the most respectable matrons was well-known fertility magic.

Certain people, such as public officials and children before baptism or initiation, required particular protection, hence the charms and talismans employed. These often took the form of small objects attached to the person, or small swinging objects, known to the Romans as *oscilla*, which could protect not only people but also crops. They could be anything from small human forms — probably a substitute for human sacrifice — to simple balls or bells. (These appear to have survived more than 2000 years to appear in the modern motor car!)

Mahavira-Jayanti (Jain). Taking place on the 13th day of the

rising moon of *Caitra* (April), the festival celebrates the birth of Mahavira, the last of the Jainas, born in 399 BC, the earlier teachers being legendary. All sects join in the celebrations of this most important of festivals which is also a public holiday. The people assemble at the local temple in the early morning. A wealthy couple is chosen to impersonate Indra and Indrani and they are expected to contribute large sums to the temple upkeep and to the needy. An image of Mahavira is placed on a small representation of the Sacred Cosmic Centre, Mount Meru, and is venerated and anointed with scented water and sandalwood. The ceremony is accompanied by chanting, throwing flowers over the image, and waving lamps. The life of Mahavira is read by a monk or nun, sacred hymns are sung and the people then return to their homes for a feast.

Makahki. See **New Year** (Oceania).

Makara-Sankranti (Hindu). Virtually a New Year festival when the sun turns North, celebrated on the fifth day of the bright half of the moon, a spring festival associated with *Makara*, equated with Capricorn; it is also a veneration of Jagaddhatri, Goddess of Spring. Makara is also an emblem of Kama, or Kandarp, God of Love. The Spring Song, *Vasant Rag*, is sung with emotion and joyousness. Food is coloured saffron and yellow clothes are worn as symbolic of spring; cattle are decorated and their horns painted. The sun is venerated as it enters Capricorn and people gather and bathe in sacred rivers, notably at the junction of the Jumna and Ganges and where the Ganges flows into the sea. Rati, wife of Kama, and Lakshmi, Goddess of Wealth and Prosperity, are also venerated.

Maori. The year has 13 months which are fixed by one or more risings of stars. Festivals are few but important and divided into two kinds, ritual and social, classified by the Maoris under the *mana* of Tu, God of War, or Rongo, God of Peace.

The first account given of a Maori festival was of an annual feast in honour of the Sun God Ra. Food was arranged in pyramids in the form of a heptagon and there were fires at each angle and a central fire on which a human sacrifice was burned. The festival took place at an ancient stone circle at Kerikeri with the stones used as posts for piles of food.

Hakari, or feasts, were said to have originated in offerings made to the gods. The whole ceremony appears to have affinities with the Amerindian **Potlatch** in the distribution of goods and the fact that it can be held to mark some special or ritual occasion, such as a marriage feast, name-giving baptismal rites, the exhumation of the bones of the dead, or when tribes cease fighting, these ceremonies being preceded by a meeting somewhat similar to a pow-pow. Preparation for a festival is considerable, requiring time for

cultivation and collection of large quantities of food, roots, sweet potatoes, fish, birds, rats, eels and shellfish. As long as a year may be needed. Messengers are sent out to other clans with invitations which are ritually chanted and replied to in a similar manner.

Food is stacked and there are cleft sticks containing money stuck in the stacks. These stacks, at ordinary feasts, are set out in long walls and presided over by a chief who indicates with his staff which foods are allocated to whom. At special festivals these stacks are placed on *hakari* stones, elaborate structures built on a framework of poles, in tiers, the stages seven to nine feet apart and diminishing in size to form a giant inverted V shape, as high as 50 to 90 feet, supporting thousands of baskets of food allotted to each clan or visitor. At the approach of the guests, and before food is accepted, there are mutual rites of prevention of evil influences. Considerable time is spent in speech-making, which is poetic, rhythmic and figurative in style; it is an essential feature of any festival. These orations are made while walking in one direction, returning in silence, then walking and speaking again. After the speeches the master of ceremonies indicates with a rod which food is allocated to which tribe or individual.

After the feast the *hakari* erection is left to go to ruin and is used for firewood. The same site is not used again. The festival is accompanied by amusements and contests, ritual combat being a feature of all Polynesian feasts. These festivals are thought to be not only offerings to the gods but also to the sun since another outstanding characteristic is the placing of large poles, with pennants, representing the rays, with a fire at the centre to represent the sun, named as *Hera*. Formerly a human sacrifice was cast into the fire as propitiation.

Fasting is practised before rites since ritual prayers performed on an empty stomach are more effective — a widespread belief and practice. Fire and water are both used in purificatory rites.

The **New Year** festival, in June, is of great importance and is held at the time of the rising of the **Pleiades**, on the east coast, and at the rising of Rigel in the north. It is greeted by women with song and dance. Spring-cleaning ceremonies are observed and the *plaza* ritually swept. It is a time of light-hearted rejoicing, pleasure, games and contests.

The Hahunga or harvest festival, is celebrated in the 10th month (March) after the crops are gathered and stored. Again it is a time of rejoicing with a feast held at the place of the planting of the crops. It is also a feast of the dead.

Mars, the Rites of (Ancient Roman). There are varying accounts of the Rites of Mars which were held from mid-March to mid-October, Mars being an earlier god of agriculture as well as of war. His birthday

was celebrated on 1 March with the relighting of the fires. This new year festival had the same freedom as the **Saturnalia**; presents were exchanged and food and drink were indulged in to excess as a symbol of plenty for the coming year. Ovid said that they gave gifts of dates, figs and honey 'that the year might in sweetness go through the course which it had begun'. The opening of the martial year, on 14 March, was celebrated by the horse-race at the Campus Martinus. Processions took place on several occasions from the 19th to the 23rd, when there was a lustration of arms. The Salii (armed priests), wearing pointed caps or helmets and carrying shields and swords, or a spear or staff, progressed through the streets in ritual dance. They invoked the legendary smith Mamurius Veturius on 14 March, dressing a man in skins to represent him then beating him through the streets; he was called the Old Man and took on the qualities and function of a **scapegoat**.

Masks. The wearing of masks is a universal custom at festivals, especially those of a carnival nature. There are various reasons for the adoption of masks and their use is ambivalent; they both conceal and reveal. They conceal the everyday personality and reveal some other hidden attribute, for example they can depict the supernatural or natural forces of the deities, characters, or animals represented and make visible the inner characteristics normally hidden by the outward personality. They destroy identity and therefore protect their wearers from being recognized by evil powers. At festivals of the dead they can both protect against malignant ghosts and frighten evil spirits away, or they can, in masked processions, actually represent the souls of the dead. Since they destroy identity, masks remove all individual and social barriers, unifying, losing the wearer in a crowd and disguising the personal traits.

When the mask attaches its wearer to some particular character it can vary from the qualities of a divinity to the merely humorous; from the divine to the profane; from the tragic to the comic, as in Greek drama, in festival processions and the European Mumming plays. (See **Plays**.)

Animal and bird masks represent the early paradisal state when communion between gods, men and animals was natural, they can also denote the instinctual and intuitive animal wisdom from which man can learn, just as the shaman puts himself in touch with these forces when wearing animal guise and the Australian Aboriginal 'bush soul' masks identify the wearer with the power of the animal or bird represented. This also applies to the wooden masks of the South Sea Islanders, to the feathered head-dress of the Amerindians and to the masks used by African tribes, though in these African communities masks can symbolize and impart a power of their own.

Since the mask disguises the true nature, so unmasking reveals the

'The wearing of masks is a universal custom at festivals, especially those of
a carnival nature' (*Mary Evans Picture Library*)

real and the mask must ultimately be removed for the understanding
of the real nature. The soul must rid itself of all disguises before
attaining true knowledge. This shares the same symbolism as
removing garments to cast off disguises and outward forms which is
a feature of the **Mysteries**.

Matronalia (Ancient Roman). The Matronalia, on 1 March, gave female slaves the same liberties as the male slaves had at the **Saturnalia**. The matrons waited on them and served meals for them. Normal restrictions were relaxed and presents could be exchanged between married women and married men at that time. The festival was in honour of the goddess Juno.

Mayan. The calendar of 18 months of 20 days gave a five-day surplus which was *Uayeb* of the solar year; this is the Vague Year, since the solar year is actually a quarter-day more, which was ignored and not intercalated. The five-day surplus was used as a great festival. The ritual year, which had 20 weeks of 13 days each, was divided into four quarters, each being under the auspices of a different quarter of the heavens while each week was under the protection of a particular deity. This lunar, religious and sacred year had 260 days and the beginning of the solar and lunar years coincided every 13 years: an occasion for a great and solemn festival. The calendar was in the hands of the priesthood.

The ancient Mayan year had various feasts, starting about January with the feast of **Ocna** which was preceded by a fast and abstinences. It was dedicated to the Rain Gods and involved renewal rites and the making of new figures of the gods and all ceremonial utensils.

In March the **Fire Festival** was also concerned with rain gods and the ceremonies were performed by old men in honour of the old Itzamna, God of Fire and Life. Animals, both domestic and wild, were sacrificed and their hearts thrown on the fire which was later ritually extinguished with jars of water as rain magic. A terraced pyramid was built and priests painted the upper steps blue, as a sky and rain symbol, while the lower steps were covered with mud.

In April there was the great feast in honour of Ekchuah, God of Merchants, and Hobnil, God of the Beehives; it was a feast of the cacao crop and the traders dealing in it. A spotted dog, the colour of the cacao-pod, was sacrificed and blue iguanas, coloured feathers and incense were offered.

In May the festival of **Pacumchac** was in honour of the God of War. There was a five-night vigil at his temple during which the war chief sat on a throne and was venerated as a deity. War dances were performed and at the end of the five days there was a fire ceremony, with the sacrifice of a dog, its heart being offered to the god by being put in one bowl and covered by another, after which large jars of water were broken to pieces. The festival ended with a great banquet and much mead drinking. The banquet was repeated in the villages during the next few weeks.

July was a new year occasion, accompanied by all the spring-cleaning rites of sweeping temples, houses and streets and removing all old utensils and replacing them with new ones. Priests, who had

fasted, kindled the new fire in a brazier before the god, and incense was burned. Later, at the Feast of **Pocam**, instruments of every sort from the books of the priests to charms, weapons and fishing nets, were reconsecrated and painted blue.

September had the **Feast of the Beekeepers** who offered honey and incense to the god Hobnil. October was the time of the great ceremony of the god Kukulcan, the Feathered Snake, the counterpart of the Aztec Quetzalcoatl. November-December had the feast dedicated to the growth of the young and imparting power to them.

Today the ancient festivals are inextricably mixed with superimposed Christianity. The new year fiesta, on 14 March, another ancient Mayan 'New Year' (see **New Year**), still celebrates the **Day of the Bearers of the Year**.

The Dance of the Little Bulls has all the ingredients of a death-and-rebirth spring rite. The bull is killed and mourned, but a lively dance greets the return of spring — a typical pastoral allegory.

Other dances at festivals symbolize the animals of the ancient kingdom: the snake, crocodile, jaguar, monkey, deer and sloth, the **deer dance** conforming to the ritual pattern of hunter and hunted, the dancers dressed in skins, masks and feathers. The **snake dance**, executed with live snakes, imitates the movement and rattle of the snake. Clowning is a feature of the festival with the performers being mimicked and, like the hobby-horse in Europe, the crocodile figure snaps its jaws and threatens the crowd.

There is a **Boundary Festival** (see **Boundaries**) which follows the ancient pattern of ritual prayer and sacrifice. The statue of the village god or Christian saint is unlocked, displayed and venerated; turkeys or chickens are killed and pieces placed in two gourds while the remainder is burned with copal. At night one of the gourds is placed on the top of the highest hill, or on an altar, again with prayer. The coming of lizards to drink the blood is regarded as a good omen. The other gourd is taken to a sacred cave and placed by water. It is a good omen if the water takes the gourd and cleans it. There is a procession, led by prayer-makers, round the boundaries where there are permanent crosses as markers, at each of which prayers are said and offerings made.

The Day of the Caves has a Christian saint taking the place of the gods for whom the caves were sacred places. Offerings, or the ashes of offerings, are placed in the caves at an annual festival. There are other festivals such as the **Day of Rain-making**, to ensure adequate rains, and the **Sealing of the Frost** to prevent damage to the growing crops, about 1 April, when the crack in the rocks, in which the frost lives, is visited and a prayer-maker is lowered to the rockface to seal the frost in.

One festival, performed annually, dramatizes in dance the Spanish Conquest, with the invaders as bearded Spaniards or Moors. The

Spaniards are repeatedly overcome, but their final conquest is greeted with mournful music. There is a ceremony of prayer and flagellation before the dancing begins.

The Christian festivals of **Lent**, **Easter**, **All Souls** and **Christmas** are celebrated and the ancient Blessing of the Animals has been adopted by the Church. Judas is hanged on Maundy Thursday and the effigy is stuffed with gifts and festooned with fire-crackers which, when exploding, release the gifts to the children. Modern festivals have dancing, processions, clowning and singing. Saints are carried high in the streets, as were the ancient gods, the processions have all the usual features of music, lights, masks and fancy dress. Roasted meat takes the place of the ancient sacrifices.

May Day. Essentially a seasonal and floral festival concerned with the spring rebirth of vegetation after its death in winter. It is a festival of all things green in nature, associated with Maia, mother of Mercury, and Flora, goddess of flowers and spring, whose festival, the **Floralia**, was held at the end of April or the beginning of May; it was a pagan spring festival welcoming the season of warmth and growth. It was also connected with the **Fontinalia**, dedicated to the spirits of the reviving waters. Girls made garlands of corn or flowers to hang on doors, where they remained until replaced the following year, as in the Greek **Thargelia** and other earlier spring festivals.

Houses, byres and stables were decorated with hawthorn, rowan, fir or birch, or other apotropaic greenery, to keep evil or unlucky powers at bay. Flowers and garlands were also thrown into the waters and springs and wells were decorated, a custom which was carried over into Christian times in Europe, the wells being 'dressed' with elaborate symbolic patterns, such as the cross, a dove, or texts from the Bible. The previously accepted powers of healing waters were attributed to the saints in place of Celtic spirits of the sacred wells and springs. The custom of well-dressing still persists in parts of England and in Europe. Nearby bushes and trees are hung with ribbons or pieces of cloth, and a piece of a sick person's clothing hung there effects a cure.

The placing of apotropaic garlands or boughs of hawthorn, rowan, etc., on doors was to protect humans and animals against the powers at large on May Eve, it was a time when fairies and witches were active and it was also *Walpurgisnacht* (see **Witches**), the great festival of witches and warlocks. The burning of witches was also a feature of May Day and bonfires were lit to drive them off. Many of these fires were lit on the ancient pagan hill-tops and in some cases battles were fought for their possession, usually a contest between youths of neighbouring parishes — youths representing the virile powers of spring growth — or there were mock battles between the powers of winter and summer, good and evil, in which winter was defeated.

In the Isle of Man a battle is fought between the Queens of Winter and Summer with clubs of gorse. Summer is first captured, then released, and finally triumphs over Winter. Crosses made of rowan are placed in front of doors to repel evil or mischievous spirits; king-cups are spread on the stable floor for the same purpose. In Ireland the May Bush is placed over houses, byres and stables and bonfires are lit on May Eve. May Balls are made of gold and silver materials to represent the sun and moon. May Day is also a 'gale' day, with the contracts of tenancy and rents and the hiring of servants; there were hiring fairs in earlier times. It is also the day for turning cattle out to pasture: this is traditional in other parts as well.

May Eve was spent in the woods and on May Morning fresh green boughs were brought home, this being called 'bringing the summer home'. The great May Tree, usually represented by the maypole, was decorated with ribbons, garlands and a crown, and brought in in procession, with singing and dancing. There were, and still are, sports, racing to the maypole, and contests, the latter being formerly of archery. Arthur's Knights and Queen Guinevere went to the woods by Westminster; Henry VI and his Sheriffs and Aldermen of London dined in the Stepney woods and Henry VIII spent May Day with his Court in the woods at Greenwich.

May Day ceremonies formerly had a King and Queen of the May. In the *Book of the Universal Kirk* (1576) Robin Hood is called King of the May, probably with Maid Marian as queen. The King and Queen also represented the Sun God, the Sky Father, and the Earth Mother, necessary to give birth to the powers of nature. The orgies of earlier times and those reputed to take place in the woods on May Eve, encouraged these powers by sympathetic magic. The marriage of the King and Queen of May conformed to the ancient **Sacred Marriage** ritual which was widespread and involved not only sympathetic magic but also the almost universal belief in the inter-communication and bond between all living things.

The May Queen outlived the King of the May and reigned alone, seated on a flower-decked throne in a bower of greenery and flowers. Attendant children, forming her court, wore wreaths of flowers and carried garlands or cowslip balls. Maid Marian and Robin Hood still took part in the ceremonies as the **Green Man**, or Jack-in-the-Green, playing an essential role. Green, being the ritual colour of the May Day festivities, was worn by most of the characters; it is also the fairy colour. Sometimes the Green Man was a sweep, with a blackened face, 1 May being a sweeps' holiday. The May Queen now survives in a few rural and urban places, appearing in pageants and carnivals, but the occasion has lost its original religious and magical significance.

The Greek *eiresione* was the same as the May-branch of Europe; both were fertility symbols. The *eiresione* was of olive or laurel and

was decked with ribbons and fruits and carried in procession then fastened to the door of the house and left there until the next year.

In Scandinavia and Germany May trees were important to both people and cattle as fertility powers; the trees, or bushes, were set up at the doors of byres or stables, sometimes one for each animal, to bring fertility. The branch, or pole, is an embodiment of the tree-spirit of vegetation and its vital powers.

May Eve was also a time for venting public opinion. 'Birchers' went round from house to house leaving appropriate decorations on the doors — pear boughs for the well-liked and popular; plum for the glum; elder for the surly; thorns for the prickly types and those scorned; weeds for the unpopular and flowering gorse for ladies of easy virtue.

It should be borne in mind that before the reform of the calendar in 1752 May Day would occur 11 days later than today, i.e. in the present mid-May, a considerably warmer time.

There is now a modern political May Day and Bank Holiday. (See also **Beltane**.)

Maypole. The history of the maypole goes back to the Phrygian pine tree of Attis, taken in procession to the temple of Cybele; it was bound with strands of wool, then set up and danced around. The ceremony passed into the Roman **Hilaria** and hence to Europe.

The dance round the pole is depicted as a round dance (see **Dance**), with alternating male and female dancers, either holding hands, dancing singly, or chain-dancing. Dancing round is invariable and dancers go in and out from the centre to the circumference in a maze movement, but the plaiting of ribbons is not so uniform, though widely associated with maypoles.

The pole is phallic, with the discus at the top as the feminine symbol. It is also associated with 'guardian trees', which were trees standing alone in some central position and which were used as focal points for meetings, council and judgements.

The Puritan Stubbs gives an excellent, if disapproving, account of the maypole ceremony:

'They have twentie or fourtie yoke of oxen, every oxe having a sweet nosegaie of flowers tyed on the tippe of his horns, and these oxen drawe home this Maiepoole (this stinckying idoll rather) which is covered all over with flowers and herbes, bounde rounde about with stringes from toppe to bottome, and sometimes painted with variable colours, with two or three hundred men and women and children followyng it with greate devotion. And this being reared up, with handkerchiefs and flagges streaming on the toppe, they strawe the ground about, binde green boughs about it, sett up summer haules, bowers and arbours, hard by it. And then fall they to banquet and feast, to leape and daunce about it

as the Heathen people did at the dedication of their idolles, whereof this is a perfect patterne, or rather the thvng itself.'

After riots on May Day and the Puritan suppression of festivals, an Act of Parliament in England, in 1644, ordered maypoles to be dismantled. There was a partial revival after the Restoration.

The maypole was actually worshipped as the Irminsul (Great Pillar) in northern Germany. Earlier than the maypole, at the Celtic **Beltane**, a fire was sometimet lit under a sacred tree, or a pole was raised and decorated with greenery: this survived in the maypole and represented the spirit of vegetation. People dressed in green leaves to associate themselves with that spirit, which was also represented by the May King and Queen.

There is little evidence of ribbons being attached to the pole in England in the earlier days as the great height of the poles would preclude it. One pole, erected in London in the Strand after the Restoration, was 134 feet high and took 12 seamen to erect it; it lasted 50 years and was finally sold to Sir Isaac Newton for use with his great telescope. Ribbons were a later development with shorter poles. The custom of attaching ribbons was prevalent in southern Europe, with shorter poles, though these were not always maypoles but could be sacred trees, or *arbres d'honneur*.

Mazes. The treading of mazes was sometimes a feature of village festivals or fairs. The maze could be an open path or a labyrinth enclosed by hedges, or it could be the Troy dance (derived from 'trois' dance of nine steps). The symbolism varies from that of the course of the sun in its decline and increase, to the difficult passage through life to reach the sacred centre, to initiation and testing the spirit, or to a death and rebirth situation, entering the darkness and re-emerging into the light.

Midsummer. The summer solstice is one of the greatest of the fire festivals; the time when the sun turns from its summer might to its autumnal decline, the *Janua Inferni*. It is also the sun festival of Mithras, God of Light. Midsummer is the most magically powerful of all times; it is the high point of the powers of the little folk and the festival is fraught with magic and divination. Its customs are general — from Iceland and Scandinavia to the Mediterranean and all over Europe. Bonfires are lit to encourage the power of the sun; there are torch-bearing processions; the throwing of flaming discs in the air; rolling blazing wheels downhill; singing and dancing round the fire sun-wise.

Although these rites are in decline or have ceased altogether in most countries, they are still to be found in parts of Europe. In earlier times people leaped over, or through, the fires and it was believed that the higher the leaping, the higher the crops would grow. Cattle

were driven through the fires for purification and fumigation and fire
repelled the powers of evil. For this purpose people dancing round
the fires also wore garlands of apotropaic flowers which were mostly
yellow in colour to symbolize the sun. The fires were often lit on high
places.

Among the Celts midsummer was a Druidical festival and Baal-
fires were lit, especially in Brittany. In Norway fires were built on rafts
and allowed to drift down the fjords; in Sweden they were lit on hills
and at cross-roads and were called Baldur-fires or Baldur's Balefires,
but midsummer fires were rare in Scotland, occurring more at
Beltane. Brands were taken home from the bonfires to rekindle the
domestic fire and torches were taken over the fields and through the
orchards, or ashes were scattered on them.

With the rise of Christianity, midsummer festivities were
transferred to St John the Baptist's Day.

Midsummer festivals often had giants as a feature: France,
Flanders, Germany and Spain, had local carnivals in which giant
figures were carried and burned on midsummer fires. It was lucky to
get hold of a charred fragment.

In some parts of Europe there were rites similar to the barley flower-
pots, or statues, of Osiris and the Greek gardens of Adonis in having
a pot of corn grown in May, then taken in procession, to be broken
against the church door at midsummer.

Midsummer is a time for gathering magic plants; they should be
plucked fasting, before dawn, with the dew still on them. This belief
is not confined to Europe, but is also known in Morocco and among
the Ainus. Apotropaic flowers were worn as garlands, as well as
golden solar flowers such as St John's wort, mugwort, fern seed and
mistletoe.

The festivals of midsummer are concerned with both fire and
water, fire to keep alive the diminishing power of the sun, and water
in the ritual blessing of the wells and springs and in bathing in dew,
a sacred water, on midsummer's night or at dawn. (See also **Fire**;
Flowers; **Solstices**.)

Min (Ancient Egyptian). There was a time of enforced leisure while
the Nile was in flood: then came the preparations for the harvest and
the festival of Min, God of Fertility, also a sky and storm god,
associated with, and sometimes a form of, Horus. His ithyphallic
statue was carried in procession by priests and hidden under
decorative hangings and preceded by the Pharaoh and a white bull.
Priests and officials followed, carrying emblems, fans and parasols.
The heir-apparent accompanied them, escorted by soldiers. At the
shrine of the god there were offerings, libations and incense. The
statue was then carried out by the priests together with the Pharaoh
and his Queen. The procession made halts as it went along; dances

were performed and hymns sung. The Pharaoh wore the crowns of Upper and Lower Egypt. Arrows were symbolically loosed to the four quarters to destroy all enemies and four birds were released. The Pharaoh was given a copper sickle to reap the first sheaf of the harvest.

Month. Months are a conventional subdivision of the year originating in early time-reckoning by the **moon.** The present Roman month has nothing to do with the moon though it is fairly near it in duration. Months were often named after the festivals which occurred in them, or the work they brought, or weather conditions, or natural phenomena. The year contains more than 12 and fewer than 13 months; this variation makes **intercalation** necessary.

Moon. Time was first reckoned by the visible lunar changes and phases which were variously divided into either, four — the waxing, waning, full and death of the moon, or, more usually, three — waxing, waning and full, or sometimes only two — waxing and waning. The moon also controls the tides and the rhythms of nature, 'the whole ebb and flow control the rhythms of all bodies whatsoever', according to Apuleius. It revolves round the earth 12 times a year and a little more, thus it moves backwards in the zodiac more rapidly than the sun. The true lunar month is the interval between two new moons, an average of 29 days, 12 hours, 44 minutes, 2.98 seconds.

The arrival of the new moon and its completion at the full are greeted in many parts of the world as a festival occasion, from Buddhism to primitive tribes. The full moon is regarded as both a time of spiritual power and of danger, just as the lunar goddesses are both beneficent and baleful. Many of the full moon festivals involve singing and dancing, as among the Bushmen; in Burma all religious festivals take place at the full moon; the Ibo of Nigeria celebrate a children's festival at the new moon; in Australia, Tasmania and Oceania festivals begin either at the new or full moon. In Ancient Greece all festivals, except those dedicated to the sun god Apollo, were tied to the period around full moon. Strabo said that the Celts celebrated a feast in honour of an unknown god at the full moon and Tacitus said that the Germans regarded the new and full moons as the most auspicious times.

The moon gives it name to the '**month**'.

Moon Festival (Chinese). On the 15th of the eighth month there is a ceremony of viewing the harvest moon. The night is spent in moon-viewing parties, poems and songs being composed in praise of the moon by scholars, while among the populace there is feasting and music and a special dumpling is eaten and wine drunk. The festival

was also taken over into Japan. (See **Jugoya**.)

Mothering Sunday (Christian). A mid-Lent break in the austerities and an occasion for family reunions with children who are away from home returning with gifts and flowers for the mother. A special cake was baked, a custom which still survives in many places, the cake being known as a Simnel (Latin — *simila*, fine flour). Servants were allowed home to take their gifts. 'Mothering' referred not only to the home but to the faithful returning to their Mother Church. It is now celebrated with gifts, flowers and cards and in many places with special services in church. The festival has affinities with the Roman festival of **Cybele**, the Mother Goddess, held on the Ides of March; gifts were then taken to her temple.

Mountains. High places hold an important place in festival rites as, being nearer to the heavens and the divinities, they were regarded as points of concentrated power. Often they were the actual dwelling place of the deities, as in the case of the Mesopotamian High Places and the Greek Olympus. When there were no natural mountains, 'high places', such as the Babylonian *Ziggurat*, were often built as an abode for the deities and as a centre of worship. In Semitic religions there are references to 'high places' and the Central American civilizations also built temples as mountains.

Mourning. The rites of mourning at the death of the dying gods, such as Tammuz, Osiris, Attis, Dionysos, etc., had as their chief objective the disclaiming of responsibility for the death of the god. (See also **Lamentations**.)

Muharram (Islam). A 10-day festival among Shiah Muslims commemorating the martyrdom of Hussain, grandson of the Prophet; it takes its name from the first month of the Islamic calendar. The incident took place at Karbala and Shiah Muslims hold meetings and give addresses on the lives of the martyrs; they dress in black for mourning and hold assemblies on each of the first nine days during which orators tell of the history and death of Hussain and his followers. On the tenth day large processions parade the streets displaying banners and models of the mausoleum of Hussain and his people and chanting 'Ya Hussain' with wailing and scourging, symbolizing the sufferings of the martyrs. The procession often includes beautifully decorated horses. During the festival drinking posts are set up to dispense free water and fruit juices to all. For Sunnites the 10th of Muharram is celebrated as the day Noah left the Ark; it is also the first day of Adam and Eve after expulsion from Paradise.

Muktad (Zoroastrian). The last 10 days of the year are Days of the Dead, Days of Released Souls, an All Souls commemoration at which

departed spirits and their guardian *Fravashis* draw near this world and bring their blessings. The dead souls are welcomed back to their former homes with joyfulness to a place specially prepared for them, cleaned and decorated with fruit and flowers, and flower 'gardens' are arranged. Shining pitchers are placed on tables and a lamp burns constantly for the whole 10 days and nights. Lights are lit as a thanksgiving to Ormuzd, Lord of Wisdom. Specially prepared food is offered — bread and *mayazda* (a term later applied to milk) and *haoma*, the sacred drink — and presented before the sacred fire and drunk by the officiating priest. Priests conduct services and burn incense at the fire temples. The *Fravashis* are ritually bidden farewell before the dawn of **No Ruz** and by sunrise they have departed. The 10 days are devoted to acts of charity.

Mummers. See **Plays.**

Music. Most nations have responded to the power of music to induce moods and sway emotions by the cosmic creative sound; it has therefore been an essential part of many festivals, often accompanying the rhythmic ritual movement and dancing. The emotions are stimulated by chanting, singing and dancing, all of which enhance the communal nature of festivals.

Music, generally held to have been of divine origin, a gift from the gods, can induce reactions varying from quiet joy to ecstatic

Music is an essential part of any festival, not least to Morris dances

abandon, from pathos or mourning to the deep sense of mystery and devotional feeling or to war-like aggression, the whole gamut of human emotions being evoked in the music of festivals of one type or another. Music is also used in magic to release different energies.

The instruments used offer the same wide variety, from the mere rattle of sticks, clashing cymbals, the banging of drums or gongs and the ringing of bells, to the elaborate stringed and wind instruments. Certain deities had their own musical instruments as attributes: the sistrum of Isis, the Egyptian harp, Apollo's lyre, the pipes of Pan and the cymbals of Cybele which played an important part in their festivities.

So important was music in Chinese celebrations that all state functions were connected wth some particular tone, according to whether the rites were conducted by the Emperor, Empress or any official, and each month possessed its particular tone which controlled the music performed in that month. In India music has held a vital position since Vedic times, the power of sound being fully recognized and employed. 'The intoned formula is the pivot point of the whole elaborate structure of Vedic offerings and sacrifice.'

Music is forbidden in Islamic festivals, although verses may be recited like a plain chant and music is used by the Whirling Dervishes (see **Dance**).

Chanting is usually the function of priests or priestesses; hymns, on the other hand, are largely communal. Festival hymns, sung in honour of the deities, are often telling of divine exploits, and myths are sung at the deities' feast days. Singing and chanting can also take the form of incantations, thanksgiving, penitence and lamentations as rhythmic beating with drums, sticks or hands — this heightens the emotional response and introduces a magical element in ceremonies, especially when accompanying dancing. Musical instruments are often regarded as possessing their own magical or sacred properties.

Mysteries. A mystery is a sacred rite to which only initiates, those to be initiated, or people who have undergone special purification, are admitted. Representing the yearning for communion with the divinity, the mysteries played an important part and were associated with the earliest form of religious rites among the Egyptians, Greeks and neighbouring people, rites which were largely feminine cults connected with the Great Mother and her son, the Dying God, and with the underworld, death-and-rebirth and the fertility of the land, its people and their flocks. The mysteries were also tied to the belief in life after death and varied from simple efforts to ensure comfort in the next world to the elaborate esoteric rituals which united the devotees with their deities and made them immortal. The chief divinities concerned were not those of the Sky Gods and the Olympians, such as Zeus and Apollo, but the Earth Mothers: Isis,

Cybele, Demeter, etc., who, with their dying, suffering, saviour-god counterparts — who were later reborn — gave, by their death and resurrection, the pattern and assurance of rebirth. It has been said that the communion with some saving deity is the object of all practices of the mysteries, and these rites were held so sacred that even invaders and conquerors of the land left them inviolate.

As they were 'mysteries', revealed only to the chosen, and wholly esoteric in their early form, knowledge of their rituals is necessarily fragmentary, though archaeological excavations have since added to this knowledge. But the mysteries of Isis, Dionysos and those of Eleusis, became so popularized and famous that they developed into great festivals for the people in general, becoming less esoteric, losing their mystery, and finally becoming holidays open to all and later even to slaves.

Though originally guarded with great secrecy and punishable by death if revealed, it is now accepted that the rites had three elements: 1) the spoken word — the teaching given to the novice and ritual incantations; 2) symbolic things revealed — the ear of corn, phallic images, sacred stones (this drawing back of curtains to reveal the holy object occurs everywhere, from Egyptian and Greek Mysteries to the Hebrew Temple and the Catholic Sacrament); 3) things enacted — ritual drama, the descent into the underworld and the return to the light, the death and resurrection of the Dying God, the main theme being suffering then triumph, the suffering saviour and the suffering human soul, its tribulations and redemption, with the intiate living through the experience. There was also the acting out of the sacramental meal: cakes and barley-drink; milk and honey; bread and wine. The rites included purifications, ordeals, initiations and esoteric knowledge and the removing of garments to symbolize the casting off of disguise, outward forms and the old nature. Plotinus said: 'Just as those who penetrate into the innermost sanctuaries of the mysteries, after being first purified and divesting themselves of their garments, go forward naked, so must the soul continue . . .'

These rituals also trained the neophyte in the interpretation of myths, symbols and allegories of nature and her hidden powers, conditions and demands which were obscured from the general public. Sophocles said: 'Happy is he that has seen those rites ere he go beneath the earth; he knoweth life's consummation, he knoweth the god-given source.' The word 'theophiles' applied to the initiates implies that they stood in some special relationship with, and shared the friendship of, the deities and were beloved by them. The sex symbols were treated with religious awe as contributing to the idea of the continuing life of the person, tribe or race beyond the limits of the earthly life.

Apuleius, an initiate of the rites of Isis, gives an account of his initiation: he was dressed in a new garment, bade farewell to the

outer world, and was conducted by a priest into the inner temple where he 'approached the confines of death, and having trod the threshold of the Underworld, returned therefrom, being borne through all the elements. At midnight I saw the sun shining with all its brilliant light: I approached the presence of the Gods beneath and the Gods above, and stood near and worshipped them'. He was not allowed to disclose what happened through the night, but in the morning he 'came forth consecrated by being dressed in 12 stoles painted with the figures of animals' [probably the signs of the zodiac]. He then ascended a pulpit in the midst of the temple, carrying in his right hand a burning torch, while a chaplet encircled his head, 'from which palm-leaves projected like rays of light'. 'Thus arrayed like the Sun, and placed to resemble a statue, on a sudden the curtains being drawn aside, I was exposed to the gaze of the multitude. After this I celebrated the most joyful day of my initiation, as my natal day [second birth] and there was a joyous banquet and mirthful conversation.'

N

Naga Panchami (Hindu). On the fifth day after the full moon of *Asarha* (June-July) the Nagas, the sacred snakes, are propitiated. Offerings are placed at snake holes and no ploughing or digging is allowed on that day. Figures of serpents are painted on walls and visits are made to Naga temples.

Nemea (Ancient Greek). The Nemean festival, known to be established by 573 BC, celebrated in the sacred grove of Nemea, and later at Argos, was a traditional occasion, taking place in the second and fourth year of the Olympiad. The prize was a wreath of fresh celery leaves. There are various legends as to its origins, one being that it was one of the occasions founded by Heracles to celebrate the slaying of the Nemean Lion, and dedicated to Zeus and Heracles; another was that the games were a funeral commemoration for a child, Opheltes, swallowed by a serpent when his nurse left him in the grove. The games were more in line with the seriousness and strenuousness of the **Olympics** than with the carnival character of the **Isthmia**, though all festivals were sacred in nature, being associated with sacred groves, temples or mounds. The simple wreath prizes prevented commercialization. Officials wore dark robes to commemorate the funereal nature of the origins of the games.

New Fire. See **Fire**.

New Year. The New Year is a universal festival, celebrated the world over from the earliest times, though the date of the New Year varies from one land to another. It has no common universal position and can depend on a variety of conditions; any of the seasons can be chosen as the beginning of the year, or it may be determined by the position of the stars. The actual 'year' may have little reference to the calendar among primitive peoples with whom it depends largely on the food supply in crops, hunting and fishing; thus there can be several new years in the space of 12 months. This dependence on the harvest also applied to more advanced cultures, most of which celebrated the in-gathering with a festival, first imposing a taboo on

the new food until it had been ritually blessed and tasted, then feasting afterwards when the appropriate rites had been performed. As different crops were reaped at different seasons in diverse lands, the New Year varied accordingly. In many countries it began at the vernal equinox, with the renewal of life in spring and in Europe this remained so until the change to the Gregorian calendar (see **Calendar**) when the New Year was transferred to 1 January.

In Ancient Egypt the year was controlled by the flooding of the Nile; in Babylon it began in the month of *Nisan*, but the harvest was also taken as a turning point and another new year; in Greece it varied from one small state to another; in Rome a religious festival began the new year in March with the rebirth of life in spring, but 1 January was instituted as a civic date for the New Year from 153 BC; among the Celts the year began at Samhain, on the eve of 1 November; in China it was, and is, controlled by the first full moon, in February; India varies the New Year between the northern and southern regions; in Oceania and among the Amerindians the sidereal year is particularly prevalent. (See **Pleiades**.)

The New Year festival, probably the most significant in the calendar, is a re-enactment of the creation of the world; a ritual regeneration and re-creation. Time is abolished and starts again, pure and untarnished as it was at the beginning of sacred time. With the regeneration of the year goes that of the individual who also makes a fresh start, 'turns over a new leaf'. It is not a matter of restoration or rehabilitation but of a completely new beginning. On the material side it is also based on the idea that a good beginning makes a good ending: *'Anfang gut, alles gut.'* Plenty of everything sets the pattern for the coming year.

The central point of agriculture was the turn of the year, either at the winter solstice or the vernal equinox, and in earlier times cities were small enough to be in close touch with, and realize their dependence on, the food supplied by the country; indeed, towns were often little more than market centres for the convenience of the agriculturalist. Greek, Roman and medieval European towns had 'town-fields', the equivalent of the modern allotments, where citizen-farmers cultivated crops and grazed stock, so that all times of agricultural significance held little difference for both town and country and the critical turn of the year was equally vital for both; all were involved in the rites of the powers and divinities which would bring about new birth. This also applied to the temple communities who owned land which was worked as 'the fields of God' by the whole community.

The New Year has always been regarded as a critical time when unseen powers are at large and the dead return to their old haunts and all require either propitiation or expulsion, hence the change from the old to the new year is heralded by loud noise, the ringing

of bells, beating drums, cracking whips, rattling bamboo canes, letting off fireworks and sounding horns, all of which help to banish not only the forces of darkness, but also the old year and its evils. The forces of chaos must be defeated by the creative powers.

The New Year was also associated with gift-giving as a sign of plenty, branches of sacred trees were exchanged, or the Druidic mistletoe, and nuts and eggs were given as symbols of immortality, or money as wealth; these customs were later transferred to Christmas.

Mircea Eliade lists the essential rites of the end of the old year and the beginning of the new as: 1) purgations, purifications, confessing of sins, driving out demons, expulsion of evil; 2) the extinguishing and rekindling of all fires; 3) masked processions (with the masks representing the souls of the dead), the ceremonial reception of the dead who are entertained with banquets etc., then led back at the end of the feast to the borders of the territory, to the sea, or the river, or whatever it may be; 4) fights between two opposing teams. 5) an interlude of carnival, Saturnalia, reversal of the normal order, orgy.

In many parts New Year's Eve is the scene of the main festivities. See also **Calendar**.

New Year (Chinese). The spring, or New Year festival takes place early in February, at the first full moon. It is a time of merry-making,

The Manoeuvring of the Dragons: at the Chinese New Year two opposing dragons, made with a framework of bamboo covered with cloth, attempt to seize the ball (representing the moon) held by a man who endeavours to evade their jaws (*Mary Evans Picture Library*)

feasting and visiting friends. Houses are spring-cleaned, accounts are settled, business suspended, the paper gods of the door are renewed and strips of red paper printed with the characters for long life, health, wealth and happiness, together with spells to ward off evil spirits, are put on doorposts and in the house. Red, the luckiest of colours, is predominant in all decorations in the house. Offerings are made to the gods and ancestors, new clothes are worn, drums and cymbals are sounded, fireworks let off in the streets, fireworks and noise being essential in most Chinese festivals, originally intended to ward off evil powers. The festival ends with the **Feast of Lanterns**.

New Year (Japanese). There are two New Year festivals, the Greater and the Lesser, the former tied to the old Chinese calendar and observed three to seven days from the first of the first month. Best clothes are worn, ceremonial visits made and greetings exchanged; Shinto shrines are visited and prayers offered; traditional food and drink, spiced *saké* and soup with rice cakes are served in family circles; pine branches, which are ritually burnt at the end of the festival, are set up in gateways. The Lesser New Year, associated with agriculture, begins with prayers to the gods of the New Year for the coming months; agricultural rites are mimed in sympathetic magic, such as ritually breaking the ground and planting the rice seedlings, these being symbolized by straws, a rite which may be carried out in snow in Northern regions. A pine branch is set up as an abode of the God of the Rice Paddy and wine and cakes are offered there. In the home a tree is set up and decorated with rice cakes made in the shape of agricultural produce, such as silk-worm cocoons and farm tools, symbolizing prosperity and good fortune. There is also a bird scaring ritual, making gestures of driving off birds which would threaten the crops. In some parts the custom of entertaining strangers at the New Year takes the form of visits by young men, dressed as demons or monsters, who are regaled with food and *saké*; they drive off evil and bring good fortune. This last custom has affinities with **First Footing**.

New Year (Oceania). The New Year is marked by the appearance of the **Pleiades** and is greeted with dancing and singing. It is the time of **harvest** with the crops already gathered in and stored before replanting. In Hawaii the Pleiades appear in mid-October and herald the great festival of **makahki**, an occasion for religious and secular festivities and a time of truce.

New Year.
See also:
Anna Perenna — Ancient Roman.
Makara-sankranti — Hindu.
Maori.

Mars, Rites of — Ancient Roman.
Mayan.
No Ruz — Zoroastrian.
Samhain — Celtic.

No Ruz or **The Great Nawroz** (Zoroastrian). The festival celebrates the end of the old year and the beginning of the new; it is also the feast of Ahura Mazda, the Lord of Wisdom, or Ormuzd Day, a festival of joy. It is a renewal of creation, 'a new day, a new month of a new year'. 'All that time has worn out must be renewed'. Innumerable fires are lit and there are lights everywhere. There are purifications and libations which originally ensured rain for the coming year. The sowing of seven sorts of grain in jars to foretell the year's harvest, as well as the fate of humans, shows similarities with the Babylonian 'fixing of lots' and is still practised by Mandeans and Yzidis. The festival is a time for the reunion of families. New clothes are worn and there is the giving of presents with meals of special foods and wine. Services are held at the Fire Temple. Poor children are given presents, money, decorated eggs, fruit and nuts.

Nudity. Nakedness is a part of early festivals associated with fertility cults and nature magic, such as rain-making. It represents the natural state, paradise and innocence, and is also connected with creation, resurrection and rebirth. The figure of a nude woman represents the Tellus Mater, Dame Nature. Ritual nudity symbolizes the re-entry to paradise and into the state of timelessness. Taking off clothes at the **Mysteries** represented the casting off of disguise, outward forms and the old nature.

　It has been suggested that the Coventry Godiva legend is a vestige of the rites of the Great Mother, from which men were excluded. At the Olympic Games men were naked and women excluded. In many tribal societies children are naked until initiated into society.

Nursery Festival (Japanese). See **Rice Planting**.

O

Oceania. Months vary from one part to another, some having 12 and others 13 months, based on lunar phases, with a name for each phase. Feasts are associated with local customs and ceremonials which differ with the occasion, rather than adhering to recognized traditional festivals, and are dependent on a plentiful food supply which consists of anything available, from flesh and fish to any edible vegetable matter. Feasting is accompanied by the drinking of *kava* and the chewing of betel-nut in many parts.

Different foods appear at different times on islands and the festival time changes with them, being tied to the vagaries of the season and not to the calendar. Generally the 'ripening or consummation of the year' is a great feast and many of the people have a feast of **First Fruits**, preceded by a fast, then accompanied by spring-cleaning, new clothes and utensils, kindling of the new fire, and the cessation of war. The feasts are usually a three-day celebration with offerings to the gods and the chief. There are dances and stylized displays by men and women, with singing, drumming and mock ritual combat. Feasts are also largely concerned with the cult of the dead, fertility and abundance, and the rites associated with them.

Borneo has two great rice festivals, one of sowing and the other for the harvest, if successful; while southern Malaysia has three: transplanting, the formation of the seed heads, and the harvest. In some rice festivals there is a Rice King, elected for the duration, in the manner of the King of the Bean in Europe.

The appearance of the **Pleiades** controls the New Year and is greeted with singing and dancing. The great festival of **makahki**, in Hawaii, is also heralded by the Pleiades, which appear there in mid-October, it is a time for religious and secular festivities and a time of truce.

There are special customs and restrictions connected with feasts in many parts, for example, in Cambodia there are days of austerity and cessation of all business before a feast.

Festivals now vary widely under the influence of the religions of Hinduism, Buddhism, Christianity and Islam.

Ocna, Feast of. See **Mayan**.

October Horse (Ancient Roman). The festival of the October Horse was the last of the various harvest festivals, the most important of which was the feast of the divine pair *Consus and Ops*, on 21 and 25 August, a celebration concerned with the storing of produce. The season of both agriculture and arms lasted from mid-March to October; both were under Mars and both employed the horse. Weapons, brought out on 14 March, were put away on 15 October, and the occasion was marked by a two-horse chariot-race in the Campus Martinus. The near horse of the winning chariot was sacrificed to Mars; it was killed with his weapon, the spear; the head was cut off, decorated with cakes, and, with the tail, was taken to the sacred hearth of the Regia which was daubed with blood and then the blood of the horse was given to the **Vestal Virgins**. Or, when a king or ruler was the greatest landowner or farmer, the head might be carried to his house and fixed there. Sometimes rival communities fought for it and the winner carried it off in triumph as good luck and fertility.

The Greeks associated the horse sacrifice with Troy. The horse is both a fertility and corn-spirit symbol and as such it continues to be represented by the hobby-horse of European fêtes; it is also the Old Hob of English fairs and often accompanies dancers; it is seen again in the Schimmel, the white horse of Germany. In some parts the hobby-horse also cavorts round the maypole. There is also a harvest custom of taking some object, such as the head of a horse, sheaf of corn, corn dolly, etc., to fix in a prominent place to ensure fertility for the coming year.

Oiche Shamhna. See **Samhain**.

Olympics (Ancient Greek). The Olympics, the most famous of the games, were founded in the eighth century BC, abolished in AD 394, and revived in 1894. Pausanias said: 'We shall not find any games greater than the Olympic whereof to utter our voice.' Pindar maintained that the games were originally funereal, founded by Heracles, at the tomb of Pelops, a vague and unidentified cult-hero, to whom athletes first sacrificed at the games. This was in pre-Dorian times and the festival was local, but the Dorians brought the political order and stability necessary for the steady and wider development of the games. That Olympia was an ancient sacred place is shown by the existence of an earlier altar to Cronos, who preceded Zeus as a high god; also a priestess of Demeter held a high place of honour at the stadium, though women were excluded from competing there.

Although some 10 miles from the sea, Olympia was accessible to the people of the colonies of Sicily and Italy, and there were traditions which associated the Cretans and Phoenicians with Olympia.

Plan of Olympia, the ancient sacred place which played host to the Olympics.

Tradition said that Heracles brought the olive from the land of the Hyperboreans and established the sacred olive grove at Olympia; another tradition maintained that the Delphic Oracle was instrumental in restoring the games after a time of feud and strife and disruption, re-establishing unity and amity. Others said that the games were founded by Oxylus and later re-established by Lycurgus, but this is denied by Xenophon.

The festival took place every fourth year, at the second or third full moon after the summer solstice (approximately August-September) and lasted for five days. There were classes for men, youths and boys. During the games a truce was declared and no one might bear arms within the sacred precincts. Everyone travelling to the Olympics was regarded as under the protection of Zeus; any violation was met with a heavy fine. Competitors had to be of pure Greek blood and not polluted by manslaughter or non-payment of fines due. Men competed naked and women could neither compete nor be present, though they could enter their horses for the chariot-races. However, they had their own festival at Olympia, the **Heraea**.

Athletic records exist for the Olympics from 776 BC and from the twenty-eighth Olympiad onwards a list of winners was recorded. This list later became a means of reckoning dates and, though the Olympics were sometimes interrupted, gave a valuable record of the development of the festival which, only a century after its inception, was attended by people from the whole of Greece and the Eastern

and Western colonies. One entry from them was Pythagoras, from Samos; he had long hair and looked so effeminate that he was rejected for the boys' boxing as too weakly, so he entered for the men's event and won it. The Olympics became a general meeting place and helped to build Hellenic unity and identity. The growth and success of the Olympics inspired the founding of other festivals at Delphi, Nemea and the Isthmus, which, from a local start, became Panhellenic. The other festivals were held in the years between the Olympiad; even years had two festivals, odd years only one, they were:

Olympia	—	late summer
Nemea	—	summer
Isthmia	—	spring
Pythia	—	August
Nemea	—	summer
Isthmia	—	spring
Olympia	—	late summer

After the Roman conquest the Olympics were at first still Hellenic, but had become professional. Later, Julius Caesar inaugurated dramatic and musical performances in which some patrician Romans took part. With the increasing Roman influence the more brutal aspects of their sports found an outlet in introducing gladiatorial shows into Greece and the East and the later Olympics were no longer Hellenic but both competitors and spectators were gathered 'from the inhabited world'. The influences were, however, two-way in that the conquest ultimately Hellenized the Roman outlook and their festivals were largely inherited from Greece, though by then degeneration had set in and produced 'a class of useless athletes and an unathletic nation of spectators'. Bribery also entered the decadent stage and caused a boycott of the Olympics on one occasion.

Prizes at the great games festivals were not only given at the actual competition and victory, but the victor's home state was also announced and basked in reflected glory. They often gave rewards to the returning hero and the populace turned out to welcome him and conduct him in triumph through the streets; songs were composed in his honour and sung in front of his house and at the temple; often a statue was set up. In some cases he had a front seat reserved for him at all public events, was given free meals and, later, lived tax-free. He was virtually worshipped, one such athlete — a boxer who won three successive Olympiads — being actually worshipped in his lifetime, but this was going too far for the gods and his statues were all struck by lightning in different places at the same moment.

Local celebrations also took place in addition to the four great athletic festivals. Various competitions were held at these and rich prizes and money were given; some were purely artistic, others athletic, but all were largely associated with some local cult-hero and

showed ritualistic characteristics, such as the torch races which were symbolic of the kindling of the new sacred fire on religiously significant occasions. These local events provided good training and fostering of local talent in preparation for the great festivals, while money prizes enabled the competitors to enter for the bigger events.

Omisoka (Japanese). A New Year's Eve festival at which temple bells are rung 108 times (a Buddhist sacred number) at midnight. Presents, or tokens of gratitude, are given to people to whom one owes obligations.

Optet (Ancient Egyptian). The Feast of Optet, in honour of Amon, took place at Karnak and lasted about 24 days. There was a trinity of Amon, Mut and their son Khonsu, to whom food and drink were offered. The boat of the god, coming down the flooded Nile bringing the life-giving waters, was represented at his shrine. Each of the trinity had a boat, Amon's adorned with rams' heads fore and aft; Mut's with female heads and a vulture skin, while Khonsu's had falcons' heads. The shrine-boats were carried in procession to the river, followed by the Pharaoh and musicians, here they were placed on a large decorated boat constructed to look like a temple, about 60 to 70 feet in length. This was towed by soldiers to the main river where it was taken over by rowing boats and taken down to Luxor. The entire festival was celebrated by the populace who joined in with the chanting priests and the dancing sistra-rattling priestesses. It was an occasion of tremendous feasting and drinking. At the end of the festivities the boats and shrines were taken back to Karnak.

Orgy. When it occurs in festivals orgy represents a destruction of identity, it limits time and is a regression into chaos and the darkness of the womb before rebirth and is thus associated with the seasonal festivals of death of the old states and birth of the new. Orgies were also used in sympathetic magic to encourage the forces of nature and fertility; they also represent the union of the Sky God with the Earth Mother and are prevalent especially at spring and May Day festivals and at the winter solstice Twelve Days of Chaos, when the sun is reborn and life begins again with the New Year.

Osiris (Ancient Egyptian). The Entry of Osiris into the Moon is a festival of the new moon which was held at the vernal equinox. Plutarch said that Osiris was the power and influence of the moon. At the new and full moons of each month the specially appointed priest of 'the Golden House' dressed and decorated the statue of Osiris in the sacred robes and ornaments of the god. The new moon was the occasion of festivals of rejoicing in Egypt, a legacy of this still continuing today in the veneration of the new moon among African tribes, making it a festive time of singing and dancing, though in some places it is welcomed in solemn silence.

Oxherd and Weaving Maiden (Chinese). On the seventh day of the seventh month there was a festival based on an ancient legend in which two lovers, separated by a fast-flowing river in life, in desperation plunged into the waters and were drowned. In sympathy the gods made them immortal and transformed them into two stars shining on either side of the Heavenly River, the Milky Way, but they are allowed to meet and become one on the seventh night of the seventh moon. Women then went out of doors, with needles with seven holes, to thread melon seeds. The needles were of silver and gold, yin and yang, and the women prayed to the Two Stars for skill in weaving and sewing. Feasts were held, poetry recited and the legend told; bamboo grass and strips of coloured paper inscribed with poems were hung on houses. The festival was carried over to Japan as the **Tanabata**.

P

Pacumchac. See **Mayan**.

Palm Sunday (Christian). The Feast of Palms, observed from the fifth century, is the first day of Holy Week and commemorates the triumphal entry into Jerusalem of the Messiah-King, riding on an ass, symbolizing humility. (Zachariah. 9.9) Palms are blessed in churches and carried in procession. In some places the figure of Christ on an ass used to be carried in the procession and flowers strewn on the way. There are striking analogies between the Palm Sunday processions and rites with those in honour of Osiris in Egypt; both followed the pattern of divine epiphany and triumphal procession, with remarkable similarity in the ritual acclamations and invocations of both Osiris and Christ. The processions also had their parallel in the earlier *Peregrinatio* of Silva and Etheria. Palms were strewn in front of Roman heroes.

Panathenia (Ancient Greek). A local, political Athenian festival was celebrated in July-August, the first month called *Hecatombaion*, for the birthday of Athena, at a time when rain was needed. There were musical competitions, recitations, athletics, horse and chariot-racing, boxing, wrestling, gymnastics and dancing, but unlike other athletic festivals which awarded garlands to victors, the Panathenic games had prizes of value and religious significance, such as jars of oil from the sacred olive groves of Attica, these were the Panathenic amphora; gilded crowns and money were given for musical prizes. There were elaborate torchlight processions, the central event being the procession to the Temple of Athena on the Acropolis; there was also a Pyrrhic dance (see **Dance**) performed in full armour, as the procession had a large military element. A bough, cut from the sacred olive tree at Athens, was festooned with ribbons and hung with fruits and cakes and was carried by a boy, and boys also carried laurel boughs.

Every fifth year a new robe, or *peplos*, was woven by aristocratic maidens for Athena; the robe was of bright colours and carried in procession. The festival was a joyous one and there was also a regatta

Horsemen in the Panathenaic procession, depicted on the west frieze of the Parthenon, *c.*440 BC (*British Museum*)

and beauty competitions — one for 'handsome old men' — and jugglers and side-shows amused the crowds. Every fourth year there was a Great Panathenia. The festival, though local, was attended by people from other parts and the colonies.

Parentalia (Ancient Roman). 13 February began the festival of the dead which continued until the **Feralia** on the 21st. The Roman dead were buried in family tombs, usually with gardens cultivated on them and roses planted as symbols of spring and resurrection. On anniversaries and at festivals the graves were inspected and a feast held there with offerings of flowers, water, wine, oil, milk and honey. The Parentalia was a state repetition of the more private family rites of the **Lemuria**, but also an occasion for family reunions. Temples were closed and altar fires extinguished and emphasis was laid on family tombs and love-feasts, all the family being present except those guilty of crimes. February, as a time of purification, was also the occasion for spring-cleaning and instruments of purification were designated as *februa*, or purifiers. As an unlucky month, associated with the dead, no marriages took place.

Parilia (Ancient Roman). The Shepherds' festival, the Parilia, took place on 21 April, and was celebrated both on farms and in the cities. Ovid refers to it as both a rural and urban festivity. He writes of it, in its rustic setting, as the shepherd at dawn purifying his full-fed sheep by sprinkling them and adorning them and the folds 'with leaves and boughs fastened to them and a long wreath decks and covers the door'. There was also a purification by fumigation with

sulphur and ashes from the head and tail of the sacrificed October Horse and beanstalks, with a ceremony of leaping through the fire and driving the flocks through it to rid them of any impurity and to avert evil influences. The bonfire had olive, pine and savine thrown on it. The shepherd then asked pardon for any trespass by him or his flocks on holy ground or graves. Cakes were baked for Pales, Queen of Shepherds (Pales can appear as either feminine or masculine); there were offerings of milk and millet and a feast followed.

Parsee. See **Zoroastrian**.

Paryushana-Parva or **Pajjusana** (Jain). Celebrated on the 12th day of the waning moon of *Shravana* (August), the festival is the most sacred time in the religious year and the longest lasting, the others being only a day long. All observe the solemn fast at a time when Mahavira said: 'a month and 20 nights of the rainy season had elapsed': a suitable occasion after the restrictions of the rainy season, both for the itinerant monks and a time of greater freedom and less stress for the laity and for conducting business. The festival lasts a week for the *Shvetambara*, and, starting in the following week, for the *Digambaras*. It is a period of restraint and fasting and visiting temples or monasteries, and on the last day all sects join in the fast and ceremonies of confession; no work is done and schools are closed while in the evening all assemble at the local temples for public confession. No conflicts may be carried over and even distant friends and relatives must be contacted to ask for forgiveness.

Passover *Pesach* (Hebrew). The Passover, or *Pesach*, begins on the eve of the 15th of *Nisan* (March-April) at the first moon of the vernal equinox; it is also known as 'The Season of Our Freedom'. The festival is one of seven days for the Reform and Israeli Jews and of eight days for the Orthodox and Conservative Jews. It is one of the pilgrim festivals. It is a spring festival, both solar and lunar and originally both pastoral and agricultural, at a time when lambs had been born and the crops were ripening. It commemorated the Exodus from Egypt (Exodus 12) and the 'passing over' of the first-born of the Jews when those of Egypt were slain. The festival was preceded by a fast for first-born males, but this was later changed to a ritual meal. There are **spring-cleaning** rites before the Passover. The occasion is combined with the **Feast of Unleavened Bread**, during which no leavened bread may be eaten. Earlier, the umblemished paschal lamb was sacrificed and its blood smeared on lintels: a widespread rite for keeping evil powers at bay and also symbolic of entrance to the new life at the beginning of the **New Year**; the sacrifice was also associated with that of the first-born. The whole festival should be symbolically carried out in haste, with loins girded and staff in hand (Numbers 28: 16-25. Exodus 23:15 and 34:18).

The Passover became more of a household festival after the Exile. On the first night there is a family gathering for a ritual meal, at which the *seder*, 'order', is used. There are various rites of ablution, eating and drinking and the sacrificial lamb is represented by a burnt shank bone. On the second night the *omer* period begins (Leviticus 23:15), a time of counting of 49 days until **Pentecost** begins on the 15th. The *seder*, on the first two nights of the festival is now a central part of the Passover; it takes the place of the sacrifice of the lamb and conforms to the biblical command to retell the events connected with the birth of the Hebrew nation. The *Haggadah*, 'narrated', which is read together, tells the story of the Exodus and also contains psalms, blessings and the Four Questions. There are also special synagogue observances which include prayers and readings concerned with the Passover and dealing with such themes as the Exodus, deliverance, sacrifice, the covenant, the birth of the nation and the Messianic hopes.

Pateti (Zoroastrian). The important festival of Pateti occurs in the month of *Farvardin* and honours the last king of the Sassanians since their calendar was instituted in his time. At one time it was the occasion for worship at the Fire Temple, fire being the symbol of God; it is now a great social affair. Getting up early, the people worship at the Temple after performing ablutions and prayers and putting on new clothes. Following worship, there is a general exchange of visits to friends and relations, joining hands and expressing good wishes. Alms are given to the poor and servants get new clothes. There are other feasts at the equinoxes which are consecrated to Mithra; and also those on the days of the new and full moons. There are also festivals of angels, in one of which the Guardian Angel of Souls is venerated and there are special ceremonies at the Towers of Silence, associated with the dead.

Patterns or **Patrons**. A specifically Irish form of pilgrimage is that of the Patterns, celebrating the day of a patron saint. Starting at the shrine, or well, devotions are performed and the shrine or holy well is ritually circumnavigated sun-wise and some token is left there. A feature of most of these gatherings is to go to some high place where there is dancing, games and trials of strength and general merrymaking, with bonfires lit in the evening, races run round them, and people jumping over them. The most famous is that in honour of St Patrick, known as *Croagh Patrick*, held on the Reek in County Mayo, where the saint fasted for 40 days and nights. Patterns are also held on the festivals of the **Virgin Mary**.

Pavarana (Buddhist). See **Vassa**.

Peach Blossom Festival (Japanese). See **Dolls Festival**.

Pentecost or the Feast of Weeks. *Shavuot* (Hebrew). Occurs on the sixth day of *Sivan* (May-June) and 50 days after **Passover**. It is a **first fruits** and **harvest** festival (Exodus 23:16) for the ingathering of the barley and fruits, offerings of which are taken to the temple. The festival is also associated with the Covenant on Mount Sinai, the synagogue being decorated with greenery symbolizing that of the Mount. The Ten Commandments and the Book of Ruth are read. Special dairy foods are eaten and the wheat harvest is also commemorated. It is a two-day festival for Orthodox Jews and a one-day for Reform and Israeli Jews, who have made the festival a Confirmation occasion for boys and girls, supplementing the *Bar Mitzvah* or *Bat Mitzvah*. After Pentecost comes a period of ritual mourning and fasting in remembrance of the destruction of the temple, in the month of *Tammuz* (June-July). Weddings are not celebrated during this time and there are special prayers and lamentations. It is one of the pilgrim festivals. See also **Whitsuntide**, Christian.

Phoenician. See **Canaanite**.

Phrygian. Phrygian religion had its **Mysteries** requiring initiatory rites and only those who had passed the tests were admitted. Demosthenes said that the rites were conducted mainly by a priestess, while a priest read from, and recited, the sacred texts. The Phrygian Mysteries were those of a largely pastoral people, while those of the Greeks were based on agriculture and when the cult of Attis-Cybele passed over to Greece it was suitably adapted.

At the vernal equinox there were ceremonies of fasting and austerities; the reversal of normal roles; license and transvestism and the reception of the newly initiated. The **Sacred Marriage** of Attis and Cybele/Rhea was celebrated underground, an all-night vigil preceded the day of the equinox when Attis, a dying god, rose triumphant, having been found by Cybele. The festival included a dramatic representation of the finding of Attis and there was a communal meal with drinking from the common cup, a rite seen later at the Greek **Anthesteria** and the 'Cups', and found widely in sacramental feasts.

At the autumn festival Attis was emasculated and there were savage orgies; followers often emasculated themselves. Attis died by a pine tree and at his festival on 25 December the pine tree was hung with presents for the God, it was swathed with fillets of wool and garlanded with violets, symbolic of his death and the death of vegetation. This pine later passed over into Europe via Germany to become the Christmas tree of Christianity. The dead god was mourned with frenzied cries, shrill music and flagellations. Plutarch said: 'The Phrygians think that in the winter the God is asleep, and that in the summer he is awake, and they celebrate to him revels, which in winter are Going to Sleep, and in the summer Waking Up.'

The cult of Attis was carried over into Greece and later, through the Punic Wars, to Rome and there was adapted to the March festivals, depicting the death and finding of Attis, at the **Hilaria**. The Roman conquests took the cult into Germany.

Pilgrimage. In all religions, and frequently in association with some festival, journeys are undertaken to sacred places such as shrines; the tombs of founders of religions, or saints; places containing or associated with a holy relic; sacred rivers or wells, etc., with the object of obtaining some sort of benefit, either spiritual or material; or in healing; or gaining merit, certain places being famous for particular benefits, such as the Hindu bathing in the Ganges to wash away sins and obtain a better incarnation, or the Christian healing at Lourdes.

Pilgrimage has been practised from early times; Babylonians and Assyrians not only made pilgrimages to certain cities and shrines, but their deities went on pilgrimage from place to place to receive homage. Hinduism, Buddhism and Christianity all set store by pilgrimages and in the Arab world the **Hajj** and pilgrimage to the Ka'aba were known before Islam.

Pilgrimages could cover vast distances and occupy years in time, as in the case of Chinese pilgrims to India to visit the sacred places of Buddhism, one such lasting 16 years and resulting in bringing the *Sutras* to China; or such prolonged journeys as those undertaken by Northern Christians to the Holy Land. More than one religion could be involved in some sacred place, for example Glastonbury, where Celtic and Christian interests were combined.

Pilgrimages are often accompanied by austerities other than the rigours of the journey. A pilgrimage could also be initiatory in character.

At religious festivals going on pilgrimage forms a bond between otherwise disparate peoples, elements and classes, festivals normally being only a community or tribal affair.

Plants. See **Flowers**.

Plays. The original function of drama was not to entertain but to give form to the cultural rites and religious ritual; it was at first liturgical, controlled by priests or monks. When, in the course of time, it became popularized it thus embodied both sacred and secular, pagan and Christian themes. Some form of sacred drama was included in most festivals, depicting events in the life of the deity or cultural hero. In the **Mysteries** the central act was dramatized and plays were a feature of all Dionysian festivals. Egyptian drama achieved the effect of the ascent of Osiris by setting up a ladder and the early dramas passed on their themes to Christianity and medieval Europe. Horus striking the crocodile and Apollo killing the Python are reflected in St George and the Dragon. Osiris, killed by

Set, is avenged by his posthumous son, and is seen again in the Irish Balor (Cronos) who kills his son-in-law but is slain by his grandson.

Many plays represented the winter-spring combat; sometimes the two could fight for a woman, but more usually spring killed winter, though it could be slain first then revived and brought back as a young boy who then slew winter, this version possibly being derived from the Oedipus myth, in which he slays his father and marries his mother, the Earth.

In the new year and spring dramas there is always the age-old struggle between life and death, light and darkness, which occurs from Babylonian, Greek and Roman times to Christian morality and mummers' plays. The sequence is one of birth, growth, marriage, defeat and death, followed by victory and resurrection — a ritual pattern. Both ancient and later plays conform to much the same plan: there is an old, unmarried woman, the old Earth Mother, often known as 'Babo', with her seven-month illegitimate wonder-child carried in a cradle (the Dionysian spring festival *liknon*) who grows rapidly to adulthood (the wonder-hero) and demands a wife (the union of heaven and earth); he is confronted by an adversary who kills him, but the doctor restores him to life. There are local and national variations, but the theme is always that of birth-death-rebirth.

In the Christian mystery and morality plays virtues and morals were inculcated. There were also the Creation, or Adam, plays and special dramas for the Nativity, the Passion, Easter and Corpus Christi. Many of the plays introduced a large element of buffoonery and farce, characteristics from earlier times, since pagan festivals were used for relief of the emotions after times of tension or seasons of hard work. In both pagan and later times the plays gradually passed out of the hands of the priesthood or clergy and churches and became secularized, controlled by the laity and performed in market places and halls instead of temples and churches.

Miracle, mystery or morality plays were associated with church festivals and gave a dramatic portrayal of Christian myth and the stories of the saints; they appeared first in France about the twelfth century. God and the Devil represented the conflict between good and evil and the plays embraced such themes as the Creation, Adam and Eve, the Resurrection and Judgement. Survivals of these are seen in children's school plays at Christmas and Passion Plays at Oberammergau and elsewhere. The Miracle Plays were acted on movable stages and taken to fairs and festivals, the stage being normally in two tiers, the lower curtained and used as a dressing room, the upper visible above the crowd, while the stage for Passion Plays was provided with three storeys representing Heaven, Earth and Hell, all connected so that God and his angels could descend to earth and souls ascend to Heaven or descend to Hell and the devil and his

Bessey and the Doctor in a Mummers' play

minions could visit the earth. Plays were often performed by the
Guilds, taking appropriate themes, e.g. Water-carriers, the Flood;
Bakers, the Last Supper.

Mummers' plays were, and still are in some parts, based on the
struggle between good and evil, light and darkness, summer and
winter, the old and the new year, the one being represented by St
George, or King George, the other by the Turkish Knight, the Black
Morocco Dog, the Black Prince, or any other locally disliked character. Yet another name was the Bold Slasher who also appeared in
other plays and could take the place of the Dragon in plays featuring
St George since sometimes the travelling wagons were too small for
the transport of a dragon. St George is largely oriental in origin and
was introduced from the Crusades; the Dragon is the hardness of the
earth in winter 'his skin more hard than brass was found', or 'his skin
more hard ase eni brass, his brest was hard ase eni ston'. The plays
were usually introduced by Father Christmas, or Beelzebub, or Molly
(a man dressed as a woman) or Old Bet, Bessey, or Dame Dorrity.
The Fool is always present, sometimes called Tommy, and can appear
in an animal skin or wearing a fox tail, a feature reminiscent of the
masks and transvestism of the Roman **Calends**.

While there are many local variations of characters the theme remains the same: the hero fights the villain and is either immediately victorious or is killed then brought to life again by the doctor who gives a life-restoring pill. The fight then continues and the hero is victorious. In other cases the fight can be between two groups, one dressed in furs as winter and the other in green leaves as spring. Additional characters are the Bungler and Toss Pot, or Happy Jack, and a melancholy man in tattered clothes. The plays are in rhyme and introduce popular songs with endless foolery and complete abandon. Mummers were also known as 'Guisers'. If played at **Christmas** Father Christmas is also present. The costumes adopted are made from long strips of paper and the head-dress completely hides the face, or, for the characters, masks were worn as 'they mustn't know who I be'. The plays have all the characteristics of the Dying God,

'Dame Jane, Bessey, or Bet, with a baby in her arms . . .'

slain and revived again.

The Plough Play, on **Plough Monday**, the first Monday after Twelfth Night, and the beginning of the agricultural year, follows the death-and-rebirth pattern of most spring dramas, earlier seen in Greece in connection with the **Mysteries**. The chief characters are, again, an old woman, Dame Jane, Bessey, or Bet, with a baby in her arms; the fool; sometimes a sergeant and a recruit, together with farm characters dressed in smocks. Often there is a hobby-horse and there can be a doctor, but in the Plough Play the slain man can revive on his own. The child is thrust at the fool who is told that it is his, this he denies. The child is the Mystery Hero of unknown origins; he grows rapidly and demands a bride and the subsequent marriage brings about the birth of the next king, the spring god born of the **Sacred Marriage**. The sword dance is often performed within the play, pointing to its original agricultural connections with Mars as both god of war and of agriculture. The play reflects magical spring rites throughout. The fool's bladder, or whip, with which he 'whiffles' takes the place of the fertility whipping of the Roman **Lupercalia**.

In Ireland, at Christmas, waits went from house to house with a Charley, 12 young blacks and a piper. There were Mummers' Plays in which St Patrick could take the place of St George.

Pleiades. The constellation of the Pleiades is an easily-recognized group of stars whose rising and disappearance coincides with important phases of climate and vegetation, thus marking the time of the rhythms of nature. The rising of stars was a means of correcting the monthly-yearly calculations among people without astrological knowledge and other methods of time-calculation and the Pleiades became the principal constellation so used; others were Orion, the Great Bear, Sirius and the Pole Star.

In ancient times the Pleiades were associated with the annual Babylonion floods which occurred at the time when they were visible. They were also widely connected with seed-time and harvest. Hesiod said: 'When the Pleiades, Atlas' daughters, start to rise again begin your harvest; plough when they go down. For 40 days and nights they hide themselves . . . and fittingly the old year dies.'

In many parts of South America the word for Pleiades and the year is the same since they coincide with the revival of nature. The rising of the constellation determined planting times in Brazil and the Amazon; the Blackfoot Indians regulate feasts by it and the Arizona Indians reckon time by it for a sacred nocturnal rite; it brings spring in Paraguay, appearing in May, and is associated with fertility and festivals.

In Central and South Africa the appearance of the Pleiades is the time for cultivating fields and the season of planting and is celebrated

with feasting, dancing and singing.

Throughout **Oceania** the new year is marked by the coming of the Pleiades and is greeted by festivals, singing and dancing; a time of sowing and feasting. In the New Hebrides it is the harvest sign for the collecting of the turtle eggs and a harvest festival; among others, such as the Dyaks, it determines the time for rice-planting.

Plough Monday. On the first Monday after the Christmas festivities ended at Twelfth Night, work began again in earlier times. The plough was beribboned and decorated and called the Fool Plough, while the ploughmen dragging it were called Plough Bullocks, Plough Stots or Jags. Farm hands followed; wearing their shirts over their jackets they were led by one disguised as an old woman, Bessy, Betty or Bet, and accompanied by a fool, often dressed in calf-skin and carrying a jester's bladder. The sword dance (see **Dance**) was a characteristic of the rites, indicating its original agricultural affinities. Bessy was sometimes Queen of the Feast which was also called Rock Monday or Distaff Day (Rock = Distaff), since as men resumed their agricultural work that day so did women return to the distaff. The ceremonies had Dionysian and Eleusinian affinities shown in the new year and spring plays (see **Plays**) performed at that time. In Europe ploughs were placed on the ship-cart of Nerthus, the Teutonic Earth Mother, or a wooden ship could take the place of the plough. The ship was also, in ancient Egyptian times, the Ship of Isis, Great Mother, Goddess of Fertility, when she searched for Osiris. In parts of Austria the plough was dragged along the boundaries and landmarks in spring.

Pocam. See **Mayan**.

Pongal (Hindu). The southern Indian New Year festival is celebrated on the first day of the Tamil year and is a sun festival of the winter solstice when the sun turns North again. The previous month, *Poh*, is unlucky so there is general rejoicing at its ending and the new beginning. Preceding the festival, offerings are made to Siva and each morning women clear a space and decorate it with flowers and balls of cow dung decorated with citrus; these are renewed daily and kept until the last day of *Poh* when they are discarded amid rejoicing and the clapping of hands. Visits and presents are exchanged and amusements provided. Married women bathe fully clothed and emerge to start boiling rice with milk; when it is ready they call 'pongal' (boiling) and offer some at the shrine; some of it is given to the cows and then there is a general distribution. More visiting takes place and the ritual question is asked: 'Has the rice boiled?' and is answered by 'It has boiled.' Cattle are sprinkled three times with water from a vat containing saffron, seeds and leaves and are then decorated with garlands and their horns painted. Prostrations are made to the four

quarters in front of the cattle who are also decorated with fruit and cakes which, when they fall off, are scrambled for and eaten. The cattle are then driven out to graze where they please, accompanied by crowds, noisy music and feasting.

Potlatch. See **Amerindian, North**.

Processions. Processions have always been a feature of most festivals, from ancient times to the present day and from primitive to cultured societies. They form a collective act of worship, homage or tribute to some divinity or hero and unite individuals by incorporating them in a social function. Sacred objects were carried in processions at festivals, some of which were only seen by the populace on these occasions and this custom is still seen in association with the major religions. Sacrifices were also accompanied by processions; processions were staged for victory celebrations, though on the other hand, processions often escorted criminals to execution. There was also a magical element involved, processions round a particular place or sacred object enclosed it in the magic circle and so protected it, and in times of crisis special processions were staged to avert plagues or frighten away evil powers. Processions round either rural or urban areas defined boundaries in the days before maps existed. Processions are an essential feature of all festivals involving **carnivals**.

Puppets. A puppet was often used as a substitute for a sacrificial victim at festivals. The Vestal Virgins threw puppets into the Tiber at the **Vestalia**; they were bound hand and foot and thrown off the sacred bridge. Puppets were frequently thrown into the sacred waters or the sea, for example, in Russia, a figure in female dress was carried on a bier to the edge of a lake or river, torn to pieces and thrown in, while the onlookers simulated mourning and grief. This custom was also present at purification rites, casting out the old in ritual regeneration, or offered as sacrifices to water deities, or as rain-making spells. Fire festivals were also accompanied by puppets being cast into the bonfires for the same reasons, either as sacrifice or to encourage the power of the sun.

Purim or **The Feast of Lots** (Hebrew). Purim, on the 14th day of *Adar*, commemorates the deliverance of the Jews from a threatened massacre in Persia, it follows the **Fast of Esther** (Esther 4:15f). Purim, largely secular and of a folk festival nature, takes the form of a typical **carnival** with transvestism, fancy dress, masks, lampooning and foolery with much eating and drinking. Haman is burned in effigy. The festival is said to be older than Esther and derived from the Babylonian new year festival when the destinies of people were determined by lots — 'puru'. There are also similarities with the pagan rites of selection of a new ruler or monarch: the parade of the

substitute king, the fast, the execution of a felon and the distribution of gifts.

Purmina (Buddhist). See **Vesakha**.

Purulli. See **Hittite**.

Pushkita or **Busk**. See **Amerindian, North**.

Pythia (Ancient Greek). The Pythian or Delphic Festival, held from 582 BC, was not of the same cosmopolitan importance and size as the **Olympics**, in spite of the fact that the Oracle at Delphi had acquired a wider reputation than the Olympic Oracle. The Pythian Games were reputed to have started as a commemoration of Apollo's victory over the Python. As Apollo had been sentenced to nine years' exile for slaying the dragon, the festival was held nine-yearly by Greek reckoning, or, by modern calculation, once every eight years. It is generally accepted that festivals associated with Apollo, such as those at Delphi and Delos, were musical and poetic events, prizes being awarded for hymns to Apollo which were chanted to the playing of the cithera. In times of war the festival had been disrupted, but was restored in 590 BC when musical items were expanded to include flute solos and songs accompanied by the flute. Horse-racing and athletics were also introduced and Delphi had a race in full armour before this event was included at Olympia. Before the stadium was built these racing events took place below Delphi on the plain of Crisa. War broke out again and once more the Pythia was disrupted then re-established, after which it was held every fourth year, in the third year of the Olympiad and it was then that the festival included chariot-racing as well as horse-racing. Horses bred in Greece were a source of great wealth. The prize at the Pythia was a crown of bay leaves from the Vale of Tempe.

Q

Quaternary. The Quaternary, the number four, representing the four quarters of the earth and the four phases of the moon, appears as a cross on sacrificial cakes and bread of festivals of lunar goddesses such as Artemis. Vestigial remains of this custom are seen in the Hot Cross Bun now made at the lunar **Easter** festival.

R

Races. Among the competitions and games indulged in at festivals races held a prominent place. The Babylonian new year, **Akitu**, festival had foot-races while the great Greek athletic festivals also had chariot and horse-races. Nor were races limited to athletic occasions but were present at the Greek **Eleusinian Mysteries**, the Roman **Robigalia** and many European festivals and the fairs attached to them. At some sacrificial ceremonies the sacrificial animal was chased and there was a race to catch it. Races were also associated with harvest festivals and at water festivals there were races for men and horses over the waters; at fire festivals people raced round the bonfires.

Ramadan (Islam). The whole month of Ramadan, the ninth month of the lunar year, is a total fast from sunrise to sunset. As the lunar and solar years differ, the month varies through the years. Only the sick, infirm, infants, pregnant women and nursing mothers are exempt from the fast. Muslims gather in mosques and spend nights in prayer and remembrance of Allah, or in recitations from the Koran, as it is related that the Prophet kept awake the entire night in worship and the revelation of the Koran began. The fast is broken at sunset, traditionally with dates and water, but customs vary from one country to another. In some parts mosques and houses are illuminated and decorated. It is a time of reconciliation, forgiveness and purification. Ramadan ends with the festival of Breaking the Fast. See **Eid-ul-Fitr**.

Ram Lila (Hindu). Preceding **Diwali** by 20 days, Ram Lila dramatizes the story of Rama and Sita, their wanderings in the forest, the abduction of Sita by Ravana and her rescue by Rama, with the help of Hanuman, and their triumphant return. Huge crowds assemble to watch and celebrate and the occasion is one especially enjoyed by children, with little boys dressing up as monkeys, and at the death of the demon Ravana fireworks explode and the demon is reduced to ashes. Finally Sita is carried off in a queen's chariot amid great applause.

Rice Planting, *Taue Matsuri* (Japanese). The Rice Planting Festival takes place on the 28th night after *Risshun* (2 or 3 May). It is also the **Nursery Festival**, making nurseries for the rice seedlings; it is the start of the working year. Rice, originally regarded as sacred, is kept in local shrines which have a paddy field attached for rice offerings to the god; the seeds are scattered over the nursery, from which people take the seedlings to grow them in their own fields. Bamboo poles, topped with pine branches, are set up in the fields with offerings of rice and *saké* for the God of the Rice Fields. Rites vary from one district to another, but the basic intent is an invitation to the god to come down to earth.

Traditional working dress is worn for the planting ceremonies and the planting is preceded by a fast and purificatory rituals; the planting is done rhythmically to the accompaniment of music. Under modern influences the sacred nature of the festival is dying. The occasion ends with a general holiday and ritual cleansing of the implements, together with offerings to the Rice God.

Rites. Rituals. Rites and rituals aim at creating a state of unity and harmony within both the particular society involved and the wider cosmic order. They confer a dignity not only on the ceremony but also on the participants. As Hsun Tzu, the early Chinese philosopher, said: 'Through rites heaven and earth join in harmony . . . they achieve order.' They are also concerned with all aspects of the human situation, both good and bad. He continues: 'Beauty and ugliness, music and weeping, joy and sorrow are opposites and yet rites make use of them all, bringing forth and employing each in turn.' They recreate the original mystical harmony between gods and humanity and humanity and the forces of nature and on the practical level they involve the individual in that which is social and local. In rites and ritual social, civic and religious occasions are formalized and regulated. Joseph Campbell writes: 'A ritual is an organization of mythological symbols; and by participating in the drama of the rite one is brought directly in touch with these, not as verbal reports of historic events, either past, present or to be, but as revelations, here and now, of what is always and forever . . . it is mythology made alive.'

Festivals are mythology brought down into time and their recitations of myths are often an important part of the ceremonies, particularly at tribal festivals, for example, the Australian Aboriginal Dream Time is 'reiterated on earth' through ritual.

Rites are also a means of control of members of a society and ritual is an oiling of the wheels of ceremonies, both religious and civic. At the same time ritual impresses the inner meaning of symbols on the minds and emotions of the participants; it is also a release mechanism for the emotions, operating on all levels of experience, from the elementary to the ethical and spiritual, both social and individual.

The apotropaic aspect is also important. Rites are designed to protect society or the individual in times of physical or psychological danger, these being known as 'rites of aversion', such as protection from ghosts of the dead, especially at festivals of the dead, or from the souls of animals slain in sacrifice or in the hunt, or from malign powers such as witches and ill-disposed fairies. The ultimate aim of rites and rituals is to reach and release a power greater than that of the performer and to put all partakers in touch with it.

Robigalia (Ancient Roman). On 25 April, the **Robigalia** propitiated the spirit of mildew, to prevent it attacking the growing crops, with the sacrifice of a puppy and a sheep.

Rogationtide (Christian). Rogation Days, occurring before Ascension Day, are a survival of the Ancient Roman **Ambarvalia** and **Terminalia** in May–June when sacrificial animals were driven round the fields and boundaries and prayers were offered to Mars for the safety of the growing crops at a time of danger from storms and blight. Beating the bounds also fixed them in the minds of the generations, an important function in societies which had no maps. The custom was adopted by Christianity and, three days before Ascension, priests and parishoners beat the bounds in procession, carrying peeled wands and praying for blessings on the crops and at the same time confirming the bounds of the parish. The liturgy was appointed to be sung and read in public. In medieval times an altar was set up at the boundary stone and a mass was said for the blessing of the crops. In cases where houses had been built over boundaries the front and back doors had to be left open for the procession to pass through. The *Book of Homilies* had an exhortation 'to be spoken to such parishes where they use their perambulation in Rogation Week, for the oversight of the bounds and limits of their town'. Sometimes the bounds were ridden at a gallop. Boys could be beaten or 'bumped' at certain points to make them take due note. The days were also known as Gang Days for the 'ganging' round to beat the bounds. The ceremony still persists in some parishes.

Roman (Ancient). From historical times until the revision by Julius Caesar, the Roman calendar was based on a cycle of four years, with a normal year of 355 days, the year starting from March. Later the beginning of the civil year was transferred to 1 January. The official calendar gave the dates of all religious festivals.

Roman festivals bore resemblances to the Ancient Greek festivals, particularly those of Dionysos from Asia Minor. Italy and Sicily had taken part in the Greek festivals from the sixth and fifth centuries BC, but the Roman temperament was less idealistic than the Greek, and Romans also regarded it as undignified to compete naked in front of spectators, so the Roman festivals became more in the nature

of spectacles performed by professionals for popular amusement. Also, the more brutal Roman nature, accustomed to incessant war, took greater interest in gladiatorial shows and blood-shedding, in which thousands of animals were ruthlessly killed, than in the more cultured, musical and gymnastic interests of the Greeks. After peace was established the people became increasingly addicted to amusement and filled their year with one festival after another. The Alexandrian Mysteries also spread to Rome from Greece and brought the Egyptian festivals of Isis and Serapis. The Phrygian cult of Cybele was also adopted, as was the Syrian Baal and the Persian Mithras. As these were largely mystery cults little is known about them but their influence was considerable; these ancient pagan festivals were not only tolerated by the Romans but actually encouraged and incorporated into the calendar, becoming part of the life of the people from the ruling bodies and priests to the general public and the slaves.

The majority of Roman festivals were concerned with urban life and the armed forces, and were associated with the summer and Mars as God of War since wars ceased in the winter. A compromise was reached between urban and rural festivals by selecting a site in the country, but near enough to the town to be attended by the town dwellers.

While the malign and death-dealing influence of Scorpio heralded the dying of the sun, the Roman Aries, or Mars, heralded the rising power of the sun and the coming of spring, so the Roman 10-month year began in March with the quickening of life and attention was focused on the growth of the crops and propitiation of the gods of agriculture. April was festive and licentious. May, a time of growth, was also a time of peril from blight or freak disasters and introduced an element of uncertainty, with the need for propitiatory rites. June and the summer saw maturity and struck a happier note. December and January were times of leisure after the harvest and had festive rites, January, continuing the leisure, also marked the entrance of the sun on its new life. Work started again in early February with the spring sowing of crops and tending of the olive trees and vines. From early December to the beginning of February the rites were of a joyful nature, but February brought a complete change with the re-awakening of life and the vital growth of crops and it became necessary to put humanity right with the gods and the ancestors and to expiate any acts of ommission or commission, hence the time became a period of preparation, purification and contact with the dead. This made February a gloomy month and unlucky since the passage opened between the worlds of the dead and the living. The year then began again in March with the resumption of both agriculture and warfare, both under the influence of Mars. The sacred fires were renewed and fresh laurels placed on the Regia and

all garlands and wreaths were renewed. In the months the Ides occurred on the day of the full moon and were sacred to Jupiter, with the **Calends**, the first day, sacred to Juno.

Festivals:
Ambarvalia
Anna Perenna
Bona Dea
Calends
Feralia
Festival of **Cybele**
Festival of Isis
Floralia
Fontinalia
Hilaria
Lemuria
Lupercalia
Matronalia
October Horse
Parentalia
Parilia
Robigalia
Saturnalia
Terminalia
Vestalia
Vinalia.

Rosh Hashanah (Hebrew). A new year festival, celebrated on the first day of *Tishri* (September), a fresh beginning at which best clothes are worn and 'Good Year' greetings are exchanged. It was originally a one-day festival, a Feast of Trumpets, at which the *shofar* sounded (Psalm 81: 3/4). It is a time of judgement, repentance and soul-searching, also of augury for the coming year, but the theme of creation and renewal is also central and signifies victory over chaos. It is an entirely public festival, in constrast to the domestic nature of most Jewish festivals, except for the domestic meal on the eve of the celebrations. Services are held in the synagogue with prayers, reading and meditation, exploring the kingship of God and His power. To emphasize this the *shofar*, the ram's horn, is ritually blown. In earlier times a ritual cleansing was enacted in casting one's sins into the waters; this survives in some parts with a ceremonial emptying of pockets and casting out the accumulated odds and ends. Orthodox Jews still assemble near water for this rite when possible. The festival begins 10 days of penitence and preparation which reach their culmination in **Yom Kippur**, these two occasions being the most solemn days of the year.

S

Sacaea (Babylonian and Assyrian). The 14th of *Adar*, or the 16th of *Lous* according to the Macedonian calendar, was a spring festival lasting five days. It was based on the God-King-Sacrifice symbolism and had the same characteristics as the Roman **Saturnalia**. A slave or a clown took the part of the king and a slave was clothed as a king in each household. General license prevailed. There was a **scapegoat**, a condemned criminal, who was given all luxuries and license until the end of the festival, when he was sacrificed. The festival also had affinities with the Hebrew feast of **Purim**, mentioned in the Book of Esther, which was a Bacchanalian fête lasting two days and falling on the 14th of *Adar*.

Sacred Marriage. The *hieros gamos* was the ritual marriage, at spring festivals, which took place between god and goddess, sun and moon, represented ritually by priest and priestess or king and queen. The feminine element symbolized the fertility of nature, or nature herself, bringing new life and growth, while the masculine counterpart represented the creative force and the patterns in nature; both joined together in the sacred marriage of Heaven and Earth which, by sympathetic magic, brought fertility to the land. It was also a teaching model and example for mortals, whose rites were a reflection of the qualities of the divinities — 'as above, so below'. In Babylon and Assyria the ritual took place at the spring festival of Tammuz and Ishtar/Inanna; in Egyptian-Graeco cults at the festival of Behdet at Edfu, between Hathor and Horus at the temple of Denderah; the vine-god Dionysos was married to his queen; at Eleusis the Sky God Zeus united with the Earth Mother Demeter; in Sweden Frey had a beautiful maiden for his wife. Humans taking part in the rite, i.e. priest and priestess, king and queen, were identified with the divine counterparts and transcended their human nature; they also brought divine power down to earth. Sometimes statues were symbolically married.

Sacred Marriage (Ancient Greek). The Sacred Marriage of Zeus to Hera was celebrated in Athens in the month of *Gamelion*, January, at

a time following the winter solstice when the turn of the year brought new life. Hera, goddess of marriage and childbirth, was a fertility divinity and was also goddess of flowers and her statues were adorned with lilies, an almost universal bridal flower. January was the month of marriages. Details of the festival are not known.

Sacrifice. Although usually associated with death, sacrifice is in fact the sanctification, or making holy, of an object, and can either be connected with paying tribute to a deity or taken as an act of communion between the people and a divine power, forming a bond between the human and the divine. Sacrifice, with altars, a sacrificing priesthood and a sacrificial meal, is a general response to the feeling of the people of a need to be in touch with their deity. Sacrifice is thus largely associated with theistic religions and is one of their most important rites. It is superseded in the metaphysical and non-theistic religions. In religions which regard the divinity as a source of annual rebirth and renewal of fertility, sacrifices have the aspect of a gift in exchange for benefits received or hoped for; they also reflect the age-old custom of any superior being approached with a gift by an inferior.

In early times sacrifice and feasting usually went together as the people made contact with the deities and joined them and the entire community together in feasting on the victims. Less frequently the sacrifice was given wholly to the deity and not shared by the people.

Sacrifice is distinct from votive offerings which take the form of gifts of treasures, images, clothing, ornaments, lit candles, etc.

Sacrifice is sometimes employed to send a message through the gates of death to the deities. This was more the case in earlier times, though still prevalent in tribal societies. Formerly human sacrifice was practised for that purpose and the human so used was generally a deformed or debased type or criminal, a person of no benefit to the community. He was first purified then sacrificed. This also applied to the sacrifice of the **scapegoat** who was regarded as a transferred guilt-carrier and was first brought into contact with the people or place to be purified before being killed, or buried, or thrown over a boundary, or cast into the waters to be carried away.

Sacrifices made to the underworld deities in ancient times were often buried or thrown into a chasm; those to water divinities were thrown into the sea, rivers or wells. Other sacrifices could be laid on the ground, hung on the trees or poured over sacred stones or objects.

Burnt sacrifice purifies the grosser elements and the cleansed and etherialized element then asends to the heavens. Fire was not employed in sacrifices to underworld deities, for example the Arkadian sacrifice to Demeter was one of natural simplicity, with no blood offerings and grapes rather than wine, honey in the comb,

wool in the grease and olive oil. There was also a fireless sacrifice to
Athene at Rhodes, but this apparently did not suit the goddess, so
she went to live at Athens where they sacrificed by fire, the
Athenians, according to Philostratos, being 'wiser in their generation
and good at sacrifice'.

Colour was important in sacrificing: white animals for sky deities;
black for the chthonic and red for fire; white at dawn and black at
sunset.

Blood sacrifice at festivals of the dead offered blood as the essence
of life, necessary for the dead to regain life in order to appear at their
festivals. It was believed, and still is in some societies, that offerings
laid on an altar are transmuted into their spiritual counterparts as
suitable for divine consumption, or, in the case of food offerings to
the divinities or the dead, the essence, or *mana*, is absorbed by them
while the actual food remains the same outwardly and can be eaten
by the devotees.

New buildings sometimes had a sacrifice, human or animal, buried
at the foundations, either to propitiate the deity or to ensure the
stability of the building. The Vikings smeared the keels of their
vessels with human blood.

In Hinduism when animals are sacrificed it is not seen as cruelty,
since the sacrificed animal escapes reincarnation as such and
becomes human in the next rebirth.

Christianity surmounted the early problem of blood sacrifice by
allowing animals to be killed for feasting at festivals or at the
dedication of churches or conversion of ancient temples to churches.

Islam still has blood sacrifices, notably at the **Hajj** pilgrimage.

Sada (Zoroastrian). Occurring on 12 December, Sada, the 'one
hundredth-day festival', is an Iranian fire festival celebrated by open-
air festivities round a large bonfire, built near water. The fire is
kindled at nightfall and symbolizes the triumph of light over
darkness, good over evil.

Saints' Days (Christian). Days dedicated to various saints occur
throughout the year and are listed as Red or Black Letter Days, the
Red being important and generally observed, the Black largely kept
only in monasteries and by priests. These days are retained in
Catholicism but were pruned back in Protestantism. The Eastern
Orthodox Church ceased to create more saints after the tenth
century, but the Roman Catholic Church continues the practice to
this day. Saints were adopted as patrons of Christian countries and
there are patron saints of parishes and cathedrals. In Sweden the
festival of St Lucia's Day, 13 December, preparatory to Christmas,
is of particular significance as it is connected with the earlier rites of
the Coming-of-Light festival. Lucia, Queen of Light, is dressed in
white and wears a crown of garlands with candles and is attended by

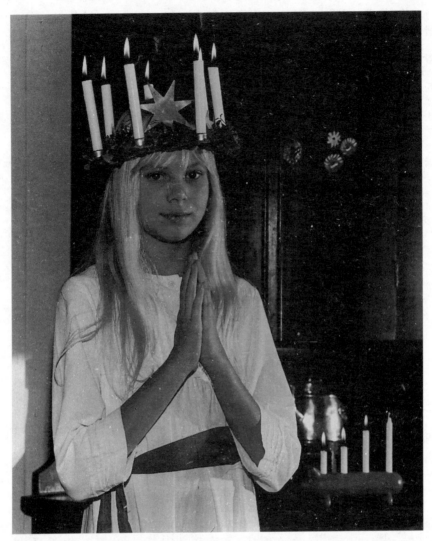

The Festival of St Lucia centres on the Queen of Light, dressed in white and wearing a crown of garlands with candles (*Swedish Embassy Information Department*)

maids of honour and star-boys wearing pointed hats. St Lucia carols are sung and mulled wine and gingerbread served. In Ireland the national holiday on St Patrick's Day, on 17 March, has parades, sports and the wearing of the green of the shamrock and St Patrick crosses. Lenten restrictions are in abeyance and there is much dancing and drinking in the 'wetting or drowning' of the green. It is highly ominous for the day to fall on Palm Sunday. In England the patron saint, St George, has his day on 23 April and other celebrated saints' days are those of St John The Baptist at **Midsummer** and St

Michael and All Angels on 29 September; this was, and still is, a time
for contracts, hiring, settlements and rents. It was also a date for
distribution of food to the poor. Michaelmas was the time of the
Goose harvest and the cusom of tenants giving a goose to the
landlord was a relic of placating the powers that be with sacrifice and
food. Various fairs were held at that time and through the year fairs
were associated with patron saints. (See **Fairs**.)

Samhain or **Samhuinn** (Celtic). 31 October, Eve of 1 November,
was the beginning of the Celtic year, the beginning of the season of
cold, dearth and darkness. It was a festival of the dead, later
Hallowe'en or the Christian **All Saints** and **All Souls**. It was also a
feast of the fairies who ruled the festival but left after it and remained
away until **Beltane**; it was a dangerous time for mortals as fairies
could 'take' them and witches and evil powers were abroad and
required propitiation. Growth was at its lowest point and cold
increasing, so bonfires were lit to encourage the sun by sympathetic
magic. As at Beltane bonfires, people jumped over them and cattle
were driven through them and witches burned on them. Going
through the fire got rid of evil influences but also acted as fumigation
to rid the cattle of parasites. Fires of the festival were called
Samhnagan.

Samhain was a time of chaos and the reversal of normal order,
symbolized by such tricks as blocking up chimneys, leading off
cattle, throwing cabbage at notable people. The hearth had to be
swept clean and a fire kept burning for the dead. It was also a season
for divination and the reading of omens such as placing two nuts in
the fire as a test for lovers, burning steadily denoted constancy,
popping was inconstancy: rites varied from one region to another.
Apples and nuts associated with Samhain and Hallowe'en were also
connected with the ancient Roman festival of **Pomona**, on
1 November, a feast of the ripening of the fruits and a time when the
summer stores were opened for winter consumption. The apple was
the Celtic Silver Bough and the fruit of the otherworld, symbolizing
love, fertility, wisdom and divination; the fruit of heaven and of wise
men. The hazel was the sacred tree of the Celtic groves and, like all
nuts, represented hidden wisdom, lovers and peace. As the Tree of
Life it grew in Avalon by the sacred pool.

In Ireland, Samhain, as *Oiche Shamhna*, was celebrated
everywhere; it was also, later, Hallowtide or Hallowe'en, the pagan
and Christian becoming indistinguishable. Again, ghosts and fairies
were both active. Food offerings should be left for both and it was
dangerous to travel on this night for fear of being led astray by fairies;
iron or steel should be carried as apotropaic.

After the advent of Christianity 'parshell' crosses were made and
fixed to house, byre and stable doors. Bonfires were lit as the

'Samhain pile' and ashes and burning brands were thrown out. There were also parties of 'guisers' going about collecting apples, nuts or money and the hobby-horse, or a horse's head, figured in the ceremonies. The evil powers were the Formorians and in earlier times human sacrifice was said to be practised; this was not only to propitiate the powers but also to bring fertility.

Traces of human sacrifice are also seen in the Welsh 'Black Sow' ceremony in which everyone ran downhill as fast as possible shouting 'the Black Sow take the hindermost', the last person being the victim. The Black Sow was the spirit of evil, cold and death. The same significance applied to the victim chosen by the carline cake at **Beltane.**

The wholesale killing of animals was not only for winter food but because there was not enough feed for them in the fields in winter. The slaughter took on a ritual and sacrificial aspect among the Celts and Teutons and bore the marks of an earlier pastoral festival with the emphasis on semi-divine animals. Feasting followed and the dead were also feasted. In Germany and Gaul boisterous processions took place and men dressed in animal masks and skins, thus gaining contact with the sacred animals and with the deities.

At Samhain a sheaf of corn, a branch of evergreen or mistletoe, symbolically carried on the dying powers of vegetation. Carrying or decorating with evergreens demonstrates that life has not died.

Pliny gives an account of a Druid festival of the cutting of the mistletoe from an oak tree: it was cut with a 'golden' sickle and caught in a white cloak, as it must never touch the ground. Two white bulls were sacrificed and a feast held.

Samhain was also a time of truce with no fighting, violence or divorce allowed, hence it was a time of marriage. Accounts were closed, debts collected, contracts made and servants hired.

Saturnalia (Ancient Roman). In Roman times November was a month of hard work in ploughing and sowing, with no time for leisure and festivals, but by December most of the agricultural work was over and arms had been put away for the winter and the people were able to relax and enjoy themselves; this saw the time of the Saturnalia, a festival which has probably left more traces on European customs than any other; it was heavily influenced in its origins by the Greek **Cronia** and adopted its practices. Saturn, the Greek Cronos, had a dual aspect, he was both sinister as Time and Death the Reaper, and benign as a God of Agriculture and ruler of the Golden Age when all men lived in accord and were equal. The origins of his festival are vague and obscure, but it became the most popular of festivals when, as Seneca said: 'all Rome went mad'. In the pre-Republican calendar the festival started on 17 December, about the time of the winter solstice, at a time when work and war were

over. The old year died and an intercalary period of chaos intervened
before the birth of the new year: a suspension of time. To symbolize
both chaos and the equality under the Golden Age, all laws, civic and
moral, were suspended and slaves and masters changed places,
slaves being waited on and allowed unlimited license and prisoners
were freed.

The festival was marked by orgies, carnivals and transvestism;
friends were visited, presents and wax candles were exchanged and
images in earthenware and confectionary were given. The freedom
and licence were also symbolized by the statue of Saturn, or Cronos,
which was fettered during the year, but having the fetters removed
for the duration of the festival. This was also symbolic of the Lord of
Misrule; a young and handsome man was chosen 30 days before the
celebrations and during that time he could indulge in any licence,
passions or fancies he chose. He was dressed in royal robes to
represent Saturn and was implicitly obeyed by his temporary
subjects. At the end of the period he was sacrificed by cutting his own
throat on Saturn's altar. This King Saturn was also considered a
burlesque on royalty. In classical times the 'King' behaved like a
buffoon, but in earlier times the rite was almost certainly that of
the God-King-Sacrifice. Also present was the idea of combat between
the old and new years, the driving out of the old being part of the
sacrifice of the temporary king. The Saturnalia, lasting 12 days,
ended with the *sigillaria* when the children were given images and
presents. Similar rites to the Saturnalia occurred in many places:
among Aztecs, in Crete, in Rhodes, Olympia and Thessaly and was
paralleled in the Babylonian **Sacaea**, the 12 days of chaos, with the
conflict between chaos and cosmos, good and evil, summer and
winter. The characteristics of this time passed from Rome into
Europe, persisting into medieval times, having also a Lord of Misrule,
and into the **Twelve Days** of Christmas.

Scapegoat. The employment of a scapegoat at festivals had the dual
purpose of being atropaic and a magical transference of guilt and
evil, or of averting evil at a time of crisis, such as plague or failure of
crops. The scapegoat could be human, an animal or bird or almost
any form of object to which the guilt or disease could be transferred
then destroyed. The custom occurs universally from the Ancient
Babylonian *kuppuru* rites to the Japanese *ohoharahi* celebrates at the
start of the agricultural year.

The scapegoat takes its name from the Hebrew rites of the **Day of
Atonement** when a goat was driven into the wilderness after the
High Priest had ritually confessed the sins of the people and
transferred them to the goat. In early times the victim was more
usually a human; sometimes a deformed or debased character who
was kept at public expense to act as a scapegoat at festivals or on

occasions of pestilence or calamity since these disasters were obviously manifestations of divine displeasure. The most famous of these rites was probably the expulsion of the *pharmakos* at the Greek **Thargelia**; he was 'a very ignoble and useless person', probably a criminal, who was ritually beaten with branches of wild figs or leeks, both having purgative properties, and the beating itself being an expulsive ceremony. This took place to the sound of flutes and the *pharmakos* was given 'pure' foods to eat: cheese, barley cakes and figs, and then expelled from the city to take the sins of the people and any evil influence with him. The same rites were employed with the Roman *Mamurius Veturius* at the **Anna Perenna** new year festival.

The Dying God has also the characteristics of a scapegoat in that he bears the sins of the people, but he also dies young to save humanity from degeneration, loss of fertility and old age.

Human sacrifice of a scapegoat has been known in modern times in some tribal societies.

Sealing of the Frost. (See **Mayan**.)

Seasons. The seasons are not only the main divisions of the year, but also the times within them, controlled by agricultural and pastoral cycles, such as ploughing, sowing, harvesting, fruit-picking and vintage, or the birth times affecting the herding or hunting of animals, either domestic or wild. The *Li Ki* said: 'All ceremonial usages, looked at in their general characteristics, are the embodiment of the ideas suggested by heaven and earth; take their laws from the changes of the four seasons; imitate the operation of the contracting and expanding movements of nature, and are conformed to the emotions of man.' They provide the rhythms of the changing year just as the rotating earth produces the rhythms of night and day. Midwinter is the point of lowest vitality; Midsummer the highest, the climax. They have positive and negative characteristics in summer and winter rites of encouraging vitality or expelling death and decay.

Festivals were largely sacred in early times and the seasons were of the greatest importance in the production of food which was provided not only by human effort but also by the aid of the gods. The year was a cyclic recurrence of times of special significance and tensions and festivals provided the calendar for these times associated with the food supply and propitiation of the controlling powers.

With agricultural people the year begins with the ploughing of the fields and sowing of the crops and the spring festivals occur with the growth of new life, the time of the ritual **Sacred Marriage** which survived in the May King and Queen rites. Midsummer sees the harvest, with universal festivals of **first fruits**, while winter brings decay and death but also, at the solstice, the rebirth of the sun and the great festivals of that time.

Seasonal festivals are either solar or lunar; the year with four seasons is solar, with the summer and winter solstices and the spring and autumn equinoxes. The lunar year is divided into the three phases of the moon. These climatic controls apply outside the tropics in which there is usually only a reckoning of colder and warmer seasons when life dies in winter and revives in spring and summer. Tropical and sub-tropical zones have also dry and rainy seasons and there are the wind seasons of Oceania.

In earlier societies there was often no calendar and little idea of time beyond the changing seasons e.g. dry, windy, raining, hunting, monsoon, animal and bird migrations, the appearance of certain **stars**, all giving their names to the seasons but not reckoning the year as a whole, thus the number of seasons varied greatly, for example, with the Algonquins there were the budding, ripening, midsummer, harvest, and winter, and there are also five seasons in the Bahamas. In rice-growing countries the seasons are divided according to the state of growth of the crop. In early tribal and Indo-European societies there were only the two seasons of wet or dry, summer or winter. The Egyptians had three seasons, rainy, cold, warm; European and Christian four, spring, summer, autumn, winter; many Amerindians had five, as above. The Greek Orthodox Church has six seasons, chiefly dependent on Saints' Days, and while early Greek reckoning had the three lunar seasons of the Horae, these later became the four solar seasons with the Horae increased to four, but a Greek treatise also gives seven seasons to include tree-planting and fruit-harvest.

A peculiarity of people of the colder regions is that the winter is the time for major festivals, the summer being devoted to work and the winter a time of rest when, in earlier times, cattle were killed off and work in the fields ended. It was the time of the great **Yule** festival of Scandinavia, the **Christmas** celebrations, and festivities among the Eskimos and North West American tribes. These are solar festivals and their celebrations are characterized by ritual combat between the powers of light and darkness, summer and winter, good and evil. Grimm says that in Europe the war was fought between two people, one clothed in ivy, the other in straw or moss, fighting until summer won, or between bands of people dressed symbolically in greenery and fur. Similar customs were known in widely divergent cultures: in Ancient Egypt and Greece, Scandinavia, Russia, among the Iroquois, the Yakut of Baluchistan, in Malaya, and the Basque plays of *Les Rouges et Noires*, the contest between St George and the Dragon, and in ritual football contests in England and Scotland.

Dances, plays and mumming all revolved round seasonal festivals, being an essential feature of the festivities.

Setsubun (Japanese). The eve of *Risshun*, in February, is the official

beginning of spring and was the New Year's Day of the old solar calendar. It is associated with end-of-year spring-cleaning and purificatory rites, driving out demons, with ritual obeisance in the Four Directions. The bean scattering ceremony takes place at shrines and temples, the bean being symbolic of good health as well as being atropaic, averting evil and bringing good luck. The formula 'In with good fortune, out with demons' bears strong resemblances to the Ancient Roman customs. In some parts beans are also used in divining the fortunes of the coming year. Prayers are offered for safety and happiness in the future.

Seven-Five-Three (Japanese). At *Shichigosan*, 15 November, boys and girls of three years, boys of five and girls of seven, are dressed in festive clothes and taken to Shinto shrines to be blessed by the priest and given a 'thousand year' sweetmeat symbolic of health and long life. At home there are ceremonies of donning special clothing signifying a change to a new state and a condition of responsibility for actions.

Sex. In festivals sex has an ambivalent function; on the one hand chastity prevents the dissipation of the energy needed for the crops and animals during fertility rites; on the other hand mating is sympathetic magic, sexuality having always been associated with all life as the seed. Ritual mating took place in fields and orchards at the time of sowing the seed and the blossoming of the trees, based on the belief that mass promiscuity encouraged new life; but while this mating had a magically beneficial effect, any sexual aberrations were unlucky and blighted the crops. Sexual abstinence and fasting, however, preserved the energy and often preceded solemn festivals as part of the purifications necessary in preparation, or during the whole length of the festivals such as in the Rites of Demeter, the Rites of Isis, the **Ambarvalia** and the **Vestalia**, when total abstinence was imposed and it was said that these feminine rites 'gave husbands gloom' as 'Cynthia has now been 10 nights continually engaged in worship'. In the Mystery religions, and in festival processions, sexual symbols were often displayed, such as the phallus of Dionysos, but they were regarded with sacred awe and reverence as demonstrating the continuation of life — personal, tribal or racial — beyond this world.

The **Sacred Marriage** at spring festivals united the solar-lunar, heaven-earth, male-female powers of fertility in the god and goddess, priest and priestess, king and queen.

Shabat (Hebrew). The Shabat or Sabbath extends from Friday sunset to Saturday nightfall and involves special ceremonies. The Jewish day begins at sunset and the mistress of the house lights candles, spreads a clean cloth on the table and places on it the Shabat

loaves, the *hallot*; a special meal is eaten and wine drunk from the *kiddush* cup. With Orthodox Jews no work may be done or journeys undertaken, but modern conditions may modify these restrictions and Reform Jews take a more liberal attitude. There is a ceremony of sanctification to keep the day holy. At the conclusion of the Shabat the 91st Psalm is read and the day ends with the *havdalah* or separation ceremony. The festival is a weekly one, and services must be attended on that day.

Shab-i-Barat (Islam). Also known as the Night of the Records, the festival is celebrated in northern India on the 14th of *Shaban*; it is the time when Allah registers the actions of all mankind, together with births and deaths for the coming year. Originally a fast, it turned into a festival celebrated by fireworks displays. Lamps are lighted on graves and at shrines with prayers for the deceased.

Shab-i-Miraj (Islam). The Night of the Ascent commemorates the night when the Prophet was transported to Heaven in a vision. This took place in the fifth year of the Call, about 11 years before *Hijra*, the migration of the Prophet from Mecca to Medina in AD 622 on the 27th of *Rajeb*. The Prophet was given divine spiritual knowledge which he imparted to mankind. Mosques, houses and streets can be illuminated and decorated with pennants and bunting. In the evening the people assemble in the mosques to pray, sing praises and glorify God. After the *Isha* prayer in larger mosques there are meetings at which the story of the spiritual ascent is told and speakers give accounts of the life and spiritual status of the Prophet. It is customary to distribute sweets after the meeting; money is given to charities and food to the poor. Devotees may spend the whole night in remembrance of Allah.

Shichigosan (Japanese) See **Seven-Five-Three.**

Shinto. Shinto is the ancient official religion of Japan, the *Kami no Michi*, the Way of the Gods. It has no historical founder or Supreme Being, but a pantheon of divinities, emperors, heroes and ancestors; nor are there any sacred scriptures. Modern Shinto has two main divisions, State Shinto and Shrine or Sect Shinto. State Shinto, to which all Japanese subjects must adhere, involves loyalty to the Emperor as a descendent of the Sun Goddess Amaterasu-Omikami. Shrine Shinto is so called since shrines are the centres of rites; they are supported by the State and are focal points of festivals at which there are processions to the shrines where priests offer prayers for successful harvests, peace and general prosperity. Many of the festivals are now fused with imported Buddhist practices.

Shrove-tide, or **Good Tide.** Shrove-tide, first observed in the Middle Ages, was a time of festivity and **carnival** before the fast of **Lent**

started. It was also a festival of the expulsion of winter, demonstrated in some European countries by the burning, burying or drowning of an effigy of winter. Shrove Tuesday, the day before Lent commenced on **Ash Wednesday** takes its name from being a day of confession of sins and being 'shriven'. During the Lenten fast no meat, poultry, eggs or dairy produce could be eaten, so foods were contrived which used up all these ingredients; in Britain these were notably pancakes, which became the traditional Shrove Tuesday food and gave the day its alternative name of Pancake Tuesday. In earlier times a pancake bell was rung and the entire household, complete with servants, joined in eating the food. Pancakes were 'tossed' and races instituted which survive today. Shrove Monday was called Collop Monday when collops of meat and eggs were served as a last indulgence before the rigours of Lent.

In Britain there were traditional ball games (see **Games**) and street football was played in towns and villages; there were no rules and no set goals, but sometimes the church, or a stream, or mill would be the objective and the contest was between two factions of the community, sometimes called up-streeters and down-streeters, the game going through the whole town or village. These games survive in some parts. The day was a holiday for apprentices. In earlier times a carnival took place, but not on the same scale as in Catholic countries, especially France, where *Mardi Gras* (Fat Tuesday) was celebrated enthusiastically with masquerades, singing and dancing. The festival still continues and has been carried over into America, especially New Orleans. A description of the pre-puritan festival in Britain is given as:

> 'Some run about the streets attired like monks and some like kings,
> Accompanied with pomp and guard and other things,
> Some like wild beasts do run abroad in skins that divers be
> Arrayed, and eke with loathsome shapes, that dreadful are to see.
> They counterfeit both bears and wolves, and lions fierce in sight,
> And raging bulls; some play the cranes, with wings and stilts upright.'

In many parts of Germany a whole week may be given over to the festival. Shrove Tuesday is *Fastnacht*, and there is a *Fastnachtsbär*, a boy dressed as a bear, going round dancing with women: an ancient fertility rite. The festival is called *Karneval* in the Rhineland and *Fasching* in southern Germany. There are processions, fancy dress, transvestism, wearing of masks and singing and dancing in the streets. A special feature is the number of huge effigies, or heads, caricaturing notable people. Some of the carnivals culminate on the Monday before Lent with huge processions. The festival is still actively celebrated in Catholic Europe and America. In Ireland it is

a time of marriage since weddings are prohibited in Lent. It is also a time for playing pranks on the unmarried who are 'chalked' or daubed.

Siberian. Festivals in Siberia are largely concerned with the reindeer and controlled by the seasons. Among the reindeer people there are festivals at the return of the herd from the summer pastures, at the first snow, and in spring when the fawns are dropped and the reindeer have lost their antlers. Fires are extinguished and the sacred new-fire kindled from the ritual fire-board and sacrifice is made to the One on High. There is also a solar festival when the sun indicates the coming of summer, after the winter solstice, and sacrifice is made to the sun. A spring celebration takes place when grass begins to grow and leaves appear on trees. Later there is a mosquito festival at the arrival of the mosquitoes when a sacrifice is made to the One on High so that the mosquitoes do not scatter the herd.

Sikh. Sikhs (disciples) are mainly established in the Punjab, but their religion is founded on belief rather than race, on the Unity of God and the Brotherhood of Man; it is based on the revelation and teaching of Guru Nanak (AD 1469–1539). Although having many points and customs in common with Hinduism, Sikhism differs from it by rejecting the caste system, the priesthood, asceticism, pilgrimages, mendicancy and bathing in sacred streams. Men and women are said to be equal and enter the community by a ritual of initiation and acceptance of the form of conduct laid down. Sikhs have 'the Five K's' as the outward sign of their religion: the *kes* —

The Sikh sacred temple and tank at Amritsar (*Mary Evans Picture Library*)

uncut hair; *khangha* — a steel comb; *kara* — an iron bracelet; *kirpan* — a short sword; *kach* — short trousers.

A series of 10 Gurus followed Nanak until Gobind Singh (AD 1675–1708), who declared that there would be no more Gurus except the One Eternal Guru — the Holy Book, the *Adi Granth*. The most celebrated point of worship is the Golden Temple at Amritsar. The religion is strictly monotheistic and God, the Name, is compassionate, a Destroyer of Sorrow, Friend of Sinners and Cherisher of the Poor.

Sikh festivals, or *melas*, follow the general pattern of the Hindu festivals of **Vaisakhi**, **Diwali** and **Holi**, but are given specifically Sikh interpretations. People assemble before the Guru and precede most rituals by ablutions, though these are not regarded as ritual purifications. Most festivals are fixed by the lunar calendar.

Festivals:
Diwali.
Gurpurbs.
Hola Mohalla.
Vaisakhi or Baisakhi.

Sirius. The helical rising of Sirius, the brightest of the fixed stars, marked by the Egyptians, reckoned the interval between one rising and the next as 365 days, 6 hours, recorded as the Sirius Year. The star was of the greatest importance to the Egyptians as it heralded the rising of the Nile, the revival of fertility and the coming harvest, and marked the New Year. In Greece the helical rising brought the dry, hot and stormy season. Homer called it an evil star and Hesiod said: 'Sirius parches head and knees'. For the Romans it was the Dog Star, marking the onset of the humid heat of summer, the Dog Days, which brought pestilence and therefore required sacrifices of placation.

Sita. See **Inca.**

Skins. The skin of an animal represents the fat which is the life-sustaining produce. Skins of sacrificial animals, or the skins of snakes, fishes, or the feathers of birds, have magical qualities and powers of purification, both moral and physical; they are also apotropaic, warding off evil powers and ghosts and can have healing properties. Skins or feathers worn ritually at festivals are usually those of some sacred symbolic or totem animal. The hobby-horse at fairs and festivals is an ancient form of disguising as an animal in festival processions. For warding off evil, skins were often carried round boundaries or fields at seed-time festivals. The qualities of the skin were transferred to the wearer, for example to wear a lion skin was to become fearless; it also put the wearer in touch with animal

instinctual knowledge. Thongs made from the skins of sacrificial animals, such as the goat and dog, used for ritual fertility whipping, were employed at fertility festivals, especially the Roman **Lupercalia**.

Snake Dance. See **Amerindian** and **Mayan**.

Snow Festival (Japanese). The *Yuki Matsuri*, held at the city of Sapporo in February, is a snow festival at which the main features are the competitive construction and exhibition of large snow and ice sculptures paraded in a huge procession. The festival is not associated with religion and, unlike other festivals, lacks the traditional *Matsuri* communion between gods and humans, but although secular in origin it has now become, according to Japanese sources, 'a natural extension of the *Matsuri* tradition'. There is also the Niino Snow Festival in January, at the Izu shrine, when snow is offered to the gods as part of a festival of prayer for a good harvest. Snow is thought to ensure good crops.

Solstices. The summer and winter solstices are the times when the sun is at its farthest from the equator and seems to stand still; they are the times of the longest day and the longest night and, in times when hunting, agriculture or pastoral interests governed the concerns of the people, they were a personal matter, closely affecting their lives. The increasing darkness brought cold, dearth and hardship to both man and beast, while the turn from darkness to light was a matter for rejoicing and the victory of light over darkness gave the assurance that spring, warmth and growth would come again.

The winter solstice was taken as 25 December when the Queen of Heaven, the Great Mother, gave birth to the Son of Light. 'The Virgin has given birth, the light grows' was the cry that went up in numerous festivals of the coming of light and life in Egypt, Greece and Rome. Virgo rises in the east and the full moon is at its nadir; this is the *Janua coeli*, the door of the gods, the growing power of the sun.

The solstices were, and in some places still are, occasions for fire festivals, both in Europe and Asia. Bonfires encourage the power of the sun and fire is a purifying force and drives away evil influences, so effigies or representations of these powers were ritually burned; witches were burned and, under Christianity, figures of Judas Iscariot, or, in Catholic regions, Martin Luther, were thrown on the fires.

Festivals of the winter solstice were marked by **plays** depicting the death of the old year and the birth of the new, or the triumph of summer over winter, light over darkness.

Spirit Festivals (Chinese). The most venerated gods are those of the ancestors and underworld and there are important festivals with rites of propitiation and expulsion of ghosts; of these the foremost are: the

Earlier Spirit Festival on the 15th day of the second moon; the Festival of Tombs, about the third day of the third moon, a time of visiting graves and keeping them in order and making offerings to the dead; the Middle Spirit Festival, on the 15th day of the seventh moon, and the Later Spirit Festival, on the 15th day of the 10th moon. All these bear close affinities with the rites of the dead among Greeks, Romans and others, when the passage opens between the two worlds, as in the mid-Autumn Festival, on the 15th day of the eighth moon, the equivalent of an **All Souls Day**. Families travel to tombs to honour the ancestors and repair the graves, to which soil is added. Incense is burned and food, wine and paper money are offered to the dead. It is also an occasion for family reunions and feasting. Willow branches are erected in doorways. On the fist day of the 10th month there is a ghost-expelling festival of the **Hallowe'en** type, the **Hsia Yuan**. Masks are worn to imitate ghosts and monsters. There are Taoist services and spells to drive off the ghosts, against whom the priest uses a magic sword. Wandering ghosts (those who have no surviving family to attend to the ancestors) are helped with spells and little paper boats bearing candles are set adrift on the waters while food and drink is offered.

Spring-Cleaning. The ritual of cleaning in spring is associated with rites of purification which precede the major festivals in most religions and cultures. At the vernal equinox temples and sanctuaries were cleaned and figures of deities ritually washed, perfumed and decorated and often, as in the Greek **Panathenia** and in Catholic Churches, given new clothes. Mesopotamian temples were cleansed; the Egyptian festivals for Osiris required the cleaning of all sacred objects; at the Hebrew **Day of Atonement** and the **Passover** spring-cleaning took pace. Eastern countries also have **New Year** cleansing rituals. Private houses were also ritually purified, being swept and all old, unclean objects associated with the old year, death and decay, were thrown out. The sweeping and ejection were accompanied by the words 'We carry death out of the house'. The person was also cleansed with ablutions, asperges with twigs and herbs, preferably hyssop, and with incense and candle-burning. It was also a time for renewing vegetation; boughs and twigs in temples were replaced by new, fresh growth, for example the Hittites brought in new green box-trees at the festival of **Puruli**; the Romans changed the laurels in the house of the *rex sacorum* at the old year on 1 March and the **Vestal Virgins** swept all rubbish from the temple and threw it in the Tiber, while at spring festivals in Europe communities brought new boughs of hawthorn and other apotropaic greenery to the houses, byres, and stables and for the maypole. These rites of purification also involved the riddance of evil powers.

Stars. The stellar year is 365 days, 6 hours, 9 minutes, 9.84 seconds.

The stars determine the recurrence of certain phenomena and fix dates with predictable exactness. It has been said that the stars are the stationary figures on the clock-face and the sun the moving hand. As the stars determined the times of recurring labours in earlier societies they also determined the times of festivals, but they give only a single point in time and do not form cyclical periods in the year. (See also **Sun, Sirius, Pleiades.**)

Sun. The sun runs through the zodiac backwards, so any particular star culminates 3 minutes, 56 seconds earlier each day, thus the exact interval between the culmination of the sun and of one particular star determines the day of the solar year. This produced a method of time-reckoning for ancient peoples, but is now abandoned in the modern calendar. The sun is employed to indicate the time of day which is also reckoned by the length of its shadows.

The sun represents supreme cosmic power and the all-seeing deity. The sun and rain are the chief powers of fertility on earth, hence festivals involving the **Sacred Marriage** are those of the Sky Father and Earth Mother, the Sun and Moon, etc. Sun festivals, especially those at the summer solstice, are characterized by fires, bonfires, torch-bearing and flaming wheels. Sun myths are associated with most founders of religions and culture heroes.

Syrian (Ancient). The chief festival of the year was the spring ceremony of the Pyre at which animals were sacrificed by being burned alive or thrown over a height to be killed by the fall.

The year began in autumn at an annual festival. At the Stygian Fountain gifts were thrown into the rivers or waters; if they sank they were accepted, if taken away by eddies they were rejected. At Syrian festivals an image of Atargatis was carried in procession to the river for purification, then back to the temple where there was feasting, the temples being places where religion and pleasure were combined. At the Temple of Atargatis at Hieropolis the sacred fish in her fish-ponds were decorated with ornaments of gold. Priests wore the fish-skin robes and the head of the fish, with open mouth, which later became the mitre of Christian bishops.

At the twice-yearly festival at Hieropolis a great concourse of devotees carried water from the Euphrates and poured it into a cleft in the temple in commemoration of Deucalion's flood.

T

Tabernacles, the Feast of (Hebrew). The Feast of Tabernacles, or
Booths (*Succoth*) is an autumn festival, the 'feast of ingathering'; a
joyous occasion associated with the escape from Egypt, 'a time of
rejoicing', celebrated at the full moon of *Tishri* (October-November),
or the autumnal equinox, when work in the fields has ended, the
grape harvest gathered in and the rains expected. It is both
the closing of the old year and the beginning of the new marked by
the coming of the rains. (Ezra 10: 9. Zech. 14:16f.) No work may be
done on the first and last days and there are religious services. In
earlier times there was a water-drawing and libation ceremony from
the fountain of Solomon, with dancing and singing and libations
poured on the altar. The festival was also known as the **Festival of
Booths**, as booths were made from boughs of evergreens, fruit trees
and palms, in which people lived for the seven days of the festival:
'Ye shall dwell in booths seven days; all that are homeborn in Israel
shall dwell in booths: that your generations may know that I made
the children of Israel to dwell in booths, when I brought them out of
the land of Egypt.' (Lev. 23:42/3.)

The custom was probably of Canaanite origin (Judges 9.27 and
21:20f.) and the festival also had close affinities with the Dionysian
celebrations of the vintage. Torch dances at night also had parallels
with the light festivals of the autumn equinox. The seventh day was
one of rituals and prayer. It was also a custom to take willow sprigs
and continue beating them until no leaves were left. The night of the
seventh was spent in prayer and reading sacred texts and an eighth
day, added in the days of the Second Temple, had affinities with the
Babylonian **Akitu** festival and the Egyptian New Year. It was a time
of renewal and a fresh start; a highly important occasion, sometimes
called *the* festival. The eighth day was a time of great rejoicing and
remained as such. The willow wands, or palm, citron or myrtle, are
now made into a bouquet which is shaken upwards and downwards
in the four cardinal directions and taken in procession round the
synagogue. In the Reform ceremony there is a consecration welcoming children into the religious school.

Tama Matsuri (Japanese). See **Bon** or **O-bon**.

Tam Kung (Chinese). At Shaukiwan, in the fourth lunar month, there is a special festival for a child god whose ability to forecast weather conditions makes him worshipped by fishermen. It is also a festival of meeting with the spirit world. It is celebrated with parades and dancing dragons; flowers, fruit and incense are offered at his shrine and there is much fortune-telling to read the future.

Tanabata (Japanese). The Tanabata festival celebrates a Chinese legend carried over to Japan; it is based on the *Oxherd and Weaver Maiden* (see **Chinese**) and takes place on the seventh day of the seventh month. In urban areas it is celebrated according to the new calendar, in July; in rural areas it may be kept a month later and its rites vary considerably from one region to another. In some parts paper dolls are made and cast into the waters, as at the **Dolls' Festival**. Freshly cut bamboos are put on roofs, or in the ground near houses, together with coloured strips of paper.

Tango no Sekku (Japanese). See **Boys' Festival**.

Taoism. For the calendar etc. see **Chinese**. Taoism is divided into two main sections, the classical, philosophical Taoism of Lao Tzu and Chuang Tzu, the *Tao chia*, which is in no way concerned with festivals and has no god or gods, and the popular *Tao chiao*, the religious and magical aspect which became so closely intermingled with Buddhist beliefs and practices and adopted the pantheon of popular Buddhism, that the two became indistinguishable in many respects; this applied to their festivals, concerned with the seasons, the pantheon and culture heroes; they appear under those of China in general.

Taue Matsuri (Japanese). See **Rice Planting Festival**.

Terminalia (Ancient Roman). The Terminalia was, appropriately, the last festival of the old Roman year before the new year began in March. The Roman god Terminus was represented by an aniconic pillar or stone; he had no anthropomorphic form, though farmers prayed to him. Boundary stones (*termini*) were set up and were then regarded as sacred, this applied in both Roman and Hebrew cultures, and anyone removing them was accursed. The festival of the Terminalia was held on 23 February when owners of fields met where they adjoined and put garlands on the boundary stones. Sacrifices were made of corn, honey and wine and there was also a blood sacrifice; the bones, ashes and incense were put into a hole below the stone and the farmer's wife brought fire from the home hearth to use on the altars set up. The feast was one of general jollification after the sombre festivals of the dead. Neighbours approached their boundaries from opposite sides and made merry together. Terminus had always been worshipped in the open air and when a great temple was

built on the site of an ancient terminus a hole had to be left in the
roof to give him his air.

Thanksgiving Day (United States of America). The celebration of
Thanksgiving Day, on the fourth Thursday in November, originated
with the Pilgrim Fathers as a **Harvest** Festival commemorating the
harvest reaped in 1621 and celebrated by a feast of four wild turkeys,
corn, sweet potatoes, nuts, berries and squash; they were helped by
the Indians. The festival was formalized in 1863 by President Lincoln
as a national holiday and is now urbanized with games, pageants,
plays, and parades. It is a gala and sports occasion, with friends
visiting and exchanging gifts, fruit, flowers and greetings. Turkey, the
sacred bird of the Aztecs, cranberry sauce, pumpkin pie, sweet
potatoes and corn muffins are traditional foods for the festival. As
with the ancient festivals, it is also a time for family reunions. There
are church services and food is provided for the poor.

Thargelia (Ancient Greek). The Thargelia, sacred to Apollo and
Artemis, was a festival of *Thargelion*, late May to early June, the time
of the harvest and, like the spring sowing, a time of anxiety. There
were processions and offerings of **first fruits**. A boy with both
parents living (i.e. having no contact with the dead) carried a branch
of olive, a harvest symbol, entwined with white and purple wool and
hung with various fruits of the earth such as figs, acorns, cakes
and a vessel of wine, and placed it in front of Apollo's sanctuary; this,
and the branches adorning houses, stayed there all year until the next
Thargelia.

   As a festival of Apollo there were musical contests. Some said that
the festival was earlier dedicated to Helios and the Horae. Aristotle
said: 'The most ancient sacrifices and meetings seem to be as it were
offerings of first fruits after the gathering of various harvests. For
those were the times of the year when the ancients were specially at
leisure.' At the Thargelia there was a ceremony of expulsion. Two
men, one, wearing a necklace of black figs, represented the men, and
the other with a necklace of white figs, for the women, represented
the whole populace; it was the **scapegoat** or *pharmakos* rite. Any man
chosen for such an occasion was 'a very ignoble or useless person',
the lowest of the low, probably a criminal. He was ceremoniously
beaten with branches of wild figs and other bushes and with leeks,
pungent plants being regarded as purgative, while flutes played. He
was given 'pure foods': barley cakes, figs and cheese, and finally
driven out of the city, taking the sins of the people with him.

Thesmophoria (Ancient Greek). Originally older than any associations with any particular deity, the Thesmophoria later became
sacred to Demeter and Kore, also to the Earth Mother Ge, together
with Athena, Aphrodite and Eileithya. It was a three-day festival in

autumn for the sowing of the crops and was held from the 11th to 13th of *Pyanepsion* and celebrated by women only but in all parts of the Greek world. The first day was the Down Going and Uprising (*Kathodos*); the second involved fasting and sexual abstinence (*Nesteia*); the third the Fair Birth (*Kalligeneia*). The whole was concerned with the fertility of the crops, animals and people. Pigs had been sacrificed in the summer by being thrown down chasms, this was said to have been in commemoration of the swineherd and his flock swallowed up when Kore/Persephone was engulfed in the chasm which opened up to abduct her to the underworld. These clefts, sometimes artificially made, were called *megera*. Phallic symbols of fertility such as snakes and fir cones were made of paste, carried about, then cast into the chasm with the pigs, themselves symbols of fertility.

At the Thesmophoria the remains of the pigs were recovered, placed on altars, then sprinkled on the seeds in the fields, acting as fertilizers. Lucian says that 'in about the chasms are snakes which consume the most part of that which is thrown in, hence a rattling din is made when the women draw up the remains and when they replace the remains by those well-known images, in order that the snakes which they hold to be the guardians of the sanctuaries may go away'. The Roman **Bona Dea** resembled these rites.

Tihar (Nepal). See **Divali**.

Tin Hau (Chinese). One of the festivals still celebrated is the Hong Kong festival of Tin Hau, Goddess of the Sea. Pilgrimage is made to her temple at Kowloon and gifts are offered to her. The Goddess herself visits the temple for three days at the festival and spells and charms may be obtained from her against death by drowning. Boats and junks are 'dressed overall' with brightly coloured flags and ritually dressed crews to sail to the temple.

Toji (Japanese). At the winter solstice, the turning point of the year, the *Daishi-ko* rites are observed on 23 December; they are based on the belief that Daishi, a child of the gods, visits each village. Offerings of rice gruel with red beans, bean curd and pumpkin are set out and the occasion is celebrated with feasting, drinking and dancing.

Tokanya (Japanese). See **Harvest Festival**.

Toltec. See **Aztec**.

Tooth (Buddhist). The Festival of the Tooth, the *Asala Parahara*, is held at Kandy, in August, and lasts for 10 days, though originally the ceremonies went on for 90 days. A proclamation is made 10 days before the festival warning the people to prepare, to clean and decorate the streets and burn incense. The Temple of the Tooth keeps special elephants for the procession, the leading and largest of them

being richly caparisoned and garlanded and bearing the basket containing the Tooth, together with a figure of the Buddha. It is flanked by two smaller elephants and followed by a train of them and the procession wends its way through the streets to the accompaniment of wildly excited shouting, cymbals, conch shells, pipes and drums and the frenzied dancing of the devil dancers. Monks watch the procession but do not participate.

Transvestism. Festivals associated with the intercalary periods of chaos, such as the Babylonian **Twelve Days**, the Roman **Saturnalia** and the **Twelve Days of Christmas**, are characterized by transvestism or 'fancy dress', as are carnival processions connected with the festivals in which the wearing of masks and transvestism are an essential feature. The same applies to festivals at which orgies take place and to religions of the androgynous deities. Transvestism symbolizes the return to the pre-creation state of chaos, the unformed, the state of dissolution before rebirth; it also identifies the wearer with the qualities of the disguise worn. Another example of the practice is seen in the Old Woman and her illegitimate Wonder Child of the Dionysian type plays; 'she' is always a man in disguise (see **Plays**) as in the medieval mummers' and morality plays. Transvestism also implies loss of identity and is sometimes used in initiation ceremonies.

Trees, the Blessing of the Trees (Hebrew). The festival, on the 15th of *Shebat*, is one of the many 'beginnings' of the Jewish year. The Blessing of the Trees festival is celebrated as a New Year of Trees. Originally a tithing and tax time, it is now commemorated by the planting of trees, usually by children, symbolizing the growth of the land. Tree planting is now sponsored by ex-patriate Jews who also eat fruit from Israel on that day. There are similar ceremonies in other countries, such as Arbor Day in the United States of America and Canada, Europe, Australia and New Zealand.

Tree Worship. A prominent part has been played by tree worship in Semitic festivals. At the annual nocturnal feast and fair at Terebinth the tree and well of Abraham were hung with lamps and libations and offerings were cast into the well. The sacred date-palm was worshipped at Nejran and, at the annual feast, was festooned with fine clothes and women's ornaments. Tree worship was frequent in Phrygia and Greece. A tree at Mecca was annually hung with weapons, clothes and gifts. The sacred pillar or pole was a surrogate for the tree and was universal among Semites. A pole decorated with greenery represented the spirit of vegetation among the Celts at **Midsummer** and **Beltane** rites, when a fire was often lit under the sacred tree or pole, the most ancient conception of the vegetation spirit being that of a tree-spirit. As a part representing the whole,

branches or twigs were placed in front of houses and farm buildings at spring festivals as a tree-spirit warding off evil forces; the same applied to boughs carried in procession at vegetation festivals. Trees associated with a Moon Goddess appear in Hindu, Phoenician, Greek, Roman, Celtic, Scandinavian and African mythology and hence in their festivals.

Tristeria (Greek). See **Dionysia**.

Twelfth Night. See **Twelve Days**.

Twelve. The number 12 was associated with the sidereal revolution of Jupiter, and there are records of reigning kings being accorded 12 years before a festival took place at which the king could be challenged by any would-be successor, he then had to defend his title with a virility-proving contest of strength. Such customs and festivals were known on the Malabar coast of south India, they occurred every twelfth year when the planet was retrograde in Cancer, a period which lasted 28 days.

Twelve Days. The festival occurring at the 12 intercalary days of the solstice is widespread: it was found in Babylon as the Twelve Days Duel between Chaos and Cosmos; in Indian traditions from Vedic times; in China; among the Celts and Teutons and in many pagan cults. The festival is one of reversal of order and roles, as in the Roman **Saturnalia**, when there was a Lord of Misrule and general license reigned. Christianity adopted the ancient pagan practices and in 567 the Council of Trent declared the Twelve Days to be a festival time and in 813 the Synod of Mainz confirmed the festival in Germany. The Twelve Days are said to forecast the meteorological pattern of the 12 months of the coming year. This also obtained in Babylon and at the Hebrew **Feast of Tabernacles** when the rainfall for each of the coming months was predicted. The Twelve Days were also a time for '**wassailling**'. In Scotland no court had any power during the Twelve Days; in Wales they were 'omen' days; in Ireland those who died in that period escaped Purgatory and went straight to Heaven. The days are also the German *Zwölften*. After **Christmas**, **Twelfth Night** was the conclusion of the festival and work started again.

U

Ullambana (Buddhist). Ullambana, the Chinese **Yu-lan-p'en** and Japanese **Urabon**, is a festival of the dead in the seventh moon of the lunar calendar, on the fifteenth day. It is a widespread and typical **All Souls** occasion. Offerings, originally made to the Buddha, became ceremonies for the dead ancestors and hungry ghosts. It also became a time for the display of riches in temples and among the public, with dramatic performances in the temples. All shrines are cleaned and at family shrines special foods are offered to the spirits together with tea and water, flowers and incense. Lights are placed in cemeteries and in front of houses to light the way for the spirits and light them back to the otherworld. The ceremonies not only propitiate the spirits but earn merit for the living and help to confer longevity.

United States of America. In addition to the Christian calendar and Jewish observances, the USA celebrates certain political events in their history as national festivals; notably **Independence Day** and **Thanksgiving Day** and there are commemoration days such as the birthdays of Lincoln, Washington and other patriots. There is also a **Mother's Day** (second Sunday in May) and a **Father's Day** (third Sunday in June). The different nationalities settling in North America also brought their countries' customs with them and so influenced the nature of the religious festivals. The original prohibitions against **Christmas** by the Puritan settlers who regarded it as pagan, gave way under pressure from emigrant groups from Catholic Europe and Christmas customs were gradually spread and incorporated until in 1890 the holiday was officially recognized. The turkey, sacred bird of the Aztecs, replaced the goose which was the traditional English food. German customs introduced the Christmas tree, as in England. The custom of gift-giving is now accepted and universal.

Up Hally A'. A Shetland festival on the last Tuesday of January. It is derived from the ancient Yule-tide festival celebrating the triumph of the sun over darkness and winter; a fire festival, with bonfires, blazing tar barrels and torch processions with the final burning of the

Viking ship, into which the torches are thrown. People wear Viking costume and sing and dance. In earlier times there was an exorcizing ceremony at midnight, with the expulsion of evil spirits who were ritually driven out of the house.

Uposatha Days (Buddhist). Conforming to the sacred character of the new and full moons, and the later inclusion of the quarters, monks should assemble at these times for a form of private mutual confession. The new and full moons are the more important occasions; they are days of rest. People in general may take part in food offerings to the monks, in visiting shrines, meditating, reading from the *Sutras* and following the Eight Precepts of Buddhism.

Urabon (Japanese). See **Ullambana**.

V

Vaisakhi or **Baisaki** (Sikh). A New Year's Day festival, held on 13 April, fixed by the solar calendar, but once in 36 years it will fall on 14 April. While for the Hindus there is barley offered from the crops to be harvested, for the Sikh it is a religious, political and social occasion for worship and listening to the teaching of the Guru. Pilgrims make their way to the temple before dawn and bathe in the pool. It is a time of relaxation before the work of the harvest. An animal fair in the neighbourhood deals in all kinds of working animals from camels to goats. It is also an occasion for initiation of new *Khalsa* members by the *pahal* ceremony. The festival also commemorates the Guru Gobind Singh's institution of the Five K.s (see **Sikh**) and the brotherhood of the *Khalsa*, the pure ones.

Valentine's Day (Christian). St Valentine's Day, 14 February, is a Christianizing of the Roman **Lupercalia** when names were drawn from a box or bag in the mid-February festivities. Presents were purchased and then exchanged after the drawing of lots; the couples then remained together for the duration of the festival. Today anonymous cards are sent to chosen people. Christianity attached the festival to a saint of that date. St Valentine's Day is traditionally the time when birds mate.

Vassa (Buddhist). In monsoon countries Vassa, or the Rains Retreat, was instituted after complaints that travelling monks damaged crops and travelling conditions were difficult for monks. The Buddha therefore ordained that there should be a period of retreat during the rainy season, from June to October. The time was one of self-examination and mutual exchange of forgiveness for any offence committed. Tibet, Burma and Thailand lay emphasis on the Retreat. In Thailand the people join in at the end of the period with a procession and decorated floats and boat-races. The Retreat ends with the ceremony of **Kathina**, or new robe, when monks are provided with new robes given by devotees. In some countries this developed into a royal occasion with sumptuous gifts to the *sangha* and temples, accompanied by processions, decorations, music and dancing. In

other parts a great feast marks the event with throngs of people celebrating in their best clothes. Pagodas and temples are festooned with lights.

Vesakha (Buddhist), **Wesak**, **Waicaka** or **Purmina** (north India). The festival is universally celebrated at the full moon in May/June, in commemoration of the Buddha's birthday, but it also celebrates the triple event of his birth, enlightenment and renunciation and passing into Nirvana; a festival of the Triple Blessing. The night before is spent in fasting and chanting; lamps are lit, temples are decorated with flowers and streamers, offerings of rice, coins and incense are made and there are processions to ritual places of worship. The Chinese pilgrim, Fa-hsien, who stayed in India in the fifth century wrote:

> 'They celebrate with a procession of images. They make a four-wheeled car and on it erect a structure of five stories by means of bamboos tied together . . . it is rather more than 20 cubits high and in the shape of a tope. White and silk-like cloth or hair is wrapped round it and then painted in various colours. They make figures of *devas* with gold, silver and lapis lazuli grandly blending and having silken streamers and canopies hung over them. On the four sides are niches, with a Buddha seated in each and a Bodhisattva standing in attendance on him. There may be 20 cars, all grand and imposing but each one different from the others. On the day mentioned, the monks and laity all come together; they have singers and skilful musicians; they pay their devotions with flowers and incense . . . all through the night they keep lamps burning, have skilful music and present offerings. All the poor and destitute in the country . . . are provided with every kind of help and doctors examine their diseases. They get the food and medicine which their cases require.'

There are also bathing ceremonies of images, processions, scattering of flowers, burning incense, flag-flying and, in China, fireworks. It is a festival of lights and events from the life of the Buddha are depicted. All temples, pagodas, streets, houses and gardens are illuminated. The Bodhi Tree, under which the Buddha attained enlightenment, is watered.

Vestalia (Ancient Roman). The Vestalia was a first fruits festival, confined to women, and was probably originally a family cult of the sacred hearth. The *perrus Vestae* was kept shut throughout the year but was opened on 7 June to all matrons; they went barefoot to the temple which only the Pontifex Maximus could enter otherwise. The Vestals offered sacred cakes, the *mola salsa*, made from the ears of the first corn reaped. The festival was a holiday for millers and bakers; mills were garlanded and donkeys were garlanded and decorated

with cakes. On 15 June the temple was swept and all rubbish taken away and thrown in the Tiber or left in some specially designated place. The Amerindians have a festival which shows distinct parallels. See also **Vestal Virgins**.

Vestal Virgins tended the sacred royal fire on the hearth of Vesta (Greek Hestia), the Hearth Goddess, at her shrine in the Roman Forum. The fire was never allowed to go out except on the last day of February when it was ritually extinguished and then rekindled on 1 March at a ceremony marking the end of the old year and the beginning of the new religious year. The Vestals, six girls chosen before puberty, had to be free-born, with both parents living (i.e. having no contact with death), without blemish and virgin. Loss of virginity entailed being buried alive. They served for five years at first, but later for 30 years, and lived under the rule of the Virgo Vestalis Maxima. Their duties also included the preparation of the sacred cakes, the *mola salsa*, for the festivals of the **Vestalia** and **Lupercalia** and they were given the blood of the sacrificial **October Horse**. Another of their functions was to throw the puppets into the river at the *Argeorum sacra*; they also took part in harvest festivals. The custom of keeping fires burning perpetually was, and still is, widespread. Frazer suggests that its origin was in the necessity of keeping a fire alight for the community to utilize at any time and that this was commonly the responsibility of the daughter of the chief.

Vinalia (Ancient Roman). There were vintage festivals in late August, September and October. In Rome, the Vinalia on 11 October, was the day of testing the new wine.

Vira-Nirvana (Jain). The death of Mahavira is commemorated on the 15th day of the waning moon of *Ashvina* (November) when Mahavira entered Nirvana; it is inaugurated by a 24-hour fast, spent in meditation, vigils and lighting lamps before the image of Mahavira. The fast is broken early next day after a service of hymns and recitations. The festival coincides with the Hindu **Diwali**, the **Festival of Lights**, which, as a public holiday, is now also celebrated by Jainas.

Virgin Mary (Christian). Festivals of the Virgin Mary are largely celebrated in the Roman Catholic and Eastern Orthodox Churches, though some are kept in the Anglican and Episcopalian Churches. *The Nativity* was celebrated from the eighth century in the Orthodox Church and later in the eleventh century by the Roman Catholics on 8 September.
The Immaculate Conception, 8 December for Roman Catholics, 9 December for Eastern Orthodox.
The Annunciation (Luke 1: 26-38) 25 March. Celebrates the Incarnation and is observed in both Catholic and Protestant Churches.

The Visitation (Luke 1: 39-49) 31 May, is a lesser festival.

The Assumption, or the *Falling Asleep*, 15 August, is celebrated in Catholic Europe with processions and fiestas.

The Solemnity of Mary, 1 January, is a purely Roman Catholic festival which coincides with the *Circumcision of Christ* in other churches.

W

Wakes. Derived from 'waking' or watching, wakes were originally a vigil kept on the eve of a feast, festival or funeral or for the patron saint of a parish in a town or village. Later, after the Industrial Revolution, wakes were made the occasion for the annual closing of mills and the holiday for the work-force. Before this tradesmen and chapmen assembled at **fairs** to display and sell their goods. The horn dance (see **Dance**) and the hobby-horse were associated with wakes.

Wassailling. The wassail was a hot spiced ale, which later changed to punch, in which healths (*was haile*) were drunk. Wassailling occurred at any time during the Twelve Days of Christmas, but more usually on the eve of **Twelfth Night**. People went from house to house singing and drinking, being entertained and given largesse. Orchards were wassailled in cider-making country regions; a legacy of the Celtic symbolism of the magic apple, fruit of the Silver Bough. Guns were fired into the branches, or in earlier times, before fire-arms, trees were beaten, both as fertility whipping (see **Flagellation**) and as waking the sleeping powers of fertility, and as warding off evil influences with the noise. Cider was poured on the roots as a libation. Customs varied widely in wassailling and anything from orchards to beehives or cattle could be wassailled. The rite still takes place as a traditional and social celebration in Somerset in England.

Waters. Associated with the beginning and end of all things, the waters represent the feminine principle, fertility and refreshment. They dissolve and wash away, purify, hence their universal employment in purificatory ceremonies at festivals. Water is also connected with light as its liquid counterpart and it is the opposing force to fire; together they symbolize the Great Contraries in the world of the elements, but are also the two forces, as moisture and heat, necessary for life. As water is the feminine Earth Mother and Moon Goddess, controller of the waters, so fire is represented by the Sky Father — though he can also personify rain. Between them they control all the elements. Waters, especially as springs and wells, are often sacred, having contact with underground powers and therefore possessing

magic forces of healing and wish-fulfilling and as such are focal points at many festivals. Water also carries away and so is used at festivals of the dead to carry the spirits back to the otherworld and in scapegoat ceremonies to carry away the sins of the people. (See **Scapegoat**.)

Weeks. The Feast of Weeks (Hebrew). See **Pentecost**.

Weeping. See **Lamentations**.

Whipping. See **Flagellation**.

Whitsuntide or **Whit Sunday** (Christian). Occurs 50 days after **Easter** and derives its name from the wearing of white by the newly baptized; it has been commemorated from the third century as **Pentecost**: the tongues of fire and the power of speaking with tongues in the descent of the Holy Ghost after Christ had risen to heaven (Acts 2.). In earlier times it was a week's holiday in which all joined, rich and poor alike, in feasting and merry-making; fasting and penance were forbidden. In England a Robin Hood Bower was built in the churchyard and decorated to enthrone the Lord and Lady of the Whitsun Ale; they were accompanied by a mace-bearer and the inevitable Fool. It was a traditional time for processions and morris dances (see **Dance**), with a hobby-horse, dragons and 'other monsters skirmishing amongst the rout'. Whit sports were wrestling, jumping, pitching the bar and handling the pike.

In some places the **maypole** was dismantled at Whit and a youth who succeeded in climbing it and getting the green, or crown, from the top was fêted with singing and dancing and drinking in the tavern. In some parts of Germany the youth was called the Whitsun King and he chose his Queen for the festivities. In France trumpets were blown to symbolize the 'violent wind' or 'mighty wind' of Acts 2. In Italy rose leaves were rained from church roofs, representing the descent of the Pentecostal flames, but this was also in the tradition of the Roman *Rosalia*. In Holland doves symbolizing the Holy Spirit were brought to the church service. In Ireland it was formerly both a religious and public holiday and a time for 'patterns', **fairs** and visiting holy wells; but it was also a particularly unlucky day, so no bathing, boating or journeys were undertaken and it was also an unlucky date for birth in humans and animals and a likely time for the sick to die. With Ascension-tide and St John's Day, Whit was a traditional time for well-dressing.

Pentecost was the High Feast of King Arthur's Court for 'all manner of strange adventures came before King Arthur at that feast afore all others'.

The festival was adopted by the Church as its birthday at the Hebrew **Pentecost**, or Feast of Weeks, which celebrated the in-gathering of the harvest.

Witches. The main witches' festivals are all on 'eves': **Candlemas Eve**, **Beltane** and **May Day** Eve, the August Eve of **Lammas**, and **Hallowe'en**. The eve of 1 May, *Walpurgisnacht*, is the greatest of their festivals; witches and warlocks were said to meet on the Brocken, in the Harz mountains, for their most important sabbath when they were given fresh powers for the coming year and planned the ruin of the country's harvest. They remained powerful for the next 12 days, making these a time of danger with woods haunted by evil spirits and beasts. On *Walpurgisnacht* one must leap over the threshold since it is a dangerous place where witches and malefic powers lurk. Hallowe'en, a witches' time, when the dead also return, does not display the fear of death and the dead as evinced in Greek and Roman festivals, but is regarded more as a joyous reunion, referring to 'our beloved ones' that 'we may meet and know and remember and love them again'. In Europe witches are said to ride to their sabbaths on broomsticks, a belief which also occurs in Mexico where the witch could ride through the air and was associated with the screech owl. Tlagoltiotl, Queen of the Witches, is depicted riding a broom and wearing a witch's peaked hat.

Wreaths. When worn at festivals wreaths symbolize the renewal of vegetative life, they had their origin in magic, being put on people, statues, images or sacred objects or attached to doors and windows to keep off evil powers. In Rome they were renewed in March, at the beginning of the year when life returned again. Later, garlands and wreaths were worn by kings, priests, notable people and victors in war or at the games; that is to say, people who, to some extent, were worshipped or revered by the populace and who were the objects of attention and therefore required protection from malign spirits. In this context they were used in connection with **May Day** rites and the **maypole** and in decorations at **Christmas**. Placed on the heads of the newly initiated, the baptized and the wedded, they are not only apotropaic but also represent the holding of secret knowledge in the head within the sacred and protective magic circle.

Y

Yom Kippur (Hebrew). Yom Kippur, or the Day of Atonement of the post-exile period, celebrated on the tenth day of the lunar month of *Tishri*, is a time of cleansing and renewal. The day is kept as a Sabbath, or Sabbath of Sabbaths, on which no profane work may be undertaken; there is fasting, sexual abstinance and ritual purification and anointing. A service is held which includes prayer, protestations, the ceremonial annulment of vows, repentance, a public confession of sins and the singing of hymns. The next day continues with services until nightfall when the sounding of the *shofar*, the ram's horn, heralds the end of the fast. There are prayers for the dead and the lighting of a memorial candle to the ancestors before the fast begins. The dead are also remembered at the end of the **Feast of Tabernacles**, at the **Passover** and **Pentecost**. In earlier times sacrifices were made to God and a **scapegoat**, dedicated to the demon Azazel, the Sin Bearer, was set loose in the desert to take away the sins of the people. Today the chief outward observance is largely one of prayers and special supplicatory psalms each morning at dawn and the purpose is to cleanse before the Lord (Lev. 16:30); a regeneration from within. With **Rosh Hashanah**, Yom Kippur represents the most solemn occasion of the year.

Yuki Matsuri (Japanese). See **Snow Festival**.

Yu-lan-p'en (Chinese). See **Ullambana**.

Yule. The pre-Christian Northern Yule-tide festival welcomed the return of the sun at the winter solstice, with the death of the old year and the birth of the new. The sun is vital to fertility everywhere, but in the Northern countries, with their cold and sunless winters, the coming of the sun and warmth at the turn of the year has always been an occasion for relief and rejoicing.

Decorating with evergreens occurs from earliest times, as a symbol of renewal and everlasting life; as it was done in temples, so is it still done in churches and homes. The only exception is **mistletoe**, the feminine counterpart of the Druidical masculine oak; it may not be

hung in churches and it retains its pagan nature, the only exception is York Minster with its Norse associations.

The Boar's Head of the Yule-tide feast is a solar animal, having bristles of gold, like the rays of the sun. The boar was sacrificed to Frey at Yule and was sacred to Woden/Odin, Frey and Freyja; it was also the food of heroes in Valhalla. Its symbolism is ancient and it is also associated with the Vedic myth of the incarnation of Vishnu and with the dying god Adonis.

The Yule Log of the Druids was of oak, but the pine of Attis was used by the Teutons and in Scandinavia an ash faggot was bound with withies and burned at Yule with predictions made from the bursting of the withies. The log is also an aniconic form of Dionysos and the ivy wound round it is the Crown of Dionysos and the Plant of Osiris. The burning of the Yule Log was a widespread custom, found in Germany, France, French-speaking Switzerland, England and among the Slavs. The log, bonfires and feasting are protective and sympathetic magic to ward off the evil powers of darkness and to mimic and encourage the summer warmth and light, and also to ensure plenty in the coming year.

Baldur, the Scandinavian god of light and joy, appeared on the eve of 25 December. See also **Christmas**.

Z

Zoroastrian (Parsee and Irani). The Zoroastrian calendar of 12 months, with an intercalary month being inserted periodically, is based entirely on festivals, each of the 12 months, with five extra Gatha days, being named after a festival associated with the pastoral year. This introduces name-day festivals (*jashans*) since the name of the divinity is continually invoked, thus there are numerous festivals but they are conducted with quiet dignity and with none of the wild enthusiasms and excesses of their Hindu counterparts but with joyful festivity and merry-making. There are no evil spirits or vengeful gods to need propitiation, no animal sacrifices, the religion being highly compassionate. Nor is there any fasting as it is regarded as inconsistent with the Good Life and also has the effect of weakening the body in the struggle against Ahriman, the Lord of Darkness.

The Heptad of Ahura Mazda, Lord of Light and Wisdom, with the Six Holy Immortals, controls Zoroastrian worship and consequently the festivals associated with them; these become Holy Days which must be celebrated and to neglect them is a sin. The festivals of the Six are the **Gahambars** which are now distributed throughout the year as six-day occasions; they are celebrated largely by the priesthood, in the Fire Temple, at the Service of All the Masters, but also by the devout laity in their own houses.

There is now also a widely used seasonal calendar of 365 days, known as *Fasli*, which fixes the new year at the spring equinox on 21 March and adopts the Gregorian calendar leap year.

Festivals:
Aban Jashan — Name-day festivals. ⎫
Adar Jashan — Name-day festivals. ⎬ See **Jashan**.
Mihr Jashan — Name-day festivals. ⎭
Muktad.
No Ruz or the Greater Nawroz.
Sada.
The Six **Gahambars**.
Tir Jashan — Name-day festivals. See **Jashan**.
Zarthust-no Diso. The Death of Zoroaster.

Bibliography

Achelis, Elizabeth, *Of Time and the Calendar*, New York, 1955.

Addison, William, *English Fairs and Markets*, Batsford, 1952.

Alford, Violet, *Introduction to English Folklore*, Bell, 1952.

——, *Sword Dance and Drama*, Merlin Press, 1962.

Anderson, Mary M, *Festivals of Nepal*, Allen & Unwin, 1971.

Apuleius. *The Metamorphoses.*

——, *The Golden Ass.*

Aristotle. *Ethics.*

Bailey, C, *Phases in the Religion of Ancient Rome*, Oxford University Press, 1932.

Barrow, Terena Tui, *Art and Life in Polynesia*, Pall Mall Press, 1972.

Beals, Carlton, *Land of the Mayas*, Abelard-Schuman, 1966.

Berndt, R. M. (ed.), *Australian Aboriginal Anthropology*, Australia Institute, 1970.

Best, Eldon, *The Maori*, Wellington, 1924.

Birket-Smith, Kaj, *The Eskimos*, Methuen, 1936.

Bloomfield, Frena, *The Book of Chinese Beliefs*, Hutchinson, 1983.

Brown, Alan (ed.), *Festivals in World Religions*, Longman, 1986.

Buck, C. H., *Faiths, Fairs and Festivals of India*, Asian Publications, 1979.

Budge, A. E. Wallis, *Osiris and the Egyptian Resurrection*, London, 1911.

Burl, Aubry, *Rites of the Gods*, Dent, 1981.

Campbell, Joseph, *Myths to Live By*, New York, 1972.

——, *Primitive Mythology*, Penguin, 1985.

——, *Creative Mythology*, Penguin, 1976.

Carpenter, Edward, *Pagan and Christian Creeds, their Origin and Meaning*, Allen & Unwin, 1920.

Chambers, E. H., *The Mediaeval Stage*, Oxford, 1903.

——, *The Elizabethan Stage*, Oxford, 1922.

——, *The English Folk Play*, Oxford, 1923.

Chaudhuri, Narad, C., *Hinduism*, Chatto and Windus, 1979.

Chaudhri, Rashid Ahmad, *Muslim Festivals and Ceremonies*, London Mosque, 1983.

Cheetham, S., *The Mysteries, Pagan and Christian*, Macmillan, 1897.

Ch'en, K. S., *Buddhism, the Light of Asia*, New York, 1968.

Christian, R., 'Old English Customs', *Country Life*, 1966.

Clark, Rundle R. T., *Myths and Symbols of Egypt*, Thames & Hudson, 1959.

Clébert, Jean-Paul, *The Gypsies*, Vista, 1963.

Coe, Michael D., *The Maya*, Thames & Hudson, 1980.

Cole, W. W. & Sambhi, Piara Singh, *The Sikhs*, Routledge & Kegan Paul, 1978.

Cornford, F. M., *The Origin of Attic Comedy*, London, 1947.

Cowan, James, *The Dream Journey*, Temenos (7), London, 1986.

Cumont, Franz, *Les Religions Orientales*, Paris, 1906.

Dabu, Daster, K. D., *The Message of Zarathushtra*, Bombay, 1956.

Danaher, Kevin, *The Year in Ireland*, Cork, 1972.

Dexter, T. F. G., *The Pagan Origin of Fairs*, New Knowledge Press, 1936.

Ditchfield, P. H., *Old English Customs*, Methuen, 1901.

Dowden, J., *The Church Year and Kalendar*, Cambridge University Press, 1910.

Drake-Carnell, F. J., *Old English Customs and Ceremonies*, Batsford, 1938.

Eliade, Mircea, *Patterns in Comparative Religion*, Sheed & Ward, 1958.

——, *Australian Religions*, Cornell University Press, 1973.

Elkin, A. P., *Aboriginal Men of High Degree*, University of Queensland, 1977.

——, *Religion and Philosophy of the Australian Aboriginees*, (Essay).

Firth, J., *Human Types*, Nelson, 1975.

Fowler, W. Ward, *The Roman Festivals of the Period of the Republic*, London, 1908.

Frankfort, H., *The Birth of Civilization in the Near East*, Williams & Norgate, 1956.

Frankfort, H. and Others, *The Intellectual Adventures of Ancient Man*, University Press of Chicago, 1964.

Frazer, J. G., *The Golden Bough*, Macmillan, 1911.

——, *The Magical Origin of Kings*, Macmillan, 1920.

Gannep nan, Arnold, *The Rites of Passage*, London, 1959.

Gardiner, E. N., *Greek Athletic Sports and Festivals*, Macmillan, 1910.

Gaster, Theodor, *Thespis, Myth and Ritual*, New York, 1975.

——, *Festivals of the Jewish Year*, New York, 1974.

Gibbons, B & Ashford, B., *The Himalayan Kingdoms*, Batsford, 1983.

Guénon, René, *Symboles fondamentaux de la Science sacrée*, Gallimard, 1962.

Gurney, O. R., *The Hittites*, Allen Lane, 1975.

Güterbach, Hans. G., 'Outline of the AN.TAH.SUM. Festival', *Journal of Near Eastern Studies*, 1960.

Guthrie, W. K. C., *The Greeks and their Gods*, Methuen, 1968.

Harrison, Jane, *Prolegomena to the Study of Greek Religions*, Cambridge University Press, 1908.
—, *Ancient Art and Ritual*, Cambridge University Press, 1911.
—, *Themis*, Cambridge University Press, 1927.
Hastings *Encyclopaedia of Religion and Ethics*.
Hesiod, *Works and Days*.
Hocart, A. M., *Kingship*, Oxford, 1927.
—, *The Progress of Man*, Methuen, 1933.
Hodge, F. W. (ed.), *Handbook of the American Indians*, Bowman & Littlefield, 1975.
Hole, C., *English Customs and Usage*, Batsford, 1941.
Hooke, S. H., *Babylonian and Assyrian Religion*, Hutchinson, 1953.
—, (Ed.), *Myth and Ritual*, Oxford, 1933.
Hunt, Cecil, *British Customs and Ceremonies*, London, 1954.
James, E. O., *Christian Myth and Ritual*, Murray, 1933.
—, *Origins of Sacrifice*, Murray, 1933.
—, *The Cult of the Mother Goddess*, Thames & Hudson, 1959.
—, *Seasonal Feasts and Festivals*, Thames & Hudson, 1961.
Jevons, F. B., 'Masks and the Origins of Greek Drama', *Folklore*, Vol.XXVII.
Jung, C. G., *Four Archetypes*, Routledge & Kegan Paul, 1972.
Karsten, R., *The Civilizations of the South American Indians*, London, 1926.
Lafaye, G., *Histoire der culte des Divinities d'Alexandrie hors de l'Egypt*, Paris, 1884.
Langdon, S., *Tammuz and Ishtar*, Oxford, 1914.
Lawson, J. C., *Modern Greek Folklore and Ancient Greek Religion*, Cambridge University Press, 1910.
Leitch, Barbara A., *A Concise Dictionary of Indian Tribes of North America*, Reference Publ, 1979.
Liu, Da, *The Tao and Chinese Culture*, Routledge & Kegan Paul, 1981.
Long, George, *The Folklore Calendar*, E.P Publishing, 1977.
Loomis, R. S., *Celtic Myth and Arthurian Romance*, New York, 1927.
MacCulloch, J. A., *The Religion of the Ancient Celts*, Edinburgh, 1911.
Macrobius, *Saturnalia*, 6 vols, fourth century AD.
Marquis, Arnold, *A Guide to America's Indians*, University of Oklahoma Press, 1974.
Mbiti, John, S., *African Religions and Philosophy*, Heinemann, 1969.
Miles, Clement. A., *Christmas in Ritual and Tradition, Christian and Pagan*, London, 1912.
Mitchell, John, *The Earth Spirit*, Thames & Hudson, 1975.
Muncey, R. W., *Our Old English Fairs*, London, 1936.
Myers, Robert J., *Celebrations. The Complete Book of American Holidays*, Doubleday, 1972.
New Oxford Dictionary of Music, The, Oxford University Press, 1957.
Nilsson, M. P., *The Mycenaean Origin of Greek Mythology*, Cambridge

University Press, 1932. (Reissued Californian Press, 1972.)
——, *Primitive Time Reckoning*, Lund, 1920.
Ochshorn, Judith, *The Female Expression and the Nature of Drama*, Indiana, 1981.
Oesterley, W. O. E., *The Sacred Dance*, Oxford University Press, 1923.
Parke, H. W., *Festivals of the Athenians*, Thames & Hudson, 1977.
Pearson, C., *The Chances of Death*, London, 1897.
Piggott, Stuart, *The Druids*, Thames & Hudson, 1968.
Plutarch, *De Iside et Osiride*.
——, *On Superstitions*.
Price, Nancy, *Pagan's Progress*, Museum Press, 1954.
Raglan, Lady, 'The Green Man', *Folklore*, Vol. L, 1939.
Raglan, Lord, *The Hero*, Methuen, 1936.
Rees, Alwyn, *The Celtic Heritage*, Thames & Hudson, 1974.
Reinach, S., *Cults, Myths and Religions*, London, 1912.
Rose, H. J., *Primitive Customs in Greece*, Methuen, 1925.
Saintyves, P., *Les Contes de Perrault*, Paris, 1923.
Sakurai, Tokutaro, *Japanese Festivals*, International Society for Education, 1970.
Scullard, H. H., *Festivals and Ceremonies of the Roman Republic*, Thames & Hudson, 1981.
Snow, Philip & Waine, Stephanie, *The People of the Horizon*, Phaidon, 1979.
Spence, Lewis, *The Myths of Mexico and Peru*, Harrap, 1917.
——, *Myths and Legends of Babylon and Assyria*, Harrap, 1917.
——, *Myths and Legends of the North American Indians*, Harrap, 1917.
——, *Myth and Ritual in Dance, Games and Rhyme*, London, 1947.
Spencer, Baldwin & Gillen, F. G., *The Native Tribes of Central Australia*, Dover, 1968.
Stama, W. E. H., 'Aboriginal Religion', *Oceania*, 1966.
Stubbs, *Anatomye of Abuses*, 1583.
Tiddy, R. J. E., *The Mummers' Play*, Oxford, 1923.
Tregear, Edward, *The Maori Race*, New Zealand, 1904.
Trevelyan, G. M., *English Social History*, London, 1946.
Unterman, Alan, *Jews, their Religious Beliefs and Practices*, Routledge & Kegan Paul, 1981.
Warner, E. T. C., *Myths and Legends of China*, Harrap, 1922.
Wasserman, Paul, *Festivals Source Book*, Book Tower, 1977.
Welsford, E., *The Fool*, Faber & Faber, 1935.
Weston, Jessie, *From Ritual to Romance*, New York, 1957.
Whistler, Laurence, *The English Festivals*, Heinemann, 1947.
Whitlock, Ralph, *In Search of Lost Gods*, Phaidon, 1979.
Williamson, R. W., *Religion and Cosmic Beliefs of Central Polynesia*, Cambridge University Press, 1933.
World of the American Indian, The National Geographic, 1974.
Young, Karl, *The Drama of the Mediaeval Church*, Oxford, 1977.